MONTROSE

MONTROSE
FOR COVENANT AND KING

EDWARD J. COWAN

CANONGATE

First published in Great Britain in 1977
by Weidenfeld and Nicolson
First published in paperback edition in 1995
by Canongate Books Ltd, 14 High Street,
Edinburgh EH1 1TE

Copyright © 1977 by Edward J. Cowan

ISBN 0 86241 556 X

British Library Cataloguing-in-Publication Data
A catalogue record for this volume is available upon
request from the British Library.

Printed in Finland by WSOY

CONTENTS

ACKNOWLEDGMENTS / vii

MAP OF MONTROSE'S SCOTLAND / viii

1 THE MAKING OF AN EARL / 1

2 TOWARDS A REVOLUTION / 19

3 CAVALIER FOR THE COVENANT / 44

4 THE CURSE OF MEROZ / 61

5 THE TEARS OF XERXES / 80

6 THE TRIALS OF JOB / 102

7 THE ADVENTURE BEGINS / 130

8 THE FIRST STRANGE COURSING / 152

9 THE SHAKING OF MACCAILEIN MÓR / 173

10 THE FREEDOM OF A KINGDOM AND A CROWN / 192

11 ASCENT TO THE MERIDIAN: KILSYTH / 213

12 DESCENT TO DECADENCY: PHILIPHAUGH / 231

13 PASSIONATE EXILE / 252

14 THE LAST CAMPAIGN / 276

NOTES AND REFERENCES / 302

INDEX / 317

In memory of Alison (1944–1994)
and for
Karen, Morna and David
who should have been thanked before

So much hath the spirit of some one man excelled, as
it hath undertaken and effected the alteration of the
greatest States and Common-weales, the erection of
Monarchies, the conquest of kingdoms and Empires,
guided handfuls of men against multitudes of equall
bodily strength, contrived victories beyond all hope and
discourse of reason, converted the fearfull passions of his
owne followers into magnanimitie, and the valour of his
enemies into cowardice; such spirits have been stirred up
in sundrie Ages of the world, and in divers parts
thereof, to erect and cast downe againe, to establish and
to destroy, to bring all things, Persons and States to the
same certaine ends, which the infinite spirit of the
Universall, piercing, moving, governing all things, hath
ordained.

Sir Walter Ralegh

ACKNOWLEDGMENTS

George Wishart, Montrose's first biographer, predicted that his hero would not lack an 'Appelles or Leucippus nor perchance a Homer' to recite his deeds. In writing this book I had no Homeric pretensions. Rather the intention was to demythologise Montrose, to depict him as a remarkable individual in a remarkable era but who suffered his own fair share of human failings and uncertainties. The idea was also to use him as a lens through which to examine the complex issues of the Covenanting Revolution.

Since this book was first published no major study of Montrose has appeared though an insightful complementary study is David Stevenson *Alasdair MacColla and the Highland Problem in the Seventeenth Century* (John Donald 1980) later republished as *Highland Warrior* (Saltire Society 1994). Two important works are Peter Donald *An Uncounselled King: Charles I and the Scottish Troubles 1637–1641* (Cambridge University Press 1990) and Allan Macinnes *Charles I and the Making of the Covenanting Movement 1625–1641* (John Donald 1991) as is *The Scottish National Covenant in its British Context 1638–1651* (ed) John Morrill (Edinburgh University Press 1990). Also illuminating are Edward M. Furgol *A Regimental History of the Covenanting Armies 1639–1651* (John Donald 1990), Kevin Sharpe *The Personal Rule of Charles I* (Yale University Press 1992) and Mark Charles Fissel *The Bishops' Wars. Charles I's campaigns against Scotland 1638–1640* (Cambridge University Press 1994). Montrose's poetry is once again available in *Collected Poems. James Graham First Marquis of Montrose* (ed) Robin Bell (The Mandeville Press 1990).

I remain indebted to all of those (some, alas, no longer with us) whose assistance I gratefully acknowledged in 1977. I must also thank the undergraduates at the University of Guelph, Ontario who took the final year option on 'Scotland's Century of Revolution' as well as the graduate students who challenged me to revise many of my views on this period. Lastly I would like to thank my reviewers whose opinions encouraged me to consider this reprint.

Glasgow   Edward J. Cowan
September 1995

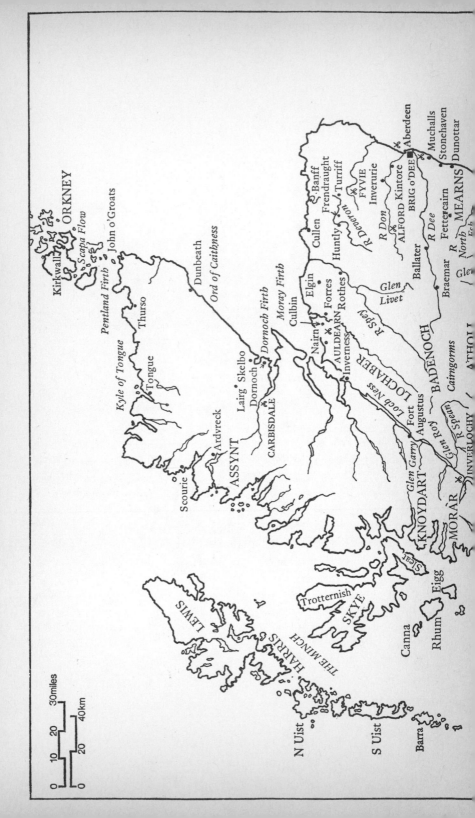

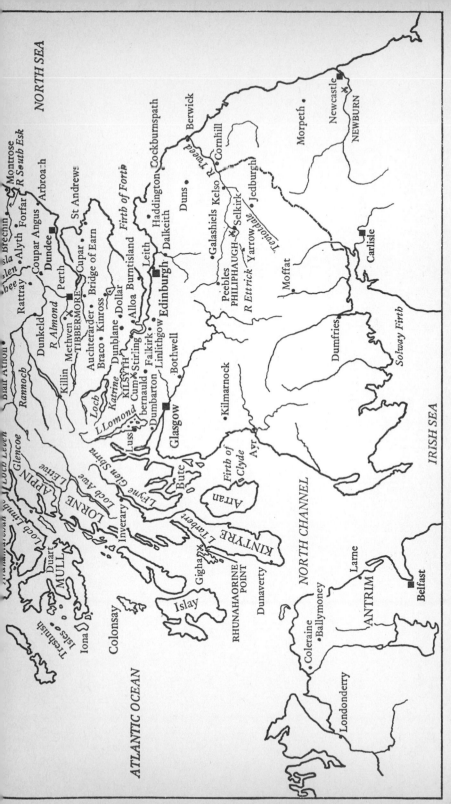

1
THE MAKING OF
AN EARL

As for that hopeful Youth, the young Lord Grahame,
James Earle of Montrose; whose war-lyke Name,
Sprung from redoubted worth, made Manhood try,
Their matchles deeds in unmatchd Chivalry.

I doe bequeath him to thy gracious Love,
Whose Noble Stocke did ever faithfull prove;
To thyne old-agd Auncestors; and my bounds,
Were often freed, from thraldome, by their wounds,
Leaving their roote, the stamp of fidele trueth,
To be inherent, in this noble Youth,

Whose Hearts, whose Hands, whose Swords, whose Deeds, whose Fame,
Made Mars for valour, canonize the Grahame.

William Lithgow, *Scotland's Welcome to Her Native Sonne, and*
Soveraigne Lord, King Charles (1633)

On the day that Alexander the Great was born the Temple of Diana was destroyed by fire. The year 1612 also witnessed certain 'prodigious works'. A cow gave birth to 'fourteene great dogge whelps'; another contained a 'deid bairne in her belly'; a man in the west vomited two toads and a serpent. Only hindsight would link such phenomena with the birth of a long-awaited male heir to John, fourth Earl of Montrose.

The history of the Grahams was the history of Scotland. William de Graham was a frequent witness to charters of David I in whose reign the family held lands in the Borders. The true founder of the family fortunes was Sir David de Graham who, in the thirteenth century, received from the Earl of Dunbar the lands of Dundaff and Strath-carron. Westwards along the Carron, Killearn, Muckraw, and Strath-blane, granted to him by the Earl of Lennox, became the nucleus of the barony of Mugdock. He also acquired the Perthshire lands on the edge of fertile Strathearn which were to form the barony of Kincardine. Two miles west of Dundaff tradition preserves the castle of Sir John de Graham, the great friend and strength of William Wallace. To the legend of patriotic perfection the Grahams added a genius for, in the main, supporting the winning side, which goes some way to explaining continuous succession in the main line without recourse to collaterals right down to the present time, a feat unrivalled in the annals of the Scottish peerage.

When Robert Bruce desired estates in the west of Scotland for his retirement he exchanged his own lands of Auld Montrose for Graham territory at Cardross on the north bank of the Clyde, 'an exchange which gave rise to the historic association between the names of Graham and Montrose'.[1] Thereafter the Grahams appeared at almost every point in the chequered history of Scotland. Raised to the peerage as Lord Graham in 1445, the Graham supported James II in his struggle with the powerful house of Douglas. When the nobility rebelled against the hapless James III, Lord Graham stood by his king. In 1503 the dazzling James IV, rejoicing in marriage with his 'rose' Margaret Tudor, created the Graham Earl of Montrose, a generosity loyally repaid with his life on the bloody field of Flodden ten years later. Montrose was conspicuous by his absence from the Reformation parliament and was the only noble to attend the first mass in Scotland of young Mary, Queen of Scots. Much distressed when the Scots deposed their queen, he was still reputed to be a papist at his death in 1571. His son, John, third earl, however, was a staunch reformer, whose long and distinguished career culminated in his appointment as chancellor in 1599. Five years later he was appointed 'supremus regni Scotiae procurator', Commissioner General of Scotland, an impressive if empty title. King James required a malleable chancellor if his new policies of governing Scotland 'with his pen' from London were to succeed. There are some indications that Montrose was opposed to James's schemes for closer union and that he was bought off with the grandiloquent title. Sandwiched between his distinguished father and his illustrious son, John, fourth earl, inevitably appears a somewhat colourless character but he achieved brief notoriety in 1595 when he engaged in combat with Sir James Sandilands at the Tron of Edinburgh to avenge the murder of his cousin Graham of Hallyards. He was thirty-five years old when he succeeded his father in 1608. Eight years later he was royal commissioner to the general assembly and shortly before his death he became president of the privy council. His health was not good and he lived rather a retiring life, preferring the management of his estates and the pursuits of the study to involvement in public affairs. He had a passion for golf which he passed on to his son and a weakness for tobacco which he did not.

On his mother's side James Graham came of a family involved to the hilt in plotting and violence. Patrick, third Lord Ruthven, had risen from his sick bed to participate in the murder of David Riccio. His son William was created Earl of Gowrie in 1581, and three years later was executed as leader of the Ruthven raid when his ultra-protestant faction forcibly removed young James VI from the papist clutches of Esmé Stewart, Duke of Lennox. William's fourteen children included a daughter, Margaret, who married the Master of Montrose in 1593. In that year young Montrose, together with the Earl of Atholl and Lady Gowrie, William's widow, was involved in another abortive protestant palace revolution, led by Francis Stewart, Earl of Bothwell. The latter, who was possessed of much of the 'valour and matchless impudence' of his famous uncle, delighted in taunting the timorous James, appearing on this occasion sword in hand in the royal bedchamber. The young Earl of Gowrie, more than somewhat distracted from his studies at Edinburgh University, departed for Padua to read law. John, Master of Montrose, was pardoned for his part in the affair and he took to wife the sister of the studious earl. Why he allowed himself to become involved at all is not clear, unless he felt obliged to demonstrate his protestant leanings following the execution of his catholic kinsman David Graham of Fintry for alleged involvement in a plot with his co-religionists the Earls of Huntly and Erroll.[2]

In 1600 John, Earl of Gowrie, and his brother Alexander perished in the ill-famed and obscure affair known as the Gowrie conspiracy. It is likely that the brothers were plotting yet another coup involving the kidnapping of the king. They lured James to their town house at Perth with tales of a pot of gold. On his arrival Nemesis struck, not at the intended victim but at the Ruthvens themselves, both of whom were slain by James's companions. Two talented youths were needlessly butchered and the earldom forfeited. Another brother, William, fled to England, where he studied chemistry and philosophy. Yet another, Patrick, spent nineteen years studying medicine and alchemy in the Tower of London, an apprenticeship which qualified him for admission to Cambridge on his release. James Graham's own intellectual endowment may have owed something to his Ruthven heritage.

Local tradition relates that James was born in Castlested, Montrose, a house in which the Old Pretender briefly stayed in 1716, but he was more probably born in the castle of Auld Montrose, west of the burgh on the edge of the Montrose basin. There had been a community at the point where the South Esk enters the North Sea since time immemorial. By the seventeenth century it had grown into 'a very handsome well-built toune, of considerable trade in all places abroad'.

According to Wishart, Montrose was in his thirty-fourth year on 5 September 1646. At Montrose on 31 December 1612 John, fourth earl, drew up a testament naming James, Lord Graham, his lawful son and executor.[3] John was present at a meeting of the privy council in Edinburgh on 18 September 1612. He did not attend again for precisely two months, missing some eleven sessions of council and, more important, absenting himself from parliament, which sat from 12 to 23 October. While it is known that John did not enjoy good health it is tempting to connect his non-attendance at such important business with the birth of a male heir. There is some evidence that a previous son, John, bearing the name customarily given to the first-born in the family, had died in childhood; otherwise the fourth earl's marriage had brought him a crop of daughters. Young Montrose sat for his wedding portrait at Aberdeen between 3 and 5 November 1629. It was delivered to his father-in-law on 2 December, duly inscribed and signed by Jamesone, who often noted the ages of his subjects, though whether the 'aetatis 17' was added in November or December it is impossible to determine. On the basis of the evidence all that can be stated with certainty is that James was born some time between 5 September and 31 December 1612. John Buchan, noting the number of charters and conveyances which he signed between 20 and 22 October 1632, tentatively assigned his birth to that month, but such subscriptions can be explained by his imminent departure for the continent. It is just possible that the date of his marriage, 10 November, was also his birthday. The marriage contract contained the rather unusual condition that the bride's father would 'entertain' the newly weds in his own family for three years.[4] The date may have been deliberately chosen so that the three years would take him to his twenty-first year, approaching the age of majority.

Lord James spent his boyhood on the various family estates at Montrose, Kincardine, and Mugdock. Time has dealt harshly with the Graham strongholds. The merest fragment of Auld Montrose survives, largely overlaid by a much later building which enjoys the same magnificent outlook over the Montrose basin, that curious expanse of sea water which somehow squeezes past the burgh of Montrose to form a great loch in the hinterland. The fertile soil of the parish of Maryton raised rich crops and staunch protestants: such great names of the Scottish Reformation as Wishart, Erskine of Dun, and Melville all had connections with the parish. Nor does much remain of Kincardine castle in Strathearn: one fragment of a wall some twenty feet high survives of this once proud fortress on an impressive site high above the Ruthven Water. The knowledge of local geography acquired during visits to Kincardine would be put to good use at a later date. All of the Graham castles were fired and razed during the 1640s; Mugdock in Strathblane, just south of the Campsie Fells, was no exception. It was described in 1877 as being in a very fragmentary condition and such remains as there were had recently been incorporated into a modern mansion house.

It would hardly be surprising if James, tagging on behind five girls, was more than somewhat spoiled. If not the baby of the family – the 'bairn Beatrix' was born after him – he was the only boy, and sisters and parents alike would be concerned to build a protective wall around the sole Graham heir. Lilias, his eldest sister, married Sir John Colquhoun of Luss in 1620. John was a man of parts. He had studied in France and had recently returned to Scotland after a visit to Heidelberg, the dazzling Renaissance capital of Frederick, the Elector Palatine, and his queen. Young James delighted in spending holidays with the happy couple on Loch Lomondside. There in the *Gaidhealtachd* proper he would hear tales of the atrocities perpetrated by MacGregors and of the treacheries of Clan Campbell.

Although Colquhoun became Montrose's good friend, circumstances prevented him from winning the place in the younger man's affections occupied by Archibald Napier of Merchiston. Napier, the son of 'logarithms John', married Margaret Graham in 1619. There is abundant corroboration for Wishart's assertion that: 'Montrose in his boyhood revered him as a most indulgent parent, in his youth as his wisest counsellor, in his manhood as his truest friend.' After studying at Glasgow University Archie devoted himself to royal service. As he progressed from courtier to privy councillor to Treasurer Depute of Scotland to Lord of Session and Commissioner of Exchequer, he became increasingly disenchanted with the duplicity and skulduggery of political life but his passionate attachment to the monarchy blinded him to the faults of the king, which, in his view, stemmed from corrupt counsellors and crooked courtiers. In spite of his disillusionment he remained politically very ambitious and at some point shortly after Charles 1's accession he actually took it upon himself to give that monarch some near Machiavellian advice on the art of ruling. After warning the king against favourites and factions, misinformations and concealed truths, he asserted that it was an easy matter for a just prince, 'by following only the bent of his own inclinations, to gyf such directions and commands upon matters perfytly known to him, as therby he may reape honour, profitt, the love of his subjects, and the reputation of wisdom and justice'.[5] Charles shared this conviction totally; it was to lead him to the block in 1649. Napier went on to advocate the establishment of an intelligence system, headed by himself, throughout Scotland, in order that the true state of affairs in this 'place remote', might be conveyed to 'your sacred ears'. Mark Napier in several studies of the period was concerned to exaggerate the influence of his illustrious ancestor upon Montrose. The latter would share some of Napier's views but he was reluctant to accept the whole theory of divine right except as a last resort in moments of near total despair. Elsewhere Napier discussed the great chain of being and showed that everything had its rightful place, cheerfully oblivious to the fact that his own recent elevation to the peerage was a negation of his own argument. Montrose was to realize that the chain had been fractured for ever; what he desired above all was a constitutional rearrangement of the links.

Of James's remaining sisters Elizabeth died in childhood and Dorothea married Sir James Rollo of Duncrub in 1628. Katherine, in one of the strangest and most notorious episodes in Graham family history, was to elope with her brother-in-law Colquhoun of Luss and was never heard of again. James also had an illegitimate half-brother Harry Graham, who was to perform stalwart service during the 'Glorious Year'.

If young Lord Graham appears to have been born with a golden sword in his scabbard it was expected that from an early age he should learn to use it. The misfortune of his mother's early death when he was not yet six years old was cushioned by the presence of so many sisters and a kindly father who seems to have been genuinely devoted to his children. Before he was eight, James's 'nags' were being shod for him by the smith at Aberuthven near Kincardine; before long the same man was sharpening and repairing his swords. In November 1624 James was domiciled in a 'great ludgin situat in the citie of Glasgow near the towne heid', where, during the next eighteen months, his education was entrusted to a Master William Forret. In preparation for his first lengthy residence away from home he was fitted out with a new wardrobe which included richly decorated cloaks and suits of camlet, paragon and sage in reds and greens. The sartorial requisites of the scholar and his pages, William and Murdo Graham, totalled over £31. Forret doubled as chamberlain, ensuring that James was furnished with the luxuries befitting his status. Detailed inventories survive of possessions and requisites transported to Glasgow for his comfort. They include silver cups and cutlery, towels, bedding, curtains and 'four pair of linning schorts'. Some of his favourite possessions also accompanied him – a sword presented by Archibald Napier, a brass handgun, a crossbow set with mother of pearl, and books gifted by his father.

The books might be expected to give some indication of James's studies, but equally they could represent the selection of a well-meaning father at the outset of his son's education, of less interest to the recipient than to the donor. They included Lipsius' commentaries on Seneca, the works of the sixteenth-century German botanist Joachim Camerarius, a treatise on knighthood, and William Strauage's *Historie of the life and death of Marie Stuart* (1624), which was pro-Mary and concerned to argue the legality of James vi's claim to the English throne. There was much to fire the imagination in the works of

Xenophon, in Marcantonio Sabellico's *Universal History*, and in the history of Godfrey de Bouillon, the eleventh-century crusader who rejected the title of king of Jerusalem out of respect for Christ's crown of thorns. Many men have dreamed of leading the ten thousand or of driving back the Saracen at the head of a great crusade. 'Every man's the son of his own deeds,' cried Don Quixote, 'and since I am a man I can become pope.' Yet he himself showed that the deeds followed the dream. Montrose never lost his capacity to dream with the passing of the years. His powers of imagination lay behind his greatest achievements. It is not perhaps surprising that a cosseted young nobleman should come to believe that all things were possible; what is remarkable is that even some of these expectations should have been realized. Gilbert Burnet was not far short of the mark when he observed that Montrose 'took upon him the port [carriage] of the hero too much and lived as in a romance'. When he matriculated at St Andrews on 26 January 1627 he took care to include in his personal baggage the most treasured book of all, Sir Walter Ralegh's *History of the World*, which stirred his imagination in youth and continued to inspire him throughout his life. One of his earliest poetic efforts was inscribed on his copy of Quintus Curtius, the Roman historian of Alexander the Great, which king figured prominently in Ralegh's history:

> As Philip's noble son did still distain
> All but the dear applause of merited fame,
> And nothing harboured in that lofty brain
> But how to conquer an eternal name;
> So, great attempts, heroic ventures, shall
> Advance my fortune, or renown my fall.

In later life he would often return to the theme and the example.

On 12 November 1626 Lord James was hastily summoned from Glasgow to Kincardine. Two days later he stood at his father's deathbed. The following January the fourth earl was buried in the Montrose mausoleum at St Kattan's chapel, Aberuthven. The Graham kindred gathered at Kincardine to be feasted on every conceivable kind of meat and game – beef, mutton, ham, veal, venison, partridge, ptarmigan, goose, and 'wylde meit' in general, washed down with claret, sack, white wine, and many gallons of ale.

Since the new earl was fourteen years of age he was entitled in law to select his own curators and it is interesting that so many Graham kinsmen figured in his choice. His curators were his cousin John, second Earl of Wigtown; his two brothers-in-law Archibald, shortly to be raised to the peerage as Lord Napier of Merchiston, and Sir John Colquhoun; the remainder were Grahams – Sir William of Braco, David of Fintry, Sir Robert of Morphie, John of Orchil, Patrick of Inchbrakie, Sir William of Claverhouse, and John of Balgowan.[6] Of the Graham estates, Braco and Orchil, the two youngest branches of the family, are both in the parish of Ardoch, Strathearn; Fintry and Claverhouse are near neighbours just north of Dundee; Morphie, the senior surviving branch, is four miles north of Montrose ; Inchbrakie is near Crieff and Balgowan is in Methven parish, Perthshire. All looked to the fourteen-year-old Graham as their chief and most would suffer for adhering to his cause. His interests were theirs. They would counsel him, share their possessions, incur ruinous debts on his behalf, fight for him, and die for him out of reverence and respect for the almost mystical concept of kinship which had its origins in the farthest recesses of Scotland's chronicled past, but which served in some way to define the present. In 1597 the fourth earl, while still the Master of Montrose, was put to the horn for refusing an assurance by which he was obliged to answer for the good behaviour of the whole of his kin. He protested that he could not make such an undertaking since his father, 'the chief and principal of their house' was still alive, having 'full commandiment' of the followers of his house. 'It wer verie ane unnaturall and undeutifull behaviour to usurp or challange to himselff the commandiment or obedience of the kin, freindis and dependaris of his house during his faderis lyftyme.' The fourth earl once paid Sir William Livingstone of Kilsyth the greatest possible compliment by telling him that he expected him to act the same as a Graham, 'whilk I have found you ever in effecte'. Iain Lom, the bard of Keppoch, would similarly honour Montrose when he referred to him as his *fearcinnidh*, his clansman. In 1605 the Earl of Montrose attempted unsuccessfully to intercede for 'certain of my cousins' who were being transported from the West March. Blood relationship between the Border Grahams and Montrose there was none, but as head of the name he was obliged to assist them.[7] Kinship constituted the main, sometimes the only, foundation on which seventeenth-century Scottish society rested.

On 28 March 1627 James was served heir to his father. Three days later he sold the estate of Airthrey, now in the grounds of Stirling University, to his uncle Sir William Graham of Braco.[8] The fourth earl had intended to place his son in fee of his estates and on the very day of his death a mandate to that effect was issued from Whitehall. The transaction may afford another small clue as to Montrose's birth date since it would appear that he could not be placed in fee until he was fourteen years old. The mandate being cancelled by the old earl's death, a fresh one granted the young heir the feudal casualties of wardship and marriage. Montrose had reason to be grateful for his monarch's generosity since he was desperately short of cash. It was said that when the third earl died in 1608 the king had ordered a funeral of great pomp and had promised to provide 40,000 merks to cover expenses. Since the money was never paid the Grahams were left with the bill.[9] Like his father before him, Montrose raised many wadsets or mortgages on different parts of his estates. The sale of Airthrey was not an isolated instance. He was forced to dispose similarly of other properties. Between 1630 and 1632 he converted most of the kindly tenancies of Dundaff and Mugdock into feu holdings. 'Kindly' is associated with 'kin' and such tenancies were often on very favourable terms. Montrose's one motive in such conversions was the desire to raise capital. If in the short term he was not exactly destitute, he was never very wealthy either.

Between 1627 and 1629 the fifth Earl of Montrose discovered, as have so many undergraduates, that his days at university were the happiest of his life. Financial burdens were borne by his curators and his programme of study was far from onerous. St Salvator's still employed the traditional regenting system whereby students were assigned to one regent throughout their three years of study. As a *bajan* or freshman he studied Greek and Latin, progressing to rhetoric followed by logic, ethics and politics, and in his final year, physics and astronomy.[10] He had ample time for his beloved golf on the links at St Andrews, with visits to the 'courses' at Leith and Montrose. There was leisure too for tennis, for hunting and hawking, for greyhound coursing, and for horse racing at Cupar. Over the years he spent a small fortune on his horses, rewarded after strenuous exercise with pints of ale. He was continually receiving gifts of dogs from kinsmen and friends. The surviving accounts of his personal expenditure at St

Andrews depict an energetic, extravagant, but above all, generous individual. His youth may explain all three attributes.

His best-known achievement at St Andrews is undoubtedly his winning of the silver arrow two years running in 1628 and 1629. The winner had a medal attached to the prize arrow and young Montrose's is still to be seen at St Andrews. The arrows of outrageous fortune seem to have found their targets in these carefree years. In 1623 the medallist was Lord Lorne, later Marquis of Argyll; the following year it was won by the future Earl of Morton, who died on the eve of Montrose's last expedition; the victor of Philiphaugh, David Leslie, took the prize in 1625; and when Montrose first went up to university the winner was Lord Elcho, who was to be driven ignominiously from the field of Tibbermore. The archery competition well illustrates the smallness of the Scottish stage: the same actors had a habit of turning up in different dramas.

The butts, golf, billiards, and any other suitable games were played for money. Montrose was a keen gambler. It is recorded that he frequently lost sums of money on the links, but larger sums, on a more regular basis, were squandered on the cards, though he tended to keep his losses, usually sums of about thirty shillings, in the family by playing in the main with his kinsmen. Through the cards he refined instincts which never left him. He knew what it was 'to put it to the touch, to win or lose it all'.

Another of his loves was music. He is found tipping violers and drummers and on one occasion a trumpeter, but his favourites were the pipers. He gave forty-two shillings to a piper and drummer who came from Stirling while he was residing at Carnock. He sought out pipers at Machany in Strathearn and at St Andrews, to reward their playing. The memorials of Montrose include the fine pibroch *Blar Allt Eirinn*, the Battle of Auldearn, still played at the present time.

Perhaps the most interesting aspect of Montrose's character highlighted by these accounts is his generosity. Not a day went by without his giving money to the poor, to beggars, to destitute Gaels, to servants bringing messages, to university porters, to boys carrying golf clubs or quivers. He never entered or departed from a town without distributing a few shillings to the poor at the gates. His gifts might be dismissed as the extravagances of an idealistic, adolescent popularity-craving profligate but behind the bald entries of his long-suffering tutor John Lambie is to be detected an individual with a genuine interest in his fellow man, a person with a true sympathy for the predicament of humanity, a young man with a genius for personal relationships. Whatever his failings in future years, he would never lose these qualities.

On 24 May 1628 Montrose suddenly became ill. Dr Arnot, the local physician, prescribed a diet of chicken but four days later Dr Maal was summoned from Dundee to add broth, posset, and whey to the menu. There was a flurry of activity around 4 and 5 June when James was given raisins and liquorice and a barber was employed 'for taking off my Lord's hair'. Thereafter he slowly recovered. Trout were sent from Kincardine and moor fowl from Orchil. By the end of the month the patient was once again playing cards. August saw him fit to enjoy an energetic vacation.

The end of term on 6 August was heralded by much settling of accounts. The college cook had to be paid, as had James Pett who supplied the earl with bows and arrows, some of them specially imported from London, He paid the *oeconomus* for board for himself and beef for his hawk, his regent the sum of £20, and to the college porter he gave a gratuity. It remained to tip a fellow removing trunks and furniture from the college chambers, to donate alms to the poor as he mounted his horse, and Montrose was off to Broughty Ferry and three months' vacation.

His first call was at Fintry, where he relaxed at the cards, despatched a boy to Montrose to collect horses, and visited Claverhouse before riding north through fertile Angus to Bonyton close to his estates at Auld Montrose. On 14 August he was playing cards at Morphie, where he remained for a fortnight, taking time out to visit Lord David Carnegie, his father-in-law-to-be, at Kinnaird on the South Esk. He also called in at Auld Montrose ordering repairs to 'ane mekle hoill in the slait-work therof'. On 27 August he was back at Fintry, thence over the ferry at Perth and west along the south bank of the Almond to Balgowan, where his kinsman presented him with a hawk. A short ride through Strathearn took him to the residence of Graham of Inchbrakie on 3 September. He visited Haldane of Gleneagles and then on to Orchil and Braco, where he sent a servant to Edinburgh to have some clothes remodelled. By mid-September he had travelled south to visit Sir George Bruce, the mine owner, at Carnock. On

19 September he lost forty-three shillings at the cards to the Earl of Wigtown at his home in Cumbernauld. From there he moved on to Dumbarton; part of his inheritance was the chaplaincy of the altar of the holy cross situated within the parish church. He seems to have stayed at Rossdhu since he spent two days at the family deer park on Inchmurrin in Loch Lomond. He then went on to Glasgow via Erskine and on 22 October he was back at Cumbernauld. Preparations were made at Kincardine for a visit by 'my Lord and his Lordship's friends'. Coals were laid in 'to be fyring in the place and to air the cleitheis'. His sister Dorothea had recently married Sir James Rollo of Duncrub in Perthshire, so James dropped in to see them. He entertained the Colquhouns together with Haldane of Gleneagles at Drumfad in Strathearn. He paid final calls upon Orchil and Braco and on 6 November he was back in St Andrews having his supper 'in William Geddes his house before his entrie in the College'. The following afternoon he was on the links. Cash was forwarded by the Graham factor to Mr Lambie for the coming term's board and lodging and for an advance of £26 13s 4d to the regent. Various necessities were bought in, such as coal, fresh bed straw, candles, and paper. Montrose's vacation was over for 1628. He had visited all of his curators except Napier, who was currently distracted with plans for a projected royal visit to Scotland. No doubt much business had been transacted; he had been brought up to date on the state of his affairs and most important of all had made personal contact with his closest kinsman. It remained for him to settle in to the pleasant round of study, archery, golf, and the supping of wine and ale with his cronies in his college chambers.

The student spent New Year's Day 1629 in the company of David Lindsay, known locally as 'David the Rosicrucian', at Balcarres in Fife. During a sojourn on the continent Lord Balcarres had imbibed the curious but, as it now seems, highly significant philosophies of the Rosicrucians who looked forward to a new age of religious and intellectual enlightenment through the media of alchemy, medicine, geometrics, and mechanics. He possessed the earliest extant British translations of the esoteric Rosicrucian tracts known as the *Fama* and the *Confessio* and he devoted his life to the study of chemistry and natural philosophy.[11] Was there talk of 'the brotherhood' over the New Year drink? Was the younger man swayed by the Rosicrucian

promise of a golden future? Did Montrose have Balcarres in mind
when he wrote:

> But as a curious Alchemist still draws
> From grosser Mettals finer and from those
> Extracts another and from that again
> Another that doth far excel the same.

Just how much time Montrose devoted to his studies is problematical. The notice of twenty-nine shillings paid to 'ane scoller quho
wretts my Lord's notes in the schooll' may suggest that he was something of an idler, unlike his fellow student Lord Ogilvie, whose
diligence was praised by his regent. Ogilvie delighted in geometry and
resented the enforced idleness of vacations.[12] In April 1627 Montrose
disbursed £19 4s on books in Edinburgh, 'Claverhouse being present'.
The purchases were unexciting – the *Meditationes* of John Gerhard,
John Barclay's romance the *History of Polyarchus and Argenis* (1621),
and the *Meditations* of William Struthers, a notorious convert to
episcopacy of whom Calderwood once observed, 'There never was a
Pharisee heard speake more arrogantly.' In June 1629 he paid for the
binding of the works of George Buchanan at a time when he was
aware that he would not be returning to university due to his impending marriage, and consequently it may be assumed that he was particularly anxious to preserve them. It was alleged that Andrew Melville
used to make his students at St Andrews read Buchanan's *De Iure
Regni Apud Scotos* more diligently than Calvin's *Institutes* and if his
popularity had declined, at least with the Establishment, he was evidently still read by the students. Montrose, in company with the bulk
of his contemporaries, digested the works of the great theoretician. Sir
James Turner averred that at the outbreak of the Troubles his name was
so universally invoked that 'I imagined his ghost was returned to earth
to meander a little among the Covenanters'.[13]

Montrose's literary patronage is briefly reflected in payments to a
somewhat improbable 'Hungarian poet' who made some verses for
him at St Andrews and to a rhymer named Croter at Braco. One of
the most interesting references is 'to Mr. Lithgow delyvering his book
to my Lord, £5 16s'.[14] William Lithgow was a magnificent original,
a genuine eccentric who claimed to have travelled some thirty-six
thousand miles in the course of his life. His mother was a Graham and
he claimed kinship with Montrose. He had dedicated publications to

James's father and grandfather. His first journey, described in his *Most Delectable and True Discourse of an admired and painefull peregrination from Scotland to the most famous Kingdoms in Europe, Asia and Affricke* (London 1614), took him from Paris to the Holy Land and on to Cairo, Malta, and Sicily. 'William of the Wilderness', as he was dubbed by a fellow poet, described his critics as mere 'vomiters of venom'. He had a device tattooed on his right arm with on one side the lettering 'the never conquered Crowne of Scotland' and on the other 'the now inconquerable Crowne of England'. The bewilderment of the Jerusalem tattooist may be imagined as he carried out the instructions of this post-union chauvinist. He had many incredible and often hilarious adventures during which he was sustained by an intense courage and a remarkable single-mindedness. Subsequent expeditions took him to Algiers and Ethiopia and he was tortured by the Spanish Inquisition in 1620. He rewarded Montrose's generosity with a eulogistic passage in a poem intended to be presented to Charles I in 1633.

Towards the end of July 1629 Montrose said farewell to St Andrews and his carefree student days to embark on his final fling as a bachelor. He was to be married to Magdalen Carnegie, youngest daughter of David, Lord Carnegie of Kinnaird, an estate some three miles west along the river from Auld Montrose. Although of a long-established Forfarshire family, Sir David Carnegie was one of the 'new men' of whom James VI tended to make use in preference to the older nobility. Such men devoted their lives to the service of the crown in confident anticipation of acquiring office and title by way of reward. In 1602 Sir David had both alarmed and embarrassed King James when, in the presence of an English agent, he toasted the union of the two Kingdoms and pledged the support of forty muskets to that end. A year later he accompanied James's 'dearest bedfellow', the rather tiresome Anne, together with Prince Henry and Princess Elizabeth on their journey south. The delicate health of the three-year-old Charles detained him in Scotland. Fêted with parties, presentations, and masques at each English city *en route*, Sir David no doubt enjoyed being a member of the royal party. He could tolerate the exasperating and precocious behaviour of his queen in return for the knighthood which awaited him in London, the first chapter in a success story which culminated in his being created Earl of Southesk in 1633. He was a commissioner for union and was active in furthering James's kirk policies, with which he was so closely identified as to become a commissioner of the detested court of high commission in 1610. Six years later he was elevated to the peerage as Lord Carnegie, at which time he was assistant to John, Earl of Montrose, as commissioner to the general assembly. Further honours followed: he became an extraordinary lord of session and a privy councillor. During his sole visit to Scotland after the union, in 1617, James resided at Kinnaird to enjoy the excellent local hunting facilities.

By his wife Margaret Lindsay of Edzell Lord Carnegie had four sons and six daughters, most of whom he married off with sagacious perspicacity to families which, like his own, were to have loyalty to the crown rewarded with peerages. His eldest son David married a daughter of Sir Thomas Hamilton, Tam o' the Cowgate, later first Earl of Haddington. Of his daughters, Margaret found a husband in William Ramsay, future Earl of Dalhousie, Agnes in James Sandilands whose son became Lord Abercrombie. Katherine was espoused to Sir John Stewart of Traquair, later Earl and Lord High Treasurer of Scotland who dithered between king and covenant throughout the Troubles. Marjorie ended life as Viscountess Arbuthnott, Elizabeth as Lady Balvaird. James Carnegie, who fought alongside Montrose, married Mary, daughter of Robert Ker, first Earl of Roxburgh, in February 1629; John, three years later, was married to the daughter of Sir John Scrymgeour of Dudhope, who became a viscount in 1641; Alexander's wife was the sister of the first Viscount Arbuthnott. With uncanny consistency the Carnegie children were conjoined to families on the make. Between 1617 and 1629 their father paid out a total of £100,000 in tocher or dowry. Of that sum £40,000 was used to purchase the greatest prize of all – a husband for Magdalen from the ranks of the established nobility. On the day that Magdalen Carnegie married the Earl of Montrose, Lord Carnegie knew that he had indeed arrived.

For James Graham's part the marriage was dictated mainly by the inexorable demands of economics; the part played by romance is difficult to determine but it is unlikely to have been large. In later years a raid upon Auld Montrose in search of incriminating documents unearthed 'some letters from ladies to Montrose in his younger years, flowered with Arcadian compliments'.[15] Some of these epistles could have emanated from the hand of Lady Magdalen. It is difficult to suggest other names, though they might be found among the Graham kindred or in the pages of the Scots Peerage. The efforts of many earnest commentators to find a Venus to set beside their Scottish Adonis have failed miserably. The silence of the evidence must imply either that his marriage was so happy as to admit of no hint of scandal where the opposite sex was concerned, or simply that he had little interest in women. He was certainly no hopeless lover. The 'pride o' the Grahams' is well exemplified in his unremarkable poem 'In praise of Women':

> But yet, fair ladies, you must know
> Howbeit I adore you so:
> Reciprocal your flames must prove
> Or my Ambition scorns to love

– lines perhaps best interpreted as hinting at a certain lack of happiness in his own domestic relationship. The Grahams, like so many of the Scottish nobility, had long settled for marrying the girl – or for that matter the boy – next door. The union with Magdalen Carnegie was in all probability a marriage of convenience, while the bridegroom's own attitude, to judge from his immediate pre- and post-marital behaviour, was totally phlegmatic. A contemporary letter confirms the tradition that Lord Ogilvie had previously been an unsuccessful rival for the lady's hand.[16]

On 1 August Montrose left St Andrews. As the recent recipient of the silver arrow for the second time and as the possessor of some specially commissioned arrows manufactured in London, he was anxious to demonstrate his prowess. In the space of a fortnight he was at the butts in Broughty, Glamis, and Montrose, calling in at Fintry and Claverhouse. There was also time for hawking, for purchasing guns in Dundee, and for the inevitable evening card session.

From Montrose he crossed the river to Morphie; his kinsman had no doubt played an important part in the marriage negotiations, since he was the husband of Lord Carnegie's sister. After a week during which he ventured briefly into the Mearns, he went direct to Kinnaird, laden with gifts and provisions. He was in Dundee the same evening before returning to Fintry, where he was measured for some fine shirts and boots, shoes, and pumps. But his other curators could not be ignored. In early September he was off to Balgowan by way of Perth and Scone. He called at Inchbrakie *en route* to Orchil and Braco. On a lightning visit to the Napiers at Gartness he patronized an acrobat and some dancers. After some ten days at Braco he rode down Strathallan to

Stirling, where he met Sir James Rollo before passing on to visit the Colquhouns. A brief sally to Govan on the Clyde preceded a call on Wigtown at Cumbernauld, then back to Stirling. The second week in October found him back at Orchil, briefly at Gleneagles, then to Kincardine and Balgowan, and across the ferry at Perth to Fintry. On 18 October he attended the kirk at Kinnaird. During two weeks in the Carnegie household there was much activity and already kinsmen were gathering for the festivities. On 3 November he rode from Morphie to Aberdeen. Morphie had decided to give his young chief a wedding portrait and James duly sat for George Jamesone. The portrait shows Jamesone 'at the peak of his powers' displaying 'an assurance in the drawing which he rarely attained and a rarely subtle interpretation of character'.[17] There is a confidence too about Montrose, as if the seriousness of the eyes was about to be betrayed by the humorous mouth; he has the face of a young man challenging the future to do its worst. The present at least was kind. The French and Spanish wine flowed when Montrose was made a burgess of the city he would later plunder.

On the day before his wedding he met Sir John Colquhoun at Montrose and they celebrated his last day of freedom on the golf course, taking a drink at John Garn's tavern before and after the game. He rode down to Kinnaird to pay a courtesy call and then returned to Morphie, where he spent the night. Unfortunately no account of the wedding has survived. Colquhoun of Luss was present, as were Graham of Morphie, Graham of Orchil, William Graham of Claverhouse, and Walter Graham of Duntroyne. Other curators and kinsmen were doubtless in attendance as well as representatives from the huge Carnegie brood. Money was liberally distributed to the poor as the company returned from the kirk to the house. Carnegie would lay on a lavish banquet of the orgiastic proportions favoured by the Scottish nobility of the period. Massive quantities of rich game dishes would be devoured, accompanied by even greater quantities of wine and aquavit. The minstrels were still playing three days later. After five days the guests began to depart and the newly-wed made a golfing widow of his wife. His trunks and furnishings had been stored at St Andrews by the local minister, one George Wishart, his future biographer. These were transported to his new home and young Montrose settled down to three years of domesticity in the castle of Kinnaird.

2

TOWARDS A
REVOLUTION

*Tis a common thing for all men to complain of the Age in which they
live as the worst of all. But no other reason can be assign'd for it except
that they have felt Nothing of the discommodities of the preceding
Ages. . . .*

Menteith of Salmonet

Chance draws a discreet, if inconvenient, veil over the private life of
Montrose during the eight years in which he moved from the nuptial
bed of Mistress Carnegie to the bed of nails that was the covenant. At
Kinnaird he had the opportunity to learn something of estate management from his astute father-in-law; he had his books, the golf links,
and the hunting park. His curators, only a day's ride away, supervised
several financial and property transactions. A letter survives dated
at Kinnaird in May 1632, asking Campbell of Glenorchy to have
his clansmen compensate for goods and beasts 'lifted' in a raid on
Mugdock.[1] Some time after 22 October the earl left Scotland for a
three-year visit to the continent. Several commentators have treated his
departure at this time as something of a mystery, since Charles arrived
in Scotland for his coronation in June 1633, and Montrose appears to
have been the kind of man perfectly suited to such glittering occasions.
They seek the explanation in a scandal which must have rocked the
family.

On 11 January 1633 Sir John Colquhoun and his German servant
Thomas Carlipis were outlawed for practising 'the crymes of sorcerie,
witchcraft and necromancie upone lady Katherine Graham . . . for
bereifing hir be divilische and unlawfull meanis of hir chastitie . . . and
lykwayis for the filthie and detestabill cryme of incest and adulterie'.
Katherine had gone to stay permanently at Rossdhu some time after

19

her father's death. It was alleged that her brother-in-law resolved to satiate his 'abominable lust and unchaste appetite' upon her and that, when his personal charm and subtle speeches failed miserably, he procured certain love philtres from his sinister manservant. Carlipis also supplied a 'golden jewel' set with diamonds and rubies which he had treated in such a way that the recipient would surrender herself to the donor. Not content with carnal copulation, shameful defloration, and the detestable vice of incest, Colquhoun with the assistance of Carlipis allegedly abducted his victim. 'We must cling to the hope,' wrote Mark Napier, as outraged by the crime as he imagined contemporaries to have been, 'that [Montrose] had made a point of discovering his ruined sister, and had provided some safe but secluded retreat for her abroad.'[2] There are, however, one or two assumptions in Napier's version of events which are untenable.

In the first place, passionate monarchist that he was, he could not understand how anyone could neglect the opportunity of attending Charles I's coronation. In fact Charles had expressed his intention of going to Scotland for that purpose in 1625 and thereafter almost annually. His Scottish policies were so unpopular that his plans were thwarted either by London advisers who feared for his safety or by disenchanted Scots who placed obstacles in his way. In the event he did not reach his native kingdom until eight years after his succession, a delay which, being of longer duration than his grandmother's personal reign, had a further deleterious effect on his relations with his Scottish subjects. Lithgow's poem 'Scotland's Welcome to Her Native Son and Sovereign Lord' states quite frankly in the prologue:

> Say, if he come this yeare say he come not,
> Yet tyme shall praise mee for a loving Scot.

Montrose could not waste his life waiting for a king who never came.

Secondly, Napier assumes that Katherine was younger than Montrose – 'a mere child when she fell within the fangs of her brother-in-law'. The fourth earl's testament, however, shows that Katherine was alive when her brother was born. She was therefore in her twenties, a respectable age by seventeenth-century standards, when the abduction took place. Many women have been tempted by less than a 'golden jewel' set with diamonds and rubies.

Thirdly, as Napier knew but chose to overlook, Colquhoun and

Katherine were long gone by October 1632. The justiciary record states that he had taken her to London in September 1631, where he had since lived with her in incest. Montrose presumably had early notice of their departure, about which he did nothing. The key to this particular mystery might simply be uncomplicated mutual lust. It is difficult to see Katherine, surely in the greatest danger of being left on the shelf, as a totally innocent victim; her maternal grandmother was a strong-willed woman and her great grandmother was married four times. John is known to have been at Heidelberg in 1619;[3] the association of German manservant, necromancy, love philtres, a hint of alchemy, and the reputed capital of the Rosicrucian brotherhood leads to the speculation (it can be no more) that Sir John Colquhoun was tarred with the same brush as Lord Balcarres. His estranged wife Lady Lilias successfully petitioned parliament for aliment in 1639. Eight years later Colquhoun returned to Scotland and craved readmission to the bosom of the Church. However 'he did somewhat decline a plain and free confession of the sin of incest with his sister-in-law till he had settled his estate in the world'.[4] There is a certain dignity about this man (family motto 'si je puis') who flew in the face of convention. Katherine was never heard of again. Montrose's departure had little to do with the Colquhoun affair; the fact that Charles chose to have his coronation during his absence was mere coincidence. The fashionable way to broaden one's horizons was to embark upon the Grand Tour and after the restrictive and rather humdrum nature of life at Kinnaird, Europe must have afforded a fair prospect.

Although little is known of his spell on the continent it is clear that Montrose intended something more than the Grand Tour. His travelling companion and lifelong friend the attractive Tom Sydserff provides a pen portrait of Montrose at this time. 'He was of a middle stature and most exquisitely proportioned limbs; his hair of a light chestnut; his complexion betwixt pale and ruddy; his eye most penetrating though inclining to grey; his nose aquiline.' Elsewhere he was to commend his noble carriage and excellent address, his acceptability to princely society, and his superb horsemanship. It may be suspected that Sydserff, soldier, poet, actor, and playwright, was painting the rather idealized portrait of a character in one of his own plays. He was the son of that Bishop of Galloway who banished the great covenanting divine Samuel Rutherford from his parish of Anwoth to Aberdeen. According to him Montrose travelled in France and Italy. 'Having rendered himself perfect in the Academies, his next delight was to improve his Intellectuals, which he did by allotting a proportionable time to reading and conversing with learned men . . . He studied as much of the mathematics as is required for a soldier.'[5]

The military academies were what drew him to France. During the winter of 1633-4 he studied at Angers. The great Gustav Adolph had perished on the field of Lutzen the previous year but already his revolutionary tactics were the subject of study. Much of Montrose's military success was attributable to the ingenious combination of text-book tactics with the traditional warfare of the clans. His mathematical studies also had a strictly military application. For example, Richard Norwood's *Fortification or Architecture Military* (London 1639), which was dedicated to the Marquis of Hamilton, aimed to show 'the application of Triangles according to that late invention of Logarithmes'. Mathematics was largely concerned with the science of siege warfare, which was why such notable figures as Argyll and Cromwell commended the subject to their sons. In visiting Angers in the Loire valley Montrose was traversing an area known to Scots for centuries. While he was there Dr Marc Duncan, principal of the protestant college at nearby Saumur, was called in to investigate the *possédées* of Loudun. The strange case of Urbain Grandier was the talk of France in 1634 and it is not impossible that Montrose made the comparatively short trip from Angers to Loudun to witness the diabolic possessions of Sœur Jeanne des Anges and her nuns. One who made a lengthier journey to witness the spectacle and to satisfy his curiosity, in 1634, was John Maitland, future Duke of Lauderdale. He was unimpressed; he had often witnessed more convincing possessions back home in Scotland.[6]

Montrose was accompanied by the faithful Lambie and by John, son of Graham of Morphie. On 27 March 1635 he visited the English College at Rome with James, Earl of Angus, whose father had recently been created Marquis of Douglas. Father and son had earned the displeasure of the authorities because Lord James's education was entrusted to catholics. Burnet relates that at some stage Montrose also met the son of the Earl of Denbigh and that together they consulted all the astrologers that they could find. Montrose's stars apparently predicted a glorious future for a time before all was lost in the conclusion.

During his absence Wigtown, Carnegie, Napier, Morphie, and

Claverhouse handled his financial affairs. They arranged bills through the Edinburgh merchant William Dick of Braid, whose factors cashed them in Paris. On his behalf the same curators paid four hundred merks towards the library and fabric of the College of Glasgow. While he toured in France and Italy, as his father had before him, Montrose was kept in touch with home affairs. Lord Archie wrote to him about the coronation and informed him of the trouble that was building up in Scotland.

The causes of the covenanting revolution have often been rehearsed. To any student of Scottish history Charles I's Act of Revocation, the reduction of the teinds, increased taxation, and ecclesiastical innovation lead inexorably towards the revolt against the prayer book and the National Covenant of 1638. Yet these are the symptoms of a much more deeply rooted malaise, the recognition of which sheds considerable light on the problem of why a man like Montrose should have given his support to the covenant.

When Bishop Burnet considered the origins of the Troubles he began with religion: 'The reformation of Scotland was popular and parliamentary.' He was correct. In most countries reformation was imposed from above by the ruler. John Knox realized that neither the young catholic Mary Queen of Scots, nor her mother the regent, was likely to establish protestantism in Scotland. There was, however, an alternative: Knox could invoke Scottish precedent. As long ago as 1320 a letter to the pope from the nobility, the baronage, and the community of the realm of Scotland, which came to be known as the Arbroath Declaration, had enunciated the possibility of deposing Robert Bruce if he did not act in the best interests of his people. This notion was itself firmly rooted in the Celtic past and in the works of several political theorists. Just as the *daoine uaisle*, or noble kindred, of a clan might remove an unworthy chief, the Scottish nobility could move against an unsatisfactory king, and consequently kingship in Scotland never quite acquired the same aura or elevated status which it enjoyed in other medieval kingdoms. The great schoolman John Major of Haddington, who may have actually taught Knox for a short time, asserted that those who 'appointed' a king had an obligation to decide 'any incident of a doubtful character that may arise concerning that king'. He believed that kings owed their institution to the people and most of all to 'the chief men and the nobility who act for the common people'. It was up to the latter sector of Scottish society to discuss 'any ambiguity that may emerge in regard to a king'.[7] Knox judged that the matter of religion constituted one such ambiguity and writing from Dieppe in 1557 he urged the nobility of Scotland to undertake 'the reformation of religion and of public enormities'. Like Major, however, Knox distrusted the nobility and in just over a year he was to spell out the justification for full-scale popular revolt. This period also marked the break from Calvin, who argued that resistance against the magistrate – i.e. lawfully constituted authority – was resistance against God. Knox's expressed views became the more extreme, the more uncertain he became about whether reformation would ever take place in Scotland. Yet once again the way had been charted by earlier writers.

In the course of the fifteenth century the nature of nobility was increasingly questioned, notably in an anonymous tract called *The Porteous of Nobleness*. The duty of the nobles was explicitly and simply stated – they were to serve their king and defend their subjects. If they failed in this task they became 'mere carls and of mair vyle condicioun than be dronkart or ruffien that sellis his land to lif in harlotry'. Also birth alone did not confer nobility; it was essential to possess noble qualities such as virtue, truth, the non-abuse of power, and so on. Major made the same point. He simply asked, 'Was Adam noble or not?', and the deafening silence of the answer opened the floodgates of social revolution. When Sir David Lindsay visited Hell in his poem 'The Dreme', he discovered that it was not reserved only for clerics, princes, and kings – 'mony ane thousand/common pepill lay, flichterand in the fyre'. In his *Satire of the Three Estates* it was John o' the Commonweal who averted the disruption of the parliament and who helped to enlighten the king as to his misrule. The superb *Complaint of Scotland* (1549) personified Noble, Clergy, and Labourer as the three sons of Dame Scotia. Again misrule was condemned, the nobility of Noble questioned, and the possibility of popular revolt implied. John Knox knew his Scotland. When it appeared that the nobles would renegue on reformation he addressed himself to the Scottish commonalty.

Albeit God hath put and ordained distinction and difference betwixt the king and subjects, betwixt the rulers and the common people, in the regiment and administration of civil policies, yet in the hope of the life to come he hath made all equal ... to you it doth no less appertain, than to your king or princes, to provide that Christ Jesus be truly preached amongst you, seeing that without his true knowledge can neither of you attain to salvation. And this is the point wherein, I say, all men is equal.[8]

Small wonder that the reformers placed so much emphasis on 'discipline'. Knox unleashed the hounds of Hell and he cut their bonds with an instrument forged on a Scottish anvil. Religion remained 'popular and parliamentary'. The danger was that the hounds might also rampage in the secular sphere. In 1488, when Major was a young man, James III met his death as the result of a revolt by a majority of the nobility; five years before Knox died the Scots deposed their young Queen Mary. At a time when theorists throughout Europe were actively discussing the legality of resistance and of deposition, the Scots carried out these exercises in practical politics. Justification after the event was provided by George Buchanan, the mentor of the Scottish revolution.

The works of Buchanan were still regarded with apprehension by the Establishment as late as the end of the eighteenth century. One of his own disapproving contemporaries considered him 'another Moses, not saved from the Nile, but born and educated among the mountains of Lennox, afterwards drinking in among the French, the error and madness of Calvin, instead of the wisdom of the Chaldees'.[9] Best known as the compiler of a vituperative attack on Mary, Queen of Scots and as the irascible tutor of her son, his most inflammatory works were the *De Jure Regni Apud Scotos* (1579) and his lengthy history of Scotland *Rerum Scoticarum Historia*, published in 1582, the year of his death. More than most historians he could be accused of using the past as a vehicle for his own bias. Although he is a difficult and often obscure writer, the clearest expression of his views is to be found in the *De Jure*. Buchanan believed that kings were originally appointed by the people, who required someone to mediate in their disputes. Experience is the greatest teacher and produces the most effective practitioner whatever the art in question. The sum of experience in the art of ruling is contained in the laws which are essential to the wellbeing of society, since he who is selected to rule 'is not only a king but a man, liable to commit errors, some involuntarily, through ignorance and many almost against his will'.[10] Therefore the people had long ago learned that it was safer to 'base their freedom upon laws than upon kings'. At the centre of Buchanan's thinking is the belief that what distinguishes the king from the tyrant is that the former is governed by the laws while the latter is not. Since the king is a mere man he is not to be given power to make law; the people must be given the right to prescribe the limits of royal authority. George, however, was no democrat; rather he favoured enlightened oligarchy. Since the people at large constitute 'a monster with many heads', only 'selected people of all classes should assemble to advise the king . . . roughly in accordance with our standing practice'. When this body has agreed upon a measure it should be referred to the people at large for their approval.

In reply to the argument that kings are born not elected and so enjoy the heritable right to have their will regarded as law, Buchanan cites examples from Scottish history to show that bad kings, or tyrants, have always been called to account. Such kings like those subjects who rebel against the good ruler have infringed a contract. 'If you bring an action against me in virtue of a contract, what should prevent me from producing those reasons which enable pacts and contracts to be ended? . . . What body of men can more justly demand restoration than a complete nation?' To emphasize the reality of the contract he cites a very interesting example. 'Those of us Scots who retain our time-honoured practice to this day, elect the chief of our clan and associate with him a council of wise men – and the chief is liable to lose his office if he does not obey this council.' At his installation a king (like a Highland chief) makes certain undertakings; he accepts the laws along with his kingship. Just as the laws create the hereditary king so they limit his powers – 'There is a mutual contract between king and people.' In another tract Buchanan once again resorts to the example of Gaeldom. The people of Scotland choose their king and confer upon him a council of the wisest 'which ancient custom the men of the Isles and others in choosing of their chiefs yet still observes. And since ever the regiment [government] of a king was admitted within the Realm, the nobility has understood that it appertained to them to correct the enormities of their princes, and all kings have acknowledged the same except when tyranny maintained them.'[11] Buchanan had no hesitation in invoking the Celtic past to justify the Scottish present.

Apart from his ideas on tyrannicide, which were more complex and ambivalent than many commentators have allowed, Buchanan bequeathed to posterity three important and interrelated legacies. The first of these was the sanctity of law. Desuetude was common in Scots law. Identical statutes were re-enacted again and again from reign to reign and it was not the case in Scotland that once a statute was placed on the statute book it remained there until it was removed by subsequent act of parliament. In the age of Bacon and Coke the Scots were to be shocked into the realization that Scotland had no fundamental law, in the sense of English common law, to which there could be a constitutional appeal. The early reformers and later the presbyterians were to place much greater emphasis upon statute than had ever previously been the case in Scotland. Indeed Buchanan's ideas, reinforced by much discussion both in England and Scotland, were enshrined in the dense second part of the National Covenant where the phrase 'fundamental law' significantly appears. Montrose's theories on law were also lifted straight out of Buchanan. Secondly, a covenant is simply a contract. The covenant represents an explicit attempt to reinstate and to restate the contract between the king and his people entered into with, and in the sight of God. The pact or agreement was in any case an everyday occurrence in Scotland in bonds of manrent or maintenance, promising reciprocal mutual aid between the parties concerned. The covenanters would elevate contract to a religious doctrine. And thirdly, Buchanan established that the nobility were the custodians of the contract. Interpretations of custodianship would differ greatly. Argyll was to opine that 'popular furies would never have end if not awed by their superiors . . . the people will soon learn their own strength . . . and from thence infer that popular power excells the power of the noblesse'. On the other hand Montrose was to address 'ye meaner people of Scotland who are not capable of a respublick', almost in desperation. 'Do you not know when Monarchical Government is shaken, the great ones strive for the garland with your blood and fortunes?'[12] Both Montrose and Argyll were caught up in a reactionary revolution where custom had the force of novelty. But perhaps no one was more conscious of the eternal conundrum that is history than Geordie Buchanan, who wrote in an early poem:

> So old the tale; but whether merely old
> I leave to each man's judgement. Some may smell
> Mustiness in anything raked out
> From ancient records; others may call that fresh
> Which matches what is green in memory.[13]

The *De Jure* was avowedly published to provide young King James with an indication of the duties he owed his subjects, but James soon revolted against the views of his old tutor. He came to realize that the reformation was anti-monarchical. 'Some fiery spirited men in the ministry . . . began to fancy themselves a democratic form of government,' and hoped, 'by leading the people by the nose, to bear the sway of all the rule.' His expressed views were totally antithetical to those of Buchanan. His *Trew Law of Free Monarchies* (1598) justifies monarchy, or at least James's definition of it, on three counts – scripture, law, and nature. Buchanan's theories on the origins of kingship are dismissed as irrelevant since King Fergus came out of Ireland, became king of Scotland by conquest, and imposed his laws on the land. According to Scotland's 'fundamental laws', a phrase of which James was inordinately fond, doubtless owing to a shrewd and envious appreciation of southern usage, the king is lord of all. Parliament is simply the king's head court where laws are 'but craved by his subjects and only made by him at their rogation'. He is bound by the law only through his own goodwill and an enlightened desire to set a good example to his subjects. His view of monarchy is thoroughly patriarchal. He cannot tolerate those ingenious spirits who identify the commonwealth with a mother who must be defended from an erring spouse. James has no fear of the explicit. No king can be so bad that opposition is preferable – 'Better it is to live in a commonwealth where nothing is lawful, than where all things are lawful to all men.'[14] In the aftermath of Major, Knox, and Buchanan, not to mention Beza, Bodin, Hotman, and a host of continental theorists, James's ideas are strikingly reactionary. He grants, as did early English medieval writers, that wicked kings are sent by God to curse his people, but like them he denies that the people may remove such rulers by their own hand. With the notion of a contract he has no sympathy whatsoever. Given its history, Scotland was just about the last place, though perhaps it deserved to be the first, for a king to articulate such extreme views of divine right. In his *Basilikon Doron* James betrayed the true source of his fears. To his chagrin, he who so often pointed out that kings would be judged by God alone, who never tired of emphasizing that the 'highest bench is sliddriest to sit upon', was forced to admit that the Scottish reformation was 'extraordinarily wrought by God, wherein many things were inordinately done by a popular tumult and rebellion'. In other countries God had sensibly used the Prince to guide his people to reformation. In Scotland the king was often 'calumniated in popular sermons, not for any evil or vice in me but because I was a king, which they thought the highest evil'. The weapon used by the ministers was parity, 'the mother of confusion and enemy to unity', which, James warned, 'once established in the ecclesiastical government, the politic and civil state should be drawn to the like'. If parity was the mother of confusion, the father of parity, so far as Scotland was concerned was James's *bête noire*, Andrew Melville.

In 1575 Melville, a brilliant academic fresh from Beza's Geneva, informed the general assembly that prelacy had no foundation in the scriptures and that originally all ministers of the gospel were equal. He almost provided an ecclesiastical mirror image of Buchanan's views on the social origins of kingship. He went on to advocate the Geneva example of presbyterian parity and the abolition of bishops in the kirk. The propagation of his famous theory of the 'Twa Kingdoms' followed, in which he envisaged the separation of the temporal from the spiritual, the one ruled by James Stewart, the other by Jesus Christ. It is little wonder that James sought refuge in divine right. Melville sought nothing less than a Scottish theocracy. Between them the two men drew the lines for a bloody and interminable battle to be fought in the next generation. The first skirmishes took place in the king's own lifetime, but his victories were pyrrhic.

The shining example of French absolutism was presented to James by the first human being to whom he gave his love, Esmé Stewart, created Duke of Lennox and suspected by the ministers both for his catholic leanings and for his unhealthy influence on the young king. The presbyterians eventually contrived the banishment of Lennox and, in 1581, forced the king and his household to subscribe the so-called Negative Confession which condemned anything remotely savouring of popery. This document later became the first part of the National Covenant. When James regained the upper hand and banished Melville and his followers to England, they delegated James Carmichael, minister of Haddington, to gather materials which would justify their actions. A concomitant of exile was legislation of 1584 outlawing presbyterianism and dubbed the 'Black Acts' by its victims. From then on the kirk was in a position of compromise as James gradually evolved his scheme of bishops in presbytery. In March 1586, in a letter to his father, Carmichael bitterly attacked any such compromise. He claimed there could be no going back on the *covenant* of 1581, apparently the first occasion on which the confession was so described. He compared it to the covenant 'maid betwene the Lord and Joas, the king and the people in the presence of Jehoida that they should be the Lord's people' (*2 Kings* 11:17). 'No posteritie did find any dowt in anie thing of that covenant since.' Carmichael's identification of confession and covenant was ingenious. A covenant joined with God could not be broken and so must attract the sanction of law in the civil sphere. He combined the appeal to scripture and the appeal to law which is at the root of covenanting ideology. Others would elaborate and amplify the concept; to Carmichael, perhaps, belongs the credit for originality.[15]

If the activities of the presbyterians might have tried the patience of a saint and driven the best-disposed king to despotism, an even greater problem threw its shadow over the reign of James VI. A recent authority has stated, 'How much demand there was in Scotland for constitutional changes before the troubles is hard to say,'[16] but this is to minimize the profound anxiety experienced by many Scots in contemplating first the prospect, and later the fact, of the greatest constitutional change of all, namely the personal union of 1603. Both James and Charles were guilty of imposing innovations in government, administration, and religion on the Scots without consultation of any kind. If there was no demand on the part of their subjects for constitutional change *per se*, which is questionable, there is no doubt that they sought a return to some notional pre-existent *status quo*.

Many of the pitfalls of the personal union were diagnosed by the outstanding Scottish feudal lawyer Sir Thomas Craig in his absorbing treatise *De Unione Regnorum Britanniae*. Although a devoted monarchist and a convinced unionist Craig preserves the contemporary arguments of those less enthusiastic than himself who feared the accuracy of Henry VII's prediction that the greater must inevitably attract the lesser. The union could be likened to a conquest. 'Our kings will be Englishmen born in England, residing in England', and preferring Englishmen as their attendants and courtiers. Few Scots would be able to advance themselves at court and then only through bribery. London would become the capital of the whole island. 'Towards London the wealth of Scotland will flow. . . . Voluntarily, therefore and in the friendliest spirit we yield to our neighbours in this union, terms such as they could not have obtained save as the result of the bloodiest war and most conclusive victory.' It was feared that Edinburgh would lose its superiority. Geography must discriminate against Scottish suitors at the English court. Towns and trade would suffer as the best craftsmen and merchants gravitated southwards. Craig concluded his account by making some suggestions on ensuring the durability of union. If his advice had been heeded the Scottish revolution might have been avoided. It was essential, in his view, that the two kingdoms be placed upon an equal footing; historical problems had arisen because England would not admit an equal nor Scotland a superior. He shrewdly reminded his readers that in the Declaration of Arbroath the Scots had pledged themselves never to submit to the English yoke, so long as one hundred of them remained alive. The religion of each country must be preserved – 'Innovations in religion are invariably accompanied by great stir and resentment among the populace.' All men in both kingdoms must devote themselves to the defence of the life, dignity, and interests of their common sovereign. 'Should the stock of his most noble majesty fail it will have to be looked to whether the two kingdoms may not again fall apart and the feuds of the past be renewed.' Craig believed that separate legal systems were not incompatible with union and, great lawyer that he was, he could not agree with Francis Bacon and others who wished to see Scots law assimilated to that of England. Each nation must be governed in accordance with its own inviolable laws and customs. Each parliament must retain its own status and authority, its sovereignty must be protected, and there must be no promulgation of new laws nor repeal of existing law without the authority of the parliament concerned. The imposition of taxation and the declaration of war must be similarly reserved. He threw out a challenge to posterity which, for good or ill, has never been accepted. 'As far as possible the public annals of the two countries should be revised. Errors and irritating expressions must be expunged (though in this matter our own histories are not so provocative as those of our neighbours) and a new history of Britain should be written with the utmost regard to accuracy.' The king was urged to spend one year in three in Scotland (James had expressed his intention of visiting Scotland every three years, which is rather different) and to employ Scotsmen in attendance during his residence. In the coming struggle almost every piece of advice tendered by Craig was rejected, with the consequences which he himself predicted.[17]

When Taylor, the water poet, arrived at Holyrood he found an inscription on the old palace which read: '106 forefathers have left this to us unconquered.' In 1607 James took the opportunity to amplify statements already made in his *Trew Law* when he told the English Commons that by 'fundamental laws' the Scots intended only those laws which maintained the king's lineage and 'the heritage of succession and monarchy . . . not meaning as you do their Common Law, for they have none but that which is called *Jus Regis*'. He went on to quote what has become one of his best-known statements: 'This I must say for Scotland and many truly vaunt it: Here I sit and govern with my pen: I write and it is done, and by a clerk of the Council I govern Scotland now which others could not do by the sword.' The staggering implications of James's words are seldom noted. After 1603 he administered Scotland like a town-bound country squire, passing on estate instructions to his factors. He proclaimed the discontinuation of the names Scotland and England except in legal proceedings. Scottish shipmasters complained that new flags which they were expected to fly prejudiced the freedom and dignity of Scotland because St George's cross was imposed upon that of St Andrew. His English subjects were no happier about the implications of union than the Scots, and James was later to reassure them that his desire was to 'conform the Laws of Scotland to the Law of England . . . my intention was always to effect union by uniting Scotland to England and not England to Scotland'.[18] He gradually reduced the membership of the privy council and ordered that records be kept of how councillors voted. In 1609 the Earl of Dunbar, Treasurer of Scotland, who together with the chancellor had been given precedence over the rest of the Scottish nobility, observed St George's day. Many of the 'ancient nobility' absented themselves from the parliament of that year, delayed for the funeral of Montrose's grandfather; the latter's heir and his peers complained of the precedence given to the bishops. An act forbade slanderous or reproachful speeches against England or English councillors, which tended to the hindrance of the wished accomplishment of perfect union. That year the court of session rose for Christmas for the first time since the Reformation. In 1610 the privy council reminded the king that copies of treaties passed to the clerk-register must be properly authenticated, unlike the recent treaty with France. The following year James scolded the Archbishop of Glasgow and Chancellor Dunfermline for being so presumptuous as to think of travelling personally to

London to offer condolences for the death of Prince Henry 'as if Scotland were a free estate'.[19] The council was alarmed when Scottish subjects were cited to appear before the English council to answer for a Border dispute.

Yet James did not have everything his own way; sometimes the factors protested that they knew more of estate management than he did. In 1607 the Scottish nobility adopted their time-honoured role and asked him to discontinue his efforts towards a closer union. They recommended that he employ officials of Scottish nationality, without prejudice, and requested that he reside in Scotland from time to time. 'We have laboured to extol all the Apparent Benefits we might receive [through union] and to Conceal and Suppress the True Ills.' They reminded the king that Scotland equalled England in dignity and the desire for liberty; the English were attempting to dominate the union. In the same year the privy council, not quite as tame as James liked to pretend, made almost exactly the same points. They claimed to have used the term 'fundamental law' only in imitation of the English. While agreeing with his interpretation of it they had invoked it in order that this 'ancient and native kingdom should not be turned into a conquered and slavishe province to be governed by a Viceroy or a Deputye'.[20]

One section of the Scottish community had already challenged James's view of the *Jus Regis*. Nineteen ministers attended a prorogued general assembly at Aberdeen in July 1605. James chose to treat this act of defiance as rebellion; he had thirteen of the offenders arrested and eight of them were imprisoned in Blackness castle. James Melville in his *Apologia* for the action of the ministers justified their conduct with reference to scripture, to the customs and constitution of the kirk, and to the laws of the realm, tracing legislation which safeguarded the privileges and freedom of the church back to the reign of James i. He opined that nothing could be more dangerous to the kirk than James's attack on general assemblics, 'at suche a tyme, namelie of the treatie of Unioun, when all the states of the realme, and everie particuler are zealous and carefull of thair right and possessions'.[21] When they were summoned before the privy council they presented a declinature, declining the competence of the council to decide a spiritual matter. Although there was perfectly respectable precedent for declinature it earned them a further charge of treason. What followed has been described as 'one of the greatest constitutional trials in Scottish history'.[22] The accused denied that their declinature in any way challenged royal authority. After a lengthy and articulate defence with much reference to the Christian duties of 'good Scottishmen', they were found guilty and banished the kingdom. Delighted with this new (and utterly unconstitutional) means of suppression, James ordered that a further eight be tried. The council, unhappy about the constitutional precedent, refused on the grounds that another trial would simply exacerbate an uneasy situation. They envisaged the fire kindled among a few spreading over the whole country with dire consequences.[23]

When Andrew and James Melville with others were summoned to London to plead the case of the Blackness ministers they were commanded to appear before the Scottish council there, which was made up of a group of noble Scottish courtiers. James Melville denied their competence. 'I am a free subject of the kingdom of Scotland which hath laws and privileges of its own, as free as any kingdom in the world. There have been no summons lawfully executed against me; the noble men here present and I, are not in our own country.' His uncle later told them that they were degenerated from the ancient nobility of Scotland who were accustomed to giving their lives and their lands for their country and the gospel.[24]

As the reign wore on James was able to fashion a kirk more to his taste with the full pre-presbyterian panoply and more besides. There was great opposition to his Five Articles of Perth which proposed kneeling at communion, observance of the Christian year, private communion, and private baptism and confirmation. Those charged with opposition to the Articles again presented the declinature and in 1620 Chancellor Seton told the king that the privy council had no competence in church matters – 'We may reason whether we sall be the bishops' hangman or not!' Ultimately the Blackness ministers won their point. In drawing up a declinature they were proposing an alternative to James's definition of the *Jus Regis*. Once he moved to England the king chose to delude himself with divine right from a distance. When his own ambitions for an integral union failed owing to Scottish and English hostility, he chose the kirk as the model for union. Much was forgiven James, 'our native king', which would not be permitted to Charles, a native raised in a foreign land, who understood nothing of Scotland and cared less. Many read great significance into the destruction by the floods of 1621 of a newly built bridge across the Tweed at Berwick. It was to bear the inscription: 'Hoc uno ponte duo regna conjunxi: Deus diu conjuncta servet.' James's final dreams of union were carried away on flood waters which surged on through the reign of his son. If the Scottish revolution had a mentor in George Buchanan and a prophet in Thomas Craig, the best evidence for the contribution of King James is the remarkable rapidity with which opposition to his son manifested itself.

James died on 27 March 1625. On 14 April John Leslie, sixth Earl of Rothes, who had been a vociferous opponent of the Five Articles, was already complaining of the straining of the ordinary customs of the privy council, of innovations in the kirk, and of the impairing of the liberties of the nobility in both council and parliament. He hoped that the new reign might produce some mitigation of these extremities to foster a unity of minds hitherto 'jangled with changes both in kirk and civil state'.[25] Charles was not the man to quench his fears. By 17 May he had drafted an act of revocation which, by the time it was fully published, had gone far beyond the traditional reservation of crown property made by the monarch in his twenty-fifth year. The act cancelled all grants of crown property made since 1540. Alarming though this was the king went farther. In pursuit of an equitable solution to the thorny problem of ecclesiastical endowment which had plagued the church since the Reformation, he revoked all grants of church lands. It was intended that all holders of such property should surrender it to the crown in return for compensation. He also proposed a scheme for the commutation of the teinds which in theory were placed at the disposal of the crown, so apparently threatening the financial security of donor and recipient alike. A concomitant of revocation would be the abolition of heritable jurisdictions. So sweeping were those measures, so tactlessly and in such an air of secrecy were they introduced, that they caused consternation not only among all Scottish landholders, but also among the clergy whom they were ultimately intended to benefit. The act passed the privy seal to become law on 12 October; a month later the privy council protested to the king that the act had been kept 'so obscure as none as yitt hes sene the same . . . nothing hes so far disquyeted the myndis of your goode subjectis and possest thame with apprehensionis and feares of the consequenceis thairof'.[26]

Charles did not rest at the act of revocation. In the first few months of his reign he succeeded in alienating almost every section of the Scottish community, blindly following the example of his father who had dinned divine right into his soul. A convention of estates cheerfully voted £400,000 Scots in taxation to finance Charles's projected visit to Scotland and to assist in the war effort in Germany and the Low Countries. Chancellor Hay offered to commute the tax for the service of two thousand troops for three years. Not surprisingly the offer was rejected, a refusal indicative of a new-found muscle on the part of the convention. Twelve miscellaneous items relating to governmental and economic matters were submitted for the convention's consideration. Some of these were referred to the privy council; a few were accepted; some were rejected. A proposal to levy customs duty of forty-eight shillings for every ton of coal exported in foreign vessels was considered to jeopardize the livelihood of the coal owners; a recommendation that all offices obtained by bribery or fraud should be forfeited was accepted, with the canny stipulation that it should have no retrospective application; a suggestion that judges of session should ride to court was thrown out as absurd since most of them lived in the closes and vennels nearby. When it was rumoured that Charles proposed some alteration in the court of session he was told that since the session was established by parliament it could not be altered without reference to that body. Charles had decided, with some reason, that the office of session judge was incompatible with membership of the privy council. When the council was reconstituted in March 1626, excluding lords of session, the list of new or reappointed councillors was ominously headed by Archbishop Spottiswood. The president was John, fourth Earl of Montrose. So unpopular was the reconstituted council, even with some of its own members, that there was difficulty in finding a quorum. 'When his Majesty begins at the College of Justice to correct any presumption of enormities what shall be the end of laws and rebellious people? Corruption in the Council is much prejudicial to a common weal; but corruption in the kirk much more impediment both to Christ, his kingdom, and his viceregent, King Charles.'[27] By attacking the council Charles had begun to sever the muscle so confidently flexed by the convention the year before.

For the remainder of Charles's peaceful reign the privy council was in a wretched situation, ground between the millstones of an over-zealous king and a recalcitrant population. It is too easy to dismiss its members, along with the king's officers of state, as a group of self-seeking opportunists. Men like Hamilton and Traquair fumbled to comprehend the unprecedented and extremely complex position in which they found themselves. Napier believed that the ends sought by Charles were often laudable in themselves, but the means were wrong. He warned the king against the elevation of churchmen to offices of state, against the employment of, and over-implicit trust in, bad counsel, against obscure and secretive legislation, and against excessive taxation.[28] His advice went unheeded.

In 1630 Charles revealed his plans for a Society of the Fishery of Great Britain, designed to harvest the rich waters of England, Scotland, and Ireland. Rothes as head of the Scottish commission on the project was warned by the privy council that the final treaty on common fishing must in no way prejudice the liberties and privileges of the crown and law of Scotland. His commission was to safeguard the interests of native fishermen and it was emphasized that the Scottish seas belonged to the Scottish crown, so that the English had no right to fish them save by the terms of the treaty. During protracted negotiations there were many wrangles over the extent of the Scottish fishing limits and the king was informed that the kingdom sustained great prejudice through the suppression of the name of Scotland in various documents issued in his name 'and confounding the same under the name of Great Britain, although there be no union as yet with England.'[29] In the sensitive climate of Caroline Scotland a humdrum discussion of fishery limits could quickly escalate into a debate on constitutional principle.

The ubiquitous William Lithgow compiled a truly remarkable poem in honour of Charles's coronation in 1633. 'Scotland's Welcome to Her Native Son' is a long sustained treatise on the country's sufferings due to the absence of the king; it inescapably recalls the predictions of Craig and its content is paralleled both in the register of the privy council and in contemporary correspondence. Scotland is personified as a widow who welcomes Charles as son, husband, and father. The king is urged to co-operate with parliament in producing good laws, to speed up justice in the courts, to settle true religion, and to remedy the abuses of the commonwealth. Towns and trade are in a state of decay – 'London robbes mee of my gaine.' The nobility squander their wealth in costly court visits to the detriment of themselves and their tenants. For their poverty Charles himself is much to blame,

> Beleeve Mee Sir, I feare this revocation,
> Make many one revoke both state and nation.

Scotland asks for legislation to prevent the nobility posting down to London whither two million pounds' worth of gold has been transported since the death of James. In the old days the nobles kept great households, unburdened with debt; now their castles and tower houses are ruined. They fritter their time in brothels and taverns, careless of the wellbeing of their children and kindred, and they cultivate the English language so that they, 'forgetting Scots can speek with gilded Spurres'. The teinding system should be reformed and the revenues used for schools, colleges, hospitals, and bridges; teinds should be commuted for money rent to alleviate a situation where crops rot on the ground before they can be teinded. Berwick has become a refuge for bankrupts – a city like Rome in its viciousness. The backbone has gone out of Scottish manhood who have

> growne effeminat, weare womens loks,
> Freize hanging combd, o're shoulders, necks and cloks,
> That many doubt, if they bee mayds or men,
> Till that their beards sprout forth, and then they ken.

Witchcraft is so rife that the burning of witches has caused a coal shortage. There is too much usury, too much begging, too much flattery, too much drinking, too much circulation of foreign currency – all because Scotland's native son is absent.[30]

Allowing for considerable poetic licence Lithgow does exemplify the dangerous degree to which Charles and his government could be blamed for all pettifogging inconveniences once initial discontent had set in. He also provides a useful backdrop for Charles's coronation and the parliament of 1633. The king did not win many admirers. His religious observance smacked of popery and his visit cost the city of Edinburgh a fortune, both at the time and subsequently, as his extravagant building schemes were carried out in Parliament Hall and the Tron kirk, as well as the refurbishing of St Giles as a fitting cathedral for the newly created diocese of Edinburgh. He placed manacles on parliament and packed its legislation with such distasteful subjects as increased taxation, innovations in religion, and the revocation. Newly prescribed apparel for churchmen recalled Rome and the tentacles of Antichrist tightened round the throat of Scotland as the bishops were granted an ever-growing role in secular affairs. The Scottish opposition produced a supplication which alluded to most of these developments. It also claimed that Charles's conduct was 'contrary to the constitution of a free parliament'.[31] Charles rejected the supplication outright and charged Lord Balmerino, who had been largely responsible for its revision, with treason. He was found guilty but reprieved from death by the king.

In the same year (1634) Charles ordered the Scots to adopt a new prayer book based on the English model. Two years later he published a new code of canons which embodied the Five Articles. At the insistence of the bishops much was inserted in the prayer book which reflected Scottish practice but it remained a thinly disguised alien liturgy imposed on the kirk by royal prerogative. It retained such presbyterian bogies as saints' days and passages from the Apocrypha; most evocative of all it pushed the communion table back against the east wall of the church and permitted the celebrant to stand with his back to the congregation. It was popularly believed that the book condoned transubstantiation. In Robert Baillie's graphic phrase Charles treated the Scottish church like 'a pendicle of the diocese of York . . . Almost all our nobilitie and gentrie of both sexes counts that Booke little better than the Masse.'[32] Petitions against the use of the book flooded into Edinburgh. Well-organized riots greeted its appearance in services on 23 July 1637 when city matrons and serving wenches stood side by side to prevent its being read; their weapons were shrill tongues and kirk stools. As the months went by the uproar increased as the disaffected converged on the capital. In response to a claim by bishops and magistrates that the tumults were caused by the numerous incomers it was agreed that commissioners would be chosen from the ranks of the multitude to wait upon the privy council. At the great convention on 15 November, one of those so chosen was the Earl of Montrose.

James Graham, 'in the flower and bravery of his age', returned from the continent in 1636. He had intended, possibly through the inspiration and example of Lithgow, to survey 'the rarities of the East if his domestic affairs had not obliged him to return home, which chanced at the time the Rebellion began to peep out'.[33] His sojourn had reinforced a good conceit of himself and many commentators point to the pride and 'stately affectation' of the twenty-four-year-old nobleman. On his way through London he was presented to the king. The Marquis of Hamilton, like so many of the anglicized Scots of the period a sadly insecure man, arranged the introduction. It is said that he warned James of the king's scant regard for Scots and for Scotland which he was intent upon reducing to provincial status. Hamilton then, fearing a rival in the king's affections, told Charles that the young earl was so powerful, so popular, and of such esteem among the Scots, that if he were not nipped in the bud he would endanger the king's interest in the north. In the event James was merely permitted to kiss the king's hand before its owner turned away. The reporter of this tale, who allegedly had it from Napier, attributed Montrose's support for the covenant to his treatment on this occasion,[34] but slighted though he doubtless felt, Montrose had profounder reasons for his commitment to the revolution.

He was in Scotland in time to witness the agitation surrounding the publication of the prayer book. In May 1637 he was at Kincardine where he listened to the arguments of Mr Robert Murray, minister of Methven, as to why he should support the cause.[35] It is unlikely that he required much persuasion. Much of Montrose's 'pride' stemmed from his rank and position as the representative of one of the older noble houses of Scotland. He could not have viewed with equilibrium the king's revocation with its implicit proposal to abolish heritable jurisdictions; his estates of Braco had been carved out of the bishopric of Dunblane and he was as jealously possessive of what he considered to be his rights as any noble in Scotland. The reduction of the teinds and the increasing burden of taxation (which fell almost exclusively on land) could only worsen his financial straits. He was acutely aware of the king's attitude towards the older nobility – Montrose was not even a member of the privy council – and he was the classic example of the Scottish nobleman who had 'too little to do'.[36] All the evidence furthermore suggests that he was a young man consciously in search of a cause. Most important of all, perhaps, he had a healthy distrust of the bishops. He signed a supplication against the prayer book on 18 October. It was said that his grandfather had been betrayed by his scant regard for the clergy, and contemporaries, unaware of the illness that was to kill him, could not understand the attitude of the fourth earl in 1626 when Charles increased episcopal representation on the privy council.[37] For the suggestion that the elevation of the clergy was the mainspring of Montrose's support for the disaffected the best testimony survives – his own.

Montrose later wrote:

This our nation was reduced to almost irreparable evil by the perverse practices of the sometime pretended prelates; who having abused lawful authority, did not only usurp to be lords over God's inheritance, but also intruded themselves in prime places of civil government; and by their Court of High Commission, did so abandon themselves, to the prejudice of the Gospell, that the very quintessence of popery was publicly preached by Arminians, and the life of the Gospel stolen away by enforcing on the kirk a dead service book, the brood of the bowels of the Whore of Babel; as also to the prejudice of the Country, fining and confining at their pleasure: in such sort, that, trampling upon the necks of all whose conscience could not condescend to be of their coin, none were sure of life nor estate, till it pleased God to stir up his own instruments, both in Church and Policie, for preventing further, and opposing, such impiety.[38]

Montrose had every reason to fear encroaching popery. His visit to the continent coincided with the victory of the 'Cardinal Infant', Ferdinand, at Nordlingen and his subsequent invasion of Picardy. But his attack on prelacy disguised a much more profound and fundamental appreciation of the Scottish constitution.

Charles's conduct from the beginning of the reign represented the whim of arbitrary rule. Montrose believed that sovereign power was as essential to government as was government to civil society. 'This Sovereignty is a power over the People, above which power there is none upon earth, whose acts cannot be rescinded by any other.' Thus far he was in agreement with James VI. Where he disagreed with that monarch and his son was over the limitation of such power, 'by the lawes of God and nature, and some lawes of nations, and by the fundamentall lawes of the country, which are those upon which Sovereign Power itself resteth, in prejudice of which a king can doe nothing'. He argued that such power was essentially the same whether it was vested in 'the person of a Monarch, or in a few principal men, or in the Estates of the People'. Such power was strong and durable when used with moderation and limited as described, but it became weak when extended beyond the bounds of law, 'which could never be at any time endured by the people of the western part of the world and by those of Scotland as little as any'. Wise rulers use their power temperately but most wish to extend it, an inclination 'fomented by advice of courtiers and bad counsellers' who 'persuade the arbitrary'. Good government results in religion, justice and peace, happiness and security to king and people alike. The effect of power too far extended is tyranny either from the king or from those entrusted with the management of affairs. Royal power restrained results in the tyranny of the subjects – 'the most fierce, insatiable and insupportable tyranny in the worlde'. He believed, as had his medieval forebears, that personal tyranny would be cured 'by good advice, satiety in the Prince, or fear of infamy, and the penns of writers, or by some event which may bring a Prince to the sense of his errors'. He would not countenance tyrannicide; if all else failed patience was the only remedy; in his view the people should never attempt to circumscribe royal power; the sword must, by all means, be avoided. The way for subjects to procure moderate government is to 'endeavour the security of religion and of just liberty'. And here Montrose was at one with Buchanan. The just liberties of the people are contained in the laws and 'parliament may advise new laws, against emergent occasions which prejudge their liberties. And if parliament be frequent, and rightly constituted, what favourite counsellor or statesman dare mislead the king to the prejudice of the Subjects' liberty, knowing he must answer upon the penalty of his head at the next ensuing parliament.'[39] Though both documents cited are retrospective accounts of Montrose's growing support for the covenant they undoubtedly represent his views in 1637 and 1638. Both may have come from the hand of Napier (the former survives in his handwriting, the latter only in a seventeenth- or eighteenth-century copy which, in wording and sentiment, is very close to Napier's other writings) but this need not in any way invalidate the identification of their contents with Montrose's own philosophies. It is quite clear that Montrose could not accept the more extreme claims of divine right, that he could not tolerate arbitrary rule, that he believed in a constitutional appeal to the laws and parliament of Scotland, and that in 1637 he believed that he was participating in an event which might bring the king to his senses. His consistency of outlook is borne out by the fact that once, in his judgement, Charles had conceded the demands of the covenanters and listened to good counsel and agreed to the meeting of both parliaments and general assemblies, Montrose parted from a faction which aimed to circumscribe royal authority much in the manner he described. He was perhaps of all his contemporaries the most scrupulous observer of the time-honoured Scottish constitutional traditions.

On 15 November 1637 the public career of James Graham may be said to have begun. He was elected as one of four representatives of the nobility to the 'Tables', committees which also contained representatives of lairds, burgesses, and ministers. Along with Lord Lindsay of the Byres he was associated with two veterans of royal opposition, Rothes and John Campbell, Lord Loudoun. The latter was a highly intelligent, impecunious, and fanatical presbyterian, one of the main architects of the revolution. The function of the 'Tables' was to monitor all that passed between the king and his council, and to circulate information throughout the country. The representatives had been chosen at a meeting in Lord Balmerino's house. Given the well-known proclivities of the host, as well as of Rothes and Loudoun, who were in correspondence with Samuel Rutherford and Alexander Henderson who was soon to draft the covenant and lead the ministerial wing of the covenanters, the election of Montrose can have been no accident. He was handpicked for the job and there can be no question that he convinced his committed colleagues of his sincerity.

That winter there were severe gales, portentous to the pious and those mindful of the storms about to engulf Scotland. Part of the tower of Elgin cathedral collapsed and a great sandbar was thrown up across the mouth of the Dee, blocking the harbour. On 22 February 1638 a proclamation from the king was heralded at the Cross of Edinburgh by trumpeters. Charles accepted responsibility for the prayer book, complained of the injury done to his royal authority, and commanded the dispersion of the 'Tables' on pain of treason. Opposite the Cross a scaffold had been erected by the disaffected; from there their own rival protestation was read out in the presence of the embarrassed royal heralds who could not escape because of the press of the crowds. Montrose, carried away by the euphoria of the moment, jumped up on a barrel placed on the scaffold. Baillie observed that 'the canniness of Rothes' had brought Montrose to the cause. That same quality made John Leslie exclaim as he laughed at the boisterous antics of his colleague, 'James you will not be at rest till you be lifted upp ther above the rest in three fathoms of rope'.[40]

3
CAVALIER FOR THE
COVENANT

The subscription of This Negative Confession at this tyme with the additions and changes which now it was published with, the whole aggregate getting the name of the Covenant, is a thing that grew so remarkable afterwards, as that it may be termed the epoch or great era of the following revolutions.

Gordon of Rothiemay

The year of the covenant was a year of protestation and counter-protestation, which began with supplication against the prayer book and ended in full-scale revolution. In his poem 'To His Mistress' Montrose vowed,

> Or if Committees thou erect,
> And goes on such a Score,
> I'll sing and laugh at thy neglect,
> And never love thee more.

From October 1637 he had ample opportunity to witness the committee in action since from then until the end of the following year he was actively involved in almost every discussion and decision of the inner council of the Tables. He frequently found himself in negotiation with, and opposition to, both Lord Napier and the Earl of Southesk. Many of the discussions were concerned with trying to persuade the officers of state to pass on grievances to the king. Men like Robert Ker, first Earl of Roxburgh, whose family a generation before had been Border reivers, and John Stewart, first Earl of Traquair, attempted Janus-like to face both the supplicants and their king. Meeting in the kirk session house at Stirling on 20 February Montrose informed his colleagues on the Tables that the councillors desired to see them removed from the town. Outrage greeted a suggestion that they should depart voluntarily

but with the persuasion of Rothes they did so peaceably on the understanding that the council should not ratify the king's proclamation
presented by Traquair. In the event when Montrose and company were
safely out of the way the councillors renegued and the proclamation was
not only ratified but read two days later in Edinburgh, eliciting the
rival protestation which so excited Montrose. It begged Charles to
release Scotland from the recent innovations introduced 'against the
laudable laws of the kingdom', and reiterated complaints about the
court of high commission. The protesters sought recourse to his
majesty to present their grievances and they insisted that no archbishops or bishops be permitted to sit on any judicatories without first
being put on trial for alleged crimes. No act passed in the presence of
the prelates was to prejudice the supplicants in any way and no one
subsequently joining them was to suffer for refusing to observe such
'acts, books, canons, rites, judicatories, proclamations introduced
against the act of General Assemblies, or act of Parliament, or the
Statutes of this Kingdom'. The protestation concluded with an affirma-
tion that its contents proceeded from conscience and a desire to preserve
the reformed religion, the laws of the kingdom, and the king's majesty.[1]

The document was a precursor of the covenant itself. The latter was
drawn up by two collaborators, the fanatical and brilliant lawyer
Archibald Johnston of Warriston and the gentler if no less committed
minister of Leuchars Alexander Henderson. Warriston would nowa-
days be described as a fanatic. Incapable of sleeping more than three or
four hours in twenty-four, he experienced a frightening intensity of
religious revelation through prayer and he confided his conversations
with God to his diary. To religious mania he added a phenomenal
expertise in Scots law, coupled with great quickness of thought and an
extraordinary memory. As his nephew Burnet put it, 'presbytery was
to him more than all the world'. He was possessed of a passionate
conviction that the second coming was imminent and that Scotland
had a divine and crucial role to play in the greatest event in world
history, which would also end that history. At a grass roots level his
conviction would appear to have been widely shared. During the early
months of 1638 the churches were packed to overflowing as the country
experienced something like religious frenzy. Many sat in their pews
from Friday to Sunday, fearful of losing their places, 'so that several,
under that religious confinement, were forced to give way to those

natural necessities which they could no longer contain, bedewing the pavements of churches with some other moisture than tears'.[2] At least one devout covenanter recalled that Knox and others had foretold that 'Christ would again be crucified in this country, but joyful and glorious should his resurrection be here.' Had not Napier of Merchiston in his commentary on the Book of Revelation prophesied that in the thirty-ninth year 'shall begin the full abolishing of all the superfluous ceremonies of the church and of all the Romish dregs of superstition'?[3] Sentiments like these led Samuel Rutherford and Warriston to identify Scotland as a second Israel. Henderson, on the other hand, sometime regent in philosophy at St Salvator's, was in his fifties (and so twice the age of Warriston) in 1638; he placed his powerful intellect at the disposal of presbyterianism only after long reflection and much study. He was no firebrand, but a man whose quiet confidence was an inspiration to others.

The covenant fell into three parts. The first consisted of the Negative Confession of 1581; the second of a long list of statutes safeguarding the reformed church. The third part repeated and amplified points previously made in protestations and supplications. Signatories undertook to adhere constantly to the reformed religion, forswearing all recent innovations until they were tried or tested in free general assemblies or parliaments. They swore that they had no intention of dishonouring God or of diminishing royal sovereignty, 'but on the contrary, we promise and sweare, that we shall, to the uttermost of our power, with our meanes and lives, stand to the defence of our dreade Soveraigne, the king's Majesty, his Person and Authority, in the defence and preservation of the foresaid true Religion, Liberties and Lawes of the Kingdom'. This was the crux of the covenant from which Montrose's three fathoms of rope would ultimately be suspended. What would happen if defence of king and defence of kirk became incompatible was not expounded, but those who remembered the teachings of Andrew Melville, Henderson among them, could have been in no doubt of the issue. This clause would in time polarize those who suspected the advancement of either king or kirk at the expense of the other. If this section of the covenant contrived to be all things to all men there was no ambiguity about what followed, the so-called clause of mutual defence: 'We shall neither directly nor indirectly suffer ourselves to be divided or withdrawn by whatsoever suggestion, allurement, or terrour from this blessed and loyall conjunction, nor shall cast in any let or impediment, that may stay or hinder any such resolution as by common consent shall be found to conduce for so good ends.' Although Montrose lived and died a covenanter and although many of his co-signatories were to depart from the letter and spirit of the covenant, he would never be forgiven for, in their view, breaking his bond in this respect. Herein lies the explanation of much of the disgust, hatred, and hysteria directed towards his later actions. Mercifully none knew what the future held on that fateful day 28 February 1638 when the covenant was first subscribed in Greyfriars churchyard, Edinburgh. Montrose was among the first to append his signature.

Shortly before the covenant was subscribed Rothes suggested that a contribution might be raised from the shires to defray such expenses as 'this business might require'. It was felt that sympathetic nobles might contribute voluntarily and Montrose was put down for approximately one hundred merks.[4] Throughout March steps were taken to organize. A group of small lairds, including Graham of Morphie, were sent to Aberdeen to meet Huntly and other notables in the north-east. Montrose signed a letter drawn up by Rothes and sent to the Duke of Lennox, the Marquis of Hamilton, and the Earl of Morton in London as 'principall members next unto the head who must prevent the imminent dangers of this state', urging them to intercede with the king. The recipients replied to their correspondents individually, Hamilton writing to Montrose, Lennox to Rothes and so on, the king having forbidden them to answer 'conjointly' lest Montrose and his colleagues 'should have thereby been acknowledged ane incorporation'. The reply was non-committal and unhelpful.

The covenanting leaders were favourably impressed by discussions which they had with Archibald Campbell, Lord Lorne. Archibald delayed his declaration for the covenant until the Glasgow assembly in November but his presbyterian sympathies were well known. As early as 1635 he had challenged the episcopal authorities over the case of the Laird of Earlston who was fined for claiming that kneeling at communion was idolatrous, and a year later he supported Samuel Rutherford when he was charged with nonconformity. His twin ideals were to safeguard the House of Campbell and the House of God in a self-sufficient Scotland. Endowed with no military gifts, he was possessed of an outstanding moral courage in spite of his reputation for vacillation and deviousness. He was the greatest politician of his age and he instinctively sought political solutions to the baffling problems which the revolution thrust upon him. According to Clarendon contemporaries regarded Montrose and Lorne 'as young men of unlimited ambition, and used to say that they were like Caesar and Pompey, the one would endure no superior and the other would have no equal'. There is little evidence of such rivalry in 1638; it would emerge only gradually. It has been sensibly suggested that Lorne was apprehensive of having his father's resignation of the family estates cancelled by the king if he adhered to the covenant. The seventh earl was dead by 4 November;[5] in that month Lorne became Argyll and a covenanter.

In April Montrose and his colleagues still complained that information was not being passed on to Charles. Their demands as outlined in a document prepared by Warriston and Henderson were becoming ever more extreme. They insisted that the discharging of the prayer book, of the canons, and of the court of high commission would no longer suffice – the liberties of the kirk must be secured by a free general assembly and by parliament. The revolutionary committee on which Montrose sat, for it can be described as nothing less, agreed that none of its members was to take part in 'divisive discussions' with Lennox or Hamilton. All were to attend punctually at committee meetings, and unanimity over further demands was agreed. It was thought appropriate to double the number of representatives of the Tables who were negotiating with the privy council, and reports on covenant subscriptions were to be forwarded to Edinburgh. There was alarming talk also about the need for arms, occasioned by rumours that Charles had sent a ship carrying cannon, powder, and ammunition to Leith.

In early June nobles, ministers, and commons lined the route from Leith sands to Holyrood to greet the king's commissioner, James, Marquis of Hamilton. Throughout that month Montrose was in frequent conference with the marquis. He was present to hear Hamilton urge moderation, begging the covenanters to trust him. 'Am I not a Scotsman of the best quality? Is not all my estate and honour in Scotland?' He promised a general assembly and a parliament but the trust was not forthcoming. Montrose's proposal that he and his colleagues should be permitted to have sight of a new proclamation which Hamilton had brought with him in order that an adequate reply might be prepared, was rejected. So, daily, the negotiations dragged on. It was decided that Rothes, Loudoun, and Montrose should interview Hamilton alone since they might have a better chance of securing free discussion. He refused to see them. Apprehensive of his intentions they tried again three days later, having persuaded Argyll to prepare the ground by airing their proposals in advance. When Hamilton joked that he had recently read more of the acts of parliament than of the scriptures, Rothes drily replied that if scripture had been more read and believed and 'men's writs less respected', it had been better for religion and law. On this occasion Hamilton's good humour made him appear co-operative but on 4 July Rothes' worst fears were realized – the king's proclamation was published. In spite of all the talk it conceded nothing; all their protestations and supplications had been ignored; it did not even provide with certainty for an assembly. The covenanters had been out-manœuvred, so caught off guard that they had hurriedly to compile a lengthy protestation when they had prepared a short one. Some nine months of agonized discussion had resulted simply in gross aggravation of the situation.

It must have been around this time that Henry Guthry, who would live through the revolution to become Bishop of Dunkeld after the Restoration, told Montrose of Hamilton's double dealing. Guthry reported that Hamilton had assured some of the covenanting leaders, 'I speak to you as a kindly Scotsman. If you go on with courage and resolution you will carry what you please; but if you faint and give ground in the least, you are undone. A word is enough to wise men.' Hamilton's own correspondence shows that he was playing a deep game. Like several of his contemporaries he mistook sheer duplicity for diplomacy or, to borrow Burnet's observation, he was one of those who 'had as little of the prudence of the serpent as of the innocence of the dove'. Within a week of arriving in Edinburgh he had advised Charles to despatch a fleet and an army to Scotland and he advocated the occupation of Carlisle and Berwick. By mid-June the marquis was actively sounding potential support for the crown in the Highlands and islands. Reports had come in that Argyll was mustering some six thousand men in the west. When challenged Argyll justified his activity by alleging that the MacDonalds of Antrim and the O'Neills were preparing to cause trouble 'upon the least stir in his majesty's dominions'. Argyll has often been accused of using the covenant to foster the interests of Clan Campbell. The fact that the 'anti-Campbell coalition' was largely the creation of Hamilton during the summer of 1638 has been overlooked. He it was who hit upon the idea of exploiting the widespread antipathy towards *Sliochd Diarmaid*. He informed the king that MacKenzie of Seaforth was willing to assume control of the Hebrides and recommended that Charles, if mustering an army, should consider the usefulness of Ranald MacDonnell, Earl of Antrim, 'as he is beloved by his name and lays claim to Kintyre and the isles'.[6] Hamilton thus shrewdly diagnosed the most likely source of royal support. He could not know that he was also pulling together for the first time the clans that would rally to Montrose during his *annus mirabilis*.

In August Sir Donald MacDonald of Sleat, better known as Donald Gorm, wrote to the commissioner informing him that he had contacted Iain Muideartach, the captain of Clan Ranald, Donald of Strome, Chief of Glengarry, and 'our haill name of Clan Donald who hes swairne to die and live with me in the kingis service'. In addition his cousin, Ranald, Earl of Antrim of the family of MacDonald of Dunyveg and the Glens, had pledged his support. Donald assured Hamilton, 'I will nowayes prove MacKay to your Lordship', a reference to Donald, Lord Reay, Chief of MacKay who had recently subscribed the covenant while assuring Charles of his loyalty and who back in 1631 had accused Hamilton of planning to use an army in Scotland to further his own interests against those of the king.[7] The thirty-year-old Ranald, Earl of Antrim, possessed an illustrious pedigree. One of his grandfathers was the great Hugh O'Neill, Earl of Tyrone, the champion of Gaelic separatism who led the Irish rebellion against Elizabeth Tudor in 1595; the other, no less distinguished, was *Somhairle Buidhe* or Sorley Boy, whose action-packed career occupied most of the sixteenth century. Somhairle, son of Alasdair mac Iain Chathanaich of Islay, fought successfully to retain possession of the Glens of Antrim which had been in his house since John of Islay's marriage to an Antrim Bisset at the end of the fourteenth century. When Ranald succeeded to his title in 1636 he inherited territories extending from Larne to Coleraine and his ambitions to recover his ancestral lands in Islay and Kintyre from the Campbells were well known. Antrim was a vain, likeable, impetuous self-seeker who detected a chance to ingratiate himself with

Charles. He rashly volunteered to raise, at his own expense, an army of Irishmen and Hebridean MacDonalds for a descent on Argyll.

Hamilton suspected that many clans would rally to Charles not out of affection for the Stewarts but because of their 'spleen to Argyll'; they would 'dou . . . just contrarie to what his men doeth'. But this explanation alone will not account for the support which certain clans now gave to the crown for the first time. After centuries of being on the receiving end of punitive expeditions, those recent victims of royal repression chose to fight and die for the Stewarts, not only during the Montrose wars but on the fields of Killiecrankie, Sheriffmuir, and Culloden.

Several historians have distinguished the acceptance and subscription of a number of statutes at Iona in 1609 by certain chiefs as the 'watershed of Highland history'. MacDonald of Islay, Hector Og, Chief of MacLean, Donald Gorm, Clan Ranald, MacLeod of Harris, MacIain of Ardnamurchan, MacKinnon of Strathordale, and MacPhee of Colonsay, among others, agreed to statutes designed to pacify the *Gaidhealtachd*. There were provisions for the maintenance of the church and of the clergy, for the establishment of inns, for curbing the number of retainers engaged by any chief, for prohibiting the use of firearms, and for discouraging the bards whose often scurrilous verses were rightly distinguished as a fertile source of strife. It was also hoped to curb Gaelic drinking habits, to reduce the consumption of vast quantities of 'strong wynis and acquavitae'. The sons of chiefs were to be educated in the Lowlands. The signatories formed themselves into a band and undertook to live together 'in peace, love and amytie'. Only six years previously those same MacLeans, MacLeods, and MacDonalds were the object of a commission of fire and sword granted to Argyll. The change of heart on the part of chiefs and government alike is neither apparent nor real. The chiefs were coerced in 1609; the Iona statutes represent the first of a long series of concerted attempts to deracinate the Gael through the deliberate and calculated erosion of his culture and language. Perspective is lent to their significance by the fact that within five years the Isles were involved in the great Clan Donald rebellion in which Colla Ciotach, father of Alasdair, played a notable part.

Although the rising represented the last great effort to keep Islay out of Campbell clutches, it stemmed from a protracted feud in the previous century between Angus MacDonald of Dunyveg and Lachlan MacLean of Duart over possession of the Rhinns of Islay. The MacLeods of Harris, the MacNeills of Barra, and the MacQuarries of Mull supported Lachlan. To the banner of Angus rallied Clan Ranald, Clan Iain of Ardnamurchan, the MacLeods of Lewis, and the MacNeills of Gigha. Sir James MacDonald, Angus's son, escaped from prison in 1615 to lead the resistance to the Campbells who waited until both sides were near to exhaustion before entering the fray. He begged the king that 'seeing my race has been ten hundred years kindly Scotsmen under the kings of Scotland and being willing to live upon one poor part of that which our forebears had', he might have the island of Islay 'to myself and my kin to sustain us'. Eloquent but unsuccessful he ultimately fled to Spain when his rising was suppressed, while Colla embarked upon the career of Hebridean pirate. As expected, the government adopted repressive measures. In 1616 MacLeod of Harris, MacKinnon of Strathordale, MacLean of Coll, MacLean of Lochbuie, and the captain of Clan Ranald entered into another band promising good behaviour on conditions similar to those of 1609 but of much greater stringency. Each had to appear before the privy council in Edinburgh when ordered to do so; the number of gentlemen in their households was to be reduced; they were to purge their lands of beggars and idlers; they were forbidden to bear weapons save on the king's service and their clansmen were not to wear swords or armour within the Isles. Each was to specify his main residence and repair his dwelling house; each was permitted to retain only one galley of sixteen or eighteen oars; the chiefs were allocated a drink ration while their followers were to abstain. As in 1609 they were to send their 'bairnis' to Lowland schools but a novel and alarming clause stated that none of their children was to be served heir unless he could read, write, and speak English.[8] The Gael was to be forced to cast off his culture, his customs, and his very language like some disused husk; naked and defenceless he would be groomed in the ways of 'civilization'. But the crown was as incapable as the clans of reforming bad old ways. Campbells and Gordons continued to hunt down 'wickit heilandmen'.

The support of the loyal clans is to be traced not to 1609 but in part to Charles's attempt to abolish heritable jurisdictions. In the nature of things the Gael had a great affection for monarchy and was genuinely upset by any suggestion that in opposing his hereditary enemy he was opposing his king. The crown representative could always give personal vendetta the cloak of legality and as a loyal servant he was conveniently placed to benefit when lands were forfeited. Feudal law created one of the greatest anomalies in the Highlands by placing MacLeans or MacDonalds under a Campbell superior. If Campbells, or for that matter the Gordons or MacKenzies, lost heritable jurisdictions, then their stranglehold on the clans would be much reduced.

Many gave their support for religious reasons. Gaelic-speaking Franciscans were active in the Hebrides in the 1620s. By 1625 the entire population of Colonsay (where Alasdair mac Cholla spent his boyhood) was catholic. A year later six thousand Hebridean conversions to catholicism were claimed. In that year Iain Muideartach, chief of Clan Ranald, picked up his pen in distant Uist to inform the Pope that his kin had recently emerged from the darkness 'introduced by the turbulent, detested followers of Calvin'. He offered to lead a crusade to restore the greater part of Scotland to catholicism. He hoped to receive aid from his holiness and promised that all Gaelic-speaking Scots and the greater part of the Irish chiefs 'from whose stock first we sprang' would wage war in his own district.[9] Clan Ranald's aspirations were what Argyll feared most – a catholic crusade on his own doorstep. Contemporaneously just such a crusade was evolving in Ireland. The catholic confederacy would spawn what bewildered Lowland covenanters distinguished as the antichristian hordes of Alasdair mac Cholla.

In view of the patterns of clan alliances which were shaping in 1638 it is of some interest that in June 1639 Charles met both Antrim and Donald Gorm near Berwick and jointly commissioned them as lieutenants of the Highlands and Islands. The former was to be rewarded with Kintyre and Islay, the latter with the Argyll holdings in Ardnamurchan and Strathordale, and the islands of Rum, Eigg, and Canna.[10] It is often assumed that the commissions were something of a dead letter until the mid-1640s but the following year Donald Gorm drew up a bond of loyalty promising absolute obedience to Charles, along with Lachlan MacLean of Duart, MacKenzie of Seaforth, John MacLeod of Harris, and Iain Muideartach himself.[11] They agreed that on the command of the king Antrim would attack Islay and Kintyre; the others would invade Lorne. The anti-Campbell coalition was therefore real enough; the charge that Argyll used the covenant to further his own interest is rather harder to sustain. One further point must not be overlooked. Argyll was hated because he was the most successful of all Highland chiefs. Although deeply involved in national politics he moved in an emphatic Highland orbit, both before and after 1638. His son and successor was fostered after the old custom by Campbell of Glenorchy and great care was taken to teach him Gaelic. Argyll took a close and lifelong interest in his clansmen and his estates, and alone of the covenanters he had the wit to perceive that if presbyterianism was to make any headway in the Isles the church must provide Gaelic-speaking ministers. He was first and foremost *MacCailein Mór*, chief of the *Sliochd Diarmaid*.

Hamilton was extremely offended 'with my Lord Montrose going to the north' at the command of the Tables and he threatened to send ships to Aberdeen to hinder his proceedings there. Rothes insisted that his mission was aimed at persuasion rather than compulsion. He commended Montrose as 'a true and noble hearted cavalier' to the Aberdeen covenanter Patrick Leslie. On the afternoon of Friday 20 July James Graham arrived in Aberdeen with a party of thirty or forty horsemen including three ministers. The provost and bailies hastened to meet their noble burgess at Skipper Anderson's house only to be told that they must sign the covenant. They gracefully declined the opportunity. The dean of gild thoughtfully provided wine and sugar for the uninvited guests 'as the toun's courtesie'. Montrose coldly refused the hospitality 'which the magistrates took in so evil part that they presently sent it to be equally distributed between their hospital and house of correction which did much offend the covenanters'.[12] The remainder of their visit was to be equally displeasing.

Aberdeen was a bastion of conservatism guarded by some very acute minds. That Friday evening a group of divinity professors from Marischal College and King's together with several distinguished local ministers presented a list of queries on the covenant promising subscription if satisfactory replies were forthcoming. The answers hastily delivered next day left much to be desired. The covenanting ministers, refused access to the kirks, preached from a gallery in Earl Marischal's town house. The crowd was somewhat unruly. If some came to pray there were many scoffers too and some merrymakers threw a dead raven into the midst of the open-air congregation. A table was set up in Marischal's yard and subscriptions were invited.

While some of the covenanters threatened violence towards those who withheld their signatures Montrose appears to have been concerned to secure as many names as possible and he allowed some to sign a limited covenant. Most were prepared to bind themselves to the maintenance of religion and the laws but they refused to disown the Five Articles or episcopal government. They also explicitly reserved their loyalty and obedience to the king. The following week was spent obtaining subscriptions throughout the north-east. Montrose personally satisfied the scruples of the presbytery of Turriff but he did not, for the present, push on from there to Strathbogie to attempt the greatest prize of all, the Marquis of Huntly, who was mourning his wife's death. Instead he returned to Aberdeen for two days of involved debate with the learned doctors before moving on to Edinburgh. His reputation was not enhanced by this brief excursion but his experience of the limited covenant was valuable.

Hamilton issued a proclamation at the mercat cross of Edinburgh on 22 September. The service book, the book of canons, the Five Articles, and the court of high commission were discharged; permission was given for an assembly and a parliament. The covenanters were still not satisfied. They countered with the inevitable protestation which although drafted by Warriston, was known as 'Montrose's protestation' because his name appeared for the noble Table. The document is of the greatest interest since, apart from its association with Montrose, it was widely discussed by a number of contemporary writers. Significantly the protestation was the subject of an important correspondence between Argyll and Thomas Wentworth, Earl of Strafford, which was copied and widely circulated as evidence of the attitude of one of the leading covenanters; one copy appears to have reached Laud.[13] Baillie affirmed that Argyll 'in some two or three well penned letters, justified our cause against (Strafford's) acute and subtill challenges'. As it happens Strafford's challenges were neither subtle nor acute but his attitude was typical of the bitter non-comprehension which the protestation engendered in many quarters. The widespread publicity which the document received ensured that the name of Montrose was synonymous with total intransigence.

The protestation rejected the royal proclamation because it did not meet the demands of previous supplications. It argued that by indicting bishops to attend the general assembly the king had limited the freedom of that body. Charles had attempted a compromise by having his privy councillors and, it was hoped, as many others as possible, subscribe the Negative Confession alone. Sixteen reasons for non-subscription of the confession were listed, most of them to the effect that a new signing was incompatible with the covenant. To sign anew would be to mock God. 'The tears that began to be poured forth at the solemnizing of the covenant are not yet dried up and wiped away, and the joyful noise which then began to sound hath not yet ceased.' Men must not play with oaths as children with toys. Subscription would lead to perjury since it would contravene the non-divisive clause in the covenant, it would imply that covenanters were guilty of rash vows, it would facilitate the encroachment of popery, and reopen the old papist charge that the faith of protestants changed with the moon. Subscription would of course imply acceptance of prayer book, canons, and Five Articles. The document concluded with seven solemn protests. The late distractions were attributed to religious innovation. It was protested that general assemblies must be free. The third protest was one which conferred a certain notoriety on the whole document. It stated that 'archbishops and bishops have no warrand for their office in this kirk'. Bishops should not be present in the assembly. This was the first occasion on which the abolition of episcopacy was publicly discussed. Solemn adherence to the covenant was protested; no covenanter was to be urged to sign the king's confession; and in future no subscription of any kind must be asked which contravened the covenant. Finally adherence to former protestations and declarations was emphasized.[14]

Charles genuinely thought that his proclamation had conceded the essential demands of the covenanters. His rage at the new protestation was boundless but his arguments show that he was as far as ever from understanding the covenanting point of view. He argued that to condemn the Scottish service book was to condemn the English one also. Since bishops were established by the laws of both countries he could not accept – nor did he attempt to answer – the argument that their presence would limit the freedom of the assembly. On the subject of subscription of the confession he was unrepentant. He dismissed mockery of God as 'some peoples' foolish thought and idle fancies'. He believed that fear of contravening the covenant's non-divisive clause was the basic reason for rejecting his proclamation and he dismissed the claim about encroaching popery as fatuous. He stood by episcopacy, berating the protesters for claiming that the covenant, 'which sure was penned by men and so but a humane writing', was of equal authority to the scriptures. Replying to the protests he stated that the rebellious distractions proceeded from the disaffected alone and not from innovations. Assemblies could not be free since the covenanters had written so many prelimitations into their protestations. He repeated that episcopacy was established by acts of both the church and of parliament. He described their solemn adherence to the covenant as 'rare and undeniable impudence . . . no such covenant or combination can come from Heaven, but from Hell, from whence cometh all faction and schism.' Charles claimed that to deny that any covenanter could subscribe another oath was high treason. With that fatal lack of tact so characteristic of the man, he attempted to justify his statement by citing the case of the Blackness ministers; he could hardly have picked a more emotive subject nor one which so well illustrated his own insensitivity. In more ways than one he had said enough – he did not trouble to answer the final two protests in detail.[15]

Strafford's arguments were so incompetent as to be barely worthy of discussion. Their importance lies in the publicity they received and the replies which they elicited. One example will suffice. He used one line in the protestation against the covenanters: 'there be no substantial difference between that [i.e. the covenant] which they have subscribed and this Confession subscribed 1581.' Strafford omits to mention that the document continues, no more difference than between 'that which is hid and that which is revealed . . . betwixt the hand closed and the hand open, betwixt the sword sheathed and drawn or . . . between the Old Testament and the New.' Argyll, who was not the most articulate of men, had little difficulty in composing a reply. He quietly concluded his letter, 'I wish your Lordship and all others of the Reformed church (not knowing the Constitutions of this) were as charitable to it, and meddled as little in disquieting her Peace as (I hope) they have carefully prevented that fault by their proceedings here.'[16] Montrose never disowned this document with which his name was so closely associated. Guthry states that when the bishops learned in November 1637 of Montrose's adherence to the disaffected 'they were somewhat affrighted, having that esteem of his parts that they thought it time to prepare for a storm when he engaged.' In the last few days of his life James Graham indicated that he stood by his earlier instincts. 'The Covenant which I took I own it and adhere to it,' he said. 'Bishops I care not for them.'

The assembly was to meet in Glasgow cathedral on 21 November. Preceding weeks were marked by feverish activity on all sides. Privy councillors attempted with a success in proportion to their personal conviction to gain subscriptions to the King's Confession; one of the most active royalists was Southesk. There is no doubt that during those weeks the disaffected attempted to rig the assembly's representation. A libel reciting the crimes of the bishops was drawn up. A 'she-prophetess' was conveniently unearthed who attracted great crowds to hear her proclaim Christ 'the covenanting Jesus' and to predict that the covenant would prosper while the confession – 'Sathan's inventione' – would be confounded. The Tables instructed presbyteries that most representatives should foregather in Edinburgh on 12 November. There they would remain for five days discussing tactics to be adopted in Glasgow.

The western city had never experienced scenes like those which took place in the third week of November as crowds descended upon it for the opening of the first general assembly in twenty years. Hamilton as commissioner was accompanied by an impressive retinue. He appointed assessors, among them Traquair, Roxburgh, Argyll, Lauderdale, and Southesk. From most of Scotland came ministers and ruling elders elected by presbyteries. Many were armed to the teeth; most were uncertain of quite what to expect. There was not a bishop to be seen. The Tables had managed the preliminaries efficiently. Henderson was appointed moderator, and Warriston clerk of the assembly, without opposition. The indefatigable Warriston produced 'five manuscript books' containing the acts of assembly from 1560 to 1590 and thus provided the Glasgow body with a written constitution. A request that Hamilton might appoint three of his assessors to a committee of ministers delegated to examine the books was refused.

Thus far all had gone according to plan. Objections were now made to certain presbytery commissioners, or representatives, who were known to be opposed to the covenant. There was a bitter dispute between Montrose and Southesk over the election of a ruling elder for the presbytery of Brechin. Two rival commissions were presented. Montrose favoured Erskine of Dun, elected by one minister and several elders. Southesk backed his son Lord Carnegie, said to have been elected by all other ministers and lay elders. The assembly sided with Montrose 'supposing the Laird Dunn to be a more fordward covenanter than the Lord Carnegye, which was true'.[17] On the back of Dun's commission was a note written by Montrose declaring the legality of Dun's election and offering to prove the illegality of the other, on the grounds that Carnegie's election was contrary to the instructions of the Tables. 'The sturre grew so great that the moderator wished both their commissions to have been annulled before such noise should have been.' Hamilton demanded that a copy of Montrose's statement be given to him but he refused, saying there was no reason to surrender a 'private note' unless the writer were willing to hand it over. Hamilton reasonably retorted that no paper could be described as private when it was presented to the assembly 'by a member of so great place and quality'. A further request for a free vote on the subject was refused. 'Let God Almighty judge if this be a free Assembly!' cried Hamilton. When Sir Lewis Stewart, advocate and one of the commissioner's assessors, attempted to contribute to the debate, Montrose claimed that he had no right to speak in the assembly. David Dickson judged that the 'back writ' had 'some negligence in it', to which Graham hotly retorted that he would 'avow the least jot that was in it'. At one point 'the contest betwixt Montrose and Southesk grew so hot, that it terrified the whole assembly so that the Commissioner took upon him the moderator's place and commanded them all to peace.'[18]

On 28 November Hamilton, unable to progress further in what had become a one-sided contest and disgusted by the covenanters' claim to competence in judging the bishops, dissolved the assembly. Just before his departure Argyll declared for the covenant. On that day the Scottish revolution began. Those who continued to sit, in opposition to the express command of the royal commissioner, were open to the charge of rebellion. As if to emphasize the point the assembly proceeded to pronounce the six previous assemblies invalid. The service book, canons, court of high commission, and Five Articles were condemned. Episcopacy was abolished and eight of the bishops solemnly excommunicated.

Hamilton told the king that of all the activists at the assembly none was 'more vainly foolish than Montrose'. Baillie asserted that Graham's 'extraordinary and evil pride made him very hard to be guided'. During the long months of 'this ominous year' Montrose had shown himself to be one of the most outspoken and intransigent of the covenanting leaders.

4

THE CURSE OF MEROZ

Curse ye Meroz, said the angel of the Lord, curse ye bitterly the inhabitants thereof; because they came not to the help of the Lord, to the help of the Lord against the mighty.

Judges 5:23

Not since 1567 had the Scots confronted a reigning monarch in the field, when the confederate lords, a label now revived for application to the covenanting faction, spent a warm June day facing Mary, Queen of Scots and Bothwell at Carberry Hill. Since that time no living Scot had experienced warfare on Scottish soil. Nonetheless the degree of professionalism which informed the covenanters' preparations for war was remarkable, particularly when compared with Charles's unhappy efforts to organize an army. For this the covenanters were indebted to the expertise of veterans of the European War who returned to continue the struggle in their native country.

Montrose's name was prominent in a circular letter sent out to the shires in January 1639. It stressed the necessity of organizing against the royal army which was designed 'to force and impose a yoke of bondage upon our consciences and turn our liberty to thraldom, if we will not willingly subjugate ourselves again to that episcopal tyranny and servitude from which God in his mercy has with an outstretched hand so mightily delivered us'. All landholders were to be acquainted with the danger to the kingdom. Committees of war were to be appointed in each county to select men for military service and to oversee all matters of organization and finance. Rolls of able-bodied men were to be kept in duplicate together with a note of such weapons as they owned or could be compelled to buy. Assessments were to be made of each parish so that the burden of paying for the levies could be equally distributed. Loans were raised to cover present contingencies until such revenues were forthcoming.[1] Early in January pikes and muskets were already being distributed in certain parts of the country and the levies were being exercised in Fife and in the environs of Edinburgh. Royal spies kept Charles informed of developments; at least one bemoaned the absence of pleasures to which he was accustomed in England – 'the best things that I can find here are wine and oysters. For handsome women there are none that I can find in Scotland'.

The Tables hastily commissioned Alexander Henderson to produce his *Instructions for Defensive Arms*. Henderson argued at length for the legality of arming against 'unjust violence'. He condemned those 'court parasites' who favoured absolute sovereignty against which the subject was powerless to defend himself. All men owed the obligation of self-defence, through obedience to God, against the magistrate if necessary. Indeed 'every soldier ought to defend the whole army against the general himself if he turn an enemy.' Henderson would not admit that tyranny was part of God's providential ordering of things. For him resistance to the tyrant was both lawful and godly. He would not subscribe to the view that 'the Lord hath ordained magistrates [i.e. kings] to be his ministers for the good of his people and their defence.' Although most of Henderson's arguments were founded upon scripture he implicitly returns to the theories of George Buchanan. 'The people make the magistrate, but the magistrate maketh not the people. The people may be without the magistrate but the magistrate cannot be without the people. The body of the magistrate is mortal, but the people as a society is immortal. And therefore it were a direct over-turning of all the foundations of policy and government to prefer subjection to the prince, to the preservation of the commonwealth; or to expose the publick, wherein every man's person, family and private estate are contained, to be a prey to the fury of the prince, rather than by all our power to defend and preserve the commonwealth.' He went on to justify the use of arms with reference to the covenant, natural law, the bible, and 'the testimony not only of popish writers, but of divines of the reformed churches, even such as be pleaders for monarchy (neither is Calvin against us, but for us)'. He stressed that there was a mutual contract between king and people as could be seen in the acts of the Scottish parliament and the coronation oath. Henderson's tract constitutes proof positive, were it required, that Montrose and his colleagues had embarked upon a revolution against the tyranny of the monarch to secure the freedom of the Scottish nation. 'The question is now, Whether we shall have a free national kirk . . . and whether we shall any longer enjoy our civil liberty . . . except we stand fast to our liberty we can look for nothing but miserable and perpetual slavery.'²

A notable opponent of the covenanters was George, second Marquis of Huntly, a cold, distant individual, extremely conscious of his rank and by instinct a private person who left to himself would always prefer the security of life on his estates to involvement in national politics. When he was approached by the covenanters in 1638 he would play no part in attacking the king. His family had risen through its attachment to the kings of Scotland and Huntly was resolved that if the king were brought down he would 'bury his lyfe, honours, and estate under the rubbidge of the king his ruines'. Predictably Charles entrusted the defence of the north to Huntly, a task easily delegated by a distant king but less easy for the man on the spot to carry out. Just as in the west the troubles ranged certain clans against Argyll, so Huntly's very commission 'did put all the north into a combustion and renewed the old deadly feudes in those parts, chiefly betwixt the Gordons and the Forbeses, who did always follow contrarie factions.'³ The Forbeses were not alone: Frasers, Grants, Rosses, Sutherlands, and Munros were similarly motivated. It fell to Montrose to attempt to contain Huntly before he received expected reinforcements from England, to secure the city of Aberdeen, and to afford some protection to those near neighbours of the Gordons who might suffer for their adherence to the covenant.

Although the covenanters placed the country on a defensive footing it was by no means certain, in those early months of 1638, that the two sides would in fact come to blows and it was widely believed that 'the English did not fancye the warre against the Scottish mutche'. Yet another manifesto gave assurances of good intentions and asserted that if the covenanters were successful 'the Englishes one day would reape the fruicts therof and who knew how soone'.⁴

In fulfilment of the instructions of the Tables Montrose was duly appointed colonel for both Perthshire and Forfarshire. He took part in a convention which met at Perth in late January and on 1 February he arrived at Forfar to carry out the assessment of the county. A meeting in the tolbooth of the ancient Angus burgh was attended by his father-in-law Lord Ogilvy, the Master of Spynie, and representatives from Dundee. Those present refused to sign a covenant abjuring episcopacy. Southesk had clearly not forgiven James for his outburst at the Glasgow assembly and when they began to discuss the assessment, or stent, of the king's lieges of Angus Southesk demanded to know by whose authority they did so. Montrose replied that they had the warrant of the Tables, requiring them to number the levies and have them suitably armed and in readiness. 'Southesk answerit thay wer all the kingis men, subject to no Table nor subject sitting therat,' a reference no doubt to his upstart son-in-law and intended to put him in his place. Their lands could not be assessed nor their men numbered save by the king's command and in his service. 'And so thay took thair leave, leaving Montrose and the rest sitting still in the tolbuith of Forfar at thair committee.' The older man must have wondered once more, as he would again, where he had gone wrong with his young ward, as he departed in high dudgeon for Kinnaird. But David Carnegie had not arrived at the earldom of Southesk by treading paths of ingenuousness. His attitude towards another son-in-law Andrew Lord Balvaird contrasts sharply with his behaviour towards James Graham. He received word that some of his 'unfriendis' were seeking his ruin by alleging that he was trying to influence adversely some of his covenanting kinsmen. He reminded Balvaird that 'I never requested you nor any of my other friends to divert you from that course.' On the contrary he had refused to give any advice to his nearest and dearest, leaving 'everyman to do as his own conscience served him, and I wished that they might do it without breach of love and duty to their friends that were of the contrary judgement.' He cannily begged Balvaird to pen a few lines to the Tables confirming his account and advising him to 'take no notice of this letter to any other'.[5] Montrose delayed somewhat longer to complete his business before pushing north to tackle Huntly the following week. He was accompanied by the most distinguished and experienced of the Scottish mercenaries, Field Marshal Alexander Leslie. Although command nominally lay with the nobleman he was to defer in all matters to Leslie's unrivalled judgement and experience.

The Frasers and the MacKenzies, fearing that Huntly was about to fortify and replenish his castle at Inverness, seized it. The northern covenanters decided to hold a committee at Turriff to agree upon the assessment and Huntly intended a show of strength. Montrose spent the night of 13 February at Muchalls on the coast five miles north of Stonehaven. Spalding relates that on the following morning he rode from Muchalls to Turriff, but a good forty-five miles separates the two places. The distance may have prompted Gordon of Rothiemay's suggestion that Montrose advanced in great haste fearing some kind of confrontation between Huntly and his neighbours; 'being desyrouse to shew himself active in his charge . . . he flyes over the Grangbean hills, with all speed possible, scarce ever sleeping or resting till he gott to Turreffe.' If such is a palpable exaggeration, since the Grampians lay well to the west of Montrose's route, it does at least suggest that he was already capable of those remarkable turns of speed for which he later became famous. 'Celeritie in ware hes ever beene a sure and happie advancer of the wictorie,' observed the didactic Gordon of Ruthven, 'nor have I ever read of a good and prosperous leader who was not adorned with this vertue of celerite and quicke despatch of action.'

On his rapid march north while Leslie remained at Aberdeen, Montrose had added recruits to the two hundred he carried with him, and arriving at Turriff he skilfully deployed these men, together with some six hundred northerners, around the town. Huntly advanced from Aberdeen where he had been attending a funeral. His party included his sons the Lords Gordon and Aboyne, the Master of Reay, son of MacKay, and several Gordon lairds. He was dismayed to discover the next day that members of his following who had made their way to Turriff found the place infested with covenanters. The committee was busy working out the stent inside the church. Some of Montrose's party politely offered Huntly the use of the Earl of Erroll's house in the town should he have any business to transact. Outraged by this cool taunt, Huntly's advisers urged that as king's lieutenant he had an obligation to attack with his superior force; failure to do so would be to hamper further recruitment and would simply encourage the impudence of the enemy. The marquis had little wish to be cast in the role of aggressor and there is some indication that the king's instructions had expressly forbidden any engagement.[6] He contained his wrath, spending the remainder of the day, as so much of his life, in hesitant inactivity, and he contented himself with a gesture, riding 'hard under the dyckes of the churchyarde, westward, within two picke lenth to Montrose company without salutatione or worde speaking on either syde'. With Aboyne he retired to Banff's house at Forglen on the Deveron, two miles from the scene of his humiliation, while Montrose, his business over, returned to Muchalls. So ended the 'first raid of Turriff'. By the time Paris was acquainted with this ignominious affair it had become the triumphant siege and sacking of the place by Huntly who, as Gordon drily observes, was better known to Frenchmen than was Turriff. Warriston was much impressed that Montrose and God had carried the day without bloodshed.[7]

The Aberdonians, expecting Montrose to descend on them on his way south, took steps to defend themselves. Watches were posted, the gates closed, guns prepared, and the university shut down. But Graham by-passed the city and the weekend found him at Dunottar receiving assurances from Earl Marischal that he had finally decided to become a covenanter. Huntly returned to Aberdeen to take part in fresh discussions with the city fathers. Early in March the king's proclamation, suppressed elsewhere in Scotland, arrived in the northern capital with Huntly's commission as Lieutenant-General of Scotland from the North Water of Esk to Caithness. Charles did not mince words. The rebels had illegally levied impositions of all kinds; he stood by episcopacy and the prayer book. Reinvigorated by the king's communication and spurred by the threat of an invasion from the north, Aberdeen prepared in earnest. Deep ditches were dug along the north side of the city from the Gallowgate to Castlehill. Ordnance was strategically placed. But diplomacy was to be tried before the sword.

On 15 March Montrose consulted with Argyll at Perth. Argyll had written to his brother-in-law Huntly urging him to attend. The ostensible reason for the Perth meeting was to deliberate methods of securing certain outlaws and 'broken men', but the true purpose as Baillie guessed was to 'take some sudden course for Aberdeen'. Argyll, having vainly offered to meet Huntly at Brechin or Fettercairn, ordered levies from his clan territories to proceed to the 'evill set pairt of the countre', the north-east.[8] If Huntly was unwilling to treat with his own brother-in-law he was not averse to discussions with Montrose, who went to Auld Montrose to prepare for a visitation to Aberdeen to proclaim the legislation of the Glasgow assembly and, in terms of its remit, to examine the two colleges there. Two of Huntly's representatives and two from the city visited Montrose at his ancestral dwelling, begging him to limit the forthcoming discussions to one hundred persons and requesting that the nobles in his own company remain as far from the city as those of the Huntly faction. It was also put to Montrose that the northern covenanters would not be molested if he would confine his activities south of the Esk. Montrose may have had some sympathy with the plight of the Aberdonians, who were uncomfortably aware of what his visitation might cost the city, but he insisted on obedience to the act of assembly. The visitors would conduct themselves in a decorous fashion, paying for all their requisites. He professed no ill will towards Huntly himself and hoped for a better understanding with him. Not satisfied with this 'delaying answer' the city fathers sent their commissioners back with a further petition on 25 March. They wished assurances that none of their citizens would be wronged in conscience, body, or goods and that the town would be left in peace. Again Montrose tried to fob them off with 'flat refusals' or 'slightings of all their proposals'. The atmosphere was tense. The townsmen of Montrose were alarmed to see fire in the direction of Edzell and they remained in arms all night, some of them threatening violence towards Huntly's envoys thinking that the marquis himself was about to attack. Dawn revealed that they had spent a sleepless night observing the muir burning on the Angus hills.

The pulse of Scotland from Tay to Moray Firth was rapid. Both Montrose and Huntly were prisoners in a play in which their parts had been sketched out but in no way developed. James Graham was manipulated by the Tables as was George Gordon by the king, and, as the puppets danced, blind men pulled the strings. Neither was quite sure what to do. Huntly withdrew to Inverurie where five thousand supporters awaited him. On reflection he disbanded his army, so further lowering his stock with the men of the north. In Fife, Perthshire, Angus, and the Mearns Leslie's influence was everywhere in evidence. The levies were exercised daily; cavaliers and musketeers were prominent; Montrose himself was having cannon prepared for the northern expedition.

Montrose, like Huntly, had his problems. The vast majority of his troops were untried. How many really understood the finer points of constitutional theory or theology? How many farm labourers from Gowrie or the Mearns could distinguish one end of a pike from the other? The Aberdeen commissioners returning from Montrose were crossing the North Esk shortly after sunrise when the sun above the sea appeared to them like a huge blood-coloured orb. How long before such suns multiplied in the breasts of soldiers throughout the country? Hitherto the battles had been fought at the court, in the Tables, and at the assembly, the weapons protestations and proclamations. 'Now they supposed they wer to dispute it withe ther enemyes in the feelds; and whatever meanes was used by the nobilitye or ther ministrye to persuade the vulgar sorte of the justnesse of ther qwarrell, yet the most pairt of them, who had been borne and bredd upp under a long peace, could hardly distinguish it from rebellione against ther kinge. This abstracted confidence from manye of the meaner sort and bredd a trepidatione in them at the hearing of their owne drummes, trumpetts, and shotte.'9 It is the measure of Montrose that he worked hard to put heart into his men, to create an *esprit de corps*. He devised the blue band worn as a sash across the chest. To these sashes the cavalry attached the spanners for their firelocks while the foot wore bunches of ribbon in their blue bonnets. Dismissed as 'Montrose's whimsy', the wearers lampooned as 'jockeys', the blue band nonetheless became the proud badge of the covenanters. And indeed the charm worked, as in the last days of March the army progressed through the Mearns, marching 'not as to a war but as to a triumph'. Camp was made at Tullo Hill, a bare three miles from Aberdeen. They could have reached the city with ease that night but with the keen eye for spectacle and pageantry that accompanied Montrose to the gallows, he delayed his triumphal entry until morning.

The agony of the unknown had almost shattered the nerve of the Aberdonians, 'daily deavit with the coming of the army', deserted by Huntly, and divided among themselves. They left off their defensive preparations, withdrew the watch, and dismantled the ordnance. Many fled the city by land and sea. Meroz awaited its fate.

At 10 am Montrose's army entered the city in battle order, led by the cavalry. The pikemen followed and behind them the musketeers. All were conspicuously well armed and well provisioned. The colours of Earl Marischal, of the Earl of Kinghorn, and of the town of Dundee were paraded. Montrose's colours bore the legend 'For Religion, the Covenant and the Countrie'. Trumpets sounding and drums beating they marched through the Overgate Port, down the Bridgegate, along the Castlegate, through the Justice Port, and out on to the Queen's

Links, blue ribbons very much in evidence. A muster taken after they had been joined by the northerners produced a total of close to eleven thousand men. Rather ostentatiously the army and its commanders dined on their own provisions on the links of Aberdeen. Some who tried to eat in the town complained that they were 'extorsioned' which grievance Montrose communicated to the unhappy provost, at the same time ordering him to have the trenches around the city filled in over the weekend 'under the paine of plundering and raising' the town. He delegated Kinghorn to secure the city and, contrary to all expectation, he marched his army out of Aberdeen that afternoon, to Kintore where he spent the sabbath. Next day he proceeded to Inverurie. The unfortunate Huntly, hearing of their march, in Spalding's words 'understood certanlie thair cuming was for him (as it wes indeid) and to bring him perforss to thair opinioun.'

Montrose was fully aware that there could be no settlement of the north which did not include Huntly. The latter equally realized that he was now totally isolated; no assistance had arrived from the king and he foresaw the dismal prospect of the firing and plundering of the Gordon territories. From the Bog of Gicht he despatched Robert Gordon of Straloch, who had represented him in the earlier meetings at Montrose, to treat with Graham at Inverurie, while he himself retired to Balvenie, well protected by the hills and glens which now feed the wealthy distilleries of Dufftown. For himself he sought peace with honour, a desire which suited Montrose's ambitions. It was agreed that the two nobles should meet, each with eleven companions armed with only one sword apiece, within three days.

On Thursday 4 April the Marquis of Huntly rode into Montrose's camp. After formal greetings and after each side had carefully searched the other, discussions commenced but rapidly degenerated into a hot exchange between the two main protagonists. Following Straloch's intervention the remainder of the debate was conducted privately between the two noblemen, a course unpopular with their respective followers, particularly those of Huntly. It was never very clear exactly what transpired between the two, nor were the precise conditions imposed on Huntly revealed, but the final outcome was in effect a private agreement between the two men and it must reflect the conciliatory attitude of Montrose. Spalding and James Gordon both believed that Huntly had subscribed a document undertaking to maintain religion and the laws and liberties of the kingdom. Spalding further understood him to have accepted the Negative Confession and to have undertaken to 'do his best' to persuade his followers to subscribe the covenant. If so it would seem that all that was required of Huntly was a version of the king's covenant, which would certainly not satisfy the bulk of the covenanters. Gordon also preserved a remarkable document, signed by Huntly, Montrose, and Kinghorn, which agreed to the non-harassment of such as were of 'contrary religion' and could not subscribe the covenant but would be willing to enter into a bond of maintenance of the laws and liberties of the kingdom.[10] The most likely explanation is that if no settlement could be made with Huntly then there was likely to be civil war between the marquis and the northern clans, which in turn might jeopardize the chances of a peaceful conclusion with the king. It is significant that as early as April 1639 James Graham was prepared to moderate. By taking religion out of the argument for whatever reasons of expediency he showed himself to be primarily interested in the constitutional questions of Scottish law and liberty, despite his known views on episcopacy and catholicism. It may be that he already had some wind of Argyll's plans for an invasion of the north-east and that his agreement with Huntly was simply intended to buy time, and simultaneously to give the impression that he was in control of the situation in the north. Montrose must have been aware that his personal triumph would not necessarily be regarded as such by his narrower colleagues and that if news of the compromise ever became public he would forfeit their confidence. The episode not only suggests that Montrose personally was possessed of a degree of religious toleration but also that the first seeds of doubt about the course on which he had embarked had been sown in his mind.

The camp at Inverurie introduced the surrounding countryside to a phenomenon which in time would wreck the economy to the north-east and of much of Scotland, and which would be the cause of much heartache and despair – armies had to live off the land. Those who 'came not to the help of the Lord' suffered severe depredation. Many in the vicinity of Inverurie had their houses plundered. Thomas Crombie of Kemnay lost four hundred and forty bolls of victual; further afield Kildrummy lost one hundred and twenty bolls; Pitmedden was similarly treated. To protect themselves many signed the covenant but much trouble was being stored for the future. Montrose was no better, and no worse, than any other general in this respect. Necessity dictated his action and in future years thousands of individuals from the loftiest members of the house of Gordon to the humblest cottar on Deeside would taste the bitter reek of smoking crops and stand helplessly by as a year's supply of young corn was consumed by the horses of ravishing armies. By the time Montrose returned to Aberdeen the city was also experiencing the rigours of enforced quarter for the first time.

En route to Aberdeen Montrose was met by twelve Highlanders from Argyll with the news that they were the advance party of a further five hundred of their kind who had come to assist in the subjugation of Aberdeen. Montrose received them graciously but expressly forbade them to enter the city, directing them instead to Drum and Pitfoddels on Deeside where they would find ample sustenance in the lands of their enemies. He was doubtless not unwilling to dispense with the dubious pleasure of having Campbells breathe down his neck as he went about his business. His refusal may have been part of his bargain with Huntly; it was hardly calculated to endear Montrose to Argyll.

The northern covenanters scented victory. Via Straloch Huntly conveyed to Montrose his fears that Frasers and Forbeses would seek to impose harsher conditions upon himself and he begged Montrose to ignore their advice. Above all he feared that they would settle old scores by demanding the seizure of his person. Montrose sympathized, maintained that he would himself undertake to fulfil his obligations to Huntly, but warned that he was not his own master since all was conducted by committee. Straloch thought that the northerners would try to persuade Leslie to take Huntly south but he believed that if Montrose took the initiative he could probably satisfy them.[11] Graham agreed to do what he could but he must have been uncomfortably aware of his predicament. In spite of his experiences during the past year he was temperamentally unsuited to government by committee.

> Like Alexander I will reign,
> and I will reign alone.

He was uneasily attempting to reconcile his own instincts and inclinations with the cause of the covenant.

Leslie was obviously dissatisfied with Montrose's terms. On 10 April

Huntly was summoned to meet him and the other covenanting leaders in Aberdeen under safe conduct. Much to the disquiet of his followers the marquis with his sons Lords Gordon and Aboyne agreed. Had Montrose not guaranteed his safety it is unlikely that he would have gone, since he believed 'it was not unlycke that his unfreendes had sett on foote ther former designe to macke him prisoner'. As soon as he was lodged in Aberdeen Leslie placed a guard on his house, conscious that impending negotiations with Charles would be fraught with even more difficulty if Huntly were allowed to lead an army from the north. He proposed that Huntly should make a financial contribution to the war effort, that he should undertake to pacify the Highlands, and that he should arrest a couple of well-known renegades who were active in the north. Leslie confidently anticipated a refusal on all three counts for agreement to the first two would imply opposition to the crown while at least one of the outlaws had received a royal pardon. Refusal would furnish an excuse to arrest Huntly. Montrose possibly intervened to overrule Leslie on this occasion and some disagreement between the two men is to be deduced from Leslie's departure from Aberdeen on 12 April, Good Friday.

That evening Montrose invited Huntly, in company with several other nobles, to dine at his lodgings 'whair thay soupit altogidder and maid myrrie'. After the meal it was suggested to Huntly that he should return his commission of lieutenancy to the king on the grounds that it had not passed the seals and consequently its legality would be called in question, 'in thir dangerous dayes'. Much to the surprise of all present, he agreed, and despatched letters to the king that very night. He returned to his lodgings in confident anticipation of departing for Strathbogie the following day. But his house was once again guarded and next morning he was again summoned to Montrose's presence. Again as in some warped fairy tale, three proposals were put to him. He should give two hundred merks to redeem the full amount of a loan made to the covenant by William Dick of Braid, the wealthy Edinburgh merchant;[12] secondly he should arrest the Highland outlaws and thirdly end the Gordon feud with the Crichtons of Frendaught. All were impossible suggestions especially the last, a long-standing affair compounded by the burning of the Tower of Frendaught in 1630 which was widely believed to have been a case of Crichton-inspired arson in which Huntly's brother perished. Huntly apparently managed to satisfy Montrose on all three points in the verbal fencing which took place and the earl changed his tactics. 'My Lord, seing we ar all now freindis, will ye go south to Edinburgh with us?' Huntly said he was going home to Strathbogie. 'Your Lordship will do weill to go with us,' insisted Montrose, who was promptly reminded of the safe conduct. 'This in my sicht seemis not fair nor honorabill,' said Huntly. On reflection Montrose enquired whether he preferred to go south as a prisoner or voluntarily. Huntly opted for the latter. Aboyne was sent back to Strathbogie for funds and Huntly with his eldest son marched out of Aberdeen with Montrose's army. The Aberdonians heaved a heart-felt sigh of relief to be rid of Montrose and Huntly alike. The contemporary commentators who recount this episode were all apologists for the Gordons and all claim that Huntly was basely betrayed. Gordon of Sallagh relates that Huntly demanded the agreement drawn up at Inverurie and 'he did tear it'. Spalding considers that Huntly was manœuvred into a position which left him no choice but compliance with Montrose's demand but he does stress that he went voluntarily. Gordon of Rothiemay is uncertain as to whether Montrose was content to allow himself to be overruled by his colleagues in order to lead Huntly to Edinburgh as a trophy of conquest or whether he was simply constrained by his fellow covenanters. He is in little doubt that Huntly's capture was the source of the later enmity between them which 'prevailed so farr as to ruinate and destroye both of them, and the kinge by a consequent'. But Montrose himself was in a delicate situation. The covenanters had taken the castles of Dumbarton and Edinburgh; they had removed the Scottish regalia from a place of safekeeping at Dalkeith to the capital, and they effectively controlled the whole of Scotland outside the Highlands. Had he allowed Huntly his freedom he was in no position to guarantee that the northern clans would honour the truce. As Baillie so graphically put it, a fifth part of Huntly's many enemies 'were able to make a disjune [breakfast] of all the Gordons when at their best'.[13]

Such considerations cannot have escaped the unfortunate Huntly. The agonizing indecision which he had displayed during recent months had lost him considerable support. By giving out that he had been forced to accompany Montrose he was neatly easing his own predicament and at the same time sparing Montrose a great deal of embarrassment. It was indeed rumoured that Huntly had gone willingly to Aberdeen, intending to be taken by Montrose, and Straloch was instructed to present Huntly's version of the story to the king.[14] As a man 'neither trusted by king nor country' there was nothing in Huntly's record to reassure either side. Montrose may have been well content to allow Huntly to issue a statement for public consumption once he was warded in Edinburgh Castle, where, if his surroundings were less comfortable than those at Bog of Gicht, he was at least safe for the moment. Huntly claimed that his only crime was loyalty and that he had been placed in his present predicament by 'unfair meenes'. He concluded his statement on a significantly melodramatic note. 'I am in your power, and resolveth not to leave that foul title of traittour as ane inheritance upone my posterity; you may tak my heid from my schuderis but not my hairt from my sovereigne.' The sentiment was worthy of Montrose himself a few years on, but in the conciliatory climate preceding negotiations with Charles on the border, Huntly's head, as he was no doubt aware, was perfectly safe. For Montrose's part the seed planted at Inverurie had begun to germinate. Events of the next few months would nurture a healthy plant.

Montrose arrived in Edinburgh to find that his name was third, after those of Argyll and Rothes, on a list of persons specifically excluded from amnesty by the king. He and the others were accused of treason, the usurpation of royal authority, arming against their king, contempt of royal proclamations, attempting to foment rebellion in England and Ireland, repealing legislation of assembly and parliament, and condemning royal supremacy. A reward of £1000 was placed on his head. Huntly's stock had never been lower. It was widely rumoured that he had subscribed the covenant and he was roundly condemned for surrendering Aberdeen without a blow. Some like Tom Windebank believed that Huntly had signed to satisfy his people 'but intends the king some secret service in it. This is a time for strategems that fills us all with strange conceits.'[15]

Within two weeks of Montrose's return to Edinburgh the north was once again seething. Young Aboyne had been persuaded by his kin that rather than follow his father south he should stay to redeem the 'heidles countrie'. Earl Marischal organized the northern covenanters who once again occupied Aberdeen. On learning that Hamilton had arrived with a fleet in the Forth, Aboyne dispersed his army and took ship for England where he made his way to the king at Newcastle, disguised as a fiddler. His supporters, 'heidles' once again but under the command of the able Lieutenant Johnstone, son of an ex-provost of Aberdeen, attacked the castle of Tollie Barclay, which had been occupied by the ubiquitous Frasers and Forbeses. The skirmish was remarkable for the death of a servant of the Gordons named David Prat, 'the first blood drawin sen the beginning of this covenant'. Three days later Johnstone drove the covenanters out of Turriff where they had gathered to hold a committee. Following the 'Trot of Turriff' as it was called, they plundered the surrounding countryside. Minor though the affair was it qualified as a royalist victory, the first in the long saga of the British civil wars. The loyal barons as they called themselves proceeded to teach the unhappy Aberdonians that a royalist occupation was as savage as any other. Cheered by hopes of assistance from Hamilton and intoxicated by their own great deeds, they planned to march on the Mearns. Turning up Deeside to Durris they were met by Lord Lewis Gordon in full Highland dress at the head of a band of Huntly's Highlanders including the Farquharsons from the Braes o' Mar and the Gordons of Glenlivet. Lewis was a mere schoolboy who had escaped the clutches of his protective grandmother by leaping the walls at Bog of Gicht to team up with Donald Farquharson of Monaltrie, Ballater. Donald Òg, the 'Pride o' Braemar', was a wild man who frequently made plundering descents on the north-eastern Lowlands, but adventurous and popular and one who could instil more of the fear of God into the citizens of Aberdeen than a dozen covenants; his brother was an advocate in Edinburgh. It was left to the faithful Gordon of Straloch to impress upon the loyalists that they had no commission for their action. He feared they might actually have jeopardized Huntly's life. 'Who,' he asked, 'was prepared to answer to Huntly for an unwarranted attack on Marischal?' Common sense prevailed; they withdrew.

It was quite obvious that Montrose's earlier visit to Aberdeen had achieved precisely nothing and when news reached Edinburgh of the Trot of Turriff he was sent north once more by the Tables. A rapid march brought him to Aberdeen once more on 25 May to find the city occupied by Marischal. Montrose led four thousand men, including the Earl of Atholl with three hundred Atholl Highlanders. The northerners provided a further one thousand and Marischal another nine hundred troops. There was on this occasion a distinct escalation of violence on the part of the occupying army. While Montrose was at his devotions part of the ruffian element in his following amused themselves in plunder. Victual was seized and salmon were stolen from the watermen of the city, leading to the death of a soldier in a brawl. The city's dogs were hunted down and slaughtered because their owners had attached bunches of blue ribbons to their pets to taunt the oppressors. Montrose fined the city ten thousand merks and scoured the town for weapons. Houses of known loyalists were ransacked. He answered the burgesses' protests with accusations that they had corresponded with the king and had sheltered the loyal barons after they had subscribed the covenant.

Having contained Aberdeen once again he marched north where he received news that a ship had appeared off Aberdeen with Aboyne and the earls of Tullibardine and Glencairn aboard. The report might initially have implied the arrival of a sizeable fleet and Montrose could well have conjectured that it signified a landing by Hamilton on the shores of the Forth. The marquis had so far managed to land only on the tiny Forth islands of Inchcolm and Inchkeith, where his troops were recovering from the ravages of smallpox. Hamilton suffered from a different scourge. His mother 'came forth armed with a pistol which she vowed to discharge upon her own son if he offered to come ashore – a notable virago!' According to English commentators she gave a lead to the women of Scotland, 'the chief stirrers of this war'. They 'doe all practise their arms, in which new kind of housewifery they are very expert . . . wishing their husbands' and children's flesh to be converted to that of dogs and their souls annihilated . . . if they refuse to come to the covenant.'[16]

If Montrose lacked the benefit of female counsel he did enjoy the confidence of Henderson and Warriston who wrote to him on 28 May expressly commanding him to levy the northern shires immediately and march post-haste to the border. The levies were to bring such weapons as were to hand and were to march day and night. Montrose was informed that Aboyne was bound for the north with officers and money but lacking men – 'we trust they shall not be able to make any such head as to hinder your Lordship to come hither presently in person . . . with all expedition.' Montrose therefore did not abandon Aberdeen to Aboyne; his orders expressly told him to entrust the city to Marischal. 'If we be lost heir the north will also be lost, but if we prevaile heir our northern losses may be recovered. There is no man acquainted with your Lordship who will think that your Lordship needeth spurring in such an exigence and therefore we remit the necessitie of speed to your Lordship's owne thochts.'[17]

Montrose never reached the army at Duns. He began to recruit, writing to the Laird of Weem from Dunnottar on 7 June, 'having desired Atholl to bring with him all the Highland men he can get for this expedition, these are to desire you to accompany him with all the people that you can possibly make to come along under his command.'[18] But the covenanters underestimated the local appeal of Aboyne to whom Huntly's commission had been transferred. Charles had sent Aboyne to Hamilton with a covering letter enjoining the latter to furnish troops for the northern expedition. Instead Hamilton gave young Gordon the services of one Colonel William Gunn, a native of Sutherland, who had seen much action in Germany. Hamilton was widely credited with the extremes of calculating duplicity and many considered Gunn to be a plant, deliberately assigned to Aboyne to ruin his chances of success. Once news of Aboyne's arrival had filtered through Buchan and the uplands, the north again rose. Lewis Gordon brought in the men of Strathbogie and the Farquharsons. Montrose would dearly have liked to take part in negotiations with the king which were about to commence on the border, but frantic messages from Marischal summoned him back to the north from Angus where he was raising levies. He arrived at the Brig o' Dee on Tuesday 18 June to find Marischal and Aboyne facing each other across the bridge. Montrose was about to fight his first battle, and that against his future ally James Gordon, Viscount Aboyne.

Perhaps 'battle' is too grand a description for what transpired. The bridge across the Dee with its seven arches built of 'hewen stone' was considered 'one of the gallantest in Scotland'. There was a gatehouse at the south end and behind it, across the width of the bridge, 'couragious Johnstone', hero of Turriff, threw up a barricade of earth and stones. The rain-swollen waters of the Dee were impassable. Montrose placed two demi-cannon weighing one and three-quarter tons each and capable of firing twenty-seven pound shot on the high ground south of the bridge. These potentially formidable weapons, supported by an assortment of lighter field pieces, pounded the enemy lines throughout the day, but they inflicted almost no damage, since as with the Scottish artillery at Flodden the shot passed harmlessly overhead. As the day wore on townswomen came out of Aberdeen with provisions for their menfolk and remained to watch the spectacle. One Aberdonian took a bullet through the head but an attempted rush on the bridge by two companies from Dundee was easily repulsed.

Night fell. The day's events had apparently given the lie to the legend:

> There's not a man in highland dress
> Can face the cannon's fire.

Montrose was being worsted and, realizing that delay was 'little better than to be beaten', he moved his cannon closer to the target under cover of darkness that 'they might brashe the gates of the porte and scoure the bridge all along'. Next morning Montrose's fire was much more accurate and the bridge took a savage pounding. Nonetheless Johnstone's musketeers and horse still held the north bank. Montrose therefore decided upon a simple feint, leading his horse westwards along the river as if to cross somewhere higher up. Although it is as well that Montrose's military reputation does not depend upon his efforts at the battle of the Brig o' Dee, he did on this occasion pioneer a ruse which would prove highly successful in later years – he set a trap with himself as the bait. Aboyne shadowed his progress along the north bank against the advice of Johnstone but in response to the urgings of 'Traitor Gunn'. Meanwhile the cannon kept up their deadly fire. One shot gave Seton of Pitmedden a place in the ballads when it carried off the top half of his body as he sat on his horse. A chunk of flying masonry shattered Johnstone's leg, and the covenanters, led by John Middleton who, elevated to the peerage, would leave his black mark on post-Restoration Scotland, charged the bridge. Johnstone and Gunn sounded retreat. The key to Aberdeen was in Montrose's grasp.

Meroz could expect little mercy as Montrose marched into the town for the third time in five months. Forty-eight loyalists were rounded up and committed to the tolbooth with 'neither meat, drink, fyre, candle nor bed'. Montrose was urged to fire the city but he would have none of it. He withstood all entreaties and his failure to commit the 'London of the north' to the flames was later held against him. Instead he fined the city £4000. He must have exerted every ounce of influence to prevent his four-thousand-strong army from ravaging the town and there is ample testimony to the fact that Aberdeen owed its salvation to his personal intervention. His troops were quartered on the city for three days and in spite of his best efforts some 'unrewly sojures' inevitably amused themselves in plunder. The town's corn was entirely consumed and many salmon were stolen. In all, the city fathers reckoned the damage in three days at about £133,000.[19] As it was, the expected conflagration was narrowly avoided. As the few dead were buried (only four individuals lost their lives, all on Aboyne's side) with full military honours, a local covenanter Erskine of Pittodrie, standing close to Montrose, was shot dead by an unknown assailant. Had this been construed as an assassination attempt on Montrose himself nothing could have saved the city. James Graham did not tempt Providence further. A ship brought news of the pacification of Berwick and without more ado he marched south. Gunn managed to escape to Berwick where he gave his host a blatantly distorted account of the battle of the brig. According to him Aboyne with three hundred men had defeated Montrose's two thousand; Montrose had come so close to death that there were shot-holes in his hat, while Marischal's hair was said to have been singed.[20] With such myths did the royalists comfort themselves in the ancient border town. Aboyne betook himself to Edinburgh where his father was now sitting as a member of the privy council. Montrose's movements are uncertain; he probably paused at Auld Montrose to catch his breath and reflect on the circumstance which had cruelly robbed him of the opportunity to meet his king.

5

THE TEARS OF
XERXES

*Your Noble and Heroicke Vertues light this Kingdome, and who can
give them light: for as the Aurore of your honoured reputation is
become that Constantinopolitan Hyppodrome to this our Northerne and
virgine Albion; so lykwise, the same singularitie of worth, hath
raised your auspicious selfe, to be the monumentall glorie of your
famous, and valiant Predecessours, justly termed 'The Sword of
Scotland': Your morning of their Summers day hath fullie enlarged, the
sacred Trophees of their matchlesse memorie; best befitting the
generositie of your magnanimous minde.*

William Lithgow to Montrose 1640

Guthry believed that when Montrose's expectations of being summoned
to Berwick by Leslie were not realized he remained at Auld Montrose
until negotiations with the king were completed. It is more likely that
he went straight to Edinburgh, but the story does suggest that there
was already some disagreement between Montrose and the covenanting
leadership, which over the next twelve months matured into open
hostility.

Meanwhile it was apparent that the articles of pacification with the
king's accompanying declaration satisfied no one. Charles claimed that
he could not ratify and approve the legislation of the Glasgow assembly
without impinging upon 'the honour and security of that true monarchical government lineally descended upon us from so many of our
ancestors'. On the other hand he was pleased to approve whatever
Hamilton, as commissioner, had promised in his name; he added to
the ambiguity by acknowledging that all ecclesiastical matters were to
be determined by 'assemblies of the kirk' and civil matters by parliament. He expressed an intention of personally attending an assembly

in Edinburgh on 6 August and indicted a parliament to meet on the twentieth of that month. His inclusion of phrases such as 'pretended Tables and conventicles' and 'late pretended general assembly' gave great offence as did his declaration – 'we neither have, nor do intend, any alteration in Religion or Lawes but that both shall be maintained by us in their full integrity.'[1] It was a simple matter for the covenanters to point to inconsistencies in the king's statement in a counter-protestation of their own. When Traquair was sent to Edinburgh to indict a general assembly, summoning the prelates as of old, 'the rude sort of people made a tumultuous outcry that they would have no bishops.'

Loudoun was sent to Berwick to account for these violent activities; he returned with a demand from the king that fourteen leading covenanters visit him to give 'satisfaction in those particulars wherein they have trenched upon his regnal authority and broken their promises'. Late on the evening of Tuesday 16 July Montrose, Rothes, Lindsay, Lothian, Dunfermline, and Warriston duly rode into Berwick. They conferred with Charles throughout the following day when he demanded that they dismantle fortifications at Leith and elsewhere, and restore royal cannon and munitions which they had seized. He also asked them to dissolve the Tables and to repeal Leslie's commission. The party returned to Scotland with instructions to bring back their colleagues for further discussions the following week. Even in the English camp great secrecy surrounded the negotiations. In the event Dunfermline and Loudoun did return to Berwick but Montrose did not accompany them and he was not present to hear Charles's announcement that he would not, after all, be attending the forthcoming assembly.[2]

On the first occasion Charles sounded out his visitors on their reaction to Traquair's appointment as commissioner and discussed possible measures leading to a lasting peaceful settlement. Burnet claimed that 'Montrose was much wrought upon, and gave his majesty full assurances of his duty in time coming: and upon that entered in a correspondence with the king.' The same authority elsewhere opined that Montrose undertook to do great services – 'he either fancied, or at least he made the king fancy, that he could turn the whole kingdom; yet indeed he could do nothing.'[3] There is no doubt that on this occasion Montrose was impressed by Charles and it was widely believed that the king had turned his head. Within the next month 'the vulgar whispered in the streets to his prejudice' and someone fixed a notice to his chamber door bearing the legend '*invictus armis, verbis vincitur*', an obvious reference to the conqueror being conquered by the words of his king at Berwick. Baillie believed that at this time Graham was 'not unlyke to be ensnared with the false promises of advancement', but he was undoubtedly under suspicion before he went to Berwick. The leadership wrangled for three days about who should be sent to meet the king. It seems to have been conceded that either Montrose or Loudoun, but not both, should be included in the party. Montrose had been criticized for his lenient treatment of Huntly and the city of Aberdeen and his recent record suggested that he might be too easily swayed; such at least may be deduced from the fact that he was strongly opposed by the western covenanters who considered restraining him by force if necessary. It could be added that, unlike Loudoun, Montrose had no experience of such negotiations. In the event Montrose prevailed and Loudoun sadly reported to Campbell of Glenorchy 'some of us hes not bein suffered to goe ther'.[4] It is doubtful if Montrose was quite as forthcoming as Burnet suggests. He had always claimed to be acting in the king's best interests, as had all the covenanters, and there is every indication that his belief was sincere. Some indication of the king's attitude towards him is to be gleaned from a letter sent by the Duke of Lennox to Traquair; it is undated but from internal evidence it clearly must be assigned to July or August 1639. 'His Majesty doubts not of Montrose's carriage in all civil points and if he would come to understand himself in ecclesiastical it would be better for him, howsoever I do not doubt but you will do your best even for the man's sake, for he hath noble parts.'[5]

Gordon of Rothiemay stated no more than the truth when he asserted that the assembly which opened in St Giles on 12 August 'was but the epitome and superstructure of the Assembly of Glasgow and a confirmation thereof, wherein the Presbyterian party gained ground palpably upon the king and his authority.' Montrose attended as ruling elder for the presbytery of Brechin. There was little novelty in the debates. A lengthy discussion of episcopacy preceded the more general business and in order to clarify the position the acts of assembly since 1575 were consulted. Traquair eventually declared himself satisfied that episcopacy was indeed contrary to the legislation of the kirk, though he felt bound to reserve the king's position by adding the rider that to declare it unlawful in Scotland 'shall never bind nor infer censure against the practices outwith the kingdom'. To this the covenanters objected but Traquair's reservation truly highlighted Charles's dilemma. As one of his Scottish supporters put it, 'Episcopacy orthodox in England, heretical in Scotland. Lord God have mercy on my soul!'[6] Charles had personally assured the Scottish bishops that though he might give way for the present he would not cease to consider the remedies in due course for these prejudices to church and state. He also made it clear that in spite of previous instructions to Traquair he could in no way approve the act 'for whatsoever is absolutely unlawfull in one church cannot be lawfull in another of the same profession of religion.'[7] The same act also rejected prayer book, canons, court of high commission, and the Five Articles. The assemblies of 1606 to 1618 were nullified and it was stipulated that in future there should be annual assemblies. Traquair subscribed the covenant as a private citizen but refused to do so as king's commissioner. Huntly also subscribed at about the same time.

Irrespective of Charles's sincerity with reference to the Edinburgh assembly it is evident that its legislation achieved all that Montrose sought. As he said himself:

We were constrained to put ourselves in a posture of arming for our own defence, till it pleased God that the king's majesty, being informed of the lawfulness of our proceedings and honest intentions, for the most part was graciously pleased to accept of our petitions, and grant us a lawful General Assembly, to be held in Edinburgh wherein the acts of the assembly of Glasgow were ratified without so much as a show of opposition by His Majesty's commissioner, conform to the conference and capitulation at the camp of Berwick. But the members of the parliament [which met at Edinburgh immediately after the assembly] some of them having designs far unknown to us, others of them having found the sweetness of government, were pleased to refuse the ratification of the act of assembly, with the abjuration of episcopacy and the court of high commission introduced by the prelates, unless they had the whole alleged liberty due to the subject; which was in fact, intrenching upon authority, and the total abrogation of his Majesty's royal prerogative.[8]

He could not know, or chose not to recognize, that Charles was once again preparing, had all along intended, to betray his word, his commissioner, and his loyal and well-intentioned subjects of Scotland.

The assembly concluded with a declaration which expressed the desirability of king and people joining in one covenant and confession of faith. It was appropriate that Montrose should be one of three nobles chosen to transmit it to the privy council for registration in the books of council. The last days of August 1639 represented the high point of James Graham's commitment to the cause of the covenant. It was short lived. A few paces separated St Giles from Parliament House, 'and fewer dayes'. The assembly ended on 30 August; parliament met the following day.

The main preoccupation of the 1639 parliament was the constitution of the lords of the articles. Since at least the fifteenth century the articles had been entrusted with the discussion, preparation, and drafting of legislation which they subsequently presented to a reassembled parliament for ratification. By the seventeenth century the articles had become the instrument of royal whim. The bishops chose eight nobles who in turn chose eight bishops; the sixteen then combined to choose eight each of shire commissioners and burgh commissioners. Since bishops were manifestly king's men representation was weighted in the royal favour. A constitutional crisis arose in 1639 since the all-important component, that of the bishops, was excluded. Charles instructed Traquair to ensure that fourteen ministers, which failing, fourteen laymen nominated by the king, be substituted for the bishops. If all else failed Traquair was to resort to his own devices, an expedient which Charles favoured since the greater the irregularities the easier the subsequent repudiation of such legislation as the articles might produce.[9]

Traquair decided to invite the nobles to deliberate with him in the choice of the lords of the articles. On this occasion, locked in bitter discussion for four or five hours, Montrose 'argued against new motions concerning the constitution of parliament'.[10] It appears that he supported Traquair's contention that noble nominations should belong to the king – Charles's own suggestions were for the moment quietly dropped – while Argyll was strongly of the opinion that each estate should elect its own representatives, a truly revolutionary departure which would, in Montrose's words, have entrenched upon royal authority and meant the total abrogation of royal prerogative. After protracted wrangling the nobles effectively chose the articles. They selected eight of their own number who were subsequently endorsed as the king's choice by Traquair; they then chose commissioners of the burghs and shires. All of the latter commissioners were covenanters but the noble representation was surprisingly diverse, including as it did, not only Argyll and Rothes and Montrose and Lindsay but such confirmed royalists as Southesk and Huntly. The composition of the articles, so far as the nobility was concerned, may be seen as a triumph for Traquair but it would be mistaken to see the debates and disagreements as a great conflict of ideologies. These were men, friends and associates, who at this point were fumbling towards a solution to unprecedented constitutional problems. United in their covenant, the similarities in their attitudes were greater than the differences. Argyll and Montrose each regarded the views of the other as misguided, but each respected the potential value of the other to the cause, and for many months to come they were more concerned to present a common front within the covenant than to publicize differences between them. This is not to deny that Montrose was well aware that many in parliament wished to go far beyond the ratification of the act of assembly which was duly approved. Both burgesses and shire commissioners made it clear that they wished to push towards more extreme demands, among them the right to nominate their own representatives to the articles, to have access to legislation for consideration prior to ratification, and to restrict the power of levying taxation to parliament. When Traquair reintroduced Charles's suggestion that fourteen laymen should replace the bishops he gained Montrose's support but the motion was narrowly defeated. William Graham, Earl of Airth, informed Charles of developments.

I find that my cousin Montrose hath carried himself both faithfully, and is more willing to contribute to his uttermost in anything for your Majesty's service, than any of these lords covenanters; for I am confident that he will keep what I promised to your Majesty in his name; wherefore I do humbly entreat your Majesty, that by a letter to him you will take notice and give him thanks and desire the continuance.[11]

Although the allusions herein are obscure and no letter from Charles to Montrose is extant it would appear from this and from Lennox's letter earlier quoted that Montrose had undertaken to support Traquair in assembly and parliament.

The articles continued to sit until late October. Much of the business was routine, concerning personal supplications (including several from

Montrose's sister, Lady Luss, seeking aliment), and matters relating to parish kirks and burghs. Montrose was appointed to a commission to treat upon the disorders in the north and also to one charged with examining the university of St Andrews. Traquair, who had suffered several setbacks in the articles, postponed the final session of parliament no fewer than eight times before proroguing parliament itself until June 1640. So ended the 'altercating parliament'. The Estates issued a proclamation claiming that this 'unexpected and unexemplified prorogation' was contrary to the constitution of all previous parliaments and contrary to the liberties of their free and ancient kingdom as well as repugnant to the king's promises in the articles of pacification.[12] The unhappy Traquair, whose brief success had turned to distress and who regarded prorogation as the only possible weapon against legislation which he knew the king would never accept, returned to court where 'he exageratts all the covenanters' deportment and actinges as tending to the destruction of the fundamentall lawes of the kingdome, and overthrow of monarchicall governiment and makes every molehill a mountane.'[13] Traquair's behaviour did not enhance James Graham's reputation either. Although the commissioner found himself out of favour, Charles had undoubtedly believed what he had to tell him. He had already recalled Thomas Wentworth, Earl of Strafford, from Ireland to advise him on the violent confrontation with the Scots which all regarded as inevitable. Even before the prorogation Charles had ordered Patrick Ruthven, Lord Ettrick, governor of Edinburgh Castle, to reduce the city by battery of ordnance if it would not supply him with provisions. Ettrick reported that the citizens were more ready to 'cut our throats than to let us have one barrel of gunpowder or match' and he suggested that powder and ammunition be sent to him disguised as barrels of beer.

On 20 November Charles wrote to Montrose stating his willingness to hear his opinion 'touching some things which may concern the king's service in Scotland' and inviting him to court 'where his Majesty's further pleasure shall be imparted to him'. James wisely did not keep this invitation to himself. He 'convened some of the nobility, shewed unto them both his particular affairs, and the king's command, and that according to his covenant of following the common resolution, and eschewing all appearances of divisive motion, nobly has resolved to follow their counsel, and has gone home to his own house and will not go to court at all.' Such at least was Warriston's version of developments. Montrose told the king on 26 December that he had been about to depart for the court –

Which coming to be here known, did so put aloft the minds of most part – being still filled with their usual and wonted jealousies – that I could expect nothing but more peremptory resolutions than is fit to trouble your Majesty withal; or me, in thinking to do your Majesty service to have occasioned. . . . I chose rather, before matters should have been made worse and the gap enlarged by my means, to crave your Majesty's humble pardon for my stay, and make you acquainted with the necessities for it: hoping your Majesty will do me the honour to think that this is no shift – for all of that kind is too much contrary to my honour, chiefly in what your Majesty or your service is concerned in, – but that, as I have ever been bold to avow, there are no things your Majesty shall be pleased to command me in . . . that I shall not think myself born to perform.[14]

Whatever the truth of the matter these two conflicting pieces of correspondence reveal Montrose to be somewhat less ingenuous than his admirers have suggested. Although he was often politically naive his attempt to convince Charles and Warriston simultaneously of his good intentions is worthy of Argyll or Hamilton. The differing accounts admirably epitomize his personal dichotomy. By now he had reached the point described in his poem on 'The Faithlessness and Veniality of the Times'.

> Unhappy is the Man
> In whose Breast is confin'd,
> The Sorrows and Distress all
> Of an afflicted Mind.
>
> Then break afflicted Hearts,
> And live not in these Days,
> When all prove Merchants of their Faith,
> None trusts what other says.

For the moment his afflicted mind told him to remain with the men of the covenant. By the end of 1640 he had fully convinced himself that his place was with the king.

In January Montrose appended his signature to an 'Information' designed to raise money for the cause. It was accompanied by a band which bound signatories to pay an unspecified sum towards the common cause and thus partially relieve those who had already contributed.

For Montrose at least the matter was of some urgency; his debts were impressive as was the extent to which his kinsmen and relations were committed on his behalf. In March 1638 he and Claverhouse borrowed £3000 from George Haliburton, a merchant in Dundee. In June of that year Napier and the Grahams of Claverhouse, Fintry and Balgowan stood surety for a loan of £10,000 which he raised from the Edinburgh merchant Archibald Sydserff. He borrowed a further £3000 from Nicholson of Carnock in August. In July 1639 Montrose with Napier and Rollo of Duncrub was loaned £6000 by John Hamilton, chamberlain of the Earl of Kinnoul, and in December he and Rollo raised £2000 from Mr Roger Mowat, advocate in the Canongate. His problems were far from over in 1640. On 24 March he and the Earl of Kinghorn drew up a bond for £1426 10s owed to James Barnes, merchant in Edinburgh, for ammunition purchased from him; in July Rollo, Claverhouse, Braco, and Orchil stood surety for £12,500 borrowed from one James Drummond.[15] By July his recorded debts amounted to some £38,000. In future years they would far exceed that sum and those who gallantly stood surety for him verged on bankruptcy.

In December 1639 Traquair had insisted on orders from the king that the covenanters appoint commissioners to travel to London for discussions, but they did not depart until the following February when a new justification was issued explaining that Scottish hopes of peace had been thwarted by malicious adversaries who branded the Scots as rebels. After further assertions that they intended no invasion of England but were merely interested in self-defence they drew up a list of wrongs and grievances suffered since the pacification. Those centred on Traquair's handling of the recent parliament. He had refused to allow the ratification of the acts of assembly as well as an act rescissory abolishing legislation which conflicted with these acts. He had refused to exclude bishops from parliament for all time and had rejected the new mode of electing the lords of the articles. His stock answer had been, 'the king will have it otherwise and will make you do it, if not worse' – 'ane ill arguement to be heard in a free parliament'. They denied that parliament had to be licensed by the king and disputed the prorogation on the grounds that much business could not be transacted without parliament – the courts did not sit, it was impossible to obtain relief from the burdens of war, church vacancies were not filled, and trade was interrupted. New fortifications were being erected, Berwick and Carlisle were being garrisoned, the king had not disbanded his forces, Edinburgh was being replenished, strangers were placed in Scottish castles, Scots abroad were forced to subscribe new oaths, the lack of stability in currency caused hardship, and all means were used to create divisions among the Scots. It concluded with an appeal to 'all good Englishmen' to plead the Scottish case and to impede the evils hanging over Scottish heads. Charles responded to the Information by having it burned by the hangman.[16]

Some time in 1639, probably May, an undated letter to Louis XIII of France had been signed by Rothes, Montrose, Mar, Loudoun, and Alexander Leslie. It related that since Louis was regarded as 'the refuge and sanctuary of afflicted princes and states' they were sending Mr William Colville to France to explain their actions and intentions 'which we desire to be engraved and written to the whole world'. Charles claimed that the letter was addressed '*Au Roy*' which he interpreted as a challenge to his own kingship. It was later claimed that Montrose was responsible both for suggesting and for drafting the letter and that Lauderdale refused to sign it because the French was defective.[17] A copy fell into Charles's hands in March 1640 when the covenanters decided to send it, with another, to Louis. The king was understandably outraged. Loudoun and the other commissioners had been instructed to have no truck with the English council which had no authority over them. They were to discuss such matters as reparation for injuries suffered since the pacification only with the king in person, but they had little chance to carry out their instructions, for Charles challenged Loudoun with the letter to Louis and confined him in the Tower. He summoned the other signatories in early April to answer for their 'very high offence', but Montrose, Argyll, Leslie, and the others refused to respond. Montrose was in any case in independent communication with Charles at this time through one of his surviving Ruthven uncles and the Earl of Panmure. Although the terms of reference are so obscure as to make speculation hazardous, if not pointless, there is a strong possibility that James was endeavouring to explain away his association with the offending letter.[18]

The divisiveness so feared by the covenanters was much in evidence during those early months of 1640. Lord Ettrick reported from the recently refortified and replenished Edinburgh Castle that there was dissension between some Angus noblemen as well as between Argyll and Seaforth, who was said to be on the point of joining the Earl of Airlie and Lord Reay in the king's service. The previous month Argyll had complained from Inveraray of some who were troubling 'this corner of the kingdom and my scurvy person'.[19] It is not unlikely that Montrose himself was involved in some of these disturbances.

Argyll was alarmed at Seaforth's *volte face*, not least because he had recently drawn up a bond of friendship with him, and he was suspicious of Huntly. He was also apprehensive that his recent arrest of Lachlan MacLean of Duart and Archibald MacColl, son of Colla Ciotach, would 'be aggravated to the full in my prejudice'.[20] In April Charles sent a proclamation to the provost and baillies of Edinburgh discharging Argyll of his justiciary of Argyll and Tarbert, ordering that none should obey him or appear in his courts or pay him taxes and feu duties until, remarkably, he should appear before the English parliament to answer charges laid against him. The king rightly recognized, following the advice of his father, that heritable jurisdictions gave too much power to individuals like Argyll. There was considerable resentment of such offices throughout the land. In 1635 and 1636, for example, the Laird of Balnagowan in Ross-shire had petitioned the king for the reduction of the 'Mairdom of Ross, for the relief of his Majesty's subjects from the Laird of Innes's suppression'. 'Lamont's declaration' of 1639 stated the desire of the sheriff of Bute and Lamont himself to be free of Argyll's justiciary. He discussed the matter with Hamilton who assured him that when the country was settled the king would 'take order as to the enormities'. Charles intended at that date to dissolve the Campbell justiciary by appointing Sir Donald Gorm Lieutenant-General of the Isles and by granting jurisdiction to Seaforth.[21] During discussion in the articles the previous September Argyll had protested that a commission to enquire into the privileges of the justiciary should in no way infringe or prejudice his office. But the whole issue was best described in a paper discussing the withdrawal of Argyll's office. 'It is fitting his Majesty should interfere out of the sense of the burden of his subjects inhabiting within the Earl of Argyll's justiciary who are forced to withdraw themselves from his Majesty's due obedience under pretext of their appearance at justice courts at Inveraray and other parts where they have no power to resist the unjust commands of the Earl or his deputies.' Argyll's two prisoners were to be set at liberty immediately or surrendered to the keeper of Edinburgh Castle.[22] The provost and baillies of the Scottish capital did not consider it appropriate in such troubled times to make proclamations against 'the persone of sic ane pryme noble man'. It would be contrary to Scots law to deprive Argyll without consulting council and parliament; furthermore no nobleman could be compelled to appear before the English parliament – he could answer only in Scotland and then to his own peers.

Times were troubled for royalist sympathizers too. The Earl of Airlie departed for the court, leaving his son Lord Ogilvie in charge of his Angus castles. Robert Maxwell, Earl of Nithsdale, was effectively in a state of siege at his castle of Caerlaverock in the Solway marshes. In August he had voiced his disappointment at Charles's lack of positive action and he continued to do so, believing that royalists like himself were being fruitlessly ignored, if not actually sacrificed, by the king. Sir Michael Ernle, charged with holding Berwick, was plagued by mutinous soldiers while Edward, Viscount Conway, entrusted with the defence of Newcastle, persisted in minimizing the threat from the north, until the very eve of invasion. He was uneasy about the significant numbers of Scots domiciled in Newcastle, notably those employed in the coal mines. Covenanting Edinburgh was much troubled by the enemy within. Ettrick received supplies of arms and men in February, and from March the covenanters mounted a guard of four hundred men nightly to watch the castle. When they began to raise modest fortifications to protect the city from bombardment, Ettrick ordered them to desist on threat of firing the town. Shots were exchanged and in the ensuing panic several prominent royalists, among them Southesk and Sir Lewis Stewart, king's advocate, were arrested. In April a royal spy reported that houses in the vicinity of the castle were being fortified by filling them with sand and horse dung. This reporter reminded the king that, according to the old chronicles, although Scotland had often been invaded it had never been conquered because the inhabitants had always been able to seek refuge in the Hebrides! Towards the end of May Montrose was sent by the Tables (now known as the Committee of Estates and consisting of twelve nobles, twelve barons, and twelve burgesses) under flag of truce to demand from Ettrick the surrender of the Scottish regalia. The governor refused and when Montrose reported back to the Estates a message wrapped round an arrow head was fired into the castle, ordering its surrender within forty-eight hours.

Such was the background to the reopening of the prorogued parliament on 2 June. In England Charles had dissolved his 'Short Parliament' a month before. Argyll had been confident that Charles would be unable to prevail upon the English Commons to 'do that to us which they would not have done to themselves'[23] and he was correct – money was refused for a war against the Scots. Charles tried unsuccessfully to prorogue the June parliament once more. He was ignored and Lord Burleigh was appointed president in the absence of a royal commissioner. Thus began one of the most significant and most revoluionary parliaments in Scottish history. In nine days, between 2 June and 11 June, a series of acts was passed 'exhibiting the reall grattest change at one blow that ever hapned to this churche and staite thesse 600 yeires bypast; for in effect it overturned not onlie the ancient state government, bot fettered monarchie with chynes.'

Much of the legislation was concerned with the affairs of the kirk. Montrose with Loudoun (now returned from England and the Tower) and Rothes presented the supplication of the 1639 assembly to parliament and council. The acts of assembly were ratified as was the subscription of the covenant and the confession of faith. The act rescissory demanded by the articles the previous year was duly passed. There was provision for the planting of kirks and the admission of ministers. There were acts against Sabbath breaking, against Monday markets which of necessity infringed the Sabbath, against observance of the Christmas vacation, and against papists and excommunicates. A Triennial act provided for parliaments every three years; voting by proxy was discouraged. But Sir James Balfour of Denmylne rightly distinguished the second act of this parliament as the most significant. It altered the constitution by effectively excluding the third estate, the bishops and clergy, from attendance at parliament for ever. The three estates were now the nobles, the commissioners of the shires, and the burgesses. The method of electing the articles worked out the previous year was approved but the lords were henceforward to discuss only those matters referred to them by a full parliament, a significant departure indicative of the long-felt animosity towards the monopolist tendencies of that body. Provision was also made for a Committee of Estates, exactly like that already operating, to handle Scottish affairs after parliament had risen. This was, as Balfour observed, 'the first positive law for committees' and, it might be added, a necessary measure for the success of any revolution. It was in vain that members of this parliament asserted 'we doe in the truth of our harts declare that it is farre from our thoughts and myndes in any sort to trinche on soveraintie or in the least touch to violat the sacred and inviolable name of his Majesty and kingly authority.'[24] Their legislation belied their protestation. Charles had truly reaped the harvest of his ignorance, neglect, and autocratic government of his native kingdom; his Scottish subjects had broken the bonds which tied them to the medieval world and had set about the creation of the new Zion.

Predictably James Graham was unhappy, if not heartbroken, at these developments. Parliament was prefaced by unofficial discussions which were concerned with the limits that existed on the loyalty of subjects to their sovereign. Argyll himself maintained that 'nothing is impossible for an enslaved people to do against tyrants and usurpers'.[25] Allowing that Argyll did not consider Charles a tyrant – though given the rhetoric and argument invoked by the covenanters since 1637 the inference that he might be regarded as such was inescapable – but merely a misguided monarch, he came up against a problem of definition. The covenanters had always envisaged a sovereignty shared by king and parliament but what was the position if one of the parts was missing? The legislation of the 1640 parliament, in spite of protestations to the contrary, came close to a deposition of royal authority. Gordon of Rothiemay considered that the Committee of Estates was set in place of king, parliament, and privy council, 'a power that Scotland had never known nor heard tell of before'. Some discussion of deposition is implied by Warriston's cryptic statement that in June 1640 'Montrose did dispute against Argyll, Rothes, Balmerino, and myself; because some urged that as long as we had a king we could not sit without him; and it was answered, that to do the less was more lawful than to do the greater,'[26] which is to be interpreted as meaning that to indict parliament without the king was more lawful than to depose him altogether. If the king ever were to be deposed there was allegedly no shortage of candidates to replace him. There were persistent rumours that Hamilton still had designs on the throne and in the aftermath of the Scots' capture of Newcastle it was reported in the Low Countries that Charles had been set aside and Queen Elizabeth of

Bohemia put in his place.[27] Argyll was said to have boasted that he was 'eighth man from Robert Bruce', and his soldiers claimed 'they were King Campbell's men, no more King Stewart's'. In the summer of 1640 a Scots translation of a Gaelic poem was in circulation proclaiming:

> I gave Argyll the praise
> because all men sees it is treuth;
> for he will tak geir from the lawland men;
> and he will tak the Croun per force;
> and he will cry King at Whitsonday.[28]

Whatever the thoughts in Montrose's mind at this juncture he had little time to ponder. The Committee became the effective government of Scotland and even some who detested what it stood for gladly served on it until the king might come back to his own. As well as Montrose himself those members who might be said to be of his circle included Wigtown, Napier, and Sir George Stirling of Keir. It was well known that some members favoured the king 'yet were nominated either to unmask them or to debauch them by their concurrence against him'.

One of the first actions of the Committee was to grant a commission of fire and sword to Argyll. Among the 'intestine enemyes' of the covenant specified were the Earl of Atholl, Lord Ogilvie, and the Farquharsons of Braemar as well as the inhabitants of Badenoch, Lochaber, and Rannoch. They were to be pursued, subdued, and rooted out of the country, their goods and victuals to be seized, and all who harboured them punished. Argyll was granted the full protection and support of the Committee in all his actions; the signature of Montrose is the first which appears on the commission.[29] That Argyll anticipated the commission by some weeks is indicated by the fact that four thousand Campbell levies rendezvoused a week after it was issued. He had a particular interest in Lochaber and Badenoch which he had received in wadset from Huntly. The Campbells therefore were not simply intent upon extending ancient clan feuds: there was an economic incentive to harry loyal Highlanders who were now obliged to pay their rents to Argyll. Feuds with the Stewarts of Atholl were of long standing while the inhabitants of the Angus glens had bitter memories of invasions during the last decade of the sixteenth century when a savage strife between the previously amicable Ogilvies and

Campbells began. So apprehensive were the men of Angus about the large force of Campbells harrying Atholl that they begged Montrose, who was raising levies in his native county and in Perthshire for the planned invasion of England, not to move his forces out of the district until the danger was passed. The local committee of Perth was of the same mind. On his own initiative Montrose decided to anticipate Argyll by taking Airlie Castle himself.

In the absence of the earl, Airlie was held by his son James, Lord Ogilvie. A year Montrose's senior, Ogilvie had been his fellow student at St Andrews and according to tradition his luckless rival for the hand of Magdalen Carnegie. The two were close friends, Ogilvie being personable and popular, 'a little light man, but always loyal'. Airlie Castle was situated ten miles west of Forfar at the point where the Melgam Water joined the River Isla. It sat on a promontory some hundred feet high formed by the two rivers and was reckoned inaccessible on all sides save the south which was protected by a ditch and a high wall. Anxious to protect his friend, Montrose rode from Forfar and demanded the surrender of the castle, warning of the possible consequences of refusal. He was later accused of having permitted Ogilvie to escape in spite of the commission which he had himself signed. The castle was entrusted to Lieutenant-Colonel Sibbald and Montrose wrote to Argyll telling him that the castle was secured and that he need not march into Angus before he advanced south to join Leslie on the border. The famous sequel was less happy. During the first week of July the dreaded Campbells marched through the glens led by *MacCailein Mór* himself, who chose to ignore Montrose's communication. He was furious to learn that he had been cheated of his prey and further enraged by Sibbald's reluctance to hand over Airlie Castle. At the first opportunity he charged Montrose 'with foul dealing before the Tables'. Lady Helen Ogilvie had remained behind and it was she who, in the well-known ballad,

> . . . looked o'er the high castle wa,
> And oh! but she sighed sairly,
> When she saw Argyll and a his men
> Come to plunder the bonnie house o Airlie.

The lady did not, however, in the words of the ballad, 'lay her doon on the hill to dee'; she was in an advanced stage of pregnancy and she was allowed to depart quietly. Alyth, Lintrathen, Glenisla, and Cortachy were also despoiled and the crops and houses of the Ogilvie tenants ruined; timber plantations were destroyed; cattle and sheep were driven off to feed the army; the best horses were taken home to Lochawe and Inveraray. It was reckoned that £7000 worth of damage was caused and the Earl of Airlie received no rents for fourteen months. When Argyll departed for Stormont he left explicit orders for the destruction of one more Ogilvie stronghold. He ordered Campbell of Inverawe to demolish the castle of Forthar or Forter which commanded Glenisla and the pass leading westwards to Glenshee. 'If ye find it will be langsome,' he wrote, 'ye shall fyre it weill, that so it may be destroyed. Bot ye neid not to lett know that ye have directions from me to fyre it.'³⁰ *MacCailein Mór* went on to carry fire and sword into Lochaber. There he burned the house of MacDonald of Keppoch, *Clan Domhnaill a' Bhraighe*. A little later the MacDonalds retaliated by lifting cattle from Campbell of Glenorchy. They fought a skirmish at Sron a' Chlachain near Killin. One who took part in 'that foray to the head of Loch Tay' was Iain Lom, the bard of Keppoch, whose poetry would immortalize the deeds of Montrose and Alasdair mac Cholla.³¹

Meanwhile Montrose joined Leslie's army near Duns where between five and ten thousand men had mustered. It was rumoured that the Scots planned to become masters of Tyneside with the intention of wringing concessions from the king by stopping the coal trade. The anxieties of the English commanders on receipt of such news were insignificant compared with those of Montrose when he learned at Duns of sinister new proposals. He was invited to subscribe a band (or three bands – the accounts are confused) 'importing the schaiking off of Authoritie, and establisching the wholl power and rule of the kingdome of Scotland in hand of Genrall [Leslie] in the fields, and the power of all besouth the water of Forth in the Marquis of Hamilton his hands, within the countrie, and the Earle of Argyle benorth Forth.' Montrose was shocked by this talk of what he called 'ane Dictatory and incantoning of the kingdome, by which the countrye was to be enslaved and reduced to all thralldom'.³² He hastened to Edinburgh where Lord Lindsay confirmed that some such scheme was afoot. A year later others were to testify that Argyll was behind these proposals. Hamilton could also have been implicated. It was said that he frequently visited Loudoun during the latter's incarceration in the Tower and Loudoun certainly took care to inform the marquis of developments within the covenanting ranks, writing to him for example on the very day that the Scottish army crossed the Tweed.[33] The time had come to mobilize moderate support and in early August Montrose drew up a band in Cumbernauld House, the home of the Earl of Wigtown.

Montrose judged 'that it was more now nor high time to us, and all honest men who respected the Libertie of the Countrye, and this Caus, to joyne themselves togither to oppose those wayes of tiranny, which in effect did tend to nothing less than the ruine of Countrye, Libertie [and] personall fredome.' The signatories declared that out of duty to their religion, their king, and their country they had been forced to subscribe the covenant, but finding that both country and cause were suffering 'by the particular and indirect practicking of a few' they bound themselves 'to study all public ends which may tend to the safety' of the religion, laws, and liberties of Scotland. They further undertook 'to contribute one with another, in an unanimous and joint way, in whatsoever may concern the Public, or in this cause, to the hazard of our lives, fortunes and estates, neither of us doing, consulting, nor condescending in any point without the consent and approbation of the whole, in so far as they can be conveniently had and time may allow.' The document concluded with a cunning echo of the covenant itself – 'every one of us shall join and adhere to others, and their interests, against all persons and causes whatsoever, so what shall be done to one shall be equally resented and taken as done to the whole number.'

According to Guthry the Cumbernauld Band was initially subscribed by – in addition of course to Montrose – Wigtown, Lord Boyd, and Lord Almond, all of whom were near neighbours. Montrose's cousin Wigtown could certainly be described as royalist. The latter's son-in-law Robert, eighth Lord Boyd, was no outstanding covenanter although many of his Ayrshire tenants were committed to the cause. The inclusion of James Livingstone, Lord Almond, is rather surprising. The third son of the first Earl of Linlithgow, Almond was a professional soldier who had enjoyed a highly distinguished career on the continent. Elevated to the peerage and created gentleman of the bedchamber in 1633, he was in 1640 second-in-command to Leslie with the rank of lieutenant-general; a year later he was created Earl of Callander. As one who 'between war and politics was much put to it in steering a course for himself', he may, like some of his co-signatories, have adopted the band as a kind of insurance. Others who signed from similarly mixed motives were Earl Marischal; Lord Johnstone of Lochwood in Dumfriesshire, later Earl of Hartfell, who rejected the band the following year; and Thomas, Earl of Kirkcudbright, who remained a zealous covenanter and who would lead a Gallovidian regiment at Philiphaugh. John Lyon, second Earl of Kinghorn, had known James at St Andrews, had entertained him at Glamis, and had been closely associated with him since the start of the troubles; friendship dictated his subscription. Those who could definitely be described as royalist, if no less vacillating than their covenanting counterparts, were John Murray, Earl of Atholl, smarting from his recent imprisonment by Argyll; John Erskine, Earl of Mar, who had spent much time at court during the lifetime of his famous father and who later claimed that he had joined Montrose under compulsion; his son Lord Erskine, another signatory, joined Montrose in 1644; Sir Mungo Murray, second Viscount Stormont, who had not long to live was another, as were John, second Earl of Perth, and his son James, Lord Drummond, both of whom suffered great financial losses in the king's service. There was no doubt of the loyalty of Alexander Stewart, Earl of Galloway; Sir John Carnegie, Lord Lour; and his son David, Master of Lour. George MacKenzie, second Earl of Seaforth, had been gravitating towards the king, and James, third Earl of Home, who supported the covenant became a fairly consistent royalist after 1640. They comprised a cavalier party, all attempting to return to the original spirit of the covenant and aiming to block the factious policies of the few. Napier and Stirling of Keir are said to have subscribed later but their names do not appear on any of the surviving copies of the band.[34] The whole document was obviously very rushed, Montrose having little time to consult much beyond a fairly restricted circle of friends and near neighbours. It remained a secret because the signatories had no wish to publicize differences within the covenanting ranks, but it did serve the purpose for which it was intended. It cleverly exploited the clause in the covenant which stated 'if any dangerous and divisive motion be made to us by word or writ, we and every one of us shall either suppress it or if need be shall incontinent make the same known, that it may be timeously obviated.' When it was subsequently discovered and burned by the hangman it did indeed foil 'the particular and indirect practicking of the few'.

All commentators agree that as Montrose approached the Tweed in August 1640, that river became his Rubicon. His 'cheerfulnesse was but seeminglye,' writes Gordon of Rothiemay, for he had 'fallen in dislycke with the Covenanters actings and was now waiting for the first opportunity to crosse them.' Menteith claims that he was unhappy about the invasion since he had observed that 'when they were deliberating upon it, those who gave their opinion against that design put the rest to a nonplus, whether it was that the affair had not been well concerted, or that the strength of their main reasons did not admit of a reply.' Nevertheless he 'suffered himself to be carried away with the violence of the stream, which would have swallowed him up, if he had made the least show of opposing it.' It is at this point that Wishart begins his heroic tale. He had recently been drummed out of St Andrews and now enjoyed a post as an assistant preacher in Newcastle. His preface points out that Scotland had always been saved 'in its hour of direst need' by the Grahams. His story continues in a similar misleading vein. He implies that his own Erastian attitudes were shared by his hero. According to him the covenanters, believing that Scotland had been too long ruled by kings, desired the extirpation of the Stewarts. 'Filled with loathing for so horrible a crime, Montrose resolved to abandon the Covenanters, frustrate their designs, reduce their resources, shake their power and with all his might preserve the king and kingly power entire and inviolate.' He neglects to mention that Montrose had no intention of abandoning the covenant. Such covenanting designs as he wished to frustrate were only those of the 'few' and Montrose's notion of preserving 'kingly power entire and inviolate' was very different from that of Charles I. Wishart further asserts that Montrose had no knowledge of the plan to invade England, which is palpable nonsense. In short he sets the tone for his entire account, a propagandist work, designed to raise support and resources throughout Europe for a renewed assault on Scotland in the late 1640s. His Montrose is a mythical figure, a hero in the classical mould, dressed in the armour and endowed with the virtues of the Old Testament.

James Graham undoubtedly did experience a *crise de conscience* in the course of 1640. The confident covenanter faltered; he had opposed the instincts of his race and rank; he had defended his kirk at the expense of the constitution; he had enabled 'great ones to aim so high as the crown', had seen sovereignty restrained, and had realized the full implications of revolt. He still owned his covenant but he could not disown his king. It is never easy for the committed to admit error, not least for a natural leader, a man of genuine conviction who had perhaps actively sought a cause for himself and who was possessed of more than his share of 'the pride o' the Grahams'. The agonies of indecision, the dull ache of disillusion, and the pain of revelation experienced by James Graham in the long months since he had joked with Rothes in the heady atmosphere of protest and proclamation are unknowable. What is clear is that for some months to come he strove to find a solution within the covenant, to win support for the king against a faction. His peace of mind could not have been eased by a poem which William Lithgow dedicated to him in 1640, but it may have reinforced his awareness of the transitory nature of human life and endeavour, and have guided him towards a decision.

The lengthy poem rejoices in the title, 'The Gushing Teares of Godly Sorrow', unjustly pronounced by Lithgow's editor to be 'a most unreadable and unsatisfactory production', which he was tempted to exclude from his anthology.[35] The theme is repentance, the futility of life without God. Man's short life 'like a shadow flees'. Man must learn to die 'that he may learn to live / for in this course his happiness consists'. There was much for James to ponder:

> Unwise is he, and thrice unhappy too!
> Who ill commits, that good thereon may follow.

The corruption of the grave awaits all men but corruption can be experienced all around, in church and commonwealth, in false reports, in ambition, in 'strained selfe contract'd opinions', in books, in princes, in courtiers, and elsewhere. Man must beware the vicissitudes of fortune which stem from sin. Peter's denial of Christ is treated at length. Who had not denied his master? 'We're apt to note the lives of other men / but not our owne.'

> Oh! if ambitious men their ends were showne!
> That like the froth, do beat on rocks of death:
> That shadow short, from a fled substance flowne,
> Much like a dreame, so vanisheth their breath:

Then would their deeds, forbeare to tyranize,
The Just might live and offer sacrifice.

In this our age, what kings have beene disthrond,
Detectd, cast downe, last banish'd from their bounds:
I could recite and where th' injust were crownd,
And Princes headlong, hurled from their grounds.
Pryde fostered spight, with them the Ulcer brecks,
Which gored the harmlesse, broke ambitious necks.

The great Xerxes wept when he realized that all his ambition, all of his mighty army, all of his fabulous wealth, and all of his people, all for which he had struggled and fought would come to dust.

Thus mournd this pagan king, whose rule may learne
Most moderne tymes, to waile the consequences.

The tears of James Graham might have mingled with those of Xerxes as he pondered the truth of Lithgow's poem. The certainty of death, which awaited him ten years later, was not matched by the certainty of the life he still had to live. If he now doubted the righteousness of the cause to which he had given his support he equally doubted the truth of the alternative. He was not the high-minded, high-principled, consistent paragon created by some of his admirers; he was a man wracked by doubts and uncertainties desperately trying to understand and come to terms with a situation created by history. At the end of his life Argyll described himself as 'a distracted man, a distracted subject, of a distracted time wherein I lived'. It was the epitaph of a generation.

6
THE TRIALS OF JOB

He teareth me in his wrath, who hateth me: he gnasheth upon me with his teeth; mine enemy sharpeneth his eyes upon me. They have gaped upon me with their mouth; they have smitten me upon the cheek reproachfully; they have gathered themselves together against me. God hath delivered me to the ungodly, and turned me over into the hands of the wicked. I was at ease, but he hath broken me asunder: he hath also taken me by the neck, and shaken me to pieces, and set me up for his mark.

Job 16:9–12

Newcastle was described in 1635 as 'beyond all compare the fairest and richest town in England . . . inferior for wealth and building to no city save London'. Situated at the main crossing point of the Tyne it was of great economic as well as strategic significance. The life blood of Newcastle was coal, which generated warmth for the houses of London and riches for the coal owners; it also fuelled the closely related salt industry of North and South Shields. Leslie planned to make the city hostage to Scottish fortune.

By the second week of August Montrose, Almond, and the others had rejoined the army at Choicely Wood, four miles south of Duns. The Tweed was in spate and at Cornhill, where the main body crossed, lots were drawn to see who should test the water. The honour fell to Montrose – 'I was, of all myself the first that putt my futt in the watter, and led over ane regement in the view of all the armie.'[1] Others used the fords at Wark and Carham. A political squib attributed to Leslie the words, 'We are now with Caesar past the Rubicon and this night you are to lie on English soil. This is the land of promise which as yet ye see but far off. Do but follow me and I will be your Joshua.'[2]

English wit provided little defence against Scottish invasion. The Scots could only pray as they crossed the field of Flodden that theirs was not to be the fate of their ancestors in 1513.

English estimates of the force differed wildly from thirty-five thousand to a more realistic fifteen thousand as they advanced through Wooler, across the Till and the Coquet to Morpeth. Montrose commanded the levies of Perthshire and Forfarshire amounting to some sixteen hundred men. Loudoun, Lindsay, and Rothes marched on foot while the other lords were mounted. The colours bore the motto 'Covenant for Religion, Crowne and Country'. Blue bonnets were worn by infantry and cavalry alike, the former armed with muskets, swords, and short staves, the latter with swords, pistols, and petronels. Some, but not all, of the Highlanders carried swords as well as bows and arrows – 'they are the nakedest fellows that ever I saw', reported a spy. There were eight large brass cannon each drawn by six oxen and two horses as well as an abundance of lighter field pieces and thirty ammunition wagons. Canvas tents had been provided by 'the dear sisters of Edinburgh'. Thousands of cattle and sheep brought up the rear. The soldiers were under strict orders to desist from plunder and 'on pain of death not to disturb man, woman or child nor to take the worth of a chicken or a pot of ale without paying for it'.[3] If any man could ensure the obedience of his soldiers it was Leslie; there were lapses and wrongdoers were hanged, but by and large the English were astonished at the exemplary conduct of the Scottish army, at least in those early days.

Before the invasion the covenanters had issued an information, declaring their intentions to 'their brethren of England', who were thanked for their refusal to believe the calumnies heaped upon the Scottish nation. Bloodshed would be avoided if possible. The Scots, tired of awaiting destruction at the hands of their merciless enemies, had resolved to explain their proceedings and desires to the king and the English people. Necessity, which 'is a sovereignty, a law above all laws', had driven them to this course of action. They undertook to harm no one, nor to take anything (from a thread to a shoe-lace) from the English without payment. They demanded only the security of the religion and laws of Scotland, according to the constitution and the acts of the late assembly and parliament. A supplementary piece recalled that the English had assisted the Scots at the Reformation, that the two peoples had lived in peace for many years, and that both had hopes 'to sie better dayis in this island'.[4] As subsequent negotiations would show the Scots genuinely desired closer union with England.

The defences of Newcastle were down. The wilfully optimistic Conway, having insisted all summer that there would be no invasion, was now forced to blame all but himself for Newcastle's unpreparedness. He was in a wretched situation for Scottish propaganda had accurately pinpointed English reluctance to engage. Charles's ambitious plans had come to nought because of an abysmal failure to recruit adequately. An army of twenty thousand foot and two thousand horse had been designed for the Border. In the event Conway complained that he was left with a mere 500 horse. Plans to fortify the city and nearby Morpeth fell through for lack of funds. Sir Jacob Astley was to send some five thousand foot from Selby but he appeared himself with only half that number and many of the troops, lacking pay and wretchedly supplied, were mutinous. Conway claimed that he feared his own 'rascally soldiers' more than he did the Scots. He received useless advice about sending ships out of the Tyne and firing the suburbs of Newcastle if the Scots attacked. Contrary counsel was given by Strafford whom he thought guilty of 'a wilful unbelief'. Conway fell back from Morpeth as the Scots approached and on 27 August Leslie looked down upon the ford of Newburn, ten miles west of Newcastle.

It is not certain that Montrose took part in the fight at Newburn. Leslie divided his forces and sent one division straight to Newcastle; since Montrose was one of the first into the city he probably accompanied it. It was later believed, through a clear case of mistaken identity, that Montrose had been killed in the battle. Conway attempted to hold the ford with seventeen hundred horse, two thousand foot, and some hastily constructed breastworks. Under cover of darkness Leslie concealed his cannon in the woody slopes of the north bank; he also placed some culverins in the tower of Newburn church. Throughout the forenoon and early afternoon of Friday 28 August the two armies faced each other across the river 'without affronting one another or giving any reproachful language'. The waiting was too much for one covenanter who galloped out from his company brandishing a sword, so antagonizing an equally impatient Welshman who shot him dead.

Battle duly commenced, Conway ordering a troop of three hundred cavalry across the river at low water. The devastating fire of the Scots guns drove them back and inflicted severe damage on those entrenched behind the earthworks. It was only a matter of time before the ford was unlocked and the covenanters advanced. The overwhelming majority of the royalist ranks broke, thus facilitating obedience to Leslie's orders for a minimum of slaughter. No attempt was made to hold Newcastle, which Leslie entered on 30 August.[5]

On 3 September Montrose, Rothes, Lindsay, and Cassilis wrote to Sir William Carnaby of Booth Hall, a prominent Tyneside royalist, asking him to visit him at their general quarters to discuss 'the weal of the country'. The victorious Scots were now less scrupulous. They sang songs which boasted that they had somehow fulfilled the prophecies of Merlin and inevitably there was some looting and pilfering with consequent executions. They demanded a daily levy of 30,000 lb of bread as well as forty oxen, one hundred sheep, and two hundred tunnes of beer from the bishopric of Durham. Meanwhile Dumbarton Castle had surrendered. In spite of Nithsdale's protests he had been left to fend for himself and after a long siege forty Maxwells were killed when Caerlaverock was stormed. Close on two hundred people had been killed in exchanges between the castle and city of Edinburgh; on 15 September Ettrick and Argyll agreed terms and the scurvy-ridden garrison – Ettrick's legs were so swollen that he could barely walk and he had lost all of his teeth – was permitted to take ship from Leith.[6]

From Newcastle the covenanting leadership petitioned the king to consider their pressing grievances, to repair their losses, and, 'with the advice and consent of the estates convened in parliament, settle a firm and durable peace', but Charles could not negotiate until the Scottish demands were more closely specified. On 8 September Sir James Mercer conveyed their terms to York where the king had gone with some notion of leading the defence of Newcastle himself. The acts of the recent parliament were to be ratified; Edinburgh and other royal castles were to be surrendered; Scots abroad were not to be censured for subscribing the covenant; 'incendiaries' responsible for the present 'combustions' were to be arrested; Scottish ships seized by the English were to be restored; there was to be reparation for all 'wrongs, losses and charges' sustained by the army; and finally the English parliament was to withdraw the charge of treason, the English army, and any other impediments towards a lasting peace. Montrose signed the conditions along with fellow members of the Committee.

The document formed the basis of lengthy negotiations which commenced at Ripon and which, transferred to London, were concluded in the Treaty of London in June 1641 with most of the points being conceded. The English parliament was party to all discussions but, preoccupied as it was with the trials of Laud and Strafford, it hoped to wring further constitutional concessions from Charles in the course of negotiations with the Scots. £300,000 were granted as a contribution towards the expenses of the Scots army which remained, inactive, at Newcastle. 'We are sadder and graver than ordinary soldiers,' wrote Lothian, who, unable to find a sober fiddler in the whole army, diverted himself with pipers. 'I have one for every company in my regiment and I think they are as good as drums.' In February the Scots began to escalate their demands. They required Charles and the Prince of Wales to spend some time each year in Scotland. Several demands aimed at closer union between the two kingdoms. Among these were the advocacy of religious unity and uniformity, triennial meetings between the two parliaments, and closer liaison on such matters of mutual interest as peace, war, and commerce. Vaguely worded and reluctant concessions gave some satisfaction on these points but the king refused the Scottish parliament the right to nominate Scottish officers of state though he did agree to discuss these matters when he visited Scotland, an intention announced in April. There was further disagreement over an act of oblivion from which certain royalists such as Traquair were to be excluded without allowing the king to exclude an equal number of covenanters; after much wrangling the king gave way. One of Charles's first acts in Scotland would be the ratification of the Treaty of London but he also hoped, somewhat vainly, to recruit Scottish support against the English parliament. Rothes, leader of the Scots commissioners in London, was offered a court post. 'He will take a place in the bedchamber and be little more than a Scottish man,' Baillie sadly predicted. But for Rothes the struggle was over. The shrewdest and perhaps the most original of the architects of the covenanting revolution died of consumption in London.

Montrose slipped a personal letter to the king into the batch of correspondence entrusted to Mercer. According to Wishart he simply assured Charles of his loyalty, obedience, and readiness to serve him but the contents of the letter were subsequently revealed to Leslie who delegated Almond to inform the offender that if he did not submit to the committee of war they would 'proceed against him capitally'. Montrose admitted the correspondence but claimed that since others were communicating with the king, he had done no wrong. Since Leslie was anxious to maintain the illusion of unanimity at this critical juncture he pardoned Montrose who now became a marked man.[7] Montrose would have sympathized with many of the sentiments expressed in a remonstrance of the faithful lords and gentlemen of Scotland which was presented to the king at York in October. The lords complained that they had been forced to flee covenanting prosecution. The 'late forged Council of State', i.e. the Committee, had issued an edict citing some seventy-five nobles, officers of state, bishops *et alia* to appear before the continued parliament on 19 November, on pain of high treason. Their only crime was refusal to concur with the 'rebellious ways' of the covenant; they had done nothing illegal. They demanded to know by what laws the edict was published, the names of Estates usurped 'to the high disgrace of royal government', sessions of parliament held, and statutes enacted; to know which laws entitled them to prorogue parliament, institute heralds, appoint judges 'in these pretended treasons, since among equals there is no supreme authority', and to ascribe powers to dispose of life and limb. 'As for their late model called the Constitution of Parliament, we absolutely decline it as diametrically opposite to our fundamental laws and the primitive institutions of our parliaments.'[8] Although Montrose was a member of the 'council of state' himself his record shows that he agreed with many of the forementioned points. The problem facing the remonstrants and Montrose alike was that by treating with the covenanters at Ripon, London, or later at Edinburgh, Charles condoned the legality of their actions and implicitly condemned his true political allies.

At Newcastle Montrose confided to Colonel John Cochrane that 'he was desyrous to follow the warris abroad and wished the business wer settled at home, that he mycht employ his talents that way.' Charles Louis, the Elector Palatine, who was at court and who was shortly to accompany Charles to Scotland, had requested Cochrane to sound Montrose, 'one of whom he muche heard', on the possibility of military service abroad. Sick at heart and now almost totally disillusioned, James asked Cochrane to communicate his interest. Once again he was taxed by Leslie with secretive correspondence and once again the matter was overlooked. Montrose told Cochrane that if he wrote again he must do so in 'covert terms, because he was a man envied and all means were used to cross him'.[9] Cochrane was also the unwilling participant in a discussion with Montrose about the Cumbernauld Band, in the hearing of no less a person than Leslie. Montrose's naivety is almost incredible, unless he was deliberately provoking a showdown. He said that he could prove that some of the 'pryme leaders' of the covenant were 'guilty of treasone in the highest maner, and that they had entered in motiones for deposing the king'. His nervous confidant wisely begged him to be quiet, but James later returned to the subject – 'think you not but I can prove what I said to you the other day?'

There was much coming and going between Edinburgh and Newcastle and Montrose was present at the parliament which met on 19 November only to prorogue itself until January. On that day Lord Boyd, on his deathbed, revealed the existence of the Cumbernauld Band and Montrose was once again called to account. Some of the ministers and other 'fiery spirits' called for his blood, but Montrose coolly produced a copy of the band – it had possibly been drawn up with just such an eventuality in mind – and Argyll, noting the names of the signatories, some of whom commanded regiments in the army, backed off. Montrose and the banders declared that their subscription implied 'no evil or divisive intention' against the covenant. Nonetheless the band was ordered to be burned by the common hangman.

By the end of 1640 Montrose was experiencing something akin to total political isolation for the first time since the outbreak of the Troubles. He was driven back upon a small circle of intimates, Napier, Sir George Stirling of Keir, and Sir Archibald Stewart of Blackhall and Ardgowan (estates in Renfrewshire), who held frequent, clandestine meetings during the Christmas period in and around Edinburgh. Keir was married to Napier's eldest daughter; his sister was the wife of Stewart, a lord of council and session. Early in 1641 Napier wrote to Charles, expressing the fears of the group. 'Your ancient and native kingdom is in a mighty distemper. It is incumbent to your Majesty to find out the disease, remove the causes and apply convenient remeads.' The cause of these troubles, 'not without some reason', was the fear of changes in religion, fear which Charles could easily disperse. He assured the king that the Scots did not intend the overthrow of monarchical government whose two-thousand-year history had bred great affection among his people. It was imperative that Charles should visit Scotland in person. 'Now is the proper time of cure, and the critical days; for the people love change, and expect from it much good – a new heaven and a new earth – but being disappointed, are as desirous of re-change to the former estate.' If he satisfied the Scots in religion and liberty all would be well and differences manifested in the recent parliament could easily be accommodated. 'Let not your authority receive any diminution of that which the law of God and Nature and the fundamental laws of the kingdom alloweth.' Napier was simply expanding upon points which he had long ago drawn to Charles's attention. On the back of the draft of this letter Napier scribbled certain axioms. 'All novations in religion, and attempts upon the laws and liberties of the subjects, produceth dangerous effects;' 'soverane power in the person of one, few or many, is the sole and only bond of human society'; 'government too much restrained is weak, too far extended is tyranny'; 'bad kings tyrannize: good kings are tyrannized by subjects'; 'sovereignty must not be disputed by subjects who must confine themselves to their own laws and liberties'; 'the king and his people make up one body politic' and so on.[10]

Robert Wodrow transcribed a letter purporting to have been written by Montrose on the subject of 'Supreme Power in Government of all sorts'. Several commentators have noted that the letter draws heavily on Napier's ideas and it appears to be a much expanded version of his 'axioms'. Much of the terminology is to be found in Napier's other writings and he probably wrote it as he did several other documents issued in Montrose's name. Wodrow was a highly expert and rigorous scholar and it is unlikely that he would have noted that the letter emanated from Montrose if it had, in fact, been signed by Napier. The letter is addressed 'noble sir' and concludes 'your humble servant'. Mark Napier (who was in no doubt that the letter was composed and written by Montrose) suggested that the recipient was Drummond of Hawthornden. The terminology makes this unlikely: 'humble servant' would be inappropriate addressed to one of lesser rank. The phrase 'noble sir' suggests that the recipient was not well known to Montrose and it is possible that the letter was written in response to a query from England of the type which Argyll and Rothes at different times received, seeking clarification of their attitudes: both in reply concocted fairly succinct statements of their respective philosophies. Implicit in the document, as in several others emanating from the Montrose circle, is the idea that the writer is trying to save the king from himself. The recipient may have been the Duke of Lennox who was increasingly involved in trying to organize a loyal party around the king. The probability that the letter was written by Napier, however, does not invalidate the identification of its sentiments with those of Montrose.

Some consideration has already been given to the first two parts of the letter in which Montrose discusses civil society and the subject of tyranny. He continues,

The perpetual cause of the controversies between the Prince and his subjects, is the ambitious designs of rule in great men, veiled under the specious pretext of religion and the subjects' liberties, seconded with the arguments and false positions of seditious preachers. 1st that the king is ordained for the people and the end is more noble than the means; 2nd that the constitutor is superior to the constituted; 3rd that the king and people are two contraries, like the two scales of a ballance, when the one goes up the other goes down; 4th that the Prince's prerogative and the people's privilege are incompatible; 5th what power is taken from the king is added to the estates of the people. This is the language of the spirits of division that walk betwixt the king and his people, to separate them whom God hath conjoined (which must not pass without some answer) to slide upon which sandy grounds those giants, who war against the Gods have builded their Babell.

He agrees that the end is superior to the means but he maintains, somewhat improbably, that the analogous argument would be to say that if a man is appointed as a shepherd or a nobleman as tutor to a poor pupil, 'the sheep should be preferred to the man, and the pupil to his tutor'. His reply to the second point is equally dubious: only the constituted can reverse his constitution. If a woman chooses a husband (a rare event in male-centric Scotland) or a people a king, neither woman nor people can free themselves from obedience or subjection. All of these examples had been used by Buchanan but Montrose slides round some of his more telling points, such as 'can he be a shepherd if he flays his flocks instead of pasturing them?' The remainder of Montrose's arguments are, however, pure Buchanan. The king and his people are not two 'but one body politic . . . so far from contrariety and opposite motions that there is nothing good or ill for the one which is not just so for the other'. The prince's prerogative and the people's privileges are mutually dependent. He dismisses the fifth point as fallacious 'for what is essential to one thing can never be given to another': the judgement or memory of the king cannot be transferred to the subjects. 'When a king is restrained from the lawful use of his power, and subjects can make no use of it, what can follow but a subversion of government, anarchy and confusion?'

Buchanan was misunderstood by contemporaries and posterity alike because it was assumed that once the legality of resistance to tyrants was accepted no king would be safe. In fact Buchanan emphasizes that tyrannicide is to be used only in the last resort. His view that 'nothing tends more towards length of power than the temperate exercise of authority which does honour to the king and is advantageous to the people' was identical to that of Montrose. Both had an essentially aristocratic view of the Scottish constitution. Buchanan feared the people at large, 'the monster with many heads' and recognized that 'the cupidity of the mob is insatiable'. He distinguished Scotland as a kingdom which for two thousand years had resisted the foreign yoke, and which had from earliest times always created lawful kings. No race was less given to sedition than the Scots. 'There have been many disputes about our laws, about the right to hold authority and the methods of administration, but our sovereignty has always remained unharmed.' Such struggles had not involved the destruction of the common people or hatred of monarchy, 'but patriotism and the desire to protect our laws'. Montrose accepted all of this and recognized with Buchanan that there was 'a mutual contract between king and people' – hence his desire to reform the king, to convince him of the error of his ways, to restore the broken contract, before, in his view, it was too late. Nowhere is Montrose's debt to Buchanan more obvious than in the concluding and most personal section of his letter on the supreme power.

Now, to any man that understands these things only, the proceedings of these times may seem strange, and he may expostulate with us thus: 'Noblemen and gentlemen of good quality, what do you mean? Will you teach the people to put down the Lord's anointed, and lay violent hands on his authority, to whom both you and they owe subjection, and assistance with your goods, lives and fortunes, by all the laws of God and man? Do ye think to stand and domineer over the people in an aristocratic way – (the people) who owe you small or no obligation? It is you, under your natural prince, that get all employment pregnant of honour or profit, in peace or war. . . . If [the people's] first act be against kingly power, their next act will be against you . . . And you, ye meaner people of Scotland, who are not capable of a Republic, for many grave reasons, why are you induced by specious pretexts, to your own heavy prejudice and detriment, to be instruments of others' ambitions? Do ye not know, when the monarchical government is shaken, the great ones strive for the garland with your blood and fortunes? Whereby you gain nothing, but instead of a race of kings who have governed you two thousand years with peace and justice, and have preserved your liberties against all domineering nations, shall purchase to yourselves vultures and tigers, to reign over your posterity, and yourselves shall endure all those miseries massacres and proscriptions of the triumvirate of Rome – the kingdom fall again into the hands of one, who of necessity must, and for reason of state will, tyrannise over you. For kingdoms acquired by blood and violence are by the same means entertained. And you great men (if any such be among you so blinded with ambition) who aim so high as the crown, do you think we are so far degenerate from the virtue, valour, and fidelity to our true and lawful sovereign, so constantly entertained by our ancestors, as to suffer you, with all your policy, to reign over us? . . . And thou seditious preacher, who studies to put the sovereignty in the people's hands for thy own ambitious ends, as being able, by thy wicked eloquence and hypocrisy, to infuse into them what thou pleases, know this, that this people is more incapable of sovereignty than any other known: Thou art abused like a pedant by the nimble witted noblemen: go, go along with them to shake the present government, – not for thy ends, to possess the people with it, – but like a cunning tennis player (who lets the ball go to the wall, where it cannot stay), that he may take it at the bound with more ease.[11]

The piece concludes by asserting that the king is the sole bond of union between England and Scotland. Montrose was concerned with 'that which I esteem truth set down nakedly, not adorned for public view'. The letter's subjective eloquence entitles him to a place with those who, through the centuries, grappled with and sought to define the vexed question of the Scottish constitution.

In February Montrose met certain ministers, including Mr John Graham, minister of Aberuthven, and Mr Robert Murray of Methven, in Margaret Donaldson's house at Perth. He attempted to clear those who had subscribed the Cumbernauld band by relating the proposals for the dictatorship and the triumvirate, doubtless aware of the preachers' potential for 'infusing into the people what they please' through their 'wicked eloquence'. When challenged by Murray he declared his willingness to defend the band before parliament or general assembly. Next day he and Murray went on to visit Lord Stormont at Scone where they met the Earl of Atholl and Mr John Stewart of Ladywell, commissary of Dunkeld. The two earls asked Stewart for information about Argyll's bands. He was able to report Argyll's alleged claim that kings could be deposed for desertion, invasion, or sedition, 'and that once they thought to have done it at the last sitting of parliament and would do it at the next sitting thereof'. Montrose naturally wanted further details and proofs but he cautioned Stewart 'to keep within bounds rather than to exceed' in what he said, promising that in return he would 'be sparing to wrang him'. Stewart and the Athollmen had suffered during Argyll's descent on the area the previous summer and Stewart subsequently sent Montrose full information about the bands and about Argyll's indiscreet discourses. He also transmitted the stories about 'King Campbell' and a translation of the Gaelic poem as well as a report that Rothes had expressed fears that he and his colleagues would be 'forced to put our intentions to execution'.[12]

At the April meeting of the presbytery of Auchterarder Mr John Graham spoke of Montrose's discussions. From there the news reached the Committee of Estates which summoned Graham to appear before it on 19 May, mainly at the instigation of an apprehensive Argyll. Graham duly reported his story, expressed the view that all were 'seeking one end', and claimed that he had cautioned his fellow ministers against pronouncing on the matter. He named Murray as his informant. The latter was 'called off the streets' to answer before the full Committee. He was reluctant to speak but Montrose came to his assistance. 'Come, come Mr Murray, emit your declaration without more ado; you know very well that you can soon put it off your hands.' Murray obliged by naming Montrose himself who admitted his involvement with alacrity. 'I named Argyll as the man who was to have the rule benorth the Forth, and as the man who discoursed of deposing the king,' said Montrose, insisting that he could name his informants, and he challenged Argyll to 'express his own knowledge of this business'. Argyll denied on oath that he knew anything of such matters so forcing Montrose to name Lord Lindsay and John Stewart of Ladywell. Four days later John Stewart, who had obviously been warned by Montrose to hold himself in readiness, appeared before the Committee. He boldly reminded Argyll of his remarks 'in the presence of a great many people, whereof you are in good memory', before signing a paper confirming Montrose's claims, whereupon Argyll 'broke into a passion and with great oaths denied the whole or part thereof'.

Montrose had consciously sought this confrontation but he reckoned without Argyll. While Stewart was confined in Edinburgh Castle the covenanters took steps to tamper with his memory. Torture altered his testimony; he begged Argyll to let him re-testify that he might give his lordship satisfaction. When he reappeared before the Committee he referred to 'the infirmitie and weiknes of my bodie and spreit' which rendered him unable to stand or walk. He recanted. Montrose was the only person to whom he had reported Argyll's opinions though on reflection he believed 'his speech was general, of all kings'. His fate was sealed. Argyll, having declared his interest but disavowing malice against any man, petitioned parliament for Stewart's trial. Baillie doubted the legality of the whole business but justified parliament's action on the grounds that Stewart was 'striving with the lives' of Argyll, Hamilton, and Rothes 'and by a consequence at the overthrow of our treaty of peace and the welfare of the whole isle; it was therefore thought necessary to make an example, the more as his friends, for whose pleasure his lies were invented, were giving out that all was but collusion between him and Argyll who undoubtedly would purchase him a free remission.' Stewart petitioned for mitigation of the death sentence on 24 July. Four days later, at three o'clock in the afternoon, he was beheaded. Guthry, who attended him in his final hours and at his execution, believed that the victim bore 'false witness against himself', so implying that his original testimony had been the true one.

After examining Lindsay at the beginning of June, the Committee concluded that 'as it is possible Montrose has mistaken Lindsay's expression . . . there is no ground for the said misconception'. Montrose had seriously underestimated Argyll's political dexterity as well as his following among the covenanters, for his record rendered him more suspect than Campbell. His confidence was shortly to suffer another crucial dent. Stewart gave one important piece of information to his tormentors which was not mentioned in his depositions. The information sent to Montrose had also been given to Lieutenant-Colonel Walter Stewart for transmission to Traquair. Sir Thomas Hope of Kerse recounted with glee that the said Walter 'was happilie rancountered betwixt Cockburnspath and Haddington, by one sent expresslie to meet him'. In his saddle-bags was discovered a letter from the king to Montrose, a letter from Colonel Cochane to Walter Stewart, and 'a signature of the chamberlainry of the bishopric of Dunkeld to Mr John Stewart, with a blank for a pension but not signed by the king's hand'. Montrose was caught by the very trap which he had set for Argyll. If the king's letter to Montrose was that of 22 May which simply informed him of his impending visit to Scotland,[13] it was innocent enough and Cochrane later testified that his epistle concerned service with the Elector, but the document concerning John Stewart was suspicious. There could, however, be no escape for Montrose. On 11 June he was arrested by the Earl of Lothian and was, according to that nobleman's account, 'without one voice disassenting, either of the Committee or noblemen or commissioners of parliament, who were present in good number, committed to the castle'. Lothian's attitude to Montrose was typical. 'In Winter, when his band was burnt, I did what I could to quiet matters and bring him off, and he thought I did him good offices. But now I took not so much pains; for his often relapses are not to be endured, and his practices will be found much to the prejudice of the public, and very malicious against particular men, who, to my knowledge, deserve it not at his hands. . . . I have no particular but the good of the public; that safe I am for all the ways of gentleness and moderation.'[14] Montrose, like Stewart of Ladywell, jeopardized the successful conclusion of the pacification, from the point of view of both the covenanters and the king, and the troublemakers were expendable. When Charles learned of Walter Stewart's arrest he immediately wrote to Argyll assuring him that his projected visit owed nothing to Montrose's overtures: nor did he intend to confer office upon Montrose and his colleagues. Napier and Keir accompanied Montrose to the castle; Stewart of Blackhall was initially not confined because, thought Baillie, he made confession to Argyll 'of sundrie of the plotters' mysteries'. Not the least of these mysteries was the one surrounding the association of the plotters with Walter Stewart, for on further investigation it transpired that he had been Montrose's means of communication with the court.

Both Montrose and Napier admitted that around Christmas 1640, when they had been meeting with Keir and Blackhall, Stewart had appeared in Edinburgh on his way to London 'for his owne privat affairis'. Montrose testified that they took the opportunity 'to desire him to represent our best respects to the Duke of Lennox'. Stewart was to advise the duke that the surest remedy for Scotland's ills was a personal visit by the king. Napier later claimed that Stewart was not so well acquainted with Lennox as he had pretended. Stewart was an enigma. He was a cousin of John Stewart, Earl of Traquair, who described him as 'a fool, or at least a timid, half-witted body'. As well as carrying letters from Ladywell and from the plotters to Traquair, he took messages from Sir William Drummond of Riccarton, one of the Scots commissioners in London, to Stirling of Keir.[15] On one occasion he arranged through Sir Richard Graham of Netherby to have himself presented to the king on Montrose's behalf and then failed to keep his appointment. His pretext was that he wished to discuss Montrose's desire to serve under the Prince Elector; Montrose did not deny writing to Graham in this connection.[16] Perhaps Stewart's most sinister association, in view of the turn events were to take, was with Hope of Kerse. At Newcastle the supposedly 'timid, half witted body' had discussed Buchanan's *De Jure Regni* with Hope and General Leslie. When Stewart expressed doubts about the legality of Strafford's trial by parliament, Hope said that Buchanan demonstrated parliament's competence to try kings. Stewart was not impressed; he considered Buchanan 'a modern writer'.[17] Secretary Vane was certain that neither the king nor Lennox knew anything of Stewart's 'foolish plot', adding that Stewart had been heard 'to speak foolishly of many'. It was believed that Montrose wanted the king to come to Scotland, sought office for himself and his confederates, and had invited Lennox 'to combine with their faction and to be accessory to their plot'. There was no evidence that Charles was implicated, 'although Colonel Stewart averred that Traquair reported to him that he had imparted Montrose's designs to the king and received his answer thereon which appeared clearly to be a calumny forged by Stewart or by Traquair, for the encouragement of those who were upon that plot'.[18]

When Stewart was arrested letters (or a letter) written in a crude cipher were found upon his person. Hope doubted Stewart's explanation 'of A.B.C. by which he says are meant the Banders, and of the viper in the king's bosom', allegedly a reference to Laud. Montrose's indictment also referred to a 'covered cabalistic way of letters of the A.B.C.'. Stewart kept changing his mind about the precise significance of the symbols. At one point he alleged that D and T stood for the Duke of Lennox and Traquair, R for the king, also represented by L which sometimes meant Liberty, as R could mean Religion. Montrose was sometimes M (which also stood for Hamilton), sometimes A and sometimes 'Genero'. The 'Elephant' was Hamilton, while the 'Dromedary' was Argyll, Cam-(pb)-el, an old joke. To confuse matters further the letters were hastily printed with a somewhat different interpretation of the code. One of them was translated as meaning that Montrose, Keir, and Napier (but not Blackhall) were prepared to 'cut off' Argyll and Rothes, and warning Lennox and Traquair that matters 'cannot go right till that serpent M [Hamilton] be cut off'. Montrose and his friends accused Stewart of writing them himself. The plotters' denial of all knowledge of the ciphers is acceptable since they had already communicated some of the material that now appeared in code to the king. In a letter of 7 June Hope described Stewart as 'my man' and rejoiced that he was 'happilie rancountered by one sent expresslie to meet him'. He mentions one letter in code and it seems probable that the number grew between Stewart's arrest and his appearance before the Committee. Furthermore they were all in Stewart's handwriting. It is difficult to escape the suspicion that Stewart was in some way a plant. Perhaps there was an actual letter from Stewart of Ladywell to Traquair or vice versa which did employ a primitive code (other examples from this period are equally unsophisticated) and Hope bribed (as Montrose alleged) or pressurized Stewart into manufacturing other correspondence designed to discredit Montrose and other royalists by association with Traquair and other incendiaries. Those identified in cipher included Wigtown, MacLean of Duart, Seaforth and the MacDonalds, all of whom were depicted as threatening Argyll and Hamilton. Charles was to disclaim all knowledge of the letters and in so doing had no choice but to dissociate himself from those mentioned. Throughout the negotiations in London Hamilton had surprisingly shown himself the covenanters' friend and there was talk of a marriage alliance between the houses of Campbell and Hamilton. The plotters repeatedly denied all knowledge of the ciphers; when the Committee of Estates solemnly assured Napier that 'Signeour Puritano' was none other than the Earl of Seaforth, 'he fell a laughing and said [Seaforth] was slandered, and they fell in a great laughter'.[19]

The situation in which Montrose and the others found themselves was no laughing matter. On 22 June the Earl of Sutherland, who headed the parliamentary commission to prepare the process against Montrose, was sent to Edinburgh Castle to command him to appear before the Committee. He replied that since he was to be questioned on matters of public concern 'the more public my trial were the further should it tend to the satisfaction and contentment thereof, that as the scandal was notour and national, so likewise should the expiation be, one way or another.' The following day, in the presence of the Committee, he refused to plead and was dismissed as 'disobedient and contumacious'. The Committee was prepared to grant Napier his liberty and freedom to return home, but he refused on the grounds that acceptance would imply his guilt.

Meanwhile a search was made of Montrose's castles for incriminating material. The task was entrusted to John, sixth Lord Sinclair, like Sutherland an old college associate, who ransacked Auld Montrose, 'violently brak up the yetts and doors thereof and sought the haill coffers, kists and trunks within the samen'. Kincardine and Mugdock were similarly investigated. Auld Montrose yielded a justification of the Cumbernauld Band in the handwriting of Mr James Graham who, like Montrose's secretary John Lambie, now taken to Edinburgh for quentioning, had been in Montrose's service since his St Andrews days. Sinclair also found, and apparently publicized, some of Montrose's old love letters.

Suitably armed with the justification and the depositions of the ministers of the Auchterarder presbytery, as well as those of John and Walter Stewart and Colonel Cochrane, the Committee prepared a charge against the plotters. The libel against Montrose was lengthy but it consisted of seven main points. Firstly he was charged with perjury, with having broken his oath in the covenant, and with dividing himself from the Committee of which he was a sworn member. Contrary to his oath he had sent Walter Stewart with private instructions to Traquair, seeking royal favours and advising the disbanding of the army of which he was a commander, in spite of his acceptance of articles of war which forbade intelligence with the enemy. The second charge was the old Scots crime of leasing making (verbal sedition) through his talk of dictatorships and suchlike. Thirdly, anyone entering into a treaty of combination or friendship with an enemy of the Estates was guilty of lese-majesty, especially when that crime was compounded with perjury. His association with Ogilvie in the Airlie episode and his alleged correspondence with Traquair were so interpreted. He was fourthly accused of 'licentious speeches', of slandering the king in the references to Charles contained in the coded instructions. Fifthly he had treated independently during the pacification. Sixthly he had impugned the dignity and authority of parliament by telling the king, through Traquair, that 'his faithful and loyal subjects will suffer no innovation in laws or otherwise to be introduced'. Such was the business of parliament, not of individuals. Lastly, refusal to answer a judge presumed guilt and Montrose had refused Sutherland as the representative of the Committee, 'in plain derision of the judicatory'. The entire libel is an excellent illustration of the ideals of the covenanting revolution. Never before had the concept of the state been so invoked in Scottish history. While some charges are rooted in medieval legislation, others such as those referring to parliament, perjury, and enemies of the state are completely novel. One could be guilty of lese-majesty without reference to the king; from there it was but a step to accuse the king of the same crime. Each of the charges represented a capital offence. By offering Napier his freedom the Committee had shown that its main target was Montrose and it aimed to silence him, if possible, before the king arrived in Edinburgh. Montrose's defence was to lack conviction, mainly because he was guilty, though not as charged.

When he appeared he 'in grate humility said he was come to know quhat wes the housse pleasure with him'. He regretted that he had the misfortune to be classed with enemies of the state and undertook to give all possible satisfaction. On being pressed twice for a fuller statement he made a speech of quiet dignity which marks the beginning of the legend of Montrose.

I am heartily sorry that it should be my misfortune to shew myself in this condition: For, as it has been far from my intention to fail in my duty to the public, so was it as much for my thought to appear here in these terms . . . For what I have done is known to a great many; but what I have done amiss, is unknown to myself. However, truth does not seek corners, it needeth no favour . . . I assure myself that both justice and your Lordships' wisdom will plead so much more strongly for me than I could express it myself. So I would only in all humility, expect your Lordships' commands. My resolution is, to carry along with me fidelity and honour to the grave; and therefore heartily wish that I may be put to all that it is possible to question me upon; and either shall I give your Lordships all full and humble content, or otherwise, not only deprecate, but petition all the most condign censure that your Lordships shall think suitable to so much demerit.[20]

However conventional the sentiments – Strafford made similar references to obedience and truth at the beginning of his defence – they were well expressed. What Montrose sought was a great show trial which would confound his enemies and reveal himself as the sole champion of monarchy, but the complete drama required the presence of the king and he employed delaying tactics until Charles should arrive. He petitioned the house to appoint advocates for his defence, for permission to consult his co-defendants and for an extension of time to prepare his case. The first point was conceded but the number of advocates and friends allowed access to Montrose was strictly limited. On 3 August Graham of Fintry requested copies of the depositions of the Stewarts and the others on his kinsman's behalf. Two days later Montrose was again summoned before the Committee. He gave his reasons for subscribing the Cumbernauld Band and once again named Argyll as 'suspected dictator' but 'being interrogat what part Argyll or any others had in these particulars, declares that for the tyme his memory does not serve him to show any more than what is before set down.' Montrose's faulty memory prevented him from remembering the precise date or number of his letters to the king though he did recall one or two during the 1639 parliament and one when the army was at Newcastle. Somewhat improbably he did not 'remember particularly the tenor of any of these letters'. He claimed that his paper on the Cumbernauld Band was not intended as a justification but was simply a private memo. He denied instructing the late John Stewart to elicit information on Argyll and his bands; he did not publicize Stewart's claims because he considered them to rest on 'too meane a ground'. He denied making arrangements with Atholl or Stewart to bring witnesses to Edinburgh, explained his letter to

Charles Louis on possible military service, and admitted his conversations with Cochrane without recalling 'particular words or expressions'. John Stewart had been the first to tell him of Argyll's remarks on deposition, but he knew nothing of Walter's 'Hieroglyphicks'. If several of these claims were obviously less than truthful, they served to gain the defendant precious time.

Parliament was incensed by the discovery of Montrose's justification of the band, 'magnifieing to the skyes his own courses and debaseing to the hells his opposites', and the matter was passed for consideration to the general assembly. Montrose did not appear in person; he was represented by a supplication and an advocate. He claimed that although the band had been destroyed the signatories were still bound by it. The assembly solemnly deliberated upon the matter and declared the band illegal, so freeing the subscribers from their oath. There was a widespread desire in the assembly to facilitate the resolution of differences among the covenanters, and those who subscribed the assembly's declaration were forgiven. Kinghorn, Seaforth, and Lour did so promptly. When Montrose was informed of the decision he 'seemed to insinuate his willingness to subscribe what the moderator would require'.

The defendant skilfully avoided demands that he should testify on oath before the house by countering with petitions that his advocate Sir Lewis Stewart be allowed to plead for him, that he be permitted to consult Napier and Keir, and that he be allowed to make extracts from the books of adjournal. He succeeded in delaying until Charles arrived, on 11 August, the day scheduled for Montrose's trial. He was 'ordained to compeir in persone at the barr, as a delinquent, in the place appointed for the common incendiaries, wich he, in all humility obayed', only to have the trial postponed until 24 August. His heart must have sunk and with it his hopes of a dramatic confrontation in parliament when he learned of Charles's opening address to the house on 17 August. 'The end of my coming is shortly this, to perfect whatsoever I have promised, and withal to quiet those distractions which have and may fall out amongst you.'[21] He undertook to settle religion and liberty and he offered to ratify the legislation of the parliaments of 1639 and 1640. Royalists, such as Lennox, were not admitted to parliament until they had subscribed the covenant. In the king's present frame of mind, prepared as he was to forgive and forget, to negotiate with what he regarded as the legitimate government of Scotland, Montrose was simply an embarrassment. Montrose might have recalled that he himself had assured Charles that the Scots had a great affection for their kings and he might have ruminated on Charles's sacrifice of such an apparently secure royal servant as Strafford in the interests of expediency. He now belonged to a faction of one, or at most of four, and his disappointment was reflected in a somewhat disspirited supplication presented to a parliament on his behalf.

He asked the house to consider his restraint and his willingness to obey whatever it might determine. After two hours of debate clarification was required on whether his supplication implied 'a submission, an accommodation or a speedy course of justice'. He replied that he desired a 'speedy, just trial'. After another two-hour debate a decision was scribbled on the back of his bill. 'King and parliament would take to their consideration his process, by way of justice, in their own time, and when they thought it convenient. And withall left him so much way in the interim to give the house satisfaction, by petitioning them for an accommodation and submission.' The door was well and truly closed on James Graham. He was simply ignored while parliament continued with its business, though it was widely believed that Charles had undertaken not to leave Scotland before Montrose was brought to trial, 'for if he leave him all the world will not save his life'.[22]

Following the publication of the acts of the last two parliaments, the ratification of the Treaty of London, and the disbanding of the army, parliament proceeded, during the next three months, to strip Charles of what remained of his royal authority. After a lengthy wrangle the covenanters obtained the right to advise upon and to approve royal appointments. When Argyll vehemently opposed the nomination of his father-in-law Morton to the chancellorship, Loudoun, whose 'freedom with the king' was widely suspected, was appointed to that office.

All of this was too much for a group of moderates who revealed themselves at the end of September when a drunken Lord Ker, son of the Earl of Roxburgh, challenged Hamilton to a duel, denouncing him as 'a juglar with the king and a traitor both to him and to his countrie', and so reviving interest in the cryptic allusions to 'the serpent in the bosom' in Walter Stewart's instructions. Roxburgh had been understandably perturbed by the covenanters' insistence that all who had left Scotland during the past three years to join the king should be debarred from office but when he protested his loyalty to king and country Argyll told him that 'comparisons were odious'. By challenging Hamilton the headstrong Ker was also threatening Argyll. Hamilton made a great show of interceding with the king, on bended knee, for Ker and his associate the Earl of Crawford, 'bot withall the wise man did make use of the injury and humblie required his Majesty's and the parliament's declaration of their judgements in the matter itself'.[23] When summoned to Charles's presence Ker initially offered to make good his allegations but he was eventually prevailed upon to admit that his accusations were 'without any ground and merely from passion'. Only the tears of his overwrought father persuaded him to appear before the house, but in the event he was accompanied by 'such a number of officers and soldiers, about six hundred, with their swords in their hands, that they frighted the parliament'. The city was called to arms; Ker's supporters were ordered to disband on pain of death; and Ker himself was forced to sign an abject retraction of his allegations. Patrick Wemyss shrewdly asserted that 'this business, if it had not been taken up, would have proved most dangerous to this kingdom (and I believe it lies but under the embers) for it has made many factions.' Two such factions were increasingly apparent: one was led by Argyll and Hamilton, the other was headed by the Duke of Lennox. The latter group, or individual members of it, decided to capitalize on the brief royalist resurgence occasioned by the Ker episode in order to destroy their opponents.

Some thought that the plot known as the 'incident' was 'but pretended' by Hamilton and Argyll who designed a public rupture 'presuming that upon their removal, the parliament should presently have broken up'. The whole affair was later dismissed as turning upon 'drunken soldiers' boasting words', an assertion of some truth since secret consultations in noblemen's lodgings in Canongate and the Cowgate were liberally lubricated with plentiful supplies of ale and wine. But there was a plot which the king knew about, and furthermore Montrose was involved. Two days after Charles's arrival in Edinburgh Colonel John Cochrane, whose evidence had earlier been used against Montrose, approached William Murray, gentleman of the bedchamber and nephew of Robert Murray, minister of Methven. He told Murray that he had important information to impart to the king. On three subsequent occasions Cochrane and Murray privately discussed the possibility of publicly accusing Hamilton and Argyll of hindering the peace. Murray also visited Montrose, who declared that if he were given the opportunity to speak with the king, he would reveal the cause of the difficulties which Charles encountered in parliament and would talk of 'things of very high nature concerning his Majesty and his state and honour'. Murray begged Montrose to write these matters down. He did so but Charles was unimpressed. Two or three days later he sent the king another more detailed letter, but again Charles ignored it, telling Murray that because many of his subjects falsely thought that he intended to foment divisions 'he would therefore let his people see that he would not entertain any motions that might seem to make interruptions'. He added that he was prepared to let bygones be bygones and he hoped for fair play in the future; he believed that any man in Montrose's situation would say much 'to have the liberty to come to my presence'. About the time that Charles received Montrose's second letter Murray contacted Cochrane, who was taken by night to the king's bedside for a private audience. Cochrane's regiment was one of three not disbanded. While drinking with his officers at Musselburgh he announced that he hoped to make their fortunes. Later he informed Lieutenant-Colonel Robert Home of his audience with Charles.

The following Sunday Cochrane and the Earl of Crawford supped at the Earl of Airth's house with Murray, Lord Ogilvie, and Lord Gray. At Murray's suggestion they took a coach to Lord Almond's residence; Almond returned home late to find his guests helping themselves to his ale. Murray asked the gathering if they had heard of Montrose's letter to the king 'wherein he undertook to accuse the Marquis of Hamilton, before the parliament, upon high treason'. Almond found Montrose's allegations 'very hard and very strange'. Crawford observed that if the marquis was a traitor he deserved the reward of a traitor. Lord Gray darkly remarked that if they had all been in France, Cardinal Richelieu would have known what to do about Hamilton. Crawford later deponed that there was no further talk 'but that they would hear more of it tomorrow as Mr Murray said'.

The morrow, Monday 11 October, was a day of intense activity. At nine in the morning Captain William Stewart and Lieutenant-Colonel John Hurry were invited to take a morning drink with Alexander Stewart who held a command in Cochrane's regiment. Hurry declined on the grounds that he was to dine with Crawford at eleven and the two Stewarts retired to a Cowgate winehouse where they called for a cup of sack. Alexander placed his pistols on the table, made sure that a box-bed in the room was empty, and swore William to secrecy. 'You have spoken much of the innocence of your uncle,' said Alexander, 'and I marvel of you who are his friends who do not petition for his release.' 'Who can petition?' asked William. 'The Marquis is of such power with the king that it is folly for any man to speak ... All was true that my uncle said and as clear as light that the marquis was a traitor.'[24] The said uncle was Sir James Stewart, fourth Lord Ochiltree, who had been imprisoned on a charge of leasing making when he accused Hamilton of trying to seize the Scottish throne. He was in ward in Blackness Castle. Captain William is thus identified as William Stewart of Corrogan in County Tyrone who married his cousin Jean, second daughter of Lord Ochiltree. William's Irish estates were among the first attacked during the Irish rebellion.[25] Alexander obviously judged that William could be relied upon to talk freely in his cups about the injustice which had befallen his uncle and he obliged by rambling on about Hamilton's power and influence with the king. He asserted as one who was 'late out at night and up early in the morning', that between them Argyll and Hamilton had five thousand followers in Edinburgh, summoned there during the Ker affair. William further alleged that Argyll, Cassilis, Loudoun, and Lindsay had been plotting before five o'clock that very morning. All of this might have passed off as idle chatter but Alexander introduced a serious element into the conversation. He believed the royalists could expect support from the earls of Home, Roxburgh, and Crawford, from Lord Almond, and from honest men in Lothian, the Merse, Linlithgowshire (now West Lothian), and Stirlingshire. He darkly suggested that it might be expedient to adopt a German solution to the problem and simply kill Hamilton. He had no doubt, at any rate, that there was now a faction strong enough to suppress Argyll and Hamilton. It was planned that Murray would, on some pretext, invite the two to the withdrawing room at Holyrood. Almond would approach by a secret stair, accuse them of assuming the whole government of Scotland, arrest them, and confine them on the king's ship at Leith. Crawford with four hundred men in the gardens would secure the palace until Home and Roxburgh sent assistance. Crawford, a blood-thirsty individual, favoured killing them on the spot – he believed that 'if the king wald stob ane with a bodkin thair sould be ane hundreth killit' – but Almond favoured the processes of law. William was not impressed by the plan, though he did agree to meet Alexander at Crawford's lodging later in the day. He also told Hurry to warn the intended victims. There were wide discrepancies in the depositions of the two Stewarts after their arrest, William's being less self-incriminating than the other. When both were freed from confinement Alexander had to promise to conduct himself in a sober and discreet manner towards William, undertaking not to molest or trouble him.[26]

At eleven there was 'ane great conference of sojors' at Jonnet Milne's alehouse in the Canongate. They included Cochrane, Alexander Stewart, Lord Kilpont, Crawford, and Hurry, who attended as Leslie's spy. Crawford invited Hurry to appear next morning 'with three or four good fellows, which would be the means to make him a fortune'. He also thanked Cochrane for his loyalty and vowed to have the traitors' throats cut. Cochrane sent for Robert Home, 'took him down a close where he renewed his promise of making him a fortune if he would follow his way', and demanded an oath of secrecy which Home refused since he was already sworn to the covenant. In the early afternoon Cochrane interviewed Lord Ogilvie who declared himself an enemy of all who hindered peace 'and these are thought to be Hamilton and Argyll'.

By convenient and well-calculated coincidence, Montrose sent a third submission to Charles that very afternoon. This time the king was impressed; he showed it to Murray who predictably concurred, since he had been the means of transmitting it. Charles decided to communicate the letter's contents to Loudoun, Lennox, Argyll, Morton, Roxburgh, and Leslie. He intended that Montrose should explain himself in their presence but James Graham was once again cheated of his moment of triumph. In Murray's words, 'his Majesty's resolution was interruptit with the incident fell on Monday at nicht' – the birds flew the coop. That evening Crawford, Home, Kirkcudbright, and Ogilvie visited Cochrane to drink some wine. 'My Lord Home lifted a glasse and said this to a good conclusionn of all thingis.

Thay ar well on a fair way of accommodating bussiness with the king, and he that hinders the peace, hanged mot he be that shall not be ane enemy to him. The rest said every one als much.' Throughout that remarkable day many a tongue must have danced to the pleasant tune of the wine. Argyll, Hamilton, and his younger brother Lanark listened, and withdrew from the city.

In spite of a lengthy enquiry contemporaries found the whole episode bewildering. Charles expressed his intense anger at the action of the fugitives. He ordered an immediate enquiry and depositions were taken from William Stewart, Hurry, and Robert Home. The plan, master-minded by Murray, seems to have involved the arrest of Argyll and Hamilton, isolating them on the king's ship at Leith and forcing them to answer charges pressed by Montrose. Responsibility for ruining the scheme lay with Charles himself. He told parliament that Hamilton had visited him in the garden at Holyrood on Monday evening 'with a petition of very small moment'. He then, having spoken in 'a philosophical and parabolical way' about the malice of his enemies, craved permission to withdraw from court. What Charles may have neglected to tell parliament was that he then challenged Hamilton with Montrose's allegations. If some such hypothesis is accepted Hamilton and Argyll fled not only because they (rightly) feared for their lives but also because they found Montrose's charges unanswerable. Charles undoubtedly believed Hamilton guilty and he made several veiled references to the fact in parliament during the next few days. The royalists favoured a public enquiry; the covenanters urged that the matter be investigated privately. When the refugees learned that Charles attended parliament on 14 October 'with five hundred gentlemen walking by his coach' they took themselves to Hamilton's residence at Kinneil near Linlithgow, fearing a royalist coup. They claimed they had done so to avoid trouble but Charles countered by accusing them of deliberately fomenting division between himself and his subjects.[27] The covenanters cunningly exploited public opinion to create an anti-royalist backlash. After a long wrangle Charles was forced to concede a private enquiry. The longer he delayed in Scotland, the less secure would be his position in England. The hearing commenced during the last week of October.

Two factors fanned the flames of covenanting apprehension. Hurry deponed that he did not respond to Crawford's invitation to join him with two or three 'good fellows' because he surmised that the intention was to release Montrose from the castle and thereafter to cause Argyll all possible mischief.[28] Such was a possibility. Of those mentioned in the depositions Almond, Home, Mar, and Kirkcudbright had signed the Cumbernauld Band, while the royalist sympathies of Ogilvie, Roxburgh, Crawford, Airth, and Lord Gray were well known. The other factor was outwith the control of the accused or their accusers. On 28 October Charles announced to parliament that the Irish were in open rebellion.

The Irish rebellion owed much to frustration, fanaticism, and fury, born of muddle-headed governmental policies, Strafford's administration, and the Lowland Scots' plantation of the province. As the atrocity stories spread, as tales of the sufferings of Scots presbyterians gained currency, all in a matter of days, the 'incident' assumed a new and insignificant perspective. On 1 November Argyll, the Scottish expert on Irish affairs, who had been planning for just such a contingency since 1638, was invited back to parliament with Hamilton and Lanark. It was judged that they had, after all, acted in good faith. Next day Montrose, Napier, Keir, and Blackhall petitioned for their release on bail. The house refused to answer until Montrose explained the wording of his letter, specifically his undertaking to 'acquaint his Majesty with a bussines wich not onlie did concern his honor in a heighe degree, bot the standing and falling of his croune lykwayes'. When questioned Montrose showed that the spirit had temporarily gone out of him. He claimed that he did not remember the meaning of his words but said that he had, in any case, already given an explanation to the king. He had not intended to accuse anyone in particular.[29] The house was still not satisfied but on 16 November Montrose and the others were set at liberty on payment of securities. Trial was set for 4 January. The Estates, however, 'that his majestie may joyfullie return a contentit prince from a contentit peopill to the setling of his royall affaires', declared that after trial they would not proceed to sentence and punishment but would remit the matter to the king.

During the first fortnight of November an impressive volume of legislation was pushed through parliament. The three Stewarts, William, Walter, and Alexander, together with Crawford, Hurry, and Cochrane, also gained their liberty. Detailed plans were made to send troops to Ireland. General Alexander Leslie was created Earl of Leven.

Argyll was given a marquisate and Warriston a knighthood. On the evening of 17 November Charles feasted the Scottish nobility in the great hall of Holyrood Palace. Self-deluded as ever, he apparently rejoiced in winning the friendship of the Scots. He had conceded every demand made of him and had elevated several of those he had earlier condemned as traitorous enemies. He hoped that the Irish crisis might promote an accommodation between himself and the English parliament, unaware that it was already well organized to turn developments to its own advantage. At eight o'clock the following morning he took the long road south; he would never set foot in Scotland again.

Montrose for the moment was safe. He retired to Auld Montrose where the strain of the past months caused his health to break down. Charles did not forget him. Writing to Traquair in January 1642 he added the postscript, 'Commend me to Montrose and desire him to give credit to what this bearer shall tell him in my name.' Next day he wrote to Montrose himself:

As I think it fit, in respect of your sufferings for me, by these lines to acknowledge it to you, so I think it unfit to mention by writ any particulars but to refer you to the faithful relation of this honest bearer: being confident that the same generosity which has made you hazard so much as you have done for my service, will at this time induce you to testify your affection to me as there shall be occasion; assuring you that for what you have already done I shall ever remain, your assured friend.[30]

7

THE ADVENTURE
BEGINS

*This league and covenant was so distastable both to God and all good
men that its remembrance, with the authors and promoters thereof in
both kingdoms, is and will be hateful to the present and succeeding
ages . . . The universality of the takers rather heightened than
diminished the guilt of that combination, which tended to, and did
really produce, the greatest rebellion that these nations was acquainted
with since they were a monarchy.*

James, eleventh Lord Somerville *c.* 1680

Throughout January and February 1642 cold winds lashed the waters
of Montrose loch. It was a sad household to which Montrose returned
for his third son David, baptized three years before, had recently died.
Magdalen Carnegie gave him four sons. John, Lord Graham was
born in 1630. James, who would succeed as second marquis, was
probably born in 1632; Robert was still a child in 1645. There was also
a daughter, Jean. The Countess of Montrose is a curiously obscure
figure about whom little is known. Loyal and long-suffering, she did
her best to raise a family, who saw all too little of their father, in
financially difficult circumstances. The Graham debts continued to
mount. Mr John Graham of Aberuthven, whose testimony had helped
to place his chief in confinement, lent Montrose £2800 against a
quarter of the town and lands of Aberuthven. Archibald Sydserff lent
£8000, Mr John Lambie £3500, and Patrick Ross, burgess of Perth,
put up £3000. The last sum was guaranteed by the Grahams of
Fintry, Morphie, Braco, Orchil, Claverhouse, Inchbrakie, Gorthie, and
Balgowan.[1] As it proved harder to find cautioners Montrose was
forced to rely more heavily on the kin. The town of Montrose was

staunch for the covenant and there is some indication that the earl could no longer depend upon the support of his Angus tenants.

Montrose and his friends were called to answer the charges against them early in February, Montrose protesting that he was only allowed 'one free day to give in my defences'. The trial took place in secret so that 'what wes done and tryit aganes thame or ather of thame wes not reveillit',[2] but Montrose's own petitions show that he was irritated by the same frustrating delays in the proceedings as before. He answered the long libel in 'two or three sheets at the most', denying perjury and arguing that the Cumbernauld Band was simply a renewal of the covenant. Communications entrusted to Walter Stewart had been intended to counter those who attempted to block the king's visit to Scotland. He defended his action at Airlie Castle, explained the plotters' attitude to disbanding the army in 1641, and denied corresponding with incendiaries. He did not attempt many specific answers to the charges libelled. At the core of his reply was the contention that a public commission in no way precluded private action. The whole document was more of a harangue than a legal argument because Montrose considered the libel 'nothing bot a rapsodie of forethought villanie . . . abortive lies begot of old malice'. He claimed that two or three years before his covenanting colleagues had threatened to remove his sword from his side 'within two months'.[3]

There was a flurry of activity towards the end of February for parliament had stipulated that the trial must take place by 1 March. Montrose argued that since Stewart had admitted to being the source of his own allegations, Stewart's deposition could not be used against him. He pointed to inherent inconsistencies in his statements which constituted *testimonium singulare* whereas Scots Law required corroboration.

This said confession of Mr John Stewart, Montrose earnestly desires that [it] may be narrowly considered, that all the world may know, what probable grounds he had to study and labour for establishing the king's authority, and liberties of the country; and to obviate all indirect practices, of the which he had jealousies and presumptions, as may appear by all the passages, declarations and depositions that have been taken in this business from the beginning.

Montrose and the others also protested that they be free of all further challenge or question since the time limit had almost expired and they appointed Graham of Morphie and Graham of Gorthie to act as procurators in all matters connected with their defence. The Committee responded by finding them guilty of breaching the covenant and of making divisive motions. The matter, as agreed, was passed to the king who granted the defendants letters of exoneration.[4] The trial as such was over; Montrose retired to Auld Montrose.

He was still a man to watch. It was rumoured in England that the king's party in Scotland increased daily, that Charles himself intended to return to Edinburgh, and that Traquair and Montrose were very strong.[5] Charles had returned to an increasingly intransigent Commons led by 'King Pym'. His abortive attempt to arrest the Five Members drove an ever-larger wedge between himself and parliament. He looked in vain to Scotland for support, but the dearly bought friendship of the covenanters brought only unwelcome offers to intervene as mediators between king and parliament. The latter body was initially unhappy about the idea of paying Scottish soldiers to suppress the Irish rebellion, rapidly developing into a mutual bloodbath. Having lost London and having sent his queen to the Low Countries for safety, Charles withdrew to York. There he received an offer of assistance from Montrose who was prepared to go to England if necessary. Charles, still hopeful of an accommodation with the covenanters, gratefully declined: 'I know I need no arguments to induce you to my service; duty and loyalty are sufficient to a man of such honour as I know you to be; yet as I think thus of you, so I will have you to believe of me that I would not invite you to share of my hard fortune, if I intended you not a plentiful partaker of my good.'[6] Two days later (9 May) he addressed himself to, in his view, a more promising source of support. 'Argyll, this is a time, wherein all my servants, that are noble and willing will have occasion to show themselves ... amongst whom, as it is well known your power wants not to serve me, so by your large expressions, at my last being in Scotland, and having, by some real testimonies, shown the estimation that I have of you I cannot doubt of your readiness.'[7] Archibald Campbell, however, had more pressing matters on his mind; nothing less than fears of a second 'incident'. The king, irritated by Scottish offers to mediate in English affairs, ordered the privy council to meet on 25 May for the express purpose of condemning the actions of the English parliament. A number of royalists converged on Edinburgh to petition the council on behalf of Charles. Once again 'a great rumour was raised of a wicked design against Argyll's person'.

A petition, partly in Napier's handwriting, doubtless represents the views of Montrose and the Banders though no commentator specifically mentions their presence in Edinburgh. Its tone is very close to that of the main petition presented by Keir, Erskine, Lord Montgomery (a converted covenanter), and the Earl of Kelly. It asserts that all are bound to maintain sovereign power according to the law of God, 'our national allegiance', the coronation oath, and the National Covenant. It asks the privy councillors to 'take some solid and vigorous resolution for re-establishing and maintaining his Majesty's authority and royal power . . . And we in all humility and loyalty, shall not be wanting to assist and second your endeavours to that end, with our lyves and fortunes, to effusion of the last drop of our blood.'[8] The councillors were spared the embarrassment of any putative plots against Argyll by the gentry and ministry of Fife 'running over in thousands' who, together with the faithful of the Lothians and Edinburgh, caused the royalists to melt away 'as snow in a hot sunshine'. They presented a rival petition urging that nothing impede the union and peace between England and Scotland; in other words the privy council should ignore the pleas of the king.

During the summer Napier drafted yet another document on the maintenance of royal authority. It was the summer in which civil war broke out in England; the summer which saw a desperate king, disappointed in his hopes of the Scottish privy council, sending Hamilton to Edinburgh with a crack-brained scheme for inviting Henrietta Maria to visit Scotland in order to mediate between Charles and his English parliament; and it was the summer during which the general assembly set up a standing commission for the public affairs of the kirk, a body which was the ecclesiastical counterpart of the Committee of Estates with powers of supervision, administration, and negotiation during those periods when the assembly was not in session. Baillie thought the commission was 'lyke to become almost a constant judicatorie'. For Napier the dispute centred on 'whether we should be dutiful subjects or no'. In his view the Treaty of London could in no way prejudice duty to the sovereign since it was 'but a civil, a legal or politic paction of men, which can never be destructive of our obligation to our prince, imposed upon us by the law of God and nature'. It was clearly emerging in the course of negotiations that the treaty was regarded primarily as a treaty between the parliaments of the two kingdoms. The English parliament petitioned privy council and general assembly for support as assiduously as did the king. Napier considered that the true bond uniting Scotland and England was the king's sovereignty, which could be defended by 'no other means but that of force, for as it is violence that has dispossessed the king of his authority, it is force on the other side that can repossess him'.[9] For Montrose, Napier's reflections represented the clarion call to action. The sword must be drawn and great deeds performed but there was, as yet, no arena where the spectacle might be staged. He had already offered to assist the king in England but apprehension about possible developments in Scotland kept the sword in the scabbard for the moment. It was possibly at this time, as Buchan suggested, that Montrose composed his best-known poem.

Mark Napier quite wrongly ascribed fifteen stanzas to Montrose's poem and, although both Edward Rimbault and W. Chappell indicated his error, he has been followed by many later commentators. In the early seventeenth century words were composed to a popular tune called 'My dear and only love take heed'. The first stanza was as follows,

> My dear and only love take heed
> How thyself expose
> By letting longing lovers feed,
> Upon such looks as those.
> I'll marble-wall thee round about.
> And build without a door,
> But if thy heart do once break out,
> I'll never love thee more.

This and a variable number of other stanzas have been added to Montrose's five-stanza original to produce a much longer poem of spurious attribution. Montrose's words and those of other versions may owe something to the early seventeenth-century answer-poem convention in which poems were set to music to gain effect by giving 'unexpected twists to the key words or phrases of the original'.[10] Almost every poet worthy of the name who wrote during Montrose's lifetime addressed at least one poem to his mistress. Examples survive from the pens of Ayton, Donne, Edward Lord Herbert, Crashaw, Herrick, Carew, Lovelace, Waller, and Andrew Marvell. The last named's 'coy mistress' is probably the best-known example of the genre. Many of these poems were explicitly erotic but others were addressed to 'an intangible mistress', a female fictitious, imaginary, unknown or unknowable who was used as a vehicle for the poet's introspection. Captain John Gwynne, for example, wrote a piece entitled 'Upon my inseparable devotion to Loyalty I called Mistress'. It need hardly be stressed that so far as is known Montrose never actually had a mistress, and the usual title for his poem 'Montrose to his Mistress' is quite misleading, doubtless deriving from the original on which he based his verse. The general assumption that it is Montrose himself who addresses his 'dear and only love' makes the poem unintelligible. Rather it is sovereignty which apostrophizes the kingdom or state of Scotland just as in Lithgow's poem of 1633 Scotia addressed her 'native son', the king. The theme is indicated in Montrose's first two stanzas.

> My dear and only Love, I pray
> This noble World of thee,
> Be govern'd by no other Sway
> But purest Monarchie.
> For if Confusion have a Part,
> Which vertuous Souls abhore,
> And hold a Synod in thy Heart,
> I'll never love thee more.
>
> Like Alexander I will reign,
> And I will reign alone,
> My thoughts shall evermore disdain
> A Rival on my throne.
> He either fears his Fate too much,
> Or his Deserts are small,
> That puts it not unto the Touch,
> To gain or lose it all.[11]

The sentiment throughout is that of a man so despairing of current developments that he could foresee the total overthrow of monarchy which he was prepared to defend at the expense of his own moderate views on the balanced constitution. These are the words of a man temporarily unhinged, who distinguished absolute monarchy as the only defence against chaos and disorder and who continued to urge the king to seek a military solution to his Scottish problems. His loyalty was rewarded with a short letter from Charles only two days after the royal standard was raised at Nottingham – 'you are one whom I have found most faithful and in whom I repose greatest trust'.

It is unfortunate that at this critical juncture in Montrose's career, documentation is comparatively scanty. Towards the end of the year he resided at Kincardine, in some uncertainty about his possible course of action. He wrote to Graham of Craigo, younger brother of Fintry, asking him to supervise certain matters at Auld Montrose. Craigo was told by his 'very loving chief' to ensure that his father-in-law MacIntosh of that ilk did not succumb to the wiles of Argyll.[12] North of Kincardine there were many indications that some unprecedented calamity was about to engulf Scotland. Folk living around the Hill of Fare in Mar heard nightly beating of drums as if armies were marching. Ghostly armies were seen elsewhere. There were similar apparitions near Banff accompanied by the thundering of shot and a clashing of arms so realistic that people buried their possessions for safekeeping. In some parts the sun shone faintly at midday or brightly at midnight; elsewhere it had the appearance of a deep loch of blood. Lakes of blood had already formed in England. The indecisive Edgehill had been fought on 23 October. In the northern kingdom the universal preoccupation of royalists and covenanters alike was the question of how soon the Scots would be drawn into the English conflict.

On 7 November 1642 the English parliament invited the Scots to provide military aid against 'the common enemy of the religion and liberty of both nations'. On learning of this move Charles immediately sent a letter to the privy council protesting at parliament's misrepresentations. A long and heated discussion took place in council in which Lanark joined with his brother Hamilton to urge the printing of the king's letter while Argyll and Balmerino favoured simultaneous publication of parliament's missive. If Montrose had had some respect for Hamilton, which he did not since he still believed him guilty of double-dealing, he might have echoed Hamilton's remarks. 'What has the king's authority come to if he may not defend himself and his government by declarations? Are you afraid that his subjects might have too good an opinion of him if they heard him speak for himself?' He carried the day; the king's letter was printed, so prompting a petition from the uneasy Fife covenanters who believed with many of the kirk party that if Charles was victorious in England, he would inevitably renegue on his promises to the Scots. A number of royalists 'crossed' the Fife petition by producing one of their own, the so-called 'Cross Petition'. Since it was the brainchild of Hamilton, Montrose was not among the forty-one nobles and lairds who signed it. They wished to establish royal authority and to continue 'that happy union betwixt the two kingdoms which can never be conceived to be intended to weaken the head, whereby it is knit together'. They coined a novel phrase – 'we British subjects' – who hoped that unity of church government might strengthen the civil union. Aware of the great calamities and irreparable evils arising out of the recent unhappy distractions, 'which if not speedily removed cannot but produce the fearful and prodigious effects of a bloody and civil war', they humbly petitioned the council to assist in removing such misunderstandings.[13] The kirk was so outraged that laymen should presume to interfere in church affairs that the petitioners were forced to offer hasty reassurances that they only intended that 'puritie of religion and presbyterial government may be propagatit throw all his Maiesteis dominions'.[14] In the welter of protest and counter-protestation during January 1643, two important decisions were taken. Five covenanters, including Loudoun and Lindsay, were sent south to mediate, as they thought, in the matter of the English civil war. As a result of the second decision a body of ministers would set off six months later to take part in the Westminster Assembly. Charles predictably rejected the representations of the well-meaning, if self-important, Scottish mediators telling them in no uncertain terms that the preservation of English church government was 'a matter of so great importance and having so near relation to the civil government and laws of England, they could not be competent considerers of it'.[15] The others were more successful; through time they would draft what became the basic constitution of the Church of Scotland.

Montrose was by now convinced that an armed rebellion in Scotland was inevitable. In February while he was in England to consult William Cavendish, Earl of Newcastle, Henrietta Maria arrived at Bridlington on the Yorkshire coast after a storm-tossed journey from the Netherlands. As commander of the king's forces in the north of England Newcastle had recently enjoyed some military success but his cheerful employment of catholics alarmed both covenanters and parliamentarians. With Ogilvie Montrose went to York to meet the queen who, some weeks before, had advised Charles to organize a loyal army in Scotland. He was actively planning a royalist rising. He told Sir Robert Gordon of Gordonstoun who, having spent the past eight months in Salisbury, was about to return to the far north, 'I shall rest very confident that you will be ready to advance his Majesty's service by all possible means both openly and in secret as occasion shall offer'. He also urged him to win the support of the Earl of Sutherland. Aboyne, second son of Huntly, also arrived in York to keep his father informed of developments.[16]

Montrose told the queen that force must be resisted with force. He assured her that many loyal Scottish subjects were ready to take up arms against the covenanters – 'all they lacked was the king's warrant, without which they would attempt nothing, with it there was nothing they would not attempt'. A stand must be made quickly to crush the 'viper's egg'; it was too late to apply medicine once poison had affected the whole body. Baillie believed that twenty-two noblemen and 'men of chief respect' had promised to support Montrose who was thus able to offer the queen a levy of ten thousand troops. She was not unsympathetic but Montrose was foiled by the arrival of Hamilton who condemned his suggestions as 'rash, imprudent, and unseasonable'. The two quarrelled violently as Hamilton spoke of treating Scotland gently, of avoiding civil war at all costs, and of the necessity for peace and reconciliation. He also indicated that no Scottish castles were in the king's hands and that the populace was rigidly controlled by the ministers. The only potentially reliable support was that of the High-landers, which, reversing his view of 1638, 'he accounted as good as none'. Huntly was not dependable. Argyll would resist the royalists. As soon as the Gaels acquired any plunder they would 'run away home to their lurking holes and desert those who had trusted them'. Finally he reminded the queen that 10,000 Scottish troops would be recalled from Ireland in the event of a royalist rising. Hamilton himself was willing to continue to act as the king's commissioner, a course dismissed by Montrose as futile and time wasting.[17]

Since Montrose regarded Hamilton as 'the prime fomenter of these misunderstandings betwixt the king and his subjects' he refused to become involved in his schemes. As Sir Robert Poyntz told the Marquis of Ormonde, 'Montrose was the only man to be the head and leader of the king's party, and being of a high spirit, cannot away with contempts and affronts.'[18] So long as the king's cause depended upon the leadership of Hamilton it would be deprived of the whole-heartedly active allegiance of Montrose. Similar jealousy and suspicion of Montrose himself would rob him of the essential support of nobles such as Huntly and Seaforth in due course. Rejected once again, James Graham returned to Scotland while his rival was given a dukedom. His disappointment was expressed in a bitter and obscure little poem on the subject of 'The killing of the Earl of Newcastle's son's dog by the Marquis of Hamilton'. The unfortunate animal was treacherously slain by the 'renouned blade' of the man who betrayed Montrose and the king. Such, at least, was the poet's view.

> Then say to eternize the curr thats gone,
> He flech't the Mayden sword of Hamiltone.

Although Montrose's break with the covenanters was not yet regarded in all quarters as irrevocable he did not cease to plot for the king. When the Earl of Antrim was arrested by Munro at Knockfergus in May, it was apparent from papers found on his own person and from the examination of two of his servants that Nithsdale and Aboyne had been in correspondence with him. It also transpired that Antrim's brother Alexander MacDonald had approached the royalists at York during Montrose's visit. At the beginning of May, following the departure of Montrose and the others, Antrim visited York where his expectations of finding a coherent plan for a royalist rising were disappointed. Ammunition intended for Viscount Aboyne had to be entrusted to the governor of Scarborough. Nithsdale reported from Carlisle that Hamilton had 'done bad office to the king' but he assured Antrim, 'I am very confident Montrose will not flinch from the king what he professed at York.' A few days later he was less certain: 'I am not altogedder disperat of Montrose, but say he were changed, I am in good hope you sall not lack well-affected subiectis in Scotland to prosecute that poynt we resolved on.' Aboyne was apparently less confident of Montrose, suspecting him of 'going back' on what he had promised, and James Stewart, one of Antrim's servitors, testified that it was openly reported in York that Montrose would not stand firm. The examinations of Antrim, Stewart, and another servant, Shane or Sean Dick, revealed an elaborate plan. A barque containing a cargo of ammunition was to be sent to the north of Scotland for the use of Aboyne and the Gordons as well as of Antrim's clansmen in the Highlands and Islands. Another was to be despatched to Carlisle for Nithsdale and his associates. Aboyne was to fight his way south to join the Marquis of Newcastle. The aim was to cause 'all mischief possible' by force of arms against the kingdom of Scotland, to overthrow the Scots forces in Ireland, and to bring Irish soldiers to England and Scotland to resist parliament and the covenant. Approaches were to be made to Colla Ciotach and his sons, to MacLean of Duart, to Sir Donald Gorm, and, if Baillie be credited, to Hamilton. Antrim testified that 'Montrose was to join them only in a legal way and would not join in raising regiments'.[19] Nothing came of the plan which differed little from those projected in 1639 or in 1644–5. While the details were undoubtedly known to Henrietta Maria, Charles's implication is more problematical though he can hardly have been entirely ignorant of the plan's existence. Nithsdale and Aboyne were accused of treason by the privy council. The reason that Montrose was suspect was that the covenanters, encouraged by reports that he had taken offence at the rejection of his proposals at York, had made overtures to him. It was widely recognized in Scotland that a convention of estates scheduled for June would pledge support for the English parliament. Montrose wrote to the queen informing her that '*les affaires en Ecosse sont en fort mauvais état pour le service du roy*', largely through her own negligence. Henrietta protested that she had acted at her husband's command but she promised to send arms 'and every possible assistance from myself, who have always greatly confided in you, and in the generosity of your character. And this confidence, be assured, is not the least diminished, although I too, like yourself, have now been made unhappy by rumours that you have formed an alliance with certain persons, which might well create apprehension in my mind.'[20] There was substance in these rumours and Montrose was in danger of once again being suspected on all sides. 'The man is said to be very double,' mused Baillie, 'which in so proud a spirit is strange.'

In April Charles instructed Huntly to assemble all his 'friends, vassals, tenants and such others as have any dependency on you' to assure them of the king's willingness to confirm all the 'graces and favours' he had of late conferred on Scotland. During the first days of June Montrose and Ogilvie met Huntly and Aboyne in Aberdeen, doubtless to work out further details of Antrim's plan, which was not yet public knowledge in Scotland. From Aberdeen they went on to Kelly to be joined by Marischal and the Laird of Banff and 'baid all nicht in joyfull maner'. It was rumoured that all except Marischal subscribed a band. Montrose and Ogilvie then went to meet Napier and Stirling of Keir at the latter's home between Dunblane and Bridge of Allan. Hamilton was still trying to win Montrose's support, only to be told by him that the Scots, instead of diverting their energies at the forthcoming convention, should be ready, if necessary, to maintain the king's interest with the sword. Argyll and some others tried to exploit the breach between Montrose and Hamilton by sending messengers to offer the former a commission in the army. His experience would be a valuable asset and the covenanting leadership was prepared to overlook 'past demeanours'. More to the point perhaps, a letter to the queen from Roxburgh, Morton, Annandale, Kinnoul, Lanark, and Carnwath had just been intercepted. None of these nobles was particularly close to Montrose but if Huntly, Aboyne, Nithsdale, and the Highland chiefs were added to the number it was obvious that there were the makings of a sizeable royalist party in Scotland. Montrose had been something of a loner during the past two years. Rejected by the king, at daggers drawn with Hamilton, spurned by his peers, might he not be prepared to join the cause? The sagacious Baillie drily observed that since Antrim, Huntly, Montrose, and the others were financially ruined they had no choice but to make 'publick commotions their private subsistance'.

Sir James Rollo and Sir Mungo Campbell of Lawers were commissioned to test Montrose's reaction to covenanting overtures. Since the death of his wife Dorothea Graham in 1638, Rollo had gained ideal diplomatic qualifications for the task by marrying Argyll's half-sister Lady Mary Campbell. He and his associate were instructed to offer Montrose the discharge of all his debts and the position of second-in-command to Leslie. When Graham pretended scruple of conscience no less a person than Alexander Henderson agreed to meet him near Keir for further discussions. Montrose had a great deal of respect for the level-headed minister, who revealed that he approached him of his own accord. Rollo on the other hand claimed that Henderson's mission was authorized by the Committee. The discrepancy in the two claims was Montrose's loophole. Having listened to Henderson outlining plans for sending a Scottish army to parliament's assistance he declared that he could give no undertaking unless the matter of authorization were clarified. Some accounts assert that he left the matter open but Montrose's irrevocable break with the covenanters had come. He told his friends at Keir of what had transpired and decided to warn the king. Montrose subsequently informed Rollo of his decision on which there could be no going back.

I could not, both from my respects to you as a particular friend and likewise as being under a kind of communing to the contrary, but freely and particularly let you know the reasons truly that do oblige me to do it. Wherefore you will be pleased to remember that in all [that] ever passed amongst us there were four points I still absolutely provided, which were first: if the third point of the covenant, the king's honour and authority to be solemnly adhered to, since our religion and liberty was already so wholly and firmly secured, which were they in hazard or by all appearance possibly questioned, I should as willingly maintain as any else alive. The second, that my honour which had been so unjustly blinded [concealed] might be repaired in some fair way. The third that whereas I had been at so great losses, all just accounts might have been acknowledged. The fourth, that those of my friends who had also suffered should be taken in and acknowledged in the same way; and there was also a fifth, as you may remember, which was the assurances I should have had for all the former. Now in this I think it is so [obvious] to us, and we so conscious of it as we cannot in common sense differ. And had this been accordingly done I should have as much passed from my life as one jot of what was communed. But since by the contrary all has not only failed, but the quite other acting, I could not for all the advantages in the world be accessory but rather take this course. Yet to show that my retreat is necessary and for no bad end, I shall wish to be no longer happy than I constantly adhere to whatsoever the country or this cause . . . are concerned. Which hoping will not only be satisfactory to yourself, but to all the world who may have greatest prejudice. I am your affectionate friend after the old manner . . . P.S. Believe I will make all good I ever professed whereof I will entreat you be confident and if any evil ensue it shall be my counterparts' fault and not mine, for I shall not be a meddlar if I be not sorely put to it.[21]

The letter well illustrates the many facets of Montrose's character. The themes of nobility and constancy are coupled with a certain wistfulness and sadness, a regret for what might have been. There is a characteristic concern with loyalty and honour, but also with friendship and money. In the postscript there is a hint of the wilfulness and self-righteousness which would shortly distinguish his actions but the overall impression is of selflessness and self-denial.

Henderson returned to a convention which spawned the solemn league and covenant. In its final form it bound signatories to preserve the reformed religion in Scotland and to strive for the reformation of religion in England and Ireland 'according to the Word of God and the example of the best reformed churches'. They were to endeavour 'to bring the Churches of God in the three kingdoms to the nearest conjunction and uniformity . . . that the Lord may delight to dwell in the midst of us'. Popery was to be extirpated. The rights and privileges of both parliaments and the person and authority of the king were to be preserved and defended. All incendiaries and malignants were to be flushed out and brought to trial. There was to be peace in both kingdoms and, as in the first covenant, there was an elaborate non-divisive clause with which the solemn league concluded.[22] The Scots bought the promise of international presbyterianism for the price of military assistance. A supplementary paper recalled that England and Scotland had leagued against popery at the time of the Spanish Armada, as they had during the Scottish Reformation. The two countries 'sailed in the same ship'; if religion was destroyed in one kingdom it must inevitably suffer in the other. English episcopacy had caused the Troubles in Scotland. The Scots were now asked to 'strike terror into the kingdom of Anti-Christ which would receive a considerable wound from this holy union'. Mutual interest overrode all other considerations; they were simply fulfilling the terms of the Treaty of London. As the tribes of Reuben and Gad crossed the Jordan in order to place their brethren in possession of the Land of Promise, the Scots would invade England 'to drive out the Canaanites and recover the liberty of the gospel'.[23]

Montrose claimed that the solemn league prejudiced religion and the liberty of the subject, that it obliged Scots to arm against their king to maintain the liberties of the English parliament, and that it involved perjury and disloyalty. He later organized a counter-band against the 'traitorous and damnable covenant' which stated that the whole Scottish nation was in danger of suffering the 'detestable imputation of partaking in this odious rebellion which misunderstanding is principally occasioned by the power which those unnatural and disloyal persons have gotten, of countenancing their most treasonable actions with the forms and glosses of public authority'. His band condemned both the convention and the projected invasion of England, denounced the signatories of the solemn league as guilty of high treason and rebellion, and called upon all faithful subjects to suppress the said rebels.[24]

From Keir Montrose went to Oxford where he found the queen no more receptive than before. Nor, it transpired, was Charles. Wishart graphically depicts Montrose as the wronged hero, a voice in the wilderness, daily maligned by worthless courtiers 'who continually buzzed into the king's ears Montrose's youth, rashness and ambition, and his hatred and envy of the Hamiltons'. The Graham was completely baffled; for months he had been warning the king to no effect. It appeared that nothing short of an invasion would bring Charles to his senses. Even his own enemies in Scotland had a greater sense of Montrose's abilities and perspicacity than the blinded monarch he so fervently wished to serve. He was apparently condemned to the misfortune of always being right but never being heard. Charles, however, had his own good reasons for not reacting immediately to Montrose's impassioned demands. The war had gone comparatively well for the royalists that summer and a cessation had been obtained in Ireland, but above all Charles was unwilling to be seen to attack first. Montrose's hour approached as correspondence from the Hamiltons gradually revealed their total failure to retrieve the situation in Scotland. When in December 1643 they arrived in Oxford where the royalists were wintering, both were arrested partly at the instigation of Montrose, some of whose long-standing criticisms of their behaviour were incorporated in an indictment which they were never called to answer. Lanark subsequently escaped to return to Scotland as a solemn leaguer but his brother was to spend the next two years in prison. The 'luckless Duke' was a curious individual who has never been understood, possibly because he was incapable of understanding himself. A man of no political ideals and of minimal ability, he was one of those most bewildered by the events which overtook Scotland in the 1630s and 1640s, a piece of flotsam swept back and forth on the tide of the Scottish revolution.

Montrose was now asked for his advice. He admitted himself that he had neither men, money, nor arms, an indication of the desperate nature of Charles's situation. Here was no great lord who could finance a campaign at his own expense; he had nothing to offer save wits and ability. He advised that Antrim, who also arrived at Oxford at the end of the year, should send Irish troops to the west of Scotland. German mercenaries should be obtained from the King of Denmark. Arms and ammunition should be sent to Scotland for the use of loyalists. Montrose himself would lead a party of horsemen supplied by

Newcastle into Scotland. Some kind of plan was gravely needed. On 19 January the army of the covenant, some 20,000 strong, having negotiated the snow-choked routes of southern Scotland, began to cross the Tweed. The Earl of Leven once again commanded with an iron hand. Secure in their new covenant the soldiers were more consciously part of the army of the Lord than the members of the very similar expedition of 1640. There was harsh punishment for thieving and whoring. Montrose was prepared, like some classical hero, to stand against the twenty thousand. Given his self-confessed limitations in manpower and resources, his action smacked to some of megalomania. His commission would ensure the defection from the king's cause of men like Carnwath in the short term and of Huntly and other great nobles, whose aristocratic sensibilities were offended by Montrose's appointment, in the longer term. If there was no very obvious candidate to lead the Scottish royalists, many were convinced that Montrose was not, and never could be, a serious contender. In spite of his remarkable successes he was never able to win the support of the vast majority of the Scottish nobility, a failure which undoubtedly detracted from, and in the final analysis possibly negated, his achievement.

For the moment Antrim was content to support Montrose's plan. On 28 January the two men drew up a bond, Montrose as Lieutenant-General of Scotland, Antrim as General of the Highlands and Islands. Two weeks later Montrose's commission was altered to that of Lieutenant-Governor and Captain-General over all the king's forces in Scotland. He was styled 'Marquis', an honour which was not officially conferred upon him until 6 May. He undertook to raise forces in the north, the east, and the Borders of Scotland and to declare against the rebels by 1 April at the latest while Antrim's task was to recruit support in the Hebrides and in Ireland and to invade Argyll's territories by the same date.[25] Having departed for Ireland at the end of January he later complained that he was expected to take orders from Montrose.

The Lieutenant-Governor left Oxford at the beginning of March accompanied by Crawford, Nithsdale, and Lords Reay, Ogilvie, and Aboyne, all of whom had signed his band condemning the solemn league. His aim was simple, if daunting. He was to receive support from the Earl (now the Marquis) of Newcastle and march into Scotland.

From York he sent Colonel John Cochrane, who since the 'incident' had been permanently employed in the royal service, ahead to Newcastle with royal letters requisitioning horsemen. Newcastle had his own problems. For two months the Scots had been threatening him and he could spare only a hundred troopers 'mounted on lean, ill-appointed horses, with two small brass pieces'. It was simply the first of many setbacks. 'It shall be no matter of discouragement to withhold us from doing our best', wrote Montrose to Sir Robert Spottiswood, an incendiary of long standing who was appointed secretary of state on the demise of Hamilton. He decided to join Newcastle at Durham.

The northern royalists had recently faced the Scots at snow-carpeted Bowdenhill in Sunderland only to withdraw to Durham. If there could be anything more romantic than a Scottish earl riding at the head of fewer than two hundred comparatively untried noblemen and gentlemen to restore Scotland to the king, it might be a female commander, sporting a black banner showing a naked figure suspended from a gibbet and the motto 'I dare'. Such a lady Montrose now met. She was Captain Frances Dalziel, the illegitimate daughter of the Earl of Carnwath, and she rode at the head of a troop of horse when Montrose persuaded Newcastle to advance once again to Hilton near Bowdenhill. Leven's banners flaunting the motto 'The Lord of Hosts is with us' faced the royalists rather ironic 'Now or Never' for two indecisive days. What could have been one of the most important and decisive battles of the British civil wars became a humiliating experience for both sides. There was skirmishing and cannon fire but nothing happened. Newcastle withdrew to York, having ordered the militia of Cumberland and Westmorland to render Montrose all possible assistance. It was almost the end of March and time to make a sortie across the border in fulfilment of the bond with Antrim.

With Crawford, Nithsdale, Aboyne, Ogilvie, and the mysterious Captain Dalziel he advanced from Carlisle into Annandale, a district with a long history of feuds with the men of Cumberland. Some such local rivalry caused a mutiny which resulted in most of his English support, a majority of his force of twelve hundred men, returning south. Nithsdale encouraged him to advance on Dumfries which he took in mid-April. Although he was warmly received by the provost of the town the south-west did not rise. The only person to join him was the catholic Lord Herries. Hartfell and other local dignitaries such as Charteris of Amisfield did not offer support. The faithful 'banders' Keir and Napier, with Lord Erskine, the Master of Napier, and the Master of Madderty sent Drummond of Balloch from Keir, urging Montrose to make a bid for Stirling Castle which they assured him would be voluntarily surrendered by its commander Lord Sinclair. The latter, however, with Campbell of Lawers' regiment, was ordered to take Dumfries and Montrose had no choice but to fall back on Carlisle. The Earl of Callender had also pledged support for the king but he proceeded to levy forces for the covenant. Montrose was understandably bitter about his failure to recruit allies and he scathingly condemned those who might have assisted him.

The only person to execute his part of the plan was Huntly who, towards the end of March, drew up a band rejecting the solemn league, and raised the standard for the king. He had hopes of support from Airlie, Southesk, Atholl, and Seaforth, anticipating that Montrose would join him from the south. Like Montrose he was to be disappointed 'for the erllis cam in and wes dung bak agane, and sic as he trustit in deceavit him and fled the causs and left him in the myre'. Having raised a force of some twelve hundred at Aboyne he marched on Aberdeen which he ransacked for weapons and ammunition. One of his officers Major Nathaniel Gordon, who was to play a prominent part in the Montrose campaigns, distinguished himself by capturing a Danish cargo vessel laden with herring, which had been seized by English pirates. The royalists wreaked havoc from Deeside to Banff. At Aberdeen Huntly commissioned banners bearing the Lion Rampant surmounted by a golden crown and the motto 'For God, the King, and against all Traitors'. He and his commanders wore black taffeta at their throats as a sign that they would fight to the death, 'bot it provit utherwayes'.

Argyll arrived at Dunnottar on 26 April. He soon commanded a force of between five and six thousand men including Campbells, levies from Perthshire, Fife, Angus, and the Mearns, detachments sent by such northern covenanters as the Forbeses and the Frasers, and a regiment of 'renegade Irish' who were singled out by Spalding on account of the vicious nature of their depredations. Based on Aberdeen, which merely exchanged one oppressor for another, Argyll systematically demolished Huntly's rising and reduced the north-east. The area now experienced fires, fines, extortions and bloodshed in the name of the covenant rather than the king. By the time Argyll returned south at the end of May, Huntly had fled to Strathnaver, where he remained for eighteen months, Gordon of Haddo, one of his chief officers, awaited execution, and various Gordon strongholds had been captured or destroyed. When Argyll, at his departure, 'went to horse, he wes convoyit with nobles, barrones, burgesses, bair heidit for the most pairt, so heichlie wes he in thir dayis exalted, little inferiour to ane king.'

The MacEwens, hereditary bards to Clan Campbell, concurred with Spalding's description of the king-like Argyll. 'From the bounds of Lewis to the coast of Ireland there is no region that pays not tribute due to thee; in the whole kingdom no kingship matches thine; thou art of the noblest of every land and lord.' To them he was 'Lord of the Gael . . . the Earl of the Saxons and of the Gael', who would 'cause his rule to run over one and all'. They likened him to Arthur and to Hector and,

He is the Pompey of the plain of Duibhne's race, he is as Cato in the fashion of his royal memory; like Caesar with omens of victory in battle; he has the traits of the lasting prince.

He is lion that leaps over every house; he is a lord who defends the faith; in Scotland's land he is a pillar of lords, whose fame is high within the church.[26]

The bards credited him with 'the learning of Aristotle' and addressed him as 'darling of the [bardic] schools and guiding star of the poets'. Like Oliver Cromwell he commended history and mathematics to his son as 'the most advantageous and proper studies' for one of his quality. He advised him to make notes on his reading as he did himself, and recommended 'that excellent recreation of Golf-ball, than which truly I do not know a better'. Though he would shortly belie the martial qualities which the poets allowed him, their poems place him firmly in the Gaelic context to which he belonged. He observed many of the old customs. His own son was fostered by Campbell of Glenorchy; he never hesitated to call upon the kin even for such matters as borrowing silver tableware on the occasion of Charles's coronation; and he took great pains to ensure that his son learned Gaelic. Argyll's views on deposition were probably conditioned by the Gaelic experience. John, Lord of the Isles, Ian MacDonald, Chief of Keppoch, and Dougal MacRanald, Chief of Clan Ranald, had all been deposed by their clansmen during the previous century and a half. He warned the Forbes kindred against 'the misthryving' of their chief in 1643. 'We are not born for ourselves. Every man knows or should know his duty and relations. . . . Moses the man of God chose rather to suffer affliction with the people of God than to enjoy the pleasures of sin for a season.'[27] Although he was undoubtedly acquisitive his instincts were identical, on a grander scale, with those of other clan chiefs; while they plundered cattle or their defeated enemies, Argyll plundered in the corridors of power.

Just before Montrose's arrival at Durham in March, Leven had taken Morpeth Castle, which he placed in the charge of Lieutenant-Colonel Somerville with five companies from Sinclair's regiment. Somerville, a relation of Montrose, was unhappy about his commission, chafing at his own inactivity while the main army advanced to the south. Newcastle supplied Montrose with two thousand foot and five hundred horse following the abortive sortie into Dumfriesshire. He hoped to create a diversion in Northumberland which might either force Leven to fall back to guard his rear or enable Montrose to break through into Scotland. In either event Morpeth would have to be taken. On 11 May, after some outlying skirmishing with Somerville's scouts, Montrose settled down before the castle which he initially attempted to storm with scaling ladders. The attack was repulsed in a fierce two-hour combat in which the ladders were pushed off the walls by the besieged who rained shot on the head of their attackers. Under cover of darkness he threw up a trench all round the castle 'within lesse than a musket-shot of the walls'. Meanwhile Leven sent eight hundred men to relieve Morpeth, a threat which Montrose met by temporarily abandoning the siege to march to meet them. The two armies skirmished indecisively before the covenanters withdrew. Montrose had feared that the besieged might join the reinforcements but they contented themselves with levelling the royalist breastworks and were soon bottled up in the castle once more. By now cannon had arrived from Newcastle to blister the fortress with shot and splintered stone. Captain McCulloch, Somerville's second-in-command, led a courageous sally out of the castle by night in an attempt to spike the enemy guns. He caused considerable damage before retreating with a pike wound in the neck. As at Brig o' Dee Montrose realized that his cannon could be used more effectively. The siege had been going on for two weeks. For three days his men laboured under fire to construct a breastwork on which they raised two batteries with three cannon on each, a hundred paces from the main wall. It was a further two days before that wall was breached 'because of the unskilfullness of the cannoneers', who aimed their shot high instead of at the base of the wall. Somerville packed the breach with earth and feather beds but the siege was effectively over. In a final fierce encounter the castle was stormed. Smoke, feathers, and flying masonry filled the air; Somerville was wounded in the head; 'two thirds of his firearms were sprung and the rest so furred by constant firing were become unserviceable.' Captain McCulloch was delegated to negotiate terms. Montrose sought to win the defeated garrison to his own side. To that end he exaggerated royalist successes and spoke of the ambition of Hamilton and Argyll. The agreed terms were generous. The officers were permitted to march out with their arms and baggage while the common soldiers carried staves instead of weapons. All swore never again to take arms against the king. On the day of capitulation Montrose entertained Somerville and his captains to a meal in the ruined stronghold which was afterwards destroyed. The siege had lasted twenty days and had cost Montrose the loss of twelve officers and one hundred and fifty soldiers.[28]

The covenanters' assessment of Montrose's military ability had been confirmed. An outraged Committee examined McCulloch and others in order to apportion blame. Callendar was chastised for not relieving Morpeth and Baillie wrote of Montrose's 'making havoc of the northern counties'. He went on to reduce another fortress at South Shields but his run of success ended with a summons from Prince Rupert to join him with all possible haste. He met Rupert at Richmond the day after the battle of Marston Moor. The defeat suffered by Rupert and Newcastle was also the undoing of Montrose. 'Give me a thousand of your horse and I will cut my way into the heart of Scotland', was his reported demand. The prince was not only unable to oblige; he also requisitioned Montrose's own troops. The king's Lieutenant-General was understandably bitter. Newcastle had failed him; there was no sign of the arms from Denmark; and Antrim had not honoured his commitment. 'The Prince when we came to him took all the force from us and would supply us with none. So we were left abandoned; neither would they do us so much as give our persons quartering on this country.' A lesser or more modest man might have given up at this point but he treated with Lord Fairfax who had distinguished himself at Marston Moor, about the exchange of prisoners and sent instructions with Ogilvie to the king at Oxford. Ogilvie never reached his destination since with several others, including Montrose's half-brother Harry, he was arrested to remain in confinement until after Kilsyth. His instructions were scathing in their condemnation of those who had 'stumbled the service', particularly the Border lords who were all accused of betraying their promises and of abusing Montrose's small force 'to the notable scandal and prejudice of that business ... Nay, though nothing was held good to us, yet we could easily have affected it notwithstanding.'[29] If Montrose lacked magnanimity in adversity he displayed no shortage of courage and tenacity. The moment had come to,

> ... put it to the touch
> To gain or lose it all.

There was no future for him in England – 'My Lord Montrose is denyit to have any command over the English because it is said to him they can hardlie trust him who was not true to his own natione.'[30] Ogilvie and Sir William Rollo, brother of Sir James, had already scouted across the border. Disguised as a groom James Graham set out to win a kingdom for Charles Stewart. Accompanied only by Rollo and Colonel William Sibbald he penetrated the western march. As in the best stories he was recognized but not revealed. A ride of four days took him through the covenanting Lowlands to arrive at Tullybelton on the northern edge of Strathearn in mid-August. This was Graham country and the home of Patrick of Inchbrakie, Black Pate. The news was not good. Huntly was hiding and 'all honest loyal subjects were crushed and prostrate under the tyranny of the rebels'. In such inauspicious circumstances, with a cause and a commission but lacking a command, the great adventure began.

8

THE FIRST STRANGE
COURSING

You heard what followed of that strange courseing, as I remember,
thryce round about from Spey to Atholl, wherein Argyll and
Lothian's sojours were tyred out; the countrie harassed by both, and
no less by friends than foes, did nothing for their own defence.

Robert Baillie

Montrose's urgently needed support was to come initially not from
Huntly, or the Graham kindred, or from the loyal Highlands, but from
Ireland. Antrim had not been idle since his departure from Oxford. He
was an impetuous, reckless individual whose contempt of all things
Irish had not prevented him from acquiring a measure of the blarney.
In 1639 he had boasted that the Irish force projected for Scotland would
live off the land, feeding their horses with the leaves of the trees and
themselves with shamrocks.[1] His task in 1644 was to coax the Irish
catholics into sending ten thousand men with ammunition, artillery,
and ships to England, or, failing that, a force of two thousand to join
Seaforth and Sir James MacDonald of Sleat, son of Donald Gorm, in
support of Montrose for an invasion of Argyll.[2] In the event he recruited sixteen hundred men mostly from his own clansmen, tenants,
and neighbours, who were placed under the command of one of the
greatest warriors of his day, Alasdair mac Cholla Chiotaich.

Alasdair's father was Colla Ciotach or Colkitto, literally 'ambi-
dextrous', who, after Sir James MacDonald's rising in 1615, fled to
Colonsay. There, the sometime home of *Clann Duib-shidhe*, hereditary
keepers of the records of the Lordship of the Isles, Alasdair spent his
youth and early manhood. Tradition relates that on the night he was
born every sword in the house withdrew a little from its scabbard and
every gun snapped. His father considered drowning him at birth for

fear he should turn out an evil man. Like Montrose he betrayed his diabolical origins by displaying a childhood penchant for toad-eating but, sadly for the folk of Argyll who preserved such stories, his father ignored the portents. Alasdair's height and strength were legendary. He could hold a cow by the horns with one hand, to sever its head with a mighty axe wielded by the other, when he was not twisting the feet off bulls with his bare hands.

When his father's household was broken up by the Campbells in 1639, Alasdair joined his Irish kinsmen in the Glens of Antrim. On the outbreak of the Irish rebellion the Earl of Antrim was initially neutral but his steward Stewart of Ballintoy, who was related to Alasdair, raised eight companies to resist the confederates. Two of these were commanded by Mac Cholla. They consisted largely of exiled catholic Scots who were not in sympathy with the protestant Stewart but who were diffident about an open break with him, on the grounds of kinship. By November 1641, Stewart having more or less contained the rebels in the vicinity of Coleraine, Alasdair decided to declare his true colours. At Portnaw, near Kilrea some sixteen miles south of Coleraine, there was an important ford on the River Bann which Stewart decided to defend against a possible confederate movement from the west. Learning that such a force was advancing from Derry, Alasdair with his two companies fell upon Stewart's six at dawn on 2 January 1642 and completely routed them. Joined by the Derry men, Alasdair set about reducing the garrison towns of Antrim with mixed success. It was rumoured that the covenanters were so impressed by Alasdair's military prowess that they unsuccessfully tried to persuade him to join Argyll.

On Good Friday 1642, 'Black Friday', at the Laney near Ballymoney, Alasdair caught Stewart in boggy ground where the Irish 'skeins', or dirks, made quick work of his small army. The victorious 'son of Anak' went on to besiege Coleraine, which would have fallen but for the timely arrival of Antrim who intervened to save the inhabitants. Soon after the earl was captured by Monro, who commanded the first contingent of ten thousand Scottish troops sent to destroy the hordes of Anti-Christ. Alasdair, powerless to resist this superior force, retired to Donegal where he suffered defeat and severe wounds at the battle of Glenmaquin which kept him *hors de combat* until he set sail for Scotland in June 1644. Throughout his brief if crowded career Alasdair was the subject of contemporary legend. An old Gaelic motif was applied to his selection as general for when he learned that the command was to be given to the one with the strongest arm, he raised his right arm, sword in hand, and said 'This is it!' When asked whose was next in strength he raised his left.[3]

Alasdair was less interested in aiding King Charles than he was in settling ancient scores with the Campbells who held his ancestral territories. Of his three colonels James and Ranald Og were Mac-Donalds of Antrim; the third, Magnus O'Cahan who covered himself with glory during the subsequent campaign, was a relation by marriage. Alasdair's own regiment of MacDonalds, MacHenrys, MacQuillans, O'Cahans, and O'Haras consisted of one thousand men. James Mac-Donald and O'Cahan commanded five hundred each, on paper at least, since none of the three quite attained full strength. Three-quarters of the force were native Irish though some were of Scottish and English descent; almost all were recruited from Antrim and northern Derry. Most fought for religious reasons; many had served in General Owen Roe O'Neill's Northern Army of the Catholic Confederation and some were veterans of the Thirty Years War, having fought for the catholics in Flanders.[4] They were accompanied by their womenfolk and there were children among the camp followers. John Baptist Rinuccini, the papal nuncio in Ireland, regarded the Irish Brigade as catholic crusaders and Alasdair as 'another Judas Machabaeus'. He remarked that although Montrose was '*religione hereticus*' he was a man without equal in the whole of Scotland. Father James MacBreck averred that Alasdair's force was 'animated by an energy derived from above' and he claimed that Montrose recognized catholics to be his most faithful and trustworthy supporters whom he welcomed the more on account of their faith, allowing the priests to exercise their functions in recognition of their allegiance to the king.[5] In short there was as much religious bigotry on the side of the Irish, as conscious a concept of a holy war, as there was on the part of the covenanters.

Alasdair sailed from Passage on the River Barrow in a frigate called the *Harp* on 27 June 1644. In the Irish Sea he captured two supply ships and a passenger vessel, the latter containing three ministers whom he hoped to exchange for his father and two brothers, then prisoners of Argyll. The force then proceeded to the Sound of Mull where they captured the castles of Lochaline and Mingarry. At the moment they reached Scotland a tremendous explosion 'as from an enormous brazen cannon of unheard of dimensions' was heard by every man, woman, and child throughout the length and breadth of the land. Both Gordon of Ruthven and MacBreck solemnly record this prodigy which told 'the whelps of Calvin' that 'a cruel, savage, and foreign enemy had invaded the country'.[6] They then crossed to Skye to recruit Donald Gorm of Sleat, but he had been dead for six months and his son Sir James refused a command in the army since he considered it too small to be effective. A report of 1640 asserted that the MacDonalds of Sleat, who were in close contact with both Ireland and the north of Scotland, could muster two thousand bowmen for the king but they were not forthcoming on this occasion.[7] It was to be the same story elsewhere. To make matters worse Alasdair's ships were captured by the covenanters, an event subsequently cursed by several Lowland writers because the Irish henceforward had no means of returning home and had no choice but to raise Cain in Scotland. There was undoubtedly an irresponsible streak in Alasdair which may have cost him his ships on this occasion. He was described as being 'so vigorous in fight that had his conduct been equal to his valour he had been one of the best generals in Europe'. Sir James Turner opined that he was 'nae sojer tho stout enough'.

Summonses directed to MacLeans, MacNeills, MacLeods, and Camerons were no more successful and, since there was little future, if much satisfaction, in harrying Campbell tenants, Alasdair decided to make for Lochaber to join up, he hoped, with Huntly. Glengarry provided beef in plenty but few recruits. Some MacDonalds of Keppoch came in and Donald Farquharson sent some of his clan from Braemar. A Scottish officer Captain Mortimer was sent to woo Seaforth who, lamenting that they had not arrived in time to join Huntly's rising, declined to assist, excusing himself 'with the malignitie of the time'. When Alasdair appeared in person to demand safe passage to Strathbogie, Seaforth prepared for military resistance. He at first promised to acquiesce but then sent the Grants and the men of Moray to guard the Spey. Thus blocked, Alasdair was forced to move south through Badenoch where three hundred MacPhersons came in with their chief Ewen Òg. When the invaders marched through Atholl the Stewarts and the Robertsons prepared to resist. 'All those considerations being seriously weighted doeth mightely afflict him, and breid a great perturbation in his courageus and undanted saule. He feared not death, for he resolved to die nobilie, but it greived him that he sould have brought so many brave and hardie men out of there native country to be heere, without hope of releife, swollowed up by the devoreing sword of there enemies.'[8] Apathy, the stranglehold of the covenant, religion (several of the clans were protestant), and suspicion of the Irish, all contributed to Alasdair's predicament. What was required was someone who could unite the disparate and divided elements. Alasdair addressed letters to Montrose whom he believed to be at Carlisle. These were conveyed to Inchbrakie and Montrose replied, as from Carlisle, ordering a muster at Blair Atholl. Gorden of Ruthven had another version from Montrose himself. He wandered in Methven Wood, living like an outlaw, 'his invincible spirit growing stronger the more it was tread upon or pressed down, his generous fortutude mounting still higher, with a matchless resolution to overcome all difficulties, although he saw nothing whereon his hopes could take hold, yet constantly relying on the justness of his cause, the integrity of his own intentions and the all-ruling providence of the Almighty.' He was grieving like Moses on the banks of the Red Sea when 'with watery eyes' he prayed to God. Just then a horseman appeared bearing the fiery cross, the ancient rallying signal of the clans.

It was late August. With Inchbrakie, Rollo, and Sibbald, Montrose rode through the hills to rendezvous at Truidh Hill in the heart of Atholl. Alasdair and the Athollmen were almost at one another's throats when they were distracted by the small party, led by a figure in Highland dress. The Irish were not convinced it was Montrose until he showed them his commission, but the Athollmen who knew him of old immediately supplied eight hundred men for the cause. His wearing of trews, shortcoat, and bonnet was shrewdly flattering to the Gaels. The proud martial record of his ancestors was also an asset. The chiefs, whose rivalries would not permit any one of their number to command, let alone Alasdair who was regarded as an upstart, were prepared to accept a man with the king's commission. They admired his pride and his conceit. As Iain Lom expressed it:

> There is beauty in your countenance, there is nobility,
> there is generosity, there is the comeliness of a
> King's son there. . . .[9]

Ever since his college days Montrose had enjoyed the gift of communication, an important asset in a society where honour was cherished and slights real or imaginary could quickly lead to bloodshed.

He was ane accomplished gentleman of many excellent parts; a bodie not tall, but comely and well compossed in all his liniamentes; his complexion neerly white, with flaxin haire; of a stayed, grave and solide looke, and yet his eyes sparkling and full of lyfe; of speach slowe, but wittie and full of sense; a presence graitfull, courtly, and so winneing upon the beholder, as it seemed to claime reverence without seweing for it; for he was so affable, so courteous, so benign, as seemed verily to scorne ostentation and the keeping of state, and therefor he quicklie made a conquesse of the heartes of all his followers, so as whan he list he could have lead them in a chaine to have followed him with chearfullness in all his interpryses ... he did wisely apply himselfe to the naturall inclination of those whom he was to command, or rather, I think, veralie he was naturally inclyned to humilitie, courtesie, gentlenes, and freedome of cariage. He did not seeme to affect state, nor to claime reverence, nor to keepe a distance with gentlemen that ware not his domestickes; but rather in a noble yet courteouse way he seemed to slight those vanisheing smockes of greatnes, affecting rather the reall possession of mens heartes then the frothie and outward showe of reverence; and therefor was all reverence thrust upon him, because all did love him, therefor all did honour him and reverence him, yea, haveing once acquired there heartes they ware readie not only to honour him, but to quarrell with any that would not honour him, and would not spare there fortounes, not there derrest blood about there heartes, to the end he might be honoured.[10]

There and then Montrose raised the standard 'for the defence and maintenance of the trew protestant religion, his Majestie's just and sacred authoritie, the fundamentall lawes and priveledges of Parliaments, the peace and freedom of the oppressed and thralled subject'. He alleged that the king insisted upon the obedience of his subjects only so long as he persisted in the maintenance of these ends.

And the farther yet to remove all possibility of scruple, – lest, whilst from so much dewtie and conscience I am protesting for the justice and integritie of his Majestie's service, I myself should be unjustly mistaken – (as no doubt I have hitherto beine, and still am), I doe again most solemnly declare, that knew I not perfectly his Majesties intention to be such and so reall as is already exprest, I should never at all [have] embarked myselfe in this service. Nor, did I but sie the least appearance of his Majesties change from those resolutions, or any of them, should I ever continue longer my faithfull endeavours in it; which I am confident will prove sufficient against all unjust and prejudicial malice.

and able to satisfie all trew Christians, and loyall hearted subjects and countrie-
men who desyre to serve their God, honour their Prince, and injoy there owne
happie peace and quyet.[11]

It was a quiet, dignified, and curiously subjective statement. Paradoxi-
cally he was employing catholics to defend the true protestant religion.
At the same time he was in the unique position of a presbyterian,
lauded as the champion of catholicism. He was a Calvinist prepared to
concede religious toleration, a superb example of what Hugh Mac-
Diarmid distinguished as 'the Caledonian antisyzygy' – 'extraordinary
contradictions of character, most dangerous antimonies and antithetical
impulses, in the makeup of almost every distinguished Scot'.[12] James
Graham believed that the end justified the means. Experience had
taught him that loyalty was not monopolized by the presbyterians.
The Irish catholics claimed, in imitation of the covenanters, that they
fought for their king and their religion. Montrose, after much heart
searching, decided that the king had priority. Judging from his treatment of Huntly in 1639 he believed that constitutional issues overrode
religious ones and if, as seems to be the case, he genuinely did come to
favour religious toleration, then in a Scottish context he was far ahead
of his time. Yet religion did not consolidate the royalist cause. In 1642
Huntly, Douglas, Abercorn, and Winton were reported to be in
communication with the Spanish ambassador Don Alonso de Carderas
concerning the conservation and augmentation of the catholic religion
in Scotland, but none of them rallied to Montrose's banner.[13] Nithsdale
was in a similar position. Such catholic nobles, and many others who
were protestant, were to avoid commitment to one side or the other
until the Restoration. It would be harsh to dismiss them all as cowardly,
double-dealing, time-servers, careless of the outcome of the civil war.
Theirs was a different reading of the situation. Although the covenanters
consistently claimed that they were as anxious as he was himself to
secure an accommodation with the king, Montrose was almost alone
in distinguishing in covenanting machinations the eventual destruction
of the monarchy. He anticipated a Cromwellian situation in Scotland
in the early 1640s. Furthermore Montrose was almost unique in
trusting Charles although his declaration betrayed some slight doubts.
Such trust was, in his case, justified but most would have agreed that
the word of Charles Stewart was a fragile foundation on which to
build. What appealed to the clans above all about Montrose was his

integrity, an ingenuousness which others would dismiss as naivety. His record suggested that alone in Scotland he would prove a fitting champion against the hated *MacCailein Mór*. Montrose had put indecision behind him. He could say with Seneca, as had his boyhood idol Sir Walter Ralegh, 'Let us satisfy our own consciences, and not trouble ourselves with fame; be it never so ill, it is to be despised, so we deserve well.'[14] Others would cultivate fame on his behalf; his conscience enabled him to pursue a kingdom for Charles I with a terrible single-mindedness.

He made one final appeal to Argyll, asking him to return to the grace and protection of his king. 'Still you may find him like an indulgent father ready to embrace his penitent children in his arms, although he hath been provoked with unspeakable injuries. But if you shall still continue obstinate, I call God to witness that through your own stubbornness I shall be compelled to endeavour to reduce you by force. So I rest, your friend if you please.'[15] The threat must have seemed empty. Montrose was regarded as a minor irritation which would soon be eradicated. An army under Lord Elcho was mustering at Perth to crush the rising. It consisted of levies from Fife, Perth, and Angus to the number of six thousand foot. Eight hundred horse were commanded by James, Lord Drummond, eldest son of the Earl of Perth.

The royalists marched south to Castle Menzies. Clan Menzies had maltreated a trumpeter sent ahead with a summons and they now harassed Montrose's rearguard. Their reward was wasted lands and fired corn. Crossing the Tay, Montrose advanced by Glen Cochill, Amulree, and the Sma' Glen to the Hill of Buchanty on the banks of the Almond where Elcho had placed a force of bowmen under Lord Kilpont, Montrose's kinsman and a son of the Earl of Airth. Surrounded by the Atholl Highlanders, led by Black Pate, Kilpont had no stomach for a fight. Instead with the Master of Madderty, husband of the 'bairn Beatrix', and Sir John Drummond, younger brother of Lord Drummond, he satisfied the instincts of his house and joined Montrose, so bringing the royalist numbers to about three thousand men, though horses were in such short supply as to be almost non-existent.

The first battle of any campaign is of crucial importance. Montrose's troops were heterogeneous and untried, and their discipline untested. The objective was the city of Perth. West of the town the rich agricultural plain of Tibbermore extends along Strathearn, the level ground rising slightly towards the south. The area was well known to Montrose for Kincardine Castle is some twelve miles south-west of the battlefield, and the Graham estates of Balgowan and Inchbrakie are situated between Tibbermore and Crieff. Sunday 1 September was hot for the time of year but there was a slight breeze; the session records of the charming parish kirk of Tibbermore record that no service was held that day. The covenanting ministers assured their troops, whose resolve was stiffened by a blood-chilling banner bearing the motto 'Jesus and no quarter', that God had promised victory. Elcho commanded the right wing, the Earl of Tullibardine the centre, and the left was entrusted to Sir James Scott 'who had served with credit in the Venetian army'. Their line, extending across the valley to protect Perth, was guarded at each end by five hundred cavalry. Montrose strung out his troops in a long line arranged in three ranks to avoid being outflanked by the larger army. He placed Kilpont on the left and Alasdair with his three regiments in the centre, while he himself 'went on foot with his target and pike', commanding the Athollmen on the rising ground of the right. The convention of the day was to fire off three volleys in succession, the front rank kneeling, the second stooping and the third standing, but Gustav Adolph had demonstrated the effectiveness of firing one volley simultaneously.

Montrose sent Madderty to proclaim his royal commission to the enemy. They were invited to return to the king's service and were informed that Montrose was 'neither covetous of honours for himself nor envious of other men's preferment, and had no designs against the lives of his countrymen'. The covenanters responded by seizing the envoy. Considering that the army had never fought as one before its success was astonishing. Montrose and Alasdair, in the face of cannon fire and greatly superior numbers, were able to discipline their men into holding their fire until they could see the whites of enemy eyes. Lord Drummond attacked the royalist left with some cavalry, only to be driven back by Kilpont's bowmen. Seizing the temporary advantage the royalists advanced. Oblivious to the shot which met them they doggedly gained ground, waiting until the last possible moment before firing a single volley and rapidly following through with dirks and clubbed muskets. Elcho's line broke in surprise and confusion. The fight was fiercest on the right where Scott and Montrose contested the higher ground, but the Atholl pikes won the day. The enemy were pursued with stones picked up on the battlefield and the rout was complete. 'God gave us the day, the enemy retreating with their backs towards us that men might have walked upon dead corps to the town.' The chase continued till nine at night. Colours, cannon, weapons, ammunition, and baggage fell to the victors. Elcho lost thirteen hundred killed and eight hundred captured while royalist losses were minimal. Montrose's book knowledge and Alasdair's practical experience combined in volley and *skein* to produce an intoxicating victory and the fall of Perth. One non-fatal casualty was the minister of Tibbermore Mr Alexander Balneaves, later defrocked for giving Montrose a glass of water on that warm autumn day. Balneaves, Black Pate's son-in-law, later defiantly told his colleagues of Perth presbytery that there was not one of them who would not have kissed Montrose's backside, on the day of the battle. Several other local ministers were also censured for associating in a less unseemly fashion with the marquis.[16]

That evening Montrose received the keys of Perth from the magistrates before domiciling himself at Margaret Donaldson's house. Black Pate prevailed upon the provost to substitute a body of royalists for the town guard. The following day three or four hundred Fife soldiers were imprisoned in St John's Kirk. Montrose sent for his old tutor Mr William Forret. Braco and Orchil brought the marquis's two elder sons to Perth. The Grahams of Balgowan, Nether Cairney, and Gorthie were much in evidence as were Alexander Robertson of Lude and Thomas Stewart, son of the late commissary of Dunkeld, both dressed 'in highland weed'. Montrose dictated to the sheriff clerk of Perth a general protection for the inhabitants, which he signed as Lieutenant-General of the king's army in Scotland. The same clerk penned copies of a letter ordering unnamed individuals to appear in arms for the king. Very few responded though Lord Dupplin, shortly to succeed as third Earl of Kinnoul, came in with a few gentlemen from the Carse of Gowrie. Both Wishart and Menteith insist that Montrose did not inflict any damage on Perth but the suburbs were despoiled, ammunition was seized, and the town was fined £60,000 and over £1300 worth of cloth, presumably to clad Montrose's 'naked runnagates'. Margaret Donaldson collected £50 from the magistrates for the use of Alasdair mac Cholla. As MacMhuirich said the Gaels 'were wealthy and rich after that battle of Perth'. But on the whole the royalists conducted themselves in an exemplary fashion. Some towns-men who visited the battlefield testified that while some sixty or seventy naked corpses lay in the field, the rest had been decently buried. On learning that Argyll was approaching with an army from the west, Montrose abandoned Perth on 4 September. Some of the prisoners accompanied him; others, having forsworn their 'rebellious ways', were released. Laden with plunder the Athollmen and some of the Mac-Phersons detoured homewards. The faithful were bewildered by defeat. John Robertson, a Perth minister, said that burgesses who fled into Perth to seek refuge in houses or cellars 'were all [so] forefainted and bursted with running that nine or ten died that night in town without any wound'. Baillie blamed the treachery of Drummond and Kilpont, the rashness of Elcho, and Argyll's dilatoriness in arriving four or five days too late.

Montrose's aim on leaving Perth was to secure the other northern cities. *En route* to Dundee he camped at the Kirk of Collace below Dunsinnan Hill – the Dunsinane from which Macbeth beheld the approach of Birnam woods. There he was joined by Sir Thomas Ogilvie, second son of the Earl of Airlie. At dawn the next day, as Wishart describes it, 'the whole camp was in an uproar, the men all running to arms, shouting and storming like madmen in their rage and indignation'. Montrose thought that a fight had broken out between the Irish and the Highlanders. Instead he found the lifeless body of Lord Kilpont. His assassin was James Stewart of Ardvoirlich, one of Kilpont's own retainers. Royalist apologists claim that Stewart, intending to assassinate Montrose, had taken Kilpont into his confidence. Although the covenanters did not scruple to use the weapon of assassination and although Stewart was later pardoned by parliament which considered that he had done 'good service', the assault seems to have been neither premeditated nor directed against Montrose, for on 4 September Argyll ordered the seizure of Stewart's cattle and livestock for joining the 'Yrishe rebellis';[17] he was clearly not regarded as an ally of the covenant. Kilpont may have been 'as learned in polite literature, philosophy, divinity and law, as he was famous for truth and courage', but he was also a recent turncoat. When tempers flared the dirks were likely to flash. A week later a reward of £20,000 was placed on Montrose's head but presumably Stewart had not anticipated collection of the prize. Montrose undoubtedly mourned his kinsman 'embracing the lifeless body again and again ... with sighs and tears', but convention demanded such public display. Stewart escaped to join Argyll in his laborious pursuit of the royalists.

Montrose demanded the surrender of Dundee but that wealthy city with its bustling harbour was well prepared for a siege and it was decided instead to make for Aberdeen, as ever the key to the north-east, which Lord Balfour of Burleigh and the Committee were attempting to secure. As he passed through Angus he was joined by the sixty-year-old James Ogilvie, Earl of Airlie, who had been, and would remain, the most consistent royalist in Scotland. Another welcome recruit was Huntly's lieutenant Nat Gordon. Between them they contributed ninety horsemen to the small army. Young Lord James who had marched with his father from Perth was deposited at Auld Montrose to continue his schooling. Montrose led his army over to Crathes Castle on Deeside, to enjoy the hospitality of Sir Thomas Burnet of Leys who had the distinction of being 'a faithful lover and follower of the house of Huntly, ane gryte covenanter also'. Graham accepted some horses and arms but he refused Burnet's offer of money.

Aberdeen had been held for the covenant since Huntly's abortive rising. Troops were now recalled to the city from Auchindoun, Kelly, Drum, and other Gordon strongholds on which they had been quartered. After the sermon on 8 September ministers throughout the north-east ordered all men between sixteen and sixty to prepare for the defence of the area. Lord Gordon and his younger brother Lewis, under the influence of their uncle Argyll, were the unwilling allies of the covenant, while Aboyne was still at Carlisle. Indeed much of the support on which the covenanters depended was reluctant. Aberdeen was not a covenanting city like Perth or Dundee as Montrose well knew, yet he was to make a tragic error of judgement in treating it as such.

Lieutenant Arnot mustered close to three thousand men, including three hundred troopers for Aberdeen's defence. Major Arthur Forbes commanded the local militia raised from each of the city's four wards. Burleigh displayed a conspicuous lack of leadership which contributed significantly to the outcome. On the Wednesday preceding the battle the covenanting army, or part of it, marched out to Two Mile Cross, now in the suburb of Garthdee.[18] The soldiers retired after one night to be replaced by Montrose's force which had marched from Crathes along the old Deeside road, in order to avoid the Brig o'Dee. As he pitched camp that night the moon rose, 'as red as blood', two hours early. Next day he sent an envoy and a drummer to confer with the city magistrates on his behalf. 'Loveing freindes. Being heir for the mainttenance of religion and liberty and his Maiesties just authority and servility thes ar to requyre yow that immediatly upon the sight heirof yow rander and give up your toune in the behalf of his Maiestie. Otherwayes that all old persons women and children doe come out and reteire themselffis, and that those who stays expect no quarter.' The provost and baillies gathered in Alexander Findlater's house at Bowbrig where the presence of Burleigh and Arnot doubtless influenced their hastily composed reply, which has been described as 'one of Aberdeen's diplomatic triumphs'. They professed qualified loyalty to the covenant.

Your lordship must have us excused that will not abandonne and render our toune so lightly, seeing we luik we deserve not censure as being guiltie of the breatche of any of the afforesaidis poyntis and speciallie of that latter article bot have beine ever knawin to be most loyall and dewtiefull sunjectis to his maiestie and be Gods grace sall to our lyves end stryve to contenew so, and in the mean tyme to be as ye use us. . . .[19]

The draft reply has also survived, exhibiting several erasures and crossings out as the writers groped for appropriate terminology. While it was being prepared the envoys were liberally plied with drink but as they were returning to their lines the drummer was shot by one over-zealous soldier. Montrose had already warned of the penalty of non-compliance; incensed by this action he ordered his men to spare no one. Spalding states that the covenanters marched from Bowbrig 'towards the bounds of Justice Mills', which were situated west of the Hardgate, the main route to Deeside, on the north bank of the How Burn and south-west of Crabstone. The area is now completely built up but such street names as Craibstone Street, Justice Mill Lane, and Holburn Street commemorate the old sites. Hardgate still survives, crossing the nineteenth-century Bon Accord Terrace close to the west end of Union Street. Discrepancies in the accounts add further confusion to a topography altered by urban development. Spalding records the circumstantial detail that at the commencement of battle, 'thair raiss ane heighe and michtie wynd out of the wast south wast in the bak of the enimy and face of oure people [i.e. Aberdonians] quhilk wes to oure preiudice'.[20] If this is correct then the dispositions plotted by

Gardiner and Buchan must be wrong since they make the covenanters face north. All battles are confusing; it would be imprudent to be too dogmatic about the 'Crabstone Rout'.

Gordon and Wishart disagree about the deployment of the royalists, Gordon placing Nat Gordon and Colonel James Hay on the left wing which Wishart entrusted to Sir William Rollo, while Nat and James held the right; John Buchan placed Rollo and Hay on the right with Nat Gordon on the left, a version for which no authority exists. Since Wishart is plainly erroneous on several points – he thought for example that Montrose took Brig o'Dee before the battle – the following account draws largely from Gordon of Ruthven.

Montrose commanded some fifteen hundred men and about seventy horse. He ordered all to thrust 'a rip of oats' from the surrounding fields into their bonnets to distinguish them from the enemy. Alasdair and his Irish were once again given the centre. The left wing was entrusted to Nat Gordon and Colonel Hay who took part in Montrose's campaign in the north of England. Gustav's defensive tactic of interspersing horsemen and musketeers was adopted, one hundred of the latter being added to thirty horse. The right, containing the rest of the cavalry, was commanded by Rollo, but this may be a mistake for it is more likely that Airlie led the Ogilvie horse. The bulk of Montrose's force was concentrated in the centre, and since his own position is nowhere mentioned it is likely that he commanded from behind in order to deploy his troops as required. Lord Gordon, in response to orders from the Committee, had summoned a muster to Kildrummy but suspicious northerners such as the Forbeses, Frasers, and Crichtons refused to follow him, preferring to make their own way to Aberdeen. He was now slowly approaching the city, having sent his brother Lewis ahead with eighteen horse. So concerned were some of the covenanters about Burleigh's lack of leadership that they contemplated offering the command to the hot-headed Lewis who declined. Burleigh embattled on the slope or hill, west of the city wall. Lords Fraser and Crichton led his left wing, with Forbes of Craigievar in the centre, while the right included Lewis Gordon, but some of the Forbeses 'stood off, not for want of good will to fight, but for want of experience, not knowing that it was their time to charge'. The remainder of the covenanting force consisted of Aberdonians and the remnants of the Fife levies who had survived Tibbermore.

The battle began when the covenanters seized some houses and gardens lying between the two armies. They tried to secure the position with lancers who were driven back by the sustained fire of Nat Gordon's musketeers, commanded by Captain Mortimer. Alasdair was meantime pushing against the enemy centre, having jettisoned his own light cannon but risking the deadlier shot of superior weapons inefficiently trained upon his positions. When the lancers finally abandoned their weapons in the gardens, a hundred covenanting cavalry and four hundred foot wheeled into a slightly elevated position to the north, which threatened Gordon's left flank as well as the exposed backs of Alasdair's Irish who were cutting their way well ahead of their original positions. Fortunately for Montrose the five hundred remained hesitantly where they were. On the right Airlie and Rollo held off a fierce attack by the foot of Fraser and Crichton of Frendraught, who were not supported by their cavalry. Lewis Gordon led his eighteen in a mad and futile charge down the slope, firing off their pistols in caracole. The finest move of the battle was master-minded by Alasdair. Craigievar, inspired or goaded by Lewis's example, led a furious charge against the royalist centre which opened to receive him and then closed behind his brigade. 'Few or none went back that durst venture with him.' Craigievar was unhorsed and captured as his men fell around him. Montrose transferred a hundred musketeers from his right to assist Nat Gordon, slowly advancing up the hill to break the covenanting right. The shooting, cleaving, clubbing, and carnage lasted two hours. Inverquharity received a lance wound in the thigh; Sir Thomas Ogilvie was unhorsed as was Kinnoul when his horse was shot from under him; Sir John Drummond was wounded in the head. Montrose ordered Major O'Lachan to bid his men jettison their pikes and guns in favour of swords and dirks. One worthy Irishman, 'his leg, so shattered at the thigh by a cannon-ball that it hung by a mere shred of skin', joked that Montrose would make him a trooper since he was now useless for the infantry, before he coolly amputated his own leg. Burleigh's horse, astonished by the sudden 'swallowing up' of Craigievar, did nothing. The 'lords, barons and gentlemen of quality were all divided in several opinions, for want of a head, whose opinion and order they ought to have followed,' says Gordon, 'but being all gentlemen, the general resolution to recover their loss, gave way to the private care of each one's safety, which brought them all to a timely flight, although they stayed till they saw the most part of the foot cut off.' There were many townsmen in the centre who were either cut to pieces or 'miserably rent and torn'. They attempted to retreat in order before breaking towards the Dee pursued by the death-despatching Irish. Burleigh fled towards the Don before beating south. Nat Gordon pursued his victims up the hill and into the city where the rest of the victorious army exacted a terrible price for the life of Montrose's drummer. For three days the army indulged in an orgy of pillage, rape, and bloodletting. Men were cut down in the streets and in their houses, having been previously stripped to avoid soiling their highly prized clothing. 'The riches of that town . . . hath made all our soldiers cavaliers', exulted one of Alasdair's officers. Nothing could be heard that Friday night 'but pitifull howlling, crying, weiping, mourning throw all the streittis'. Naked bodies lay where they had fallen. Women were forced where they were found or sent back to join the camp followers. Spalding listed ninety-eight non-covenanting townsmen by name, who were slaughtered in the sack of Aberdeen. They included advocates, burgesses, merchants, maltmen, fishermen, tailors, wrights, millers, websters, a piper, cordiners, a cooper, a student, a cook, and a gardener. There was hardly a man left to bury the dead.

Montrose remained at the camp until the following day when he entered the city to lodge at Skipper Anderson's, having vainly ordered an end to the carnage. God alone knows what was in his mind as he sat with his son Lord John that Friday night. He must have heard the agonized screams of the city which had made him a burgess fifteen years before, and which he had refused to burn in 1639. It was a brutal, tragic irony that Aberdeen, of all the cities in Scotland, should have been crucified for the covenant. Her citizens had been 'harllit out, sore against their wills, to fight against the king's lieutenant'. Many of them were among the eight hundred dead who lay on the battlefield or its environs but no tally could be placed on the human misery experienced by the town. Frustrated by the lack of support he attracted, desirous of making an example, anxious to manifest his authority, he may have been, but he was guilty of one of the most unforgivable atrocities of the Scottish war. He could not even plead religious extenuation, as the covenanters would do when their turn came. On that 'Black Friday' a part of the 'gentle Montrose' perished forever.[21]

All the signs are that he was unrepentant, possibly exonerated by his conscience and the single-mindedness which had inspired him since the first doubts troubled his mind and which had led him to put himself forward, a man alone, as the champion of monarchy. His commission was proclaimed at the mercat cross, declaring that his task was to bring the king's subjects to obedience 'by fair means or by fire and sword'. The citizens, denied even the comforting prayers of their ministers who had fled, pathetically donned the protective badge of the 'rip of oats' to save themselves. By Monday it was time to be moving on. Word had arrived of Argyll's approach and as Spalding so beautifully expressed it, 'mony who lovit the king wes glaid of thir newis, utheris of the covenant was no less sorie.'

Montrose marched to Kintore and Inverurie where he was joined by several troubled gentlemen who favoured the Gordons, though he was disappointed of further support from that quarter since most were 'restrained by the example and influence of Huntly himself'. He sent Rollo off to the king to inform him that he could not hold out much longer without relief from England and elsewhere. Since mobility was essential he buried cannon captured at Aberdeen, and divested his troops of as much surplus baggage as possible before withdrawing through Strathbogie to Speyside. If the mouse jumped the cat was more ponderous. Argyll reached Brechin on 16 September to be joined by Marischal and Lords Gordon, Forbes, Fraser, and Crichton. On the eighteenth he had a proclamation read out at the mercat cross of Aberdeen declaring Montrose and his followers traitors and offering a reward of £20,000 for the Lieutenant-General, dead or alive. Argyll had his own problems since such northern covenanters as Marischal, Forbes, and Fraser displayed no eagerness to support him. There was trouble between the Campbells and members of Lothian's regiment. Lothian was a sensitive, scholarly man, educated at Cambridge and Paris, whose travels had taken him to Italy and Switzerland. He was dedicated to the covenant but detested campaigning. He kept a diary of the pursuit which now commenced. By the time Argyll eventually advanced to Strathbogie on 23 September there was not a horse to be had in the vicinity of Aberdeen to bring in the corn or the peats. A war of attrition now began as Argyll attempted to ensure that Montrose would never recruit from Gordon dependants. Lord Gordon and Lewis were forced to watch helplessly as their uncle plundered and burned Strathbogie and Strathisla. Without sustenance there could be no resistance. Regiments left behind at Drum performed a similar service throughout the length and breadth of Deeside.

Montrose, unable to cross the Spey since the ferry boats had all been beached on the west bank, and uncomfortably aware that the northerners could raise a considerable force to resist him if they wished, retreated along the eastern bank to the woods of Abernethy in the foothills of the Cairngorms. The Laird of Grant who barred his way protested his loyalty, explaining that he awaited instructions from Seaforth who, in turn, depended upon a signal from Huntly, with whose royal commission Aboyne had entrusted Montrose at Carlisle. Montrose is often criticized for not passing the commission to Huntly, but he doubtless suspected that there was little likelihood of the Gordon agreeing to serve under his supreme command. If Huntly would join Montrose of his own volition some compromise might be concluded. Argyll meanwhile was beating through Huntly and Bog of Gicht, both of which he systematically destroyed. Lord Gordon's patience, or conscience, could stand no more. He demanded to know the necessity for such devastation when it appeared they could easily march to seize Montrose. Argyll assured him that 'the settling of the north in security against future invasion detained him in this sort, entreating him for the present to have patience.' He promised that the Gordons would receive compensation 'even to the last farthing' from the Estates.[22] Montrose withdrew to Rothiemurchus and Badenoch to tempt Argyll from the havoc he was creating, but in the wilds of Badenoch he fell sick for some days.

By the first week of October Montrose was in Atholl where Alasdair left him to attend to the garrison in Mingarry Castle which was under attack by Campbells, and to recruit clan support in the west. As Montrose progressed through Badenoch and Atholl some few individuals joined him before he wheeled eastwards through the passes to Angus. Argyll halted in Forres to consult with Sutherland, Lord Lovat, and various northern lairds. Seaforth was also supposed to be present but he absented himself – 'it was thocht that he and sum utheris had correspondence privatlie with Montrose' at Abernethy. If so it was possibly some of those 'utheris' who addressed an anonymous letter to Montrose admitting that they had not waited upon him 'according to his expectation . . . with our swords in our hands', but pleading their dependence upon Huntly who had forbidden any association with Montrose.[23] Argyll briefly visited Inverness before scorching his way through Badenoch and Atholl into Angus where Montrose was firing the holdings of such covenanters as Lord Coupar, brother of Balmerino, and Erskine of Dun.

There was consternation once again in Aberdeen, some of whose citizens fled the city in a snowstorm, but for the moment they were safe for Montrose crossed the Dee at Mills of Drum to avail himself again of the hospitality of Crathes Castle. Having decided upon another effort to win over the Gordons he laid down a smoke-blackened trail to Strathbogie. The houses, steadings, and cornyards of Echt were fired, as was Pittodrie on the slopes of Bennachie and several other estates. Monymusk, with whose lady, the daughter of Burnet of Leys, he dined, was spared but the Forbes estates which lay in his path were ravaged, as were those of Crichton of Frendraught, east of Huntly. For a week his army pillaged and plundered in retaliation for Argyll's earlier depredations, hoping thereby to coax Gordon support, but his efforts were in vain. He had temporarily based himself on the Earl of Dunfermline's splendid Renaissance castle at Fyvie by 27 October when he suffered a near fatal failure of intelligence of the type which was to cost him Philiphaugh a year later. He believed Argyll to be far to the south of the Grampians when he was actually just over the next hill.

Accompanied by Lothian Argyll took the familiar route via Inverurie and advanced towards Fyvie on Monday 28 October to find the royalists 'lying soe strong in a wood, that they could not be forced out of it by ane army'. Montrose removed himself from the castle, a building designed more for comfort than defence, not wishing to invite a siege. He positioned his main force on the hill to the east of the castle so that he was protected by the River Ythan and the woods of Fyvie Glen, while his left found cover in a series of ditches and dykes previously constructed by local farmers moved by an early spirit of agricultural improvement. Argyll's two thousand, five hundred infantry and thousand cavalry halted at Crichie on the south side of the river to view Montrose's thousand foot and fifty horse. The few Gordons among the royalists immediately deserted. Argyll, for once, did not delay, promptly sending a force against Montrose's positions. 'We beate in and killed at least fifteen or sixteen', wrote Lothian, rejoicing both that his own casualties were few, and that Robert Keith, the royalist brother of Marischal, was killed. The royalists were losing heart when

Montrose sent Magnus O'Cahan to drive off the attackers, though in Gordon's version the honour fell to Donald Farquharson. Irish muskets had little difficulty in repulsing Lothian's horse, severely hampered by dykes and ditches. Although Wishart, eager as ever to depict heroic endeavour, recounts amusing tales of royalists melting down the castle's pewter vessels and chamberpots to manufacture bullets on the following day, both Lothian and Gordon testify that there was no activity. 'No invitation we could make could drawe them out', says Lothian while Gordon states that Argyll 'the nixt day was not sein to appear in the fields'. Spalding was astonished that such a small force could hold off the might of the covenant – 'a mater mervalous and wrocht by Godis owne fynger, as wold appeir'. But Gordon was correct when he said that Fyvie 'deserved not the name of a battell'; in spite of the claims of later commentators it never ranked among Montrose's six victories. In 1649 Forbes of Tolquhon petitioned parliament for compensation for aid rendered to sick and wounded soldiers after the conflict at Fyvie and for supplies requisitioned by Argyll.[24] On the Wednesday Argyll withdrew and Montrose moved north to plunder Turriff and Rothiemay. Sensible utilization of terrain and Argyll's timidity had saved him from potential disaster. Lothian wished that those who censured the army's slowness were in their places. 'I wish I were disengaged,' he told his wife, 'but I must bide it out till it be donne handsomely, for death is better than discredit.'[25] One thing that came out of the skirmish at Fyvie was a fine ballad, whose subject, 'The Bonnie Lass o' Fyvie', fell in love with the captain of 'a troop of Irish dragoons'. Her sweetheart was killed – was he modelled upon Major Christopher O'Cahan whose mortal wound was recorded by MacBreck? – and the 'floo'er o' Fyvie' was left to mourn her loss.

Montrose was summoned back to Strathbogie by a letter from one of Huntly's baillies expressing a desire to parley. He responded with alacrity hoping that the long-sought accommodation might be imminent. This may have been an Argyll-inspired ruse to negotiate a truce. The year was drawing on, the first snows had already fallen, and it would be well nigh impossible to maintain armies in the field during the winter. Argyll rapidly followed Montrose to Huntly where there were further insignificant skirmishes between the two armies. More important, he made overtures to some of the royalists, promising them free passes and safe conducts. Montrose jokingly demanded a passport to visit the king, but Argyll's offer was accepted by Forbes of Craigievar who had travelled with the royalist army on parole since Aberdeen and who now deserted to the enemy. Nat Gordon, with Montrose's connivance, went to Aberdeen. Argyll was undoubtedly exhausted and his desire for truce was genuine; what is more, he honoured his word. Nat Gordon was free to come and go as he pleased as were Lord Dupplin, Sir John Drummond, Ogilvie of Inverquharity, and Colonel Hay. Montrose would have no truce. He fired his camp at Strathbogie and retreated along the Deveron to Balvenie Castle. Argyll fell back to Aberdeen, sending one thousand of his Campbells home for the winter. Back in Edinburgh he and Lothian resigned their commissions to the Committee of Estates, which formally thanked them for their services, 'all the more deserved because there had been so little bloodshed'.

Wishart has a story that Montrose marched twenty-four miles through the snow from Badenoch in a single night to surprise Argyll at Dunkeld, but allowing for Wishart's reckoning the distance would be nearer thirty-two miles and it is doubtful if Argyll was ever at Dunkeld. Montrose in any case had the greatest difficulty in holding his small army together. 'Some of them pleaded ill-health, others declared themselves unequal to such winter marches, through wild, pathless mountains beset with rocks and thickets, and mostly buried in snow, where the foot of man never trod; and therefore unwillingly, they said, and only through absolute necessity, they begged to be dismissed. He refused leave to none that asked it, but more with an air of indignation and scorn for their degeneracy, than indulgence and approval!'[26] He spent about two weeks at Rothiemurchus from where he was daily expected to make a descent upon Moray,[27] but it was not to be. The north held no attractions for him. During the last week of November he led the small force which remained towards Atholl.

9

THE SHAKING OF
MACCAILEIN MÓR

This so hard and difficulte interpryse begane that trembling ague
which brocht the most pairt of that great flourisheing name of
Campbell to the grave, and did shaike the grandour of M'Allan with
such terrible and shivereing fitts, as that great oak did bow lyke a reid
befor the wind.

Gordon of Ruthven

Such was the reputation of the royalists that 'Montrose and MacKoll [were] in every manes mouth . . . and if a few goates be seen uppon the topps of hills in twilight it concluded to be Coll Coll MacKoll.'[1] Alasdair recruited much valuable support in the west. Neil Mac-Mhuirich, bard and *seanchaidh* to Clan Ranald, wrote his invaluable Gaelic account of the wars because 'those who treated of the affairs of the time have made no mention at all of the Gael, the men who did all the service'. He rejoiced in the exploits of his patron Iain Muideartach who joined Alasdair at Mingarry to ravage Sunart, carrying off the spoils to Iain's island fortress of Castle Tirrim in Loch Moidart. Some of the Irish who had marched from Atholl took over the garrison duties at Mingarry so that the relieved soldiers could accompany their leader through Arisaig and Morar to Knoydart, where they unsuccessfully tried to recruit MacLeod of Dunvegan and Harris, and Angus MacDonald of Knoydart. Although both chiefs refused, some of the MacDonalds responded. At Loch Nevis Donald Glas of Keppoch came in, as did some of the Appin Stewarts, Clan Ian of Glencoe, and the Camerons of Glen Nevis. From the Great Glen they marched through Keppoch country and the Braes of Lochaber to Drumochter, and so to Atholl to rejoin Montrose whose spirits lifted at the sight of Alasdair's eight hundred Gaels, well equipped with mailcoats, breast plates, and targes. Their weapons included firearms, bows, swords, and Lochaber axes.

Montrose's one thought was to leave the hill country for the Lowlands but Alasdair offered a startling ultimatum. If Montrose would not agree to attack the territories of Argyll the Gaels would go nowhere except home. The marquis was astonished by, and opposed to, the idea, but he agreed to a council of war, trusting the Lowlanders present to take his part. He argued that 'Argyll was separat from the rest of the continent by a continued rigge of high cragie and unaccessable montaines, the straight passes wherof might be easely kept by fyve hundreth against tuantie thousand.' The Campbells would block them up in the vast bowels of those deserts 'till famyne had consumed them every man'. Even if they penetrated that inhospitable area the sea lochs and firths 'divided it like the teeth of a comb', necessitating at least one sea crossing for every day's march, a disadvantage which the enemy would exploit. Alasdair replied that the Highlanders were familiar with both the countryside and the passes into it. They knew that the Campbells possessed 'neither braines to forsee the danger, nor judgement to apprehend what was fitteing for resistance'. The simple truth that what they were proposing was unprecedented sufficed to indicate the glory which awaited those who would attempt it. He begged Montrose to consider Argyll's massive contribution to the covenant; if his wings were clipped the whole of the Highlands would rise for the king. It did not escape Alasdair that the Campbells 'had long been the fiercest persecutors and, whenever they could, the murderers and assassins of the catholics in the north of Ireland and the whole of Scotland.' He passionately wished to avenge the souls of their victims. 'The entire conduct of the war and the whole hazard of their cause turned upon this single point, and they considered that they would effect nothing worthy of their efforts unless they crushed the Campbells, devastated Argyll with fire and sword, and administered a terrible and telling chastisement to this hideous receptacle of bandits, plunderers, incendiaries, and cut throats.'[2] Montrose was almost persuaded. Alasdair called in Angus son of Alan Dubh, one of the *daoine-uaisle* of Glencoe, to dispel his lingering doubts. 'Will we find sufficient victuals and place to camp?' asked Montrose. Angus replied that there was not a township in all the lands of Argyll that was not known to him and that if 'tight houses and fat cattle' would suffice, there would be no difficulty in procuring them.[3] The breathtaking boldness of the scheme captured Montrose's imagination. If they were successful the Campbells' proud boast, 'it's a far cry to Loch Awe', would ever after sound very hollow.

Father James MacBreck, who believed Argyll to be the only area of Scotland into which catholic missionaries had not penetrated since the Reformation, conceived of the whole episode as a crusade. In his eyes Alasdair becomes a saintly figure who had the benediction recited in Latin before he dined, who fasted three days in the week, and who received the Holy Eucharist after confession. Impressed by his example a Uist MacDonald 'went down on his knees in thick snow in his ardour to cleanse his soul by confession', at Blair Atholl, on St Andrew's day. Although MacBreck's account frequently strains credulity he had his information from a priest who accompanied the expedition, and while Alasdair was never the Gaelic-speaking Loyola he imagined, he does preserve much fascinating circumstantial, and accurate, detail.

The army moved out during the first week of December towards Loch Tay and Breadalbane, marching along both sides of the loch to plunder and burn the lands of Glenorchy, 'ane of Argyll's speciall kinsmen'. Although Glenorchy fostered Argyll's son he had his own disagreements with his chief, not least the matter of the covenant to which he was much less committed than *MacCailein*. As they pushed westwards they were joined by the MacNabs of Glen Dochart and the MacGregors.

For those Lowlanders present, who considered Badenoch to be remote, the western Highlands were the back of beyond. Scotland was a small country, made even smaller by Montrose's phenomenal route marches, but in the eighteenth century travellers in the Highlands still took care to make their wills before setting out. The seventeenth-century attitude is well brought out by MacBreck.

The centre of Scotland is divided by ranges of mountains some of which are almost impassable. In summer and early autumn, they are frequented for the purpose of hunting stags and shooting the wild fowl, and men of rank engage eagerly in these pursuits, but in winter they are covered with immense masses of snow, through which it is impossible even to find a footpath. Argyll is the wildest country of all . . . And even before it is reached, a short distance takes many days to traverse, with no regular road, with continually alternating ascents and descents, and long detours, and numberless streams to be crossed, equally difficult for ferry or ford. There are few trees to conceal or adorn the landscape. There is no track which the traveller can follow, except along the shore, and this is frowned upon by rocks, and interrupted by pools of water, alternatively spreading and subsiding, and the whole region seems to devour the wayfarer rather than carry him through it. The soil is full of caves and holes, and barren spots, or covered with mosses, with innumerable bog holes of black and brackish water, quite unadapted for the plough, though in places turned up with a hoe, the hillsides being low and abrupt. You continually come upon lakes, the waters of which are kept in movement and made difficult to cross by the streams which flow between the higher hills ... It seemed at first sight the height of folly and rashness to attempt to march an army through such country in the depth of winter, where the snow alone is sufficient to overwhelm multitudes of human beings.[4]

The inhospitable landscape sustained a way of life as old as recorded Scottish history. As Bishop Lesley noted in his *History* published in 1578 the inhabitants had preserved their institutions for two thousand years, their language, clothing, and customs altering little, in his view, during that time.[5] It was a language which few of the Lowlanders presently on the expedition understood and to them many of the customs were mysterious. At any moment screaming Campbells might throw themselves down the hillsides and the invaders would die forgotten in a Celtic desert. When Argyll learned of the invasion he could scarcely believe his good fortune, hastening from Edinburgh in confident anticipation of picking off his exposed and starving enemies in the passes. He was at Inveraray when breathless scouts brought the incredible news that Montrose and Alasdair were advancing down Glen Shirra. His galley lay waiting in Loch Fyne and he did not stay to greet them. The Glencoe guides had done their work well. At Loch Awe the force divided, for Iain Muideartach went his separate way as far as Kilmartin in Glassary where he raided the estates of Campbell of Auchinbreck at Carnassary Castle.

Inveraray Castle was well garrisoned and was ignored by the exultant raiders who proceeded, quite simply, to rape Argyll. Montrose had as well cried to the wind as to have tried to prevent the carnage which followed. All armed men were put to the sword and 'they did not desist until they had hunted every man fit for service out of the country, or driven them into secret lurking holes.' The town of Inveraray and all the countryside round about was consumed with fire; barely one house was left unburned. They left 'not ane four footed beist in the haill lands, and sic as wold not call thay hochit and slew.' Robert Baillie tempered disbelief with philosophy: 'the World believed that Argyll could have been maintained against the greatest armie, as a country unaccessible, but we see there is no strength or refuge on earth against the Lord.'[6] Clan Ranald destroyed the estates of Lochnell and Barbreck, driving a thousand cows back to Montrose's camp. At least nine hundred Campbells were killed in all.

Alasdair earned the label *'fear thollaidh nan tighean'*, 'the man who holed the houses', by dint of destroying every Campbell dwelling which he came upon. Many were the atrocities attributed to the son of Colkitto as Campbells gathered round the peat fires in future years; his name was used, like that of the Black Douglas in an earlier century, to terrify the children of his enemies into sleep or silence. The clans indulged in an orgy of blood and plunder for which they had been preparing for over a century. The bloodlust spawned by naked hatred was almost insatiable, a primitive painful appetite sharpened by religion which time alone could quench. For those who required it mass was available in Argyll 'for the first time since the churches were destroyed by the madness of the Calvinists'.

Later in exile on the continent, Montrose told Wishart that he considered the withdrawal from Argyll his most remarkable experience of the infinite mercy of God. Had the passes been defended he would have been trapped; if the herdsmen had driven off the livestock to a place of safety his force would have starved. Even the winter was milder than usual. 'My march was through inaccessible mountains, when I could have no guides but cow-herds, and they scarce acquainted with a place but six miles from their habitations,' Montrose informed the king. 'If I had been attacked with but one hundred men in some of these passes I must certainly have turned back, for it would have been impossible to force my way, most of the passes being so straight that three men could not march abreast. I was willing to let the world see that Argyll was not the man his Highlanders believed him to be, and that it was possible to beat him in his own Highlands.'[7] After celebrating Christmas at Inveraray his force rampaged through Lorn, negotiating the comb-fretted landscape of which he was so apprehensive. Only Campbell of Inverawe attempted any resistance and he was driven to Dunstaffnage to lick his wounds. The narrow straits of Loch Etive threatened to halt their progress or to cut them off altogether for 'the country behind them was all burnt and no provisions were to be obtained'.[8] They were rescued by the Prior of Ardchattan who brought protection for his lands by furnishing the army with ferry boats. Here again they might have been surprised in the confusion of loading men into small boats and of forcing horses and cattle to swim the chilly narrows, but they crossed safely. Through Benderloch and into Appin via the old hill track from Loch Creran to Glen Fiddich, they arrived at Ballachulish where they were joined by a further contingent of Appin Stewarts. Montrose's intentions are not altogether clear. His own account reflects his uneasiness while the army remained in Argyll. His subsequent route march through the Great Glen may suggest that he had designs on Inverness, but he may have hoped that the Gordons, inspired by his recent success, would at last join him. There was one more great obstacle to negotiate. Loch Leven was a dangerous place to linger. Argyll sent a ship armed with brass guns to bombard the royalists on the shore but fortunately for them it was wrecked. Montrose obviously judged that it was simply a matter of time before Argyll recovered sufficiently to put together an army bent on revenge. Although Glencoe was friendly – and there, to their delight, the priests found a man who could recite the Lord's prayer and the Angelic Salutation in Gaelic – it was a potential death-trap, 'reached only by a single passage between precipitous rocks, and has only one exit. The mountains are so high that only eagles' flight can reach them. An arm of the sea extends at their feet, and into this a deep and rapid river flows, too deep for fording after rain. This is signified by the name of the place, which means "moist with tears or rain".'[9] Similar topographical considerations were not lost upon those who, in 1692, inflicted partial revenge for the rape of Argyll by falling upon the inhabitants of the 'Glen of Weeping'. Boats were once again obtained, however, and at Ballachulish the raiders crossed into the hospitable territory of the eastern Camerons, on 8 January 1645.

Since Marston Moor, royalist fortunes in England had been mixed. Charles managed to secure the south-west and Wales but the north was lost. A commander among the victorious Scots when Newcastle fell on 20 October was General William Baillie of Letham in Stirlingshire, a veteran of the European War, of Newburn, and of Marston Moor. He was recalled to Scotland by the Committee which wished him to assume supreme command of the army in Scotland since Argyll,

Lothian, and Callender had declined that honour. Baillie accepted with some reluctance, taking care to stipulate that he would not take orders from Argyll who, as Baillie said in a most informative 'Vindication' which he later presented to parliament, 'seemed to be displeased, and expressed himself unto some, that if he lived he should remember it.' When the news reached Edinburgh of the descent on Argyll, Baillie was sent with Leven's regiment to rendezvous with *MacCailein* at Roseneath on the Firth of Clyde. Eleven hundred men were transferred to Argyll's command while Baillie returned to Perth. It was only proper that the chief of Clan Campbell should personally attempt to exact retribution for the late devastation suffered by his people.

Montrose rested his followers at Inverlochy, a medieval fortress guarding the head of Loch Linnhe. Tradition made it an ancient Pictish capital but the MacDonald songs affectionately recalled a great victory won there by their clan under Donald Balloch at the expense of the Earls of Mar and Caithness in 1431. Sir Lachlan MacLean of Duart arrived at Inverlochy with thirty clansmen including the Mac-Leans of Coll, Kinlochaline, Ardgour, and Kingairloch. With him also was Ewan MacLean of Treshnish, the tiny but spectacular islands at the mouth of Loch Tuadh in Mull. Ewen had just returned from Ireland where he commanded a company in the Scots army, suppressing Irish catholics. The MacLeans, unlike other clans, were represented only by this small contingent of gentlemen.[10] Eachann Bacach's fine elegy for Sir Lachlan, '*A' Chnò Shamhna*', describes him as 'most esteemed in the camp of Montrose', praising his generosity and the splendour of his court at Duart Castle with 'pot-still whisky being poured into goblets of silver' to the accompaniment of the haunting music of the harpists.[11] Lachlan explained that he would have come sooner had he not found the greatest difficulty in penetrating Argyll; he was undoubtedly much impressed by the recent 'shaking of Mac-Cailein'. The Camerons of Locheil had also hesitated to join the royalists. Their chief Ailean mac Dhomnaill Dhuibh was a very old man and his grandson Ewen was being fostered by Argyll who was the Cameron superior. Nevertheless, Locheil, although too old to participate in person, sent some of his Camerons to Inverlochy. He was the 'old fox' who prophesied that a defeat would be sustained at Inverlochy 'by them that came first to seek battle'. It may be doubted whether he felt disposed to recite the remainder of the prophecy to Argyll's face.

It was predicted that a red-haired, squint-eyed earl would be the last of the line, and that if the Campbells took arms against their king, the family would be completely extinguished.[12]

From Inverlochy the army advanced up the Great Glen to Kilcumin, now Fort Augustus, at the foot of Loch Ness. There, in the last days of January, Montrose drew up a band of union, mutual assistance and defence. As MacBreck observed – and though the band survives he is the only contemporary authority to mention it – Montrose imitated 'the example of the rebels, adopting the mode thay had instituted, in order to draw them over to the king's cause'. The band is reminiscent of the National Covenant though care was taken to ensure that it was acceptable to the catholics, Montrose's catholic secretary William Leith consulting the priests on his behalf. It constituted a covenant without partisan religion and as such it may be said to represent one aspect of Montrose's constitutional ideal. The band swears 'all faithfull and loyal subjects' totally to eschew the wicked, traitorous, unjust, and unnatural 'rebellious faction', and to join with Prince Maurice or Montrose 'to use all the best and most vigorous opposition against the actors and instruments of those abominable and monstrous crimes'. Echoes of the covenant are most obvious in the second part of the document. Subscribers undertook to –

Bind and obleige our selfs – lykas we ar by God and Nature tyed – with our lyves, fortunes, and estates to stand to the maintenance of the power and authoritie of our sacred and native soverain, contrarie to this present perverse and infamous factione of desperatt Rebells now ine furie against him; and that we shall ... be ever readie to use all our best and most active endeavours for that effect: As also each and everie one of us doe faithfullie promeis, mutuallie to assist one another heirin, as we shall be desyred, or the occasione requyr: All which befor God and his angells we most solemnlie, and from our consciences and just sense, voluntarlie and sincerlie vowe and promeis firmlie till adher to, and never to swerve from, as we would be reputed famous men, and Christians, and expect the blessing of Almighty God in this lyf, or his eternall happiness hereafter.[13]

The Almighty God of the Kilcumin Band smiled, or frowned, upon protestant and catholic alike. Although several of the signatures, such as those of Seaforth and Lord Gordon, were added later, the subscriptions are of the greatest interest. There, side by side, are the signatures of Montrose, Airlie, Alasdair mac Cholla, MacLean of Duart, the heir of

Glengarry, the fiar of Appin, the tutors of Locheil and of Strowan, Donald Farquharson, Donald MacDonald of Keppoch, Patrick Mac-Gregor, and MacLean of Lochbuie, as well as those of Gordons, Grahams, Drummonds, Grants, Robertsons, and several purely Lowland lairds. There too is the simple 'Graham', the fourteen-year-old Lord John, whose experiences at Aberdeen and in Argyll must have hastened a premature manhood. Montrose was trying to forge a nation, uniting Highlander and Lowlander, protestant and catholic, in the name of the king. It was a courageous and intriguing experiment. Yet the conflict of the 1640s cannot be seen purely in terms of catholic and protestant. Airlie, the Macleans, Robertsons, Stewarts, MacGregors, and MacNabs were protestant without being presbyterian, in favour of episcopacy but not episcopalian. Such people, if pressed, would have admitted a preference for the Jacobean ecclesiastical settlement but there was some truth also in the covenanting assertion that 'some of place and power, formerly were neither professed enemies to religion or never took religion to heart';[14] for them loyalty to the king transcended religious matters.

At Kilcumin Montrose learned that Seaforth was advancing from Inverness. At least Seaforth is always credited with the command although he had no deep commitment to the covenant. Hitherto he had managed to avoid implicating himself but Argyll had wintered part of Lawer's and part of Lothian's regiments at Inverness. Seaforth was probably pressured by the commanders of these regiments and by the Earl of Sutherland, the Frasers, the Rosses, the Monros, and the men of Moray, who now marched down Loch Ness-side. Throughout the previous summer the clans beyond the Great Glen had seized upon the excuse of raising musters for one side or the other, to indulge in private feuds and vendettas. Coigach MacDonalds, the MacLeods of Assynt and Gairloch, the MacKenzies, and the Frasers all raided one another's lands. Rumour had it that Seaforth was in communication with Montrose; he certainly corresponded with Argyll.[15] Montrose prepared to meet his challenge. His intention was altered by a message, sent some say by Locheil, telling him that Argyll had arrived in Lochaber with a sizeable army and had occupied Inverlochy. A well-attested tradition claims that the messenger was none other than Iain Lom, the bard of Keppoch, whose magnificent poetry would reflect the major events of Scottish history through the Restoration, to Killiecrankie and the Union of 1707. A hastily convened council of war concluded that since the lands of Keppoch, Clan Ranald, Locheil, and Glengarry were at risk, it was essential to double back to tackle the threat to the rear.

Argyll had indeed followed Montrose's trail through Benderloch, Appin, and Lochaber where he was now firing the Braes, but when he injured his face and arms in a fall from his horse the command was entrusted to Sir Duncan Campbell of Auchinbreck, a highly experienced and respected soldier recently returned from Ireland. He commanded some three thousand men. On 31 January Argyll wrote from Inverlochy to the Captain of Dunstaffnage, ordering him to send ammunition, supplies, and boats as quickly as possible.[16] That same Friday morning Montrose 'began that flank march which is one of the greatest exploits in the history of British arms'.[17]

A less resourceful leader would have been trapped between two armies with no obvious means of escape. Instead he took to the hills in the depths of winter. From Loch Ness his army entered Glen Tarff, turning south-west at Cullachy to march parallel to the Great Glen, concealed by the long ridge of Meall a'Cholumain. Guards were posted to watch 'the beaten roads' at Cullachy and Aberchalder while the main body advanced up Glen Buck. At the head of the glen the steep pass of Allt na Larach put them well over the two thousand-foot contour. They continued southwards by the headwaters of the Turret and into Glen Roy whose steep sides took them down to Keppoch where the Roy meets the Spean. There they encountered and killed some of Argyll's troops who had been harrying the Braes. The survivors fled to Inverlochy with the incredible news. Having waited three hours to allow the slower part of his force to catch up, Montrose crossed the Spean at the ford of Dalnabea and led his army through Leanachan to command a view across Acha a'Chatha, 'the field of battle', towards Inverlochy Castle. In thirty-six hours his followers had marched a good thirty miles through 'country known to none but drovers and hunters in pursuit of deer'. Most of them had 'not taisted a bitte of bread these two days, maircheing high mountaines in knee deepe snow, and widdeing brookes and rivers up to there girdle.' Wet, weary, and hungry they stood to arms throughout the frosty moonlit night, the silence broken only by the odd skirmish between rival scouts, exchanges deliberately encouraged by Montrose, it was said, for fear that Argyll would withdraw during the night. According to tradition the guide on this heroic march was Iain Lom. When Alasdair asked him, 'Iain will you go with us?', he replied, 'No, I shall be a spectator of your prowess, and if you do well today, I will tell it as well as I can to your praise tomorrow.'[18] So it was that on the morning of Sunday 2 February, Iain climbed 'the brae above the castle of Inverlochy'. His superb poem contains a reference to 'the enthusiam' generated by the bravery of Clan Donald as they ascended the 'spur of Culachy', which would suggest that he was indeed present on the march.

Iain Lom's poetry and Gaelic tradition both testify that the march from Kilcumin, culminating in the rout at Inverlochy, transcended the struggle between king and covenant. The exertions of Montrose and Alasdair were nothing short of epic. In another poem '*Soraidh do'n Ghramach*', a song of greeting to the Graham, Iain flattered Montrose by listing all those who rallied to him – the MacLeans, the men of Atholl, Clan Chattan, the Lamonts, the MacLachlans 'and all who are allied to them', with John Stewart of Appin and MacNab from Glen Dochart. Most important of all were Clan Donald, 'the men with the fair locks and red shield-bosses'. MacMhuirich also included a proud roll-call of the heroes of Inverlochy. In addition to Alasdair, Sir Lachlan MacLean and Iain Muideartach with his son, there was Angus Mac-Donald of Glengarry whose grandfather, Domhnull MacAonghais mhic Alasdair, was to die on the day of the battle over one hundred years of age. There too was 'a good man of the nobles of Scotland', the Earl of Airlie with his son Sir Thomas. Airlie and Montrose breakfasted on 'a little meale, mixt with cold water, which out of a hollow dishe, they did picke up with there knyves for want of spoones'.[19] Nor did MacMhuirich forget the Irish contingent: Magnus O'Cahan, 'son of the Giolla Dubh Mac Cathan', commanded his regiment on the left wing, while Colonel James MacDonald, descendant of the great Somhairle Buide, commanded the Irish reserve behind the van. Colonel James planted his colours on a small knoll beside the main road opposite Auchandaull Farm; its name, Tom na Brataich, the banner knoll, still commemorates the event. Alasdair's regiment was given the right wing and Montrose commanded the centre comprising Clan Ranald, the Mac-Donalds of Glengarry and Glencoe, the MacLeans, the Athollmen, and the Appin Stewarts. Sir Thomas Ogilvie led the few horsemen whose mounts, their 'hoofs worn to pieces', had survived the long march.

During the night Argyll withdrew to his galley *An Dubh Luidneach*, which lay in Loch Linnhe, a prudent action thought Gordon of Ruthven who criticized Montrose's folly in hazardously exposing himself at Fyvie, and who refused to believe the widely circulated stories of Argyll's cowardice. Sir James Rollo, Sir John Wauchope of Niddrie and Mr Mungo Law, a preacher, all of whom found themselves appointed as observers in these unfamiliar surroundings by the Committee, found similar shelter on the loch. Auchinbreck commanded his clansmen in the centre with a reserve behind. A detachment of Campbells was placed on both wings, the six companies of Leven's regiment being equally distributed between them. Forty or fifty men were placed in Inverlochy Castle and a field piece was placed on the vantage point just north of the modern hotel from where a good view of the battle-site can still be obtained. To the south-east Glen Nevis is guarded by *Beinn neamh-bhathais*, popularly etymologized as the mountain with its summit in the sky. Auchinbreck's line is today bounded on the right by the aluminium works, on the left by a railway goods yard. The royalists approached from the direction of Leanachan woods to the north-east, as at Tibbermore employing a long line extending across the valley.

Montrose commanded about fifteen hundred men but some of the Farquharsons, Clan Ranald, and the Athollmen had returned home with booty. Catholic prayers were offered before battle commenced. O'Cahan was sent against Auchinbreck's right with orders to withhold fire until he could shoot lead into the breasts of the enemy. He went one better and held off until he 'fired their beards'. The Campbells could no more stand their ground than could the veterans of Marston Moor. Alasdair assaulted the left wing which also broke. The van, led by Montrose himself, advanced against Auchinbreck's centre, firing at close quarters and charging 'in a close bodie with such strength and furie as they ware forced to give backe upon there reire', which, instead of either opening to receive them or standing to present covering fire, turned and ran. Some tried to escape the merciless claymores and Lochaber axes by making for the castle but Sir Thomas Ogilvie headed them off.

'A little after the sun was up both armies met,' wrote Montrose, 'and the rebels fought for some time with great bravery, the prime of the Campbells giving the first onset, as men that deserved to fight in a better cause. Our men, having a nobler cause, did wonders, and came immediately to push of pike and dint of sword, after this first firing.' He claimed that he would have prevented the ensuing slaughter had it been within his power to do so. Fifteen hundred of the enemy reputedly lost their lives. Many died where the waters of Nevis enter the loch. Some tried to escape into Glen Nevis where their graves are still pointed out. Others fled to what is now Fort William to be cut down at the foot of the Cow Hill. Alasdair pursued the defeated along the upper Auchintore road which skirts the Mamores on its way to Loch Leven. Near Loch Lundaura he gave up the chase. There, according to tradition, he erected a cairn 'Clach nam Caimbeulach'; 'every Campbell or sympathiser with Argyll throws down the topmost stone, every MacDonald or admirer of Montrose with equal duty replaces it.'[20] Ewen of Treshnish was wounded when he intervened to prevent an Atholl sword despatching Campbell of Skipness, one of his late comrades-in-arms in Ireland. Few of Sliochd Diarmaid were so fortunate. Auchinbreck was given the choice of death by the rope or the sword. His reply became proverbial, 'dha dhiu gun aon roghainn', 'two evil alternatives that give no room for choice'.[21] Alasdair understood that kind of language. Tradition says in any case that Auchinbreck died by his own hand.

Iain Lom exulted on his hillside.

The most pleasing news every time it was announced about the wry-mouth Campbells, was that every company of them as they came along had their heads battered with sword blows.

When the great work of blood-letting came to a height at the time of unsheathing slender swords, the claws of the Campbells lay on the ground with sinews severed.

He celebrated the prowess of Iain Muideartach 'of the bright sails' and condemned the faithlessness of the Gordons, but for him the hero of the hour was Alasdair, 'of the sharp venomous blades'.

Alasdair, son of handsome Coll, expert at breaking castles asunder, you routed the sallow-skinned Lowlanders, and if they had drunk kail you knocked it out of them.

Were you familiar with the Goirtean Odhar? Well was it manured, not by the dung of sheep or goats, but by the blood of Campbells after it had congealed.

Perdition take you if I feel pity for your plight, as I listen to the distress of
your children, lamenting the company which was in the battlefield, the
wailing of the women of Argyll.[22]

This victory 'much diminished Argyll's credit among his own followers,
to whom this day was very fatal,' wrote Menteith, 'because it broke
the band wherewith he kept those poor Highlanders attached to
his interest.' When the fortunate Campbell of Skipness was brought
before Montrose he condemned the cowardice of his chief. According to Montrose himself the prisoners laid 'all the blame on their chief'.
But the cruellest, most tragic, and most bitter indictment of all
was articulated in the 'Lament of the Widow of Campbell of Glen
Faochain'.

> O, I am sorely wounded since the day of the Battle of
> Inverlochy. The Irishmen's onset was searing, they
> who came to Scotland empty-handed, who owned not even
> a cloak; they gave mettle to Clan Donald.
>
> They slew my father and my husband and my
> three fine young sons; my four brothers hewn
> asunder, and my nine comely foster-brothers.
>
> O, I am spent on account of Campbell of Glen
> Faochain. Every man in this land weeps for you;
> Here and there about Inveraray women wring their
> hands, their hair dishevelled.
>
> O, I am despoiled on account of the rider of
> bridled and pillioned horses who fell in battle
> with his followers. Great MacCailein took himself
> off to sea, and he let this stroke fall on
> his kin.[23]

For his part Montrose lost four men (MacMhuirich says seven) with
two hundred wounded, though royalist apologists were notoriously
generous in their underestimates. One casualty was Sir Thomas
Ogilvie who died a few days after the battle from a leg wound.
Even if Montrose's figures are suspect his casualty list was surprisingly
small. He was beginning to appear invincible. The depredations suffered by the Campbells in Argyll placed them at a psychological disadvantage which the failings of their natural leader intensified. The
hardened troops of Leven's regiment could not cope with a force that
materialized in the dead of winter out of snow-covered mountains,

'a region which no army had ever yet traversed'. They were totally unnerved by the steady, determined advance of warriors who appeared impervious to shot and who held their fire until the last possible moment before laying about them with broadswords and battle-axe. They were opposed by a new kind of combatant, employing ancient time-honoured methods but showing scant regard for the conventions of contemporary warfare. Several prisoners admitted that 'they had been seized with so great a panic at the sight of the royalists and papists that their weapons fell from their hands'.[24] Perhaps above all the Lowland companies were defeated by the environment, gripped by the old near-superstitious phobias about the unknown deserts of mountain, moor, and loch west of the Highland line. There is a suspicion that many of the Lowlanders who fled towards Inverlochy Castle surrendered a shade too readily in order to save themselves from the murderous blades of the Gaels. They were certainly prompt to accept Montrose's offer of parole, an alternative not presented to the hapless Campbells.

On 3 February the aged chief of Clan Cameron arrived in person to congratulate Montrose. That same day the victorious general conveyed the good news to his king. He expressed his uneasiness about reports that Charles would shortly reach an accommodation with parliament:

I am in the fairest hopes of reducing this kingdom to your Majesty's obedience. And, if the measures I have concerted with your other loyal subjects fail me not, which they hardly can, I doubt not before the end of this summer I shall be able to come to your Majesty's assistance with a brave army, which, backed with the justice of your Majesty's cause, will make the rebels in England, as well as in Scotland, feel the just rewards of Rebellion. Only give me leave, after I have reduced this country to your Majesty's obedience, and conquered from Dan to Beersheba, to say to your Majesty then, as David's General did to his master, 'Come thou thyself, lest this country be called by my name'. For in all my actions I aim only at your Majesty's honour and interest, as becomes one that is to his last breath, your Majesty's most humble, most faithful and most obedient Subject and Servant.[25]

After giving his army a well-deserved rest he marched up the Great Glen once again 'with incredibill diligens'. His route lay through Stratherrick on the southern side of Loch Ness and into Strathnairn where he paused to consider a descent upon Inverness. Since the town was well prepared to withstand a lengthy siege, he doubled back past

Loch Moy into Strathdearn which led him from the mountains down into Moray. The estates of Culbin (to be totally buried in drifting sand by the end of the century), Brodie, Lethen, Grange Hill, and Duffus, all in the vicinity of Forres, were plundered and burned, a punishment inflicted on all who still refused to join him. Just short of Elgin he was met by three hundred Grants sent by their vacillating laird. At Elgin the northern covenanters, including the Laird of Innes, Seaforth, and his brother MacKenzie of Pluscardine, were holding a committee. Many in the district sought refuge in Innes's Spynie Castle while Seaforth and the 'rest of the committee men fled their own ways' on Montrose's approach. He ordered all true subjects to join the army 'under the pain of burning and slaying of all and whatsoever disobedient persons'.[26]

There was much rejoicing when the army reached the ancient see of the bishops of Moray for Nat Gordon arrived to report that he had put Argyll's safe conduct to good use. He had succeeded in recruiting the support of Lord Gordon who rode rapidly from Gordon Castle to receive a rapturous welcome from Montrose, and they 'supped joyfully together'. The sudden switch of George, Lord Gordon, puzzled contemporaries. Some thought that his honour had been offended by the Estates, others that his father was displeased by his unlikely alliance with the covenant, but he had undoubtedly been alienated by Argyll's harsh treatment of Gordon lands, and his uncle's humiliation at Inverlochy enabled him to declare for the king. Gordon of Ruthven distinguished the ambition of the nobility, 'the pest and plague of the bravest minds', as the curse of Scotland. It was also the personal tragedy of James Graham. While many nobles could see clearly through 'the dazzling mist of the covenant', had no delusions about 'the alluring freedom in anarchy', and confessed their allegiance to monarchy, Ruthven was amazed that they had apparently degenerated so far from their 'birth, blood and gentry, and greatness', as to endure patiently the slavery of the covenant with all its concomitants. He thought that the flaw was present in the very concept of nobility. 'As they are noblemen, they will be all free princes, every one will command, none will they obey. They scorn to be followers, or to receive orders from one whom the king may appoint to be general.' Such, he opined, had always been the old and incurable disease of the Scottish nobility and he cited historical examples which would not have disgraced the works of John

Major. Lord Gordon, however, for the moment, was not possessed of 'this vain estimation of grandeur, this chimera of greatness'. He came in with Lewis and a number of personal dependants. He had little choice. His father remained in self-imposed exile while the Gordon estates were ravaged by king's men and covenanters alike. Montrose was capable of deep friendship, freely given to those who would accept it. Lord Gordon was one such although the two men would know one another intimately for only four-and-a-half months.

There might have been further cause of rejoicing when George MacKenzie, Earl of Seaforth, presented himself at Elgin, but he was suspect and Montrose had him arrested. He was released on signing the Kilcumin Band, undertaking to raise the MacKenzies 'from Lewis and every other country he possessed'.[27] Montrose took care to defend himself against possible attack from the south or east by drawing all the Spey ferry boats to the northern bank and by guarding all the fords on the river. Elgin bought protection at a cost of £1300 but the Grants could not be restrained from burning the town, a pleasure to which Montrose left them as he marched to Bog of Gicht. Fearful of further trouble in the vicinity of Inverness, he sent Seaforth to hold it and, as it turned out, to betray his word. MacKenzie as ever was too preoccupied with local feuds, too distracted by the presence of a covenanting garrison, to meet his obligations to Montrose.

At the Bog, Montrose suffered the sad loss of a veteran of Aberdeen, of the long march, and of Inverlochy. There his fifteen-year-old son Lord Graham died of a 'seiknes' nurtured by the hardship and exposure of a Highland winter. He was buried in the graveyard of nearby Bellie parish kirk. Two months later his cousin Lady Keir still wore mourning. His father had to keep his grief to himself. The new heir was Lord James who, two weeks later, was seized by the covenanters at Montrose and carried off to Edinburgh Castle. Before the end of April, Southesk was ordered to present his grandson Robert to the Committee. Young Robert was then returned to his mother's safekeeping at Auld Montrose.

From the Bog the Farquharsons, eager for action having missed Inverlochy, were sent to raid the Earl of Findlater's estates at Cullen. The earl departed, leaving his lady to preside over the heartbreak of a rifled household. When Montrose arrived she begged him not to burn the mansion, offering a payment of 20,000 merks for fifteen days' grace.

A quarter of that sum was accepted in advance. The army moved along the northern coast, looting all in its path from the books and goods of the local minister at the Boyne to everything of value in Banff, including the clothes of its inhabitants, but the support which should have followed Gordon's switch of allegiance was not forthcoming and Montrose turned south along the Deveron to Turiff.

Argyll reached Edinburgh on 12 February 'sore lamenting the loss of his kin and friends, but chiefly the loss of his honour' and still sporting his arm in a sling. It was said the *MacCailein* 'pretended that he had not actually been beaten, though he acknowledged he might have been'.[28] Lord Balmerino risked the charge of perjury by informing the Committee that only thirty covenanters had perished at Inverlochy. Argyll once again received the formal thanks and admiration of the men who thought themselves to be his masters. The Committee ordered Baillie to advance from Perth with six companies of foot. Two companies which Argyll had quartered on Aberdeen were now scattered throughout the north-east. These were to rendezvous with Balcarres' horse and Sir James Halket's horse at Aberdeen under the command of Sir John Hurry, a man whom Baillie could not abide. Not for his right hand would he have recommended Hurry for state service though in spite of that soldier's chequered career, Baillie 'doubted nothing of his honesty'.[29] After the 'incident' Captain Hurry joined the parliamentarians, only to desert to Rupert. He received his knighthood for passing on useful information about the movements of his late employers and though he fought for the royalists at Marston Moor he once again attached himself to parliament. An Aberdonian, he was recalled to Scotland about the same time as Baillie. His remarkable career was to include yet another switch of allegiance for though he opposed Montrose at Auldearn he later joined him, accompanying him into exile, and he returned to defeat and execution in 1650. With Sir James Turner he had swallowed the dangerous maxim, 'so we serve our master honestlie, it is no matter what master we serve'.[30]

On 11 February the Estates formally forfeited the honours and property of James Graham, a doom to which was added a renewal of the sentence of excommunication. Robert Baillie admitted that the defeat at Inverlochy 'did extreamlie amaze us. I verilie think had Montrose come presentlie from that battell, he should have had no great opposition . . . scarce till he came to Edinburgh. But God, in mercie to us, put other thoughts in his heart: he went incontinent northward.' To the consternation of Baillie and his fellows, however, James Graham, having conquered 'from Dan to Beersheba', proceeded to march 'incontinent' southwards.

10

THE FREEDOM OF A KINGDOM AND A CROWN

We need not praise thee, let thy passive Foes
Tell their destruction; whilst our Nation owes,
In compensation for the blood that's spilt,
Memorials of thy glory, and their guilt;
Who tempted first thy Loyaltie, to dare,
With private valour, t'undertake a Warre
Against a Multitude, Fortune alone
Favouring to bring future successes one;
But now thy sword hath so destructive been,
In spight of force and danger, that the sinne
Of bolder Treason henceforth seemes to bee
The presage of thy further Victorie.
Whilst thy successful Arme sustaines alone
The freedome of a Kingdome and a Crowne.

'Some lines upon Montrose',
George, Lord Gordon 1645

The canny Aberdonians, heedful of yet another royalist descent upon their city, sent representatives to Turriff to remind Montrose of the hapless plight of their citizens. After hearing them patiently he assured them that he wished nothing except entertainment at his own expense and he promised to forbid the Irish to approach within eight miles of the city. Nat Gordon had already visited Aberdeen, confiscating weapons and skirmishing haphazardly in the vicinity; he returned to join his leader in plundering Frendraught of livestock and victuals. The Aberdonians were ordered to muster at Inverurie for the king's service as were individual Gordons who still failed to rally to the banner. The response, while gratifying, was not wholly satisfactory. Each parish in the shire was then ordered to furnish two commissioners with an accurate roll of all feuars, heritors, and liferenters in order that they might be assessed for supply.

Nat Gordon went back to Aberdeen with Donald Farquharson, Captain Mortimer, and some eighty horsemen, apparently intent upon nothing more serious than a few days 'on the town', neglecting to post guard or watch while they sought out liquid refreshment. Spies promptly reported their presence to Hurry who immediately brought one hundred and sixty of Balcarres' horse from the North Water of Esk. He marched calmly into Aberdeen, closed the gates, and took the carousers completely by surprise. The 'pride o' Braemar' was shot dead in the street. Several others were killed, wounded, or captured, the royalist horses seized, and Gordon himself escaped only with the greatest difficulty. Hurry's action was as spontaneous as that of the royalists for he withdrew at once to the town of Montrose. His prisoners included Farquharson's brother-in-law Angus MacQueen of Corrybrough who joined Donald Òg and Alasdair when they entered Strathdearn. John Douglas who carried the *clàrsach* or harp for his master Neil Campbell had been forced to accompany the royalists since his capture at Inverlochy. James Low, 'a poor tailzeour boy', had gone to the city to seek a master. Thomas Leyes of Elgin was a groom who swore he had never borne arms. Another captured in the stables was George Lobban, forced to accompany the king's men on pain of hanging. Alexander MacCall was a boatwright whose useful talents had been recruited at Inverlochy by a loyal Stewart who promised 'he should cutt the head aff him lyk a dog' if he resisted. An Irish prisoner Duncan Gilmour did not attempt excuses but Hew McVayne of County Tyrone, a surgeon in Captain Mortimer's company who had travelled with Alasdair to Ardnamurchan and Skye, deponed that at the battle of Aberdeen 'he wes sitting on a know-heid, looking on'. He missed Inverlochy since he had gone to Blair Castle to tend to wounded and had been arrested while visiting Aberdeen to purchase some drugs; he was illiterate. Cormac MacIver, born in Trotternish, Skye, claimed that Hurry had made a big mistake for when taken he was 'begging throw the cuntrie with two bairnes'; he knew no one in Aberdeen or its environs.[1]

Gordon of Ruthven who might have enjoyed a distinguished career as an obituary writer, testifies to Donald Òg's loyalty, courage, and popularity. A shamefaced Nat Gordon miserably reported the loss to

Montrose. When the Aberdonians speedily protested that his death was not their fault, Montrose, 'hard thame patientlie with ane wo hairt, yit knew weill aneuche who wes innocent or guiltie of this mater within the toune'.[2] Alasdair quartered his troops at Brig o' Dee and Two Mile Cross, and Donald, who had been one of the first to rise for the king back in 1639, was buried with full military honours, 'trailing of pikes and thundering volley of muskets', in the chapel on Castlehill. On the whole Alasdair's men were well behaved, confining themselves to spoiling the houses of two notorious covenanters, but their presence invalidated Montrose's promise and the fears of the Aberdonians were realized. When Mac Cholla withdrew, some of his 'Irishes' remained behind searching for cloaks and plaids in order to indulge their craving for cloth and fabrics. Although Alasdair whipped them out of town he appropriated £1440 worth of apparel himself.

When Airlie fell ill with fever, he was sent with a guard of three hundred men to Lethenty, the home of his daughter and her husband, to convalesce while Montrose advanced to Durris where he was rejoined by Alasdair for a further bout of plundering. Since the northern clans were again attacking Strathbogie, five hundred men were detached to defend the area. At Dunnottar Marischal sheltered no fewer than sixteen ministers. Although Marischal's brother George Keith participated in discussions with Montrose and Gordon, the earl at the prompting of his wife and his devout guests refused to join them. He had to watch helplessly as Dunnottar's sustenance was systematically destroyed. Urie, Cowie, and Stonehaven were mercilessly ravaged, ships and fishing boats were sunk, and cottars fled from their smoking dwellings crying for mercy. 'But the poor people gat no answer, nor knew thay quhair to go with thair children.' Nearby the ancient settlement at Fetteresso was plundered, its superb hunting park fired, and its highly prized deer slaughtered like cattle. The pillage continued south to Drumlithie. The month was March. Those who lost their seed and young livestock in such a season faced the certainty of famine. It was a month of unusually severe gales which spread the stench of burning from Strathdearn to Stonehaven and it may be surmised that, as on an earlier occasion, 'the reek infected as mony as it blew upon'. Montrose, like Argyll, failed to realize that the sword and the torch were not the most effective means of winning friends for the cause.

On 22 March the army reached Fettercairn in the Howe of the

Mearns. Hurry encountered a party of troopers sent out from Fettercairn to harass the surrounding countryside but was forced to withdraw when reinforcements were sent to their assistance. The citizens of Brechin hid their possessions in the castle and the kirk steeple before fleeing from the invaders who vented their wrath by burning sixty houses while a detachment was assigned to seek supplies at Montrose. At Brechin it was learned that Baillie was close by with a large contingent drawn from the regiments of Lothian and Loudoun. In addition to the horse commanded by Hurry he expected to receive reinforcements of fifteen hundred 'redcoats' from Ireland. His commanders included Lord Lindsay (who had usurped the Earl of Crawford's title), Balmerino, and the earls of Cassilis and Kirkcudbright. Both sides were evenly matched in infantry with about three thousand each but the covenanters had twice the number of cavalry – between six and seven hundred – well horsed and well trained since they benefited from considerable experience in England. Montrose was not dismayed. He marched in full view of the enemy along the northern bank of the Esk before striking through Kirriemuir, Airlie, and Ruthven towards the Isla where the two armies occupied opposite banks 'within musket shot', but without conflict save for the odd skirmish between scouting parties. Baillie was either content, or was forced by his noble associates, to play a waiting game which had a corrosive effect on royalist nerves. At a point on the Isla between Alyth and Coupar Angus both armies stood all night in battle formation. When Montrose challenged Baillie to pitched battle on chosen ground the covenanter quite properly retorted that 'he would mind his own business himself'.

On learning of Inverlochy, Charles sent a bearer to Montrose indicating his intention of joining him in the Lowlands. Although the bearer was intercepted and subsequently executed his message must have reached Montrose for he now attempted to oblige the king.[3] He went to Dunkeld in hopes of crossing the Tay but Baillie effectively blocked the route to the south. Some of the Highlanders, wearying of the forced marches in battle order, were beginning to desert and a number of Gordons obtained leave to return home. Such men were always uneasy south of the Highland line. Montrose had no choice except to retreat to the north but 'that it might not appear that he had advanced to the banks of the Tay for nothing, and to keep up the reputation of his arms . . . he was resolved by the way to take Dundee, one of the most disaffected towns to the king that was in the kingdom, and the usual receptacle of all covenanters,'[4] a course made possible by reports that Baillie was south of the Tay. He sent the main part of his army back to Brechin and with Gordon and Alasdair at the head of a force of two hundred horse and eight hundred foot, he advanced towards the city on 4 April.

Wishart asserts that many English and continental students of Montrose's campaigns preferred the march to Dundee to his most famous victories. 'Whether such an account will be believed abroad or in after ages I cannot pretend to say, but it rests on the most certain information and the best of evidence,' wrote Wishart who was less than scrupulous about some of the other adventures that he described. Robert Baillie, on the other hand, rejoiced that at Dundee Montrose experienced a 'great and reall disaster', a point also made by a propagandist, but sober contemporary pamphlet. Neither Gordon nor Spalding dwelt upon the episode and MacMhuirich did not mention it at all. A good twenty-six miles separate Dunkeld and Dundee. Wishart had Montrose cover the distance in ten hours, Menteith in twelve, and the pamphlet in fourteen, any one of which estimates is impressive. On arriving at the town about noon on 5 April, Montrose ordered John Gordon, lying 'halfe sleeping with the rest of Lord Gordon's regiment about Dundee', to take a paper to the magistrates demanding surrender on pain of the by now familiar fire and sword. Gordon later testified that he obeyed but that before he could receive an answer the assault began. Montrose's intelligence had once again failed him for Baillie had halted at Perth from where, on learning of the royalist advance, he sent warning to Dundee, promising that reinforcements were on their way. The wall behind Corbie Hill in the north-west corner of the town was under repair, so enabling Montrose to seize that important vantage point with ease. Corbie's ordnance, which had dissuaded Montrose from attack the previous September, was now trained upon the city's defenders. There Montrose remained while the Highlanders and the Irish broke in through the Western Port and the Nethergate Port. Dundee's defence was led by Lieutenant Cockburn who conducted operations from a chair placed in the street since he suffered from acute gout.[5] By all accounts there was skirmishing throughout the afternoon between the royalists and Cockburn's musketeers, but the Gaels, as was their wont on these rare visits to cities, fell to plunder and drink. About five in the afternoon Montrose was alarmed to see Hurry's horse advancing from the west. He immediately decided upon as orderly a retreat as possible though some urged him to save himself, others that they should prepare to die fighting. 'Montrose concurred with neither. Nothing could ever induce him to abandon his bravest men in their hour of utmost peril. He preferred an honourable death among his men to a base regard for his own safety.'[6] But some of his men were drunk, while others had indulged in other forms of excess with the wenches of Dundee. The town later received a colossal grant of £54,477 for its losses at this time which suggests that the royalists looted more than alcohol. Much plunder, baggage, and ammunition was abandoned in panic. The drink-assisted instinct of some of the Irish was to stand and fight. When two of their officers were killed there was allegedly 'a terrible howling among them, and they fought desperately to recover their bodies [and] one of their faces was so disfigured and mangled by the Irish themselves not being able to carry away his corpse, that it was not possible to discern who he was – some say it was Colkitto, some O'Cahan.'[7]

There can be little doubt that Montrose's presence of mind turned a rout into an orderly, if hard fought, retreat. He sent four hundred ahead and remained himself to command a rearguard consisting of two hundred foot and the horse. This line of horse and musketeers dissuaded Hurry's troopers from over-assiduous pursuit. Baillie fulminated that Hurry failed to charge 'the rebells with our whole horse'; neither would he assign his horse to his superior, 'notwithstanding I did require him to it at several times'.[8] Nonetheless there was fierce skirmishing between Hurry and Montrose before darkness assisted the retreat. Although covenanting claims that Montrose lost four or five hundred killed were grossly exaggerated his losses must have been considerable. Many like John MacAllane, an Antrim man, were captured. Donald MacGregor, 'born in the clachan at the head of Loch Awe' and sometime servant to Captain Hugh MacDougal, slain at Inverlochy, was taken some six miles from Dundee. He had been elevated to the position of Alasdair Mac Cholla's footman and when captured was 'carrying his maisters hatt, cloke and a paire of gloves'![9]

Several commentators such as Murdoch and Simpson and Buchan have needlessly complicated Montrose's route by mistranslating

Wishart's Latin, turning the army south-west at Arbroath to double back to the north later, apparently as some elaborate ruse to outwit their pursuers. Wishart plainly states however that near Arbroath the army marched north-west, *'in occidentem aestivum'*, that is by way of Friockheim, Guthrie, and Melgund Castle in the parish of Aberlemno. Hurry caught the weary royalists at Careston, a ford on the South Esk. The covenanter had sensibly allowed his troops a modicum of food and rest but Montrose's men 'were so overwhelmed with drowsiness that pricks and wounds could hardly stir them up'. Although glossed over by Wishart the last part of the march must have been a nightmare. Hastily beaten and prodded into movement, harried by Hurry's cavalry, 'they did never so much as turn faces about, but marched from one plain to another, many of them fallen from the rest and many were killed by our horse and some of the country people. We have pursued them so quickly that they got neither leave to harm the country nor to take rest or meat to refresh them.' By the time they reached the welcome haven of Glen Esk they had marched over seventy miles in forty-eight hours without food or sleep, exhausted by pillage, whisky, skirmishing, and enemy harassment. Wishart was correct. The Dundee episode was heroic, but it was also misconceived and unnecessary. The capture of the city would have achieved nothing unless Montrose intended joining the king by sea, a possibility nowhere suggested. The most serious flaw was a failure of intelligence similar to that which had let him down at Fyvie. If, in retrospect, the retreat seemed glorious, it was a weary, humiliating, and bitter experience for his loyal followers. Some were killed at Edzell before they could reach the safety of the mountains. The detachment sent to Brechin had taken the precaution of withdrawing to the hills. Montrose was now faced with the task of reorganizing his dispersed and dispirited army.

Lord Gordon and Lewis, both of whom contrary to Wishart's assertions had taken part in the attack on Dundee, were sent to Strathbogie to raise levies, and Alasdair was entrusted with a similar task in Mar. Montrose personally displayed a remarkable amount of energy. Spalding 'had no certainty quhair Montrose went, he wes so obscure', but with five hundred foot and fifty horse he tracked a good fifty miles to Dunkeld, hugging the hilly fringe of Strathmore. On 16 April he was at Borlick in Strathbrane, west of Dunkeld.[10] Through Amulree and the Sma' Glen he passed to Crieff where a small brush with Baillie did not prevent him from moving westwards along Strathearn to Loch Earn which he reached on 18 April. He had so far attracted little new support but he confidently anticipated the imminent arrival of some important recruits.

It can be no coincidence that both Aboyne and the Master of Napier broke through to join Montrose at the same time. Since Marston Moor Sir Thomas Glenham had been holding Carlisle against the Scots. Aboyne had remained with him when Montrose donned his groom's disguise to enter Scotland. On the night of 14 April Aboyne, fired with rumours of Montrose's success, broke out of the besieged city with fourteen followers. He managed to survive 'ane unknown masse of dangeres and ane insnairing laborinth of difficulties', cutting through Annandale, Clydesdale, and Stirlingshire to arrive at Cardross, just south-east of the Lake of Menteith, between 19 and 21 April. At the same time the seventeen-year-old Master of Napier's escape from the confinement of Holyrood Palace, where his father and his brother-in-law Stirling of Keir had been held since the previous autumn, was organized by the two sons of William Alexander, first Earl of Stirling. Montrose was delighted to welcome young Napier and 'ane other stronge branche of that great oak of Huntly', a consistent if ineffectual royalist, with whom his relations would prove not altogether happy. The party withdrew to Loch Katrine in the shelter of the Trossachs.

Charles had promised to send five hundred horse under Sir Philip Musgrave to Montrose's assistance. 'Had I but for one month the use of those five hundred,' wrote Montrose to one close to the king on 20 April, 'I could have seen you before the time that this could come to your hands with twenty thousand of the best this kingdom can afford.' He complained that he had 'continued this half year bygone without the assistance of either Men, Arms, ammunition', or the necessities of war. 'Howsoever though you have not assisted me, I will yet still do my best to bar all assistance coming against you . . . they have been forced presently to draw four regiments of foot from Newcastle down here to oppose me. So long as it pleases God I am alive and free, there shall nothing trouble [the king's] affairs from this.'[11] However desirable the south, the north was again beckoning for word arrived that Gordon was threatened by Hurry. In response Montrose and his party embarked on another of those remarkable marches for which he is so famous.

They crossed the old track by Bealach a' Chonnaidh to the Braes of Balquhidder, up Glen Ogle and along Loch Tay-side to Atholl, thence through the passes to begin the long haul through Angus. Wishart asserts that they went down the strath of Glen Muick 'into the very heart of Mar'. If so they followed the South Esk up to Glen Clova, taking the Capel Mounth track through the hills to Glen Muick. It would have been strange if they had not used the more obvious and direct route by Glenshee and the Cairnwell but perhaps they did. Only Wishart supplies anything like an exact itinerary and his knowledge was not precise. It is also possible that on these long forced marches, dependent upon local guides, Montrose himself was sometimes none too sure of the country through which he passed. There is still a fine network of tracks and paths through the Grampians, one looking much the same as another to those unfamiliar with the landscape. In Cromar, well over one hundred miles from Cardross, the party joined Gordon and Alasdair both of whom had enlisted some support. On 1 May they marched down Deeside to Skene. Since they were short of powder Aboyne was given the chance to prove his mettle with a swift raid on Aberdeen.

During Montrose's absence Gordon had based himself at Auchindoun Castle near Dufftown, in order to avoid unauthorized conflict with Hurry who, with twelve hundred foot and sixty horse, ravaged Strathbogie and Enzie from 20 April to 2 May. Baillie was ordered into Atholl by the Committee at the beginning of May. During that 'unnecessarie voyage', as he called it, he harried the area and, having decided against an attempt on the military hospital at Blair which doubled as a prison, he began a steady advance through the Grampians. On 2 May Montrose broke camp at Skene to push forward through Strathbogie to Elgin. Although Wishart asserts that the royalists surprised Hurry, the historians of the north-east, who are generally much better informed on these matters, describe his orderly retreat, first across the Spey and then from Elgin to Forres, deliberately baiting his pursuers all the way. When James Gordon of Rhynie was wounded in one of several skirmishes between the two sides, he was left in a cottar's house to recuperate, only to be discovered by a group of Inneses who murdered him. Hurry continued his westward march to Inverness where he called up Lawer's, Buchanan's and Loudoun's regiments and consulted Seaforth who 'wes thocht to be ane perfidious traittour efter he was deiplie suorne be Montross to the kingis service'.[12] He was joined by the earls of Sutherland and Findlater and by the Inneses, Rosses, Munros, Frasers, Dunbars, MacIntoshes, and the followings of other northern lairds, a total in all of about four thousand foot and five hundred horse. On the night of Thursday 8 May Montrose's force of three thousand foot and horse camped at Auldearn. Montrose later estimated Hurry's force to consist of three hundred horse and between four and five thousand foot 'whereof there were four of the best trained regiments they had in the three kingdoms'. He also claimed that he himself commanded 'horse and foot about fourteen hundred men', a figure possibly dictated by the necessities of propaganda.

The presbytery of Forres in 1649 described Auldearn as 'a large landward paroch consisting of 16 hundreth communicable'. The language of the parish was partly English and partly Gaelic.[13] The village, two miles from the sea, is the same distance east of Nairn. The Boath Doocot stood and still stands on the Castlehill on the west of the township, flanked from south to north by what must have been very boggy ground before agricultural improvement, several place-names in the area testifying to the marshy nature of the terrain, though the ground is rolling and undulating rather than level. A road to Newmill, Kinsteary, and Brightmony lies to the south; another runs south-west to Grigorhill and west of it is the farm of Kinnudie. A dip behind the woods now flanking the east side of the Newmills road would provide sufficient concealment from an army marching from the west. Auldearn is the most fully documented of all Montrose's battles. Suitably interpreted there is broad agreement between the various accounts while, significantly, even the most partial writers are generous in praise of others; the glory was equally distributed.

Montrose's system of intelligence was such that he was probably unaware of Baillie's advance through the Grampians. He did post scouts but his consistent neglect of adequate intelligence, particularly in hostile territory, was one of the most surprising, and potentially dangerous, aspects of his military career. It is clear that he was taken unawares by Hurry's rapid night march through torrential rain from Inverness. He received advance warning only by chance when the covenanters fired their sodden muskets to clear them before the attack. Although they took the precaution of testing them by the sea to deaden the noise, the shots were heard by royalist scouts, Nat Gordon among them, who promptly raised the alarm. Montrose put to good use a hasty survey of Auldearn's topography carried out the previous night. He placed Alasdair on strong ground 'a little before the town', a location confirmed by Wishart's description of 'ground which happened to be defended by dykes and ditches, brushwood and rocks' as the dog-leg hollow south-west and south of Castlehill.

Confusion about the exact disposition of the Gordons probably arose from Montrose's interesting tactics, for he effectively established two lines. Alasdair commanded the MacDonalds, the Irish, and a detachment of Gordons, his line extending south-east and south across the present main road and protected by existing dykes and ditches which were supplemented by hastily constructed trenches. Mac Cholla entrusted his right wing to Aboyne who placed himself on the Castlehill. This explains why MacMhuirich, for example, credits Alasdair with command of the left wing of the entire army – he was positioned on the left of the Boath line while Aboyne and Nat Gordon were on the right. The Clan Ranald *seanchaidh* has a story about the Gordons approaching Alasdair, 'the red-armed knight', to ask him to allow a number of Gordons and MacDonalds to exchange positions in obscure fulfilment of an ancient agreement to the effect that neither clan ever struck a blow against the other. Alasdair obliged because the Gordons had none of the experience of his own veterans. After a hesitant beginning the alliance worked. Some of the Gordons, who 'could not hear the sough of an arrow or the whistling of a ball without bowing their heads or flying about', were cut down by their own officers to prevent flight but the remainder recovered sufficiently to perform heroic feats, inspired by that 'good knight and fortunate warrior' Nat Gordon, *Gordonach Caoch*. The royal banner was planted behind Alasdair's line to draw the main fire, while Montrose himself, having given Alasdair strict instructions not to move from his position, withdrew to the concealment of the hollows east of the Newmills road, from where he commanded the remainder of the foot. Lord Gordon, who specifically requested Ewen of Treshnish as his personal bodyguard, commanded the cavalry. The plan, and it was brilliant, was to lure Hurry towards Alasdair's lines whereupon Montrose would launch a flank attack.

Hurry advanced to Kinnudie, due west of Montrose's position. There is also some difficulty about the exact deployment of his troops. The most confident contemporary statement about their positions occurs in Gordon of Sallagh – 'Hurry ordered his men thus: the Laird of Lawers hade the van; Hurry his own hors from the south were appointed to preserve the right wing of his foot; and the hors of Murray, and of the north countrie, were appointed to guard the left wing; and one Captain Drummond was directed to be their leader. The Earls of Sutherland and Seaforth were with Hurry in the reserve.'[14] That Sir Mungo Campbell of Lawers, recently returned from Ireland, held the centre is certain. He also commanded detachments of Lothian's and Loudoun's which had wintered at Inverness. Buchanan's men may, as Sallagh and Montrose assert, have remained behind to guard Inverness, but the former must be wrong in giving Drummond command of the covenanting left; it will become clear that that unhappy officer must have led the right. MacMhuirich asserts that in the battle Alasdair's men encountered MacKenzies, who were probably among the northern levies on Lawer's left. Hurry himself stayed in the rear with Sutherland and Seaforth. Although the covenanters took the lure, Alasdair almost ruined everything.

'A brave man, but readier with his hand than with his head, hasty in battle and bold to rashness, stung by the taunts and scoffs of the enemy, he disdained to shelter himself behind dykes and bushes, and contrary to orders, threw himself with his men, outside of their strong position.' Twice his yellow banner advanced against the Campbells and twice he was forced back into his original position. Precluded from movement to the left by marshy ground and hampered by hesitant Gordons on his right, his weakened ranks were subjected to a frontal assault by Lawer's regiment. The 'valiant Alasdair' was a giant in the fight; 'covering himself with a huge targe, single-handed he withstood the thickest of the enemy.' He broke his sword but seized another to scythe through pikes embedded in his shield. The enemy bowmen rained arrows on his position. By his side died a brother-in-law MacKay of Ardnacross, as did an Irishman Feardorcha Magee and several others before he could reoccupy his original position. Ranald mac Domnuill from Mull took an arrow through both cheeks, was wounded by no fewer than five pikes when his sword stuck in his scabbard, and narrowly escaped death at the hands of a pikeman who, stooping to pass through a doorway, had his head sliced off by Alasdair; but Ranald lived to tell of his experiences. Alasdair, even in retreat cutting swathes in enemy ranks, achieved 'what was unpossible to be don by any other but himselfe', but fearing that all was lost he prepared to die on the spot.

> Health and joy to the valiant Alasdair who won the battle of
> Auldearn with his army;
> You were not a feeble poltroon engaging in the crossing of swords
> when you were in the enclosure alone.
> Helemeted men with pikes in their hands were attacking you with all
> their might until you were relieved by Montrose.[15]

Montrose had been about to attack Hurry's flank as planned when he received word that Alasdair had been routed. In his hesitation his position was detected by Hurry who ordered his right wing to meet the threat. To his horror the order was misheard by Captain Drummond and the line turned left instead of right, so exposing their backs to the royalists. Montrose seized his opportunity. 'Our friend MacDonald on the right has routed the enemy and is slaughtering the fugitives!' he cried to Lord Gordon. 'Shall we look on idly and see him carry off the honours of the day?' He immediately sent in Gordon's cavalry who jettisoned their pistols and carabines to execute a very successful sword charge to cries of 'Remember Donald Farquharson and James of Rhynie!' Simultaneously Aboyne, recognizing Alasdair's desperate situation, charged the enemy left, heedless of a hail of fire 'as he semed by the thick smok throw which he went, to assalt a terrible cloud of thunder and lightening'. He captured the covenanters' colours but neglecting to furl them he distracted his brother from pursuit since the latter thought they represented a fresh enemy assault. Alasdair paused to praise the valiant Gordons before, joined by Montrose, he crashed over the dykes to fall upon the centre. 'The bold and warlike clan of the MacDonalds and of the truly fierce, very brave, powerfully spirited band of the Clan Ranald, forced the enemy manfully and bravely without the fear or terror of strokes or shots.' Hurry's cavalry fled though he himself was last to leave the field. Lawer's and Lothian's courageous veterans stood their ground to die in the fury of 'killing and goring underfoot'.[16] Montrose related a somewhat different version of the battle.

Allwayes finding myselfe ingaged, and that the longer I delayed they should increase and I diminish, I resolved to fight, but chosed my posts and all advantages of ground, and to bide them at the defence. So they being confident both of their men and their number fell hotly on, but being beat backe, seimed to coole of their fury, and only intended to blocke us up (as it wer) till more number should come, which perceiving, I divided myself in two wings (which was all the ground would suffer) and marched upon them most unexpectedly, and after some hot salvyes of musket and a litell dealing with sword and pike, they took the chase.

The old prophecy had been fulfilled with a vengeance –

> Betwixt Arr, Boath and the Sea,
> Many a corpse shall buried be,

for the covenanting casualties were put at two thousand. Montrose optimistically exaggerated enemy casualties – 'they left three thousand of ther foot slaine in the place, and had all ther horse killed and scattered'. MacMhuirich is one of the few to concede that royalist casualties were significant. Wishart on the other hand says that Montrose lost one soldier and a few Irish, while Spalding debits twenty-four gentlemen and a few Irish, Gordon notes sixteen casualties of which fourteen were Irish, and only Sallagh estimates a more realistic two hundred dead with Hurry losing one thousand men. William Baillie states that Hurry lost all of his twelve hundred foot at Auldearn and Robert Baillie puts the figure at one thousand. When Iain Lom describes Alasdair in the enclosure 'alone', he refers poetically to the severe casualties to which both MacMhuirich and Highland tradition allude. In the view of Lowland writers the Gaels were expendable and possibly Highlanders and Irish were excluded from the final totals. It is certain that many of the covenanting deaths were needless. 'No quarter' was the revenge for Farquharson and Rhynie and a majority of the two thousand perished in the pursuit which continued as far as Inverness. Covenanting Scotland was well represented in the carnage. Lord Gordon arranged an honourable burial for Sir Mungo Campbell of Lawers, 'a good Christian and expert commander'. With him there died a Colonel Campbell, captains Campbell, Bruce, Cashore, and Shaw, and five lieutenants. Captain Drummond was subsequently court martialled for misinterpreting Hurry's order and was shot on the high road to Tomnahurich. From the Borders the dead included Murray of Philiphaugh, 'two Gledstanes of Whitelaw and nine nephews of Douglas of Cavers'.[17] Many MacKenzies were slain,

Seaforth escaping 'on horseback after losing his men and his honour'.
At least eighty-seven Fraser widows mourned their husbands.

> There was not a Dunky or Kenny in the land of MacKenzie, who did
> not abandon his firearms on the moorland moss.
> There was not a Tommie or Simmie in the lands of Lord Lovat who
> did not escape into hiding holes everywhere.

Lord Lovat who was 'in deep mourning for relations who died a
natural death by the hand of God', had now to lament 'for such of them
as are killed by the hand of men'. A cousin had died earlier in the year
'being sick of the times we live in', and he was sure his own time was at
hand.[18] Many were killed in the vicinity of Kinsteary and Brightmony.
Local tradition, which betrays no affection for catholic Gaels, has it
that Alasdair tricked Hay of Kinnudie in a hand-to-hand struggle by
telling him that he was being attacked from behind, whereupon he
stabbed him in the back.[19]

> Many a blue eye'd youth, wounded by the naked blades, lay
> beyond speech at the gates of Kinnudie.[20]

These and others found a mass grave in Dead Man's Wood just
south-west of Auldearn. Captains Crichton and MacKenzie were distinguished in death by monuments erected above them in Auldearn
churchyard. In terms of tactics, military genius, and sheer heroism,
Auldearn probably ranks as the finest victory of Montrose and Alasdair;
it was also one of the bloodiest.

Montrose allowed the victors two days' rest before advancing to
Elgin to seek medicines, and surgeons to tend the wounded. The
flames of Nairn and Elgin spread to Cullen and Frendraught as the
royalists were quartered throughout the district. Any thoughts of a
rapid march on Inverness to capitalize on the victory were dispelled by
the news that Baillie had arrived in Cromar where he was joined by
Balcarres with two regiments of redcoats. Baillie advanced to the
Wood of Cocklarachy two miles south of Huntly to be joined by
Hurry who, with one hundred horse, had managed to penetrate
Montrose's lines. Hurry, however, had fought for the covenant for the
last time. Pleading sickness he left Baillie and shortly thereafter he
transferred his allegiance, once again, to the royalists. The royalists
prepared for battle, withdrawing to 'places of advantage about the

yards and dykes', supplemented by hastily constructed breastworks. The covenanters stood embattled throughout the night of 21 May only to discover next morning that Montrose had slipped along the Deveron to Mortlach and Balvenie Castle. As Baillie followed, Montrose moved south-west through Glen Rinnes to Glen Livet where the two armies were in sight of one another. Next morning the quarry had again disappeared but Baillie 'by the lying of the grass and heather, conjectured they were marched to the wood of Abernethy upon Spey'.[21] From Invereshie on the south bank of the Spey Montrose wrote to Robertson of Inver, intimating his imminent arrival in Atholl and ordering an exchange of prisoners. He was particularly anxious to secure the release of John, Lord Napier's stepbrother, 'against whom they intend to insist and proceid in ane seiming legall way, which gif they doe . . . I will use the lyk severitie against some of ther prisoners'.[22] Negotiations were already under way for the release of Montrose's natural brother Harry, captured at Newcastle and sent to Edinburgh, and for that of Colla Ciotach and two of Alasdair's brothers confined by Argyll since 1639.

Montrose camped at Ruthven of Badenoch near Kingussie while Baillie's troops looked on hungry and helpless as the royalists consumed meat and provisions seized on the march. Desultory skirmishing gained no advantage for either side. Baillie was forced to visit Inverness for supplies; by 3 June he had once again crossed to the east bank of the Spey and was camped at Newtown in Garioch, 'distroying the countrie, and eating the grein growing cornes to the very clod'. Meanwhile Montrose, having learned that Crawford-Lindsay was at Newtyle, rapidly marched to Angus on the proven principle of 'divide and conquer', sweeping through Glen Feshie and the Forest of Mar to Linn of Dee and south through Clunie and Glen Shee to Glen Isla. His planned attack was foiled by instructions from Aboyne recalling the Gordons to the north. Nat Gordon was despatched to Strathbogie, followed at a short interval by Lord Gordon who, with Aboyne, later rejoined Montrose in Cromar. The Lieutenant-General retraced his steps through Glen Shee to the Braes of Mar. At Braemar itself where Glen Clunie meets the Dee Alasdair departed across the mountains by the Glen Tilt route to recruit further support in the west. On clearing the mountains east of Ballater, Montrose, having learned that Crawford-Lindsay had joined Baillie farther down Deeside, led his depleted force across Glen Gairn to 'the ruined castle of Corgarff' situated near Cockbridge on the Lecht road, leading to Tomintoul, where 'he felt himself safe, being near the mountains'.

Baillie was chastised by letters from the Committee censuring his 'slow prosecution of the warre' and his failure to subdue the enemy. He responded by requesting to be relieved of his command on the grounds that he was inadequately equipped to fulfil their demands and that he was 'altogether unwilling to ruine the forces committed to my charge in wayes both against reason and common sense'. In spite of these misgivings Baillie was tempted to provoke battle with Montrose but some of the covenanting veterans, unpersuaded by the lure of booty and blood, began to question their right to resist the king. These troops, 'on whose valour he most relied', were doubtless suffering from the fatigue of consecutive and apparently pointless marches and were demoralized by successive royalist victories. They claimed they could discern 'no just quarrel' since they felt bound to agree with Montrose, the Gordons, and the Irish who were simply maintaining the king's royal prerogative. If such stories were not simply royalist propaganda, Baillie efficaciously overcame the dilemma of disobedient, not to say mutinous, troops by obeying the strange orders of the Committee, which commanded him to exchange over one thousand of his own veterans for less than half that number of Crawford-Lindsay's raw recruits and to proceed with his depleted force against Montrose. The newcomers thus exchanged a depredatory descent upon Atholl for the furies of the battle of Alford.

At Corgarff Montrose was informed that Baillie was intent upon attacking Gordon Castle. Gordon of Ruthven had a story that the Lieutenant-General had instructions from the king to avoid engaging the enemy before the twenty-fourth of June, 'by reason of some over-ture made to his Majestie by some noblemen of the south, for certane reasones that were very considerable'. But ten days before the deadline expired Charles's cause was irretrievably shattered at Naseby. Montrose moved along Strathdon, turning northwards at Kildrummy, fifteen miles south of Huntly, in order to make some token gesture towards defending the Gordon estates. Baillie was entrenched 'in a narrow difficult pass', now overlaid by the new town of Keith laid out by the Earl of Findlater in the eighteenth century. The royalists threw them-selves into indeterminate skirmishes which achieved nothing owing to the covenanters' strong position. An invitation to pitched battle was hotly rejected by Baillie. Montrose withdrew to Pitlurg a few miles south of Keith and then marched fifteen miles south to Druminnor, seat of Lord Forbes. Montrose was the willing quarry, tempting Baillie after him by pretending retreat. The advancing general had learned that Alasdair was absent and he prepared to press his advantage. Montrose spent two days at Druminnor until he was certain that the bait was taken and then crossed to the Howe of Alford to intercept Baillie's forces, marching due south along the ancient Suie road which crosses the eastern flank of the Coreen Hills at a height of some twelve hundred feet. A local ballad tradition says that Montrose spent the night before the battle in the castle of Asloun.

The River Don irrigates the fertile Howe of Alford. A mile west of the village, a nineteenth-century railhead, the Gallow Hill looks down on the Bridge of Alford and the junction of the A980 and the A944. From the summit long fields sweep down to the cross-roads where Baillie was to take up his positions. Early on the morning of 2 July Montrose placed his army on the alert on the Gallow Hill while he investigated the defensive potential of the ford (at the modern bridge). There he received word that Baillie was making for the ford at Montgarrie a mile to the east, which has also been replaced by a bridge. Baillie was intent on 'buckling the enemy', hoping to outflank Montrose whom he believed to be in retreat. Montrose left a guard at the ford of Alford and swiftly established his positions. To Lord Gordon and Nat Gordon he assigned the right wing, to Aboyne the left, both flanked by Irish musketeers. The centre consisted of some of Clan Ranald, the men of Badenoch, some Athollmen, and a number of other Highlanders, but chiefly those of the Huntly following from Strathbogie and Upper Deeside. Who commanded is uncertain. The honour most likely fell to Angus MacDonald, chief of Glengarry. Wishart also allowed a command to George Drummond of Balloch but Gordon of Ruthven thought that if such was the case 'his part in command could not be much, since he wanted the language and for the most part was unknown of all the Highlanders'. The point is interesting but there is little doubt that one with estates in Perthshire would have Gaelic at this period. Gordon believed that the centre was entrusted to James Farquharson of Inverey, an obscure person but a man whom the Highlanders allegedly both loved and understood, 'for he had their language', was a kindred spirit of Donald's, and was a dependant of the house of Huntly. Montrose took a stance on the rising ground behind his lines, placing the reserve under the Master of Napier out of sight behind the Gallow Hill. He turned his line towards the north-east as Baillie approached from Montgarrie, so that the royalist rear was protected by 'a march intersected by ditches and dykes', commemorated in the modern farm name Muir of Alford.

For the first time Montrose with close on two thousand men outnumbered the enemy infantry while his two hundred and sixty horse almost matched their cavalry. His line extended some six hundred yards across the side of the Gallow Hill, his foot drawn up in files six deep. The disposition of Baillie's force is uncertain apart from Balcarres' horse which, arranged in three squadrons, were placed on the left. Baillie's plan was to tempt Gordon from his strong position by exposing two of these squadrons and then, when he charged, to send in the third, held in reserve while the infantry entrenched in the dykes, ditches, and marshy ground in the vicinity of Ardgathen cross-roads.

MacMhuirich alone asserts that a party of the men of Badenoch was first sent to try the enemy; all others agree that the honour fell to Lord Gordon, enraged, according to one of his name, by the sight of Strathbogie cattle in the possession of the covenanters. 'I shall bring you Baillie by the neck from the midst of his party', boasted Lord George before hurling himself and his hundred Gordons upon Balcarres. The two sides struggled 'at close quarters, fighting hand to hand so stubbornly that none could advance a foot or a nail's breadth but over the body of his foe, while retreat was impossible, so great was the crush of men pressing on behind.' Baillie ordered the reserve to advance but they failed to engage though Balcarres himself, 'one of the bravest men in the kingdom', refused to give ground. Although the Gordons cut a passage through the covenanting horse the outcome was still in the balance until Nat Gordon called upon the musketeers. '*Agite commilitones*', cried he in Wishart's Latin. 'Hunt them down comrades. Throw away those useless muskets and stab or hamstring the rebel horses with your dirks.' Thomas O'Lachan and his foot set to with a will. Their task was hazardous for the cavalry by now were 'seizing each others heads with their left hands and striking one another on the heads with their pistols. and the foot did not know what to do for the raging of the horse'. Aboyne smashed Baillie's right leaving

O'Cahan and Colonel James MacDonald to complete the carnage. On the left Irish swords and dirks mercilessly despatched the hated enemy; on the right the Irish used the same weapons as they dived under horses' hooves to open their bellies and render them useless. Hard on these two cavalry charges, Montrose led out the reserve and the centre also engaged. The two armies crashed into each other, firing at close quarters. Such was the confusion that Alasdair MacRanald later said himself that he stood for a time with the point of his sword 'to the earth', not knowing where to strike a blow and unable to distinguish between friend and foe. 'Our foot stood with myself and behaved themselves as became them, until the enemy's horse charged in our rear, and in front we were overcharged with their foot,' wrote Baillie. The covenanting line was completely broken. More than any other battle Alford was a Gordon victory, yet they were cruelly robbed of their moment of triumph for Lord George Gordon, charging behind the enemy lines, was shot in the back. He fell dead (according to MacMhuirich just as he was putting his hand on Baillie's sword belt) at the Gordon Stane, midway between the Gallow Hill and the modern village of Alford. If Farquharson and Rhynie had been the excuse for the massacre at Auldearn, the defeated at Alford could expect little mercy. 'They were so mortified at the fall of Lord Gordon that they ordered that no quarter should be given to any man that day.' Many fell at Feight Faulds on the western edge of the village; the Buckie Burn east of Alford flowed red with the blood of the victims; others were cut down at Bloody Faulds in the parish of Tough, four miles east of Alford. Baillie lost about seven hundred dead; the royalist losses, as usual, were slight. Besides Gordon only three others were killed. Several glory-seeking baggage boys also perished.[23]

The death of Lord George Gordon was a real and severe blow. The support of the Gordons was no longer assured since Aboyne was not the measure of his brother. Montrose 'mourned bitterly over the melancholy fate of his dearest, only friend; grievously he complained that the pride of his race, the ornament of the Scottish nobility, the stoutest champion of royal authority in the north, his best and bosom friend, should be thus cut off in the flower of his age.' Montrose might have shed a tear for himself; the depth of his grief for a friend of barely five months adequately reflects his plight. If Gordon of Ruthven was correct in distinguishing Lord George as 'too rich a jewell to adorne so unhappie ane age', then Scotland was almost totally bereft of treasure. In spite of his victorious progress and a success that seemed unstoppable, Montrose still failed to win the support of the nobility. The eye at the centre of his storm was stunningly calm.

With heavy heart James Graham moved that night to Cluny Castle. Next day he pitched camp at Craigton, on the Dee, seven miles from Aberdeen.

11
ASCENT TO THE
MERIDIAN: KILSYTH

*Divinitie laughs and playes with human affaires. For now the great
and formidable successes of this worthie and valiant and fortunate
leader were mounted to his zenith, and being come to his meridian,
begins to discend; and in his decadencie, to sett as low in the occident
of a few malhoures, as he arose in the orient of so many prosperous
actiones.*

Gordon of Ruthven

Alford added another victory to the impressive battle honours of
James Graham and he resolved to carry the war to the south with his
'small but never conquered army'. He was nonetheless anxious to
avoid engaging the enemy until Alasdair returned from the west
while Aboyne was despatched to Strathbogie to procure reinforcements. At Fordoun in the Mearns Montrose was rejoined by Black
Pate and his Atholl Highlanders, who had departed before Auldearn
to investigate the damage which Baillie had inflicted on their district.
More important, Alasdair came in fresh from recruiting in the *Garbh
Chriochan*, the 'Rough Bounds' of the western Highlands. With him
was Donald Muideartach, son of old Iain of Clan Ranald, and over five
hundred of his clansmen from Uist and Moidart. Sir Lachlan MacLean
of Duart brought seven hundred MacLeans from Mull. Appin Stewarts,
MacGregors, MacNabs, Farquharsons, and a further contingent of
Glengarry MacDonalds brought the total to close on three thousand
men, but Montrose expressed dissatisfaction that the Gaels had not
brought more supplies with them. Muideartach promptly remedied
the deficiency by obtaining them from the surrounding countryside.
MacMhuirich explains that no clan made more preys on Angus and
the Mearns than Clan Ranald. Many of the other clans conveyed their

213

spoil back to their native glens but Donald would 'not do any such thing, nor would he allow any of his men to go away from him with a prey or spoil'. He adds rather disarmingly that it was not easy in any case 'for the men of the Isles to come with spoils to their own country from the Low Country'. A perceptive old man, in a neat example of oral transmission, told Donald that the Mearns had not been pillaged since Donald Lord of the Isles had invaded the area at the time of the battle of Red Harlaw in 1411. 'And I suppose, young man, that you are descended of him, if you be the captain of Clan Ranald.'

The miserable Baillie, still attempting to shed his commission, marched to Stirling to attend a parliament driven out of Edinburgh by the plague. Those attending were amazed 'that it should be the pleasure of our God to make us fall thus the fifth time, before a company of the worst men in the earth', but they exonerated Baillie although refusing to accept his resignation until the matter could be discussed at a further parliament in Perth on 24 July, when new levies from counties south of the Tay were to present themselves.[1]

Montrose determined to mount a show of strength outside the walls of Perth. Following the familiar route which hugs the Highland line, he crossed the Tay at Dunkeld and striking south across the Almond camped in the Wood of Methven, quite close to the site of Tibbermore. He was gambling on being joined by much-needed cavalry, daily expected from Aboyne and Airlie. Indeed he was forced to utilize every mount in his army including those from the baggage train to convince the terrified occupants of Perth of the superiority of his horse. The ruse worked but with only eighty decent horses and a hundred pack ponies he could not risk attack; under cover of darkness he fell back to Dupplin, south-west of the city. He was playing a very dangerous game. There can be little doubt that he chafed at the non-appearance of Aboyne whose horse might have permitted a final victory over the indecisive covenanters. The royalists were forced to retreat very quickly when Baillie called his bluff and rapidly marched on the camp in Methven woods. Both Gordon and Wishart imply that the royalist retreat was planned and orderly, an impression belied by the latter's account of how a number of Highland and Irish womenfolk and camp followers were 'most foully and shamefully' butchered by the advancing army. Baillie himself states that 'upon sight of us the enemie retired to the hills', and suggests that if his own orders had been executed with greater alacrity Montrose might not have escaped from Methven so easily. But Montrose was not panicked; he organized an effective rearguard action as he retreated northwards to Dunkeld. His Highlanders harassed the enemy, driving them off 'like a herd of deer before the hunters' and one, Angus mac Ailin Duibh, earned himself a place in tradition by killing an over-persistent covenanter with a single shot at great range.

The long-awaited Aboyne arrived at last with four hundred horse and eight hundred foot. Airlie added a contingent of mounted Ogilvies. It was now or never. Montrose tested intelligence reports informing him that some of the covenanting recruits had disbanded and gone home (as in fact they had) by parading his cavalry in full view of the enemy who observed, decamped by night, and retreated across the Earn. The royalists followed.

Not for the first time nor for the last there was consternation among the people of the Lord. Baillie, 'upon consideration of the many contests and hot disputes, which were at every meeting betwixt the prime men of parliament', finally demitted his charge but against his better judgement, which Kilsyth would brutally endorse, he was prevailed upon to continue with the army for a further fortnight. Levies continued to be raised in Fife while recruiting proceeded in Lanarkshire, Ayrshire, and Clydesdale.

Lieutenant-General Baillie later related how his troops entrenched at Kilgraston a mile south-west of Bridge of Earn, hoping to be joined by the Fife levies. Montrose approached, but finding the position too well fortified he moved 'up towards the hills on the right hand' – that is presumably Montrose's right, behind Dron. Next day Graham marched towards the Mills of Forth, says Baillie, while he, with the advice of the Committee, moved eastwards to Lindores to rendezvous with the Fife levies. In an effort to unsettle further the good folk of Fife Montrose marched up Glenfarg to Kinross. If he was intending to prevent the Fife regiments from joining Baillie he failed. On the other hand, if the western levies now being mobilized by the Earl of Lanark, Cassilis, and Alexander, Earl of Eglinton were to cross the Forth, he would be trapped in the Kingdom of Fife. Experience had taught him, however, that it was imperative to keep his Highlanders on the move if he was to avoid desertions, particularly in the Lowlands, and west of Kinross by way of Crook of Devon and Rumbling Bridge there was a particularly attractive lure for his Gaels. At Dollar was situated the magnificent Castle Campbell which popularly retained its ancient name of Castle Gloom long after it was acquired by the Campbells in 1493. Argyll had recently strengthened the garrison and one report suggests that he was himself in the castle at this time with his foster-son young Ewen Cameron of Locheil. Ewen was to enjoy a splendid career during which he fought for another Graham at Killiecrankie, and he lived through the Jacobite rising of 1715 to die four years later. The MacLeans had much to avenge on the Campbells and in full view of the helpless garrison they devastated the surrounding countryside, wasting the parishes of Dollar and Muckhart, though the castle itself was not sacked. The royalists had neither the time nor the resources to mount a full-scale attack and they swept on to Alloa which was plundered by Alasdair's Irish in spite of the loyalist sympathies of its owner the Earl of Mar, who invited Montrose, Airlie, and his own son-in-law the Master of Napier to a banquet in Alloa Castle while Alasdair marched westwards. They had barely dined before word came of Baillie's approach. Montrose did not delay; he rejoined Alasdair, crossed the Forth above Stirling, and struck south towards the Graham estates of Dundaff and on to Kilsyth, 'the field of the desperate battle', where he camped on the evening of 14 August.

Baillie halted at Stirling to be joined by the Fife regiments and the covenanting lords. Argyll enquired as to their course of action but Baillie, beset by rumblings of mutiny, hamstrung by the Committee, and doubtless fearful of yet another defeat, disclaimed responsibility – 'I answered that the direction should come from his Lordship and those of the Committee' – and he gave his reasons. Prisoners were exchanged without his knowledge, others usurped the command in his presence, and victuals which could have been used by the army were destroyed without his express order. He would give his advice but would follow the judgement of the Committee. Having cleared the air, they marched to Bridge of Denny and camped at the farm of Hollandbush some five miles east of Kilsyth.

The parish takes its name from the estates of the Livingstones, viscounts Kilsyth. Equidistant between Forth and Clyde it is well described as 'altogether an extended strath between two lines of hills'.[2] The area must have been very familiar to Montrose and he chose a brilliant site on which to make his stand, pitching camp in the meadows now covered by the waters of a reservoir built to feed the Forth Clyde canal which slices through the valley parallel to the Antonine wall. He was positioned on the frontier of ancient Alba looking south to the magnificent panorama of southern Scotland, the prize which would fall to the victor. On his right he looked down towards Glasgow to the route along which the western levies must come if they were to join Baillie. Eastwards he could glimpse the waters of the Forth and the rich Lothian plain. From the reservoir the ground rolls gently east towards the red roofs of the small village of Banton, situated in the mouth of a steep and wooded ravine which has its source in the Kilsyth hills. On the west the field is similarly demarcated by parallel and almost identical burns feeding the Colzium estate. An excellent view of the field may be obtained by taking one of the charming paths through the grounds of Colzium House and climbing to the ridge behind Riskend farmhouse. From that point at an elevation of some four hundred feet the ground rises northwards to over one thousand feet before dropping down into the Carron valley.

Surviving accounts of the battle are not incompatible. The most reliable version is without doubt that of the unfortunate Baillie who presented a justification of his conduct to a mystified and understandably embittered parliament. Royalist commentaries suffer from an over-concentration upon the exploits of individuals or individual kindreds. Gordon of Ruthven, for example, piqued because Wishart's circumstantial account made no mention of the Gordons, purported to remedy the deficiency by giving 'the true relation of those who were at the battle'; but Wishart is not without value. MacMhuirich's version, although containing several palpable exaggerations, possibly represents the view of an eye-witness. Both Wishart and Gordon agree that Montrose considered it vital to engage the enemy before they could be joined by the western levies, but it was not in his power to dictate battle since the initiative lay with the covenanters.

Baillie implies that he did not intend to march from Hollandbush until he was reinforced by Lanark's troop, fifteen hundred of whom were reported to be only twelve miles away. When Argyll asked Baillie if they might not advance closer to the enemy, he was told, 'we were near enough if we intended not to fight and that his Lordship knew weell enough how rough and uneasie a way that was to march in.' In discussion Baillie was overruled by Argyll, Burleigh,

Tullibardine, Balcarres, and Elcho, all of whom had already been on the receiving end of Montrose's victories and who relied on six thousand foot and eight hundred horse to inflict a much-desired revenge. Crawford-Lindsay alone had not previously faced Montrose in the field. Baillie therefore 'marched with the regiments through the corns and over the braes, untill the unpassible ground did hold us up.' He embattled 'where I doubt if on any quarter twenty men on front could either have gone from us or attack us'. His position faced northwest, from Banton on his right to a point south of the significantly named farm of Craigs on his left. At an elevation of some two hundred and fifty feet, in broken ground of scrub and boulders he looked across Banton Burn towards Montrose's lines. He positioned Balcarres' regiment on the right, with Lauderdale's next to it, Home's on the left, and on the extreme left wing Loudoun's. Crawford's regiment was positioned behind Lauderdale and Home in the centre and behind it stood the Fife levies whose lack of experience kept them out of the battle.

There is little specific information as to how Montrose deployed his forces. He commanded some five thousand foot and six hundred horse. He placed Huntly's following under Nat Gordon on his left, but he took great care to situate Aboyne at the rear, probably at a point between the farms of Auchinrivoch and Auchinvalley to judge from later developments. Between the two armies were a number of cottages and enclosures, traces of which may still be seen in the vicinity. Montrose ordered Ewen MacLean of Treshnish with a hundred of his clansmen to occupy one such enclosure, ahead of his lines and on the other side of the burn, probably, as has been suggested, close to the site of the mill in the bend of the road between Banton and Craigs.[3] 'In sending you upon this service I feel it is my duty to tell you that the post I assign you is of such importance as to require all your courage and tact to overcome your danger.' 'Danger! my Lord,' replied MacLean, 'the more dangerous the more honourable: call it desperate, so is my resolution.'[4] Each would have something to remember or fabricate about this battle. The main body of the MacLeans together with Clan Ranald, both commanded by Alasdair, seem to have been in the centre with two regiments in the rear for support. Airlie and his Ogilvies may have been on the right but no precise information about either the latter position or the earl is available. Montrose must have orchestrated his victory from the high ground behind his centre. The accounts allow him a brief council of war at which 'the defending, stout hearted, clean armed, army of the Gael' urged battle. He commanded them to throw off their plaids to fight unencumbered in their pale shirt-like tunics, tails tied between the legs; the day promised to be warm; in the heat of battle none need hesitate to distinguish friend and foe.

About a mile to the north of Baillie's right, at High Banton, the ground begins to rise steeply from the five-hundred-foot contour. Although Baillie shunned the elevated position it was a tempting bait for his colleagues. All except Balcarres, shy of hills since Alford, urged that the hill be seized. Baillie could see no point in attempting to take it – 'the loss of the day would be the loss of the kingdom' – but once again he was overruled. His regiments faced right and marched up the east side of the burn, halted in a line between Banton and High Banton and faced due west towards the royalists. Corroboration of the positions of both armies is given by Baillie's reply to the charge that he should have marched from one ground to the other in battle order; it was not possible, he said, 'to have marched with single regiments, embattelled from the north side of the water to the hill, but by turning ane narrow flanke of sex deep unto the enemy, against common sense.' He there-fore marched along the south-east bank of the burn 'making the flanck the front so that even upon our march, the faceing again to the left hand should have put us in our former posture and battell, if the enemy had attacked us on that way'.[5] The move brought his left, Loudoun's and Home's, close to the enclosure occupied by the MacLeans. Baillie undoubtedly intended to outflank Montrose to the north once the movement towards the hill was imposed upon him. He ordered a Major Haldane on his far right to advance along the hill from High Banton with a group of musketeers; Balcarres and Lauderdale were to follow. Haldane however marched unordered to 'a house near the glen' oblivious of the fact that Montrose had despatched some of his forces up that glen 'through the bushes' to combat the challenge posed by the covenanters' new position. Home's and Loudoun's had been told to hold their position but to his alarm Baillie saw them advance towards the enclosures. The musketeers attached to those regiments wasted a great deal of shot fired at the MacLeans secure behind their dykes. There was some dispute about precedency between Clan Ranald and the MacLeans in the centre, but so hard pressed was Ewen in his enclosure that support was essential. Donald, son of Hector Òg

MacLean and the captain of Clan Ranald with Patrick Caoch Mac-Gregor, 'leapt over the dyke, and with down heads fell on and broke these regiments' of Home and Campbell, and 'the first man of them that leaped the enemy's wall was Donald that son of Iain Muideartach, followed by his men'. A praise-poem by Cathal MacMhuirich in honour of Donald would commemorate his feat, 'I would know his footstep, leaping swiftly over the dykes'.[6] It was fitting that it should, for at the dykes the battle was lost and won.

While the murderous claymores of the clans hacked the pathway to victory an equally fierce encounter was taking place on Montrose's left. Nat Gordon on the high ground advanced to check the attack by Balcarres' horse supported by Lauderdale's and Crawford's. He was extremely hard pressed and in danger of being cut off. Aboyne, cooling his heels in the rear, considered the Gordon action rash but seeing the chance for action he despatched a messenger to Montrose requesting support for his kinsmen, and himself charged into the fray. He veered to the left to avoid disciplined ranks of lethal pikes and surviving three volleys of musket fire he broke through the lines to relieve the Gordons. Gordon of Ruthven alone relates that Aboyne managed to regroup and launch a further attack. Meanwhile in response to his messenger, Montrose sent the indefatigible Airlie to his assistance. When some of Montrose's officers, seeing the Gordons so hard pressed, 'flatly refused the task of supporting them', Montrose (presumably ignoring this slight to his generalship and rank disobedience in the face of the enemy) turned to Airlie. 'You see my Lord, those rash men of ours have plunged into desperate danger, and will soon be cut to pieces by the cavalry unless at once supported. All eyes and hearts are upon your lordship, as the only man fit for the honour or beating back the enemy, saving our comrades, and repairing by your veteran courage, the error of their headstrong youth.' It was a fine speech to hear above the clash of steel, the crash of gunfire, and the screams of the dying and wounded, but Airlie responded to the appeal. The Ogilvies threw their weight behind the Gordons and the combined force drove through Crawford's regiment. Thus all of the main participants, or at least those lucky enough to attract any kind of partial chronicler or historian, succeeded in acquiring a piece of the action; the honour of posterity was satisfied.

Baillie, trying to support Home's unpremeditated attack on the dykes, frantically galloped across the burn to bring up the Fife levies, only to find that they had already fled. The battle of Kilsyth was over.

> Like the short-lived web of the spider when facing tempest, not more enduring is that host laid low on knolls: thousands are slain.

> Bodies like clothes a-bleaching are stretched on hill-sides, ignoble of aspect; they have left Saxon women wet of cheek and not joyful.[7]

There remained only the exultant carnage of the victors. To Denny and Falkirk the vanquished were pursued. Many were cut down in Dullatur Bog one-and-a-half miles south of the reservoir, on the line of the Antonine Wall. The glen where the fiercest fighting took place, where Home's and Loudoun's were bled in the enclosures, still rejoices in the name Slaughter Howe. Within a radius of three miles bones and bullets were frequently excavated at the end of the eighteenth century. Local tradition says that a cottar and his four sons, lacking the protection of the white 'sarks', were butchered at the roadside. In 1829 a quantity of bones 'mostly of small size' were dug up in a field near Auchincloch farm, on the main road east of Craigs. 'The tradition that the drummers and fifers were buried there was thus confirmed.'[8] The covenanting casualties must have run to thousands though rather more than the traditional 'few hundred' must have escaped, among them, as usual, the bulk of the leadership, who lived to apportion blame to all except themselves. Argyll 'for the third time, took boat and escaped aboard a ship'. Two days later he wrote to Stewart of Grantully from Burntisland in Fife, 'who knows but it pleased God to deal so with us (because of some that trusted too much in the arme of the flesh) that both his glory and our weaknes may bee the mor evident.'[9]

Within a few hours of the battle the victorious general wrote to Glasgow Town Council commanding that their citizens 'remain in their own houses and that they make ready all sort of provisions for the passing of the Army; which giff they do, they shall be assured to be protected as good and loyal subjects; but giff they do otherwayes, they shall oblige us to proceed against them as rebels and enemies to his Majesties service.'[10] He had once again 'conquered from Dan to Beersheba'. The climax of weeks and months of exhausting campaigns was to be the submission of the rich cities of the Lowlands. Two representatives from Glasgow rode out to congratulate Montrose. It was rumoured that the city compounded for enormous sums ranging from £18,000 to £66,000. Montrose remained at Kilsyth for two days before making his triumphal entry into the western capital to the accompaniment of 'the joyous acclamation of the people'. There he summoned a parliament for 20 October. The city which in later centuries proved a magnet for the people of the Highlands held no such attractions then. The clans had been promised the pillage of Glasgow but, trapped in the dual role of Highland leader and royal liberator, Montrose was forced to deny his veterans. Murdo MacLean of Lochbuie could not even prevail upon the Glasgow merchants to supply clothing without prior payment.[11] Violence was strictly prohibited; several wrongdoers were executed and already the rift between Montrose and Alasdair mac Cholla was apparent. James Graham had used the natural talents of the Gaels to win the war; these same talents would not serve to win the peace. The clans had little time for the niceties of tact and diplomacy; it was not to their taste to sit down with their recent enemies. To spare Glasgow and himself further embarrassment and to avoid the hazards of the plague, James withdrew to the Kirkton of Bothwell in Clydesdale where he established camp and the royalist headquarters in Scotland.

Both at Glasgow and Bothwell he received the accolade that was his due; the king had come back to his own. The waverers were among the first to come in. The Marquis of Douglas appeared, a man given to agonizing interminably about where to place his stake and then infallibly backing the loser. He was the sad representative of a once great house (motto *Jamais arrière*), a catholic who had joined the covenanters the previous year. From Dumfriesshire came Hartfell who had signed the Cumbernauld Band and who with his neighbour Annandale, who accompanied him, had refused to join Montrose in April 1644. Gordon of Ruthven shrewdly remarks that several who appeared at Bothwell were sent by their fathers, intent on hedging their bets and securing the family estates against future contingencies. Such were Seton, son of the Earl of Winton, though filial loyalty to the king had already cost the family £40,000; James, Lord Drummond, son of the Earl of Perth, veteran of Cumbernauld and Tibbermore; Wigtown's son John, Lord Fleming; Lord Erskine, son of the Earl of Mar, and Linton, son of Traquair. The earls of Queensberry and Airth and Montrose's brother-in-law James, Lord Carnegie, afterwards seecond Earl of Southesk, made up the faceless number, and those who did not actually appear in person, such as Home, Roxburgh, and Traquair, committed their loyalty to parchment. Many of these names represented the most powerful families in the south of Scotland, essential to Montrose's efforts to consolidate his hold on the kingdom, but most had hitherto shown themselves a poor lot and there can be little doubt that stalwarts like Alasdair and Aboyne chafed at the attention given to such people at the expense of themselves. They had risked life, limb, and fortune to find themselves supplanted by a group of time-servers. It must have been at this time that Montrose received overtures from potentially the greatest ally of all. Argyll claimed at his trial in 1661 that in 1645 Montrose and he 'were fully agreed upon articles and conditions contained in a treaty past betwixt us; the gentleman is yet alive who carried the messages both by word and writing betwixt us and it was neither his fault nor mine that the business did not end at that time.'[12] If such negotiations really did take place at Bothwell they were the most closely guarded secret of the entire war.

Montrose's true supporters lay festering in covenanting dungeons and he took immediate steps to release them. On 20 August the Master of Napier and Nathaniel Gordon were sent to Linlithgow with two hundred horsemen and dragoons to proclaim a parliament in the town. They were also to summon Edinburgh but were to avoid 'all places suspect to be spoyled with the Infectione as you will answer on the contrarie at your hiest perrell'. At Linlithgow the Master freed his wife, his two sisters, his brother-in-law Sir George Stirling of Keir, and his aged father. Parliament had actually provided for their liberation the week before but the order had not been carried out. Napier was able to obtain the release of others from the tolbooth of Edinburgh, among them George Wishart. Lady Helen Ogilvie had petitioned for the transference of her husband to safer quarters than those which he occupied at Edinburgh Castle on the grounds that he was attended by a boy 'whoise father latlie died of the pest', that his food came from an infected household, and that he often spent forty-eight hours without so much as a cup of water. The Master's timely visitation saved Ogilvie from transportation to the plague-free, but ague-nourishing Bass Rock.

Napier and Gordon received express instructions to obtain the submission of Edinburgh peacefully. Their approach drove many of the citizens to implore the mercy of the prisoners 'so lately exposed to the bitter abuse and contempt of the vilest of the mob, eager to have them tortured and gibbeted'. Ogilvie and the Earl of Crawford were released to negotiate terms with their deliverers on behalf of the town council. Edinburgh's submission cost her a fine, the promise of loyalty and obedience, the surrender of the castle, and the release of the remaining prisoners. Among those so freed were Lord Graham, Montrose's brother Harry, and his sister Lilias.

Stirling and Dumbarton held out but the magazine at Leith was captured. Renfrew also submitted and after an expedition into Ayrshire by Alasdair and Drummond of Balloch which frustrated the efforts of Cassilis and Eglinton to recruit for their regiments, Irvine, Ayr, and many other towns in the western shires sent commissioners to Bothwell. Over three hundred protections to towns and individuals survive in a book which once contained twice that number. Many were granted to friends and allies such as Stirling of Keir, Wigtown, Stewart of Blackhall, and the sons of Sir Robert Spottiswood. The earls of Callendar, Mar, Airth, and Abercorn were included as were several ministers and many burgesses and merchants. Lewis Stewart was among the advocates and lawyers. Montrose's creditor Archibald Sydserff was not forgotten; nor were Airlie's brother, James Ogilvie, and William Drummond of Hawthornden. Although the bulk of those listed were gentlefolk from the west of Scotland and the central Lowlands there were a number of poorer people as well, small tenants and widows, for example, all eager to enter the king's peace.[13] These must have been happy days for James Graham towards the end of August 1645. The reality had followed the dream. His position was apparently unchallenged; Scotland was at his feet; he was reunited with those closest to him who had suffered so much for the cause. It was tempting to agree with Drummond of Hawthornden, who wrote to Montrose at Bothwell that 'the Golden Age is returned, his Majesty's crown re-established, the many-headed monster near quelled'. To celebrate the event James invited him to bring or send 'some pieces vindicating Monarchy from all aspersions, and another named *Irene*' in order that they might be printed. The muse would compound the peace. Hearts and minds are seldom conquered by the sword. In those crowded days after Kilsyth it is remarkable that literature should have been one of Montrose's priorities. How much time he had found for verse during the past sixteen months is impossible to ascertain but he had doubtless enjoyed the brilliant poetry of the Gael during his sojourn in the north. He is said to have sent a letter to Iain Lom immediately after the battle which concluded 'your very loving and trew friend to command'. The most explicit statement which the poet made on their friendship is tantalizingly obscure:

> Chalk white were your teeth, well and closely set,
> underneath slender eyebrows that showed no frown;
> although often did a tryst with you rouse me
> from sleep, I will not reveal that to others to-night.[14]

In the aftermath of Sir Walter Scott, the German poet and essayist Heine was to remark on the 'strange whim of the people – they demand their history distilled back into the original poetry whence it came'. Such distillation still took place in Gaeldom and Montrose's exploits were duly processed by the bards. Montrose provided a symbol of hope for a culture under siege just as Dundee and Charles Edward Stewart would do. More important perhaps he provided the opportunity for the Gael to assert himself, for Alasdair, for the MacLeans, for Clan Ranald, and the MacGregors, for the very clans who had suffered most during the *Linn nan Creach* to seize the chance to halt the seemingly inexorable process of land-grabbing carnage so successfully manipulated by the partnership of crown and Campbell under the guise of 'civilization'. Yet within a month of the glories of Kilsyth the 'Golden Age' had turned to dust.

On 14 June Cromwell's New Model Army proved its devastating power at Naseby. Apart from Oxford only Celtic Britain stood for the king; Montrose commanded the Scottish Highlands, while Charles still controlled the West Country and part of Wales. In the north of England the situation was no more promising. On 28 June Leven took Carlisle, which success was followed by a squabble as to whether the ancient frontier fortress should be garrisoned by Scottish troops or by their parliamentary allies. As Leven put it, 'wee know not but the Enemy may, according to their former resolution, endeavor to send a flying Armie into Scotland.'[15] Leven's concern to protect the frontier had all along exacerbated deteriorating relations with the English. Ever since Inverlochy the royalists in England had hopes of linking up with Montrose and the latter's successes owed much to the dissipation of Scottish strength in the service of the south.

The king decided to attempt a rapid march to join Montrose. With two thousand horse he reached Doncaster on 18 August where for two halcyon days he was buoyed up by the promise of support from Yorkshire. But Major-General Poyntz, fresh from his triumph at Scarborough, was bearing down from the north and Lieutenant-General David Leslie, despatched by Leven from Hereford reached Rotherham. Close to checkmate, Charles withdrew to Huntingdon. Kilsyth preserved him from pursuit; on learning of Montrose's victory Leslie made for Scotland. He received a depressing letter from Loudoun informing him that the royalists were now masters of the field, 'running over and destroying the country'. If they were not checked they would ruin the kingdom and, by pressing recruits into their army, would be in a position either to invite Charles to Scotland or else march south to join him. Loudoun's suggested remedy was the speedy return of the Scots army from England for 'suppressing these bloody rebels and the recovery of their native kingdom'. Leslie did not hesitate. On 26 August he sent a letter to the Scots commissioners in London telling them of his actions, acknowledging that some would censure him but assuring them that it was essential to both kingdoms that he deal with Montrose. Leslie intended to take only half his troops north with him but so concerned were they about the Scottish situation that all insisted on going, much to the perplexity of their allies. Scottish requests for support from Leven's army besieging Hereford were flatly refused – 'it seemed Hereford was of more consequence than the kingdome of Scotland'.[16] Leslie was of the New Model breed, a brilliant, ruthless soldier who had no time for the niceties or chaos of amateur warfare. He was a veteran of Marston Moor and credited by some with engineering the victory. It is remarkable that Montrose did not take the threat which he posed more seriously.

The ever-perceptive Patrick Gordon distinguished Montrose's greatest error as proceeding with too much confidence and trusting too much 'to his happie fortoune'. Montrose, who had been fascinated by the concept of fortune ever since his college days, beautifully described the predicament in which he found himself in August 1645.

> Some friends as shadows are,
> And fortune as the sun;
> They never proffer any help
> Till fortune hath begun:

But if in any case
Fortune shall first decay
Then they, as shadows of the sun
With fortune run away.

A good number of 'shadow friends' had already joined him at Bothwell. One of his associates considered that the defeat of his enemies was the least of his problems, 'he hath more to do with his own seeming friends', while James alluded to the same group when he complained of those who schemed to avoid involvement, who would act on assurance of victory but 'dare not hazard any thing for Religion, Prince or Country ... and are so stuffed with infidelity that they can believe nothing but what they see and can commit nothing to God'.[17] It was essential that he make others believe in his fortune in order to gain and hold the much-needed support of the Lowlanders. The time had come to emphasize his orthodox presbyterianism and to play down his dependence upon catholic allies. His impressive battle record greatly facilitated his task but there are indications that it also deluded him into believing in his own propaganda and invincibility. His interest in fortune is a further indication of his own peculiar brand of Calvinism. 'Fortune and adventure are the words of Paynims, the signification whereof ought in no wise to enter into the heart of the faithful,' wrote John Knox, echoing Calvin's *Institutes* – 'if all success is blessing from God, and calamity and adversity are his curse, there is no place left in human affairs for Fortune and chance.'[18] Montrose's alleged belief in astrology and his propensity for gambling sit uneasily with his religious views, but he never hesitated to invoke divine sanction for his achievements. While his English associates hailed his victories as miraculous, 'rather like dreams than truths', while his enemies tearfully searched their aching hearts for reasons as to why the Lord had abandoned them, Montrose himself wrote 'it may be sensibly seen to be the Lord's doing, in making a handful to overthrow multitudes'. Shakespeare's Edmund had condemned the practice of blaming the stars for lack of fortune as 'the excellent foppery of the world'; for Bacon fortune had no existence. If an adherence to Fortuna be distinguished as backward-looking, Montrose's quixotic spirit, restlessly striving for something beyond a fatalistic acceptance of a pre-ordained albeit God-ordained existence, is indicative of a new era. He was a man who dearly loved and valued his God but who refused to live in a religious strait-jacket.

Nonetheless Montrose took good care, in a remonstrance penned by Napier after his release from Linlithgow, to stress his adherence to the covenant. He seems to have believed that given sufficient encouragement, most Lowlanders would declare for the king. Ironically he was partly correct but he was quite oblivious of the virtual impossibility of a rapprochement between Charles and the Scots which depended upon himself. Six times he had destroyed Gideon's army and shattered the strong right arm of the Lord. The profound psychological effect which his action had on the covenanters cannot be minimized and is reflected in the vituperative hysteria of their attitude towards him. To make matters worse, Montrose was avowedly a covenanter himself, albeit one who had utilized the antichristian hordes of Gaeldom and Ireland.

The remonstrance, although it was never published, would have simply intensified the bitter contempt reserved for him by his former allies, who were unlikely to be impressed by Montrose's attempt to justify the lawfulness of his proceedings against those 'malicious and bloody persecutors' who had ordered his excommunication, forfeiture, and death. Mark Napier, for once disenchanted with his hero, described the remonstrance as 'as unjustly severe against Episcopal government as the bitterest Covenanter could desire'. The 'perverse practices of the prelates' were roundly condemned as was the 'dead service book – the brood of the bowels of the Whore of Babel' – and the bishop's usurpation of civil authority. It is truly remarkable that on the eve of a planned link-up with Charles, Montrose should not only have employed such emotive language, but that he should have taken such pains to stress his adherence to the covenant. In the words of that document he would return to Charles sworn to 'the same cause of maintaining the true Religion and his Majesty's authority'. He claimed that the occasion of his own revolt from the covenanters had been 'their revolt from their National Covenant' as manifested in the solemn league.

Montrose argued that the Scottish church was as much threatened by Independency as it had been by episcopacy – 'the outcasting of the locust' was 'the inbringing of the caterpillar'. He was resolved to 'eschew the extremities and keep the middle way of our reformed religion', maintaining it with the hazard of life and fortune – 'it shall be no less dear to us than our own souls'. But Independency, which by vesting authority in individual congregations implied the separation of church and state, was anathema to the most fanatical covenanters just as it was to Montrose. Furthermore there were no signs of it developing in Scotland. To suggest that Argyll or Warriston was veering towards Independency was as ludicrous as accusing Montrose of recusancy. The ultimate failure of the Scottish revolution is to be detected in the non-development of religious radicalism such as evolved in England. Oliver Cromwell, the Independent, laid presbyterianism prostrate; its revival was temporarily and wrong-headedly entrusted to Charles II at the Restoration.

Montrose was anxious to reject the charge of malignancy, of being a traitor to his country. He argued that on the contrary he was 'for' his country unlike those who stood on the sidelines while 'their misleaders, like unnatural countrymen, or vipers, are wasting the bowels of their native nation for their own benefit, and as they have unnaturally killed many sent forth by them, so let them take malignancy to themselves, as having kindled the coal, fomented the flames, and by disturbing the peace of the country, like salamanders live in the fire of contention.' The question of who had kindled the coal or fomented the flames was irrelevant. Neither side was disposed to concede points on this issue. To attribute the deaths of those men defeated by Montrose to their leaders was the over-subtle assertion of one convinced of his own righteousness, a conviction difficult to escape in an age which equated might with right and in which victory vindicated the just. He would have been less than human if his spectacular record had not turned his head. It was believed that he had 'cut off (and killed most of) twenty-five entire regiments ... since his coming into Scotland with his inconsiderable strength'.[19] Gordon of Ruthven considered his achievements miraculous since 'it hath seldome or never been herd before that ane armie, still the waiker and lesser number, sould fight sex bettelles, against sex sundrie armies, ever stronger then themselves ... and in all those battells, not to losse ane hundreth of these men; there being killed of there enemies above fyfteine thousand.' Yet his very success was the main barrier to some kind of compromise with the Lowlanders. One of the main factors tipping the scales in favour of the solemn league had been reports of the catholic atrocities in Ireland. In the popular view the very men responsible for these outrages now fought alongside Montrose. What kind of covenanter would employ Irish catholics against his fellow countrymen? Montrose made little effort to defend himself convincingly against the last charge, simply asserting that Alasdair had been employed by Colonel Munro in Ireland – 'we marvel why they should think that which is lawful for them should be unlawful for us, as if they had greater liberty to make use of his Majesty's subjects than he himself had.'

Montrose denied that he was either traitor or 'bloody rebel'. Rather the traitors are those that 'brangles his Majesty's authority ... that meddle with his revenues and employ them to their own use, that traduce his Majesty to his subjects as an enemy to religion, that carry arms against him to cut short his authority in England.' As for the charge of bloodletting – 'never did we shed the blood of any but of such as were sent forth by them to shed our blood and to take our lives, whose blood we shed in our own defence', momentarily overlooking the hapless inhabitants of Aberdeen and Argyll. What was done was the Lord's doing. 'Neither will the Lord's sword be put in till the rebels repent of their rebellion, perjury, and oppression; and what the sword does not the Lord will by his other plagues perform, till those that be secrete in their holds perish with those that are in the fields, and the tall cedars fall with the little bramble.' The remonstrance concludes with an appeal to all to join with him and the promise of retribution which will surely follow on refusal.[20]

This was the high point of Montrose's career. The master of Scotland prepared to march in triumph into England. The role of Deliverer was one which he relished. But as Patrick Gordon observed, 'Divinitie laughs and plays with humane affaires'. On 12 September the Scots commissioners in London presented a submission to the English on behalf of their fellow covenanters: 'such as were most zealous for the covenant and cause of God are forced to fly for their lives and to leave their habitations, possessions, and all that they have in this world to the cruelty and spirit of the enemy ... As we are not willing to conceal or extenuate their miseries in this day of the Lord's visitation, so are we not able sufficiently to express them; the yoke of their transgressions is bound by his hand, they are wreathed and come upon their neck, he hath made their strength to fail, the Lord hath delivered them into their hands from whom they are not able to rise up.'[21] 12 September was the eve of the battle of Philiphaugh; God was about to indulge in laughter.

12
DESCENT TO DECADENCY: PHILIPHAUGH

Tis now that Montrose, after so much prosperity, must go through some cross Fortune, and by one fatal day, learn, that the Fortune of war is uncertain, and that victory does not always attend the valour of the combatants, nor the goodness of the cause.

Menteith of Salmonet

Among a number of circumstances leading to the defeat at Philiphaugh were poor communications with the king. Charles did not receive news of Kilsyth until 24 August at Huntingdon. Since the camp at Bothwell was abandoned on 3 September there was comparatively little time in which to send instructions to Montrose. Messengers reached him from Oxford, which the king had not visited since 7 May. One of these, Sir Robert Spottiswood, president of the court of session and a long-standing opponent of the covenanters, carried with him a commission confirming Montrose as Lieutenant-Governor and Captain-General. Sir Robert had taken a long circuitous route via Wales, Man, Lochaber, and Atholl. Another messenger, a Mr Andrew Sandilands, 'a Scotsman educated in England, where he had entered holy orders, an upright, loyal man', was possibly despatched direct from Huntingdon, since he was rector of Scrayingham in Yorkshire.[1] Very soon after his release Ogilvie was sent with Douglas to the Borders to sound out Home, Roxburgh, and Traquair. The lack of resolution displayed by Home and Traquair was by now almost legendary. Roxburgh's third wife, sixty years his junior, was to become the bride of James, second Marquis of Montrose. According to Menteith the three Border peers declared 'that they were all ready to serve in person, and to join him with their friends and vassals, but . . . they begged of him to advance towards the Borders, where they would do their utmost

231

to hasten the levies.' Montrose delegated Ogilvie and Douglas to join Annandale and Hartfell in Dumfriesshire where they were to raise such horse as they could before marching eastwards. They were evidently considering a strike for Carlisle, where their fellow peer the Earl of Queensberry was a prisoner,[2] a course from which they were deflected by their leader who commanded them to advance through Tweeddale and the Merse to meet him in East Lothian. Douglas established a base at Galashiels. But still the Borderers refused to come in, allegedly because Montrose himself was not present, and the raw farm hands already recruited by Douglas also wavered in his absence.

Alasdair, with his Highlanders and Drummond of Balloch, was sent into the covenanting country of the south-west to foil the efforts of Cassilis and Eglinton to raise the levies. He was welcomed with open arms by the Countess of Loudoun who provided a magnificent banquet and promptly despatched a servant to Montrose to assure him of her loyalty. Thus the Campbell countess entertained the greatest living MacDonald at her castle on the banks of the Irvine. Alasdair also relieved her of 8500 merks which preserved the parishes of Loudoun, Galston, and Mauchline from pillage. Eglinton's factor compounded for 4000 merks after a nasty moment when Alasdair suspected him of double-dealing. All weapons and ammunition at Eglinton House were transferred to Bothwell. The lairds of Rowallan and Cunninghamhead eventually compounded for 1000 merks and 1200 merks respectively but not before Alasdair had caused an estimated £10,000 worth of damage. The town of Kilmarnock was also harshly treated *pour encourager les autres*, but once he had given his word he kept it. He returned to Bothwell laden with plunder and booty. Always uneasy in the Lowlands, many of the Gaels, ever since the entry to Glasgow, had been homesick for their native glens. There were women and children to protect, harvests to secure, and loot to be deposited. Alasdair was disappointed by Montrose's failure to allow him the plunder of Glasgow and he was also offended by the prominence given to new-comers. Neither Mac Cholla nor his followers had any desire to pursue the war to the land of the *Sassunnach* and as ever he was concerned about potential developments on his ancestral estates for he had heard disturbing reports that Argyll had been dealing harshly with his kinsmen. Antrim was preparing to go to Scotland and he had invited Alasdair to join him in the west. Despite Montrose's entreaties he was adamant about his departure but he did leave five hundred of the Irish behind and he did promise to return. His failure to do so earned him severe castigation, as well as accusations of betrayal, from Wishart. On the day before he struck camp Montrose knighted Alasdair. He publicly commended the bravery of, and acknowledged his indebtedness to, the warriors of the Highlands and Islands and in particular he praised the martial qualities of Alasdair mac Cholla Chiotaich with whom he had written one of the most stirring chapters in Scottish history. Between them they had also done more than any others to widen the rift between Gaelic-speaking and Lowland Scotland. They unwittingly confirmed the portrait of the blood-thirsty savage who could be tamed by only the harshest methods, and so must bear some of the responsibility for the destruction of one of the oldest cultures in Europe so assiduously pursued throughout the following century and particularly in the aftermath of Culloden. Alasdair now returned to the west Highlands with some two thousand Gaels and the remainder of the Irish. The two men would never meet again.

Two days later, at Calder Castle, Montrose suffered a similar setback. Aboyne announced that he also wished to withdraw; he had received letters from his father who, as ever, was wary of the intentions of the northern covenanters. Aboyne too was undoubtedly unhappy about the favour shown to newcomers and it was rumoured that he was particularly outraged because he was cheated of the post of General of the Horse, promised him by Montrose but already conferred by royal commission upon the recently released Earl of Crawford.[3] In Spottiswood's words he 'took a caprice'. Montrose's entreaties that he should delay his departure for a week were to no avail. They had done all that could be expected of them – 'it was reasonable that the southern shires should have their share of the fatigue.' Aboyne withdrew with five hundred Gordons.

The defection of Alasdair and Aboyne on the verge of what promised to be his finest hour – the breakthrough to England – raises many questions not only about Montrose's qualities of leadership but also about the nature of the Gael. The natural distaste of the latter for warfare far from home is sufficient to explain their withdrawal. What is remarkable is Montrose's apparent inability to stop them; his famous charm and powers of persuasion deserted him; he was not a leader that his men would follow blindly; his triumphs had always depended upon mutual respect and co-operation. He seems to have been naively optimistic about the amount of support he might recruit as his march progressed, discounting the fact that the plague debarred him from the cities which would have provided a sound base for his activities as well as a fertile recruiting ground. He was apparently quite unaware of the threat posed by Leslie and, perhaps most surprising of all, in spite of his own strictures about 'seeming friends' he appears to have placed almost total trust in Roxburgh and Home.

Skirting pest-ridden Edinburgh and avoiding Dalkeith, Montrose advanced towards Gala Water. Meanwhile Leslie was resting at Berwick, having marched some four hundred miles in twenty days. There he was joined by Argyll who was about to experience the exhilarating, and for him unusual, experience of being on the winning side. At Galashiels Douglas awaited his leader with the news that his troops were daily diminishing. Traquair arrived to greet Montrose, to promise him support, and to return with alacrity to his house near Peebles. Montrose approached the castles of Home and Roxburgh in an effort to learn some news of those remarkably silent peers. Wishart, Menteith, and Gordon all agree that Home and Roxburgh deliberately surrendered themselves to Leslie in order to escape their obligations to Montrose, yet still appear loyal to the king. The correspondence of the covenanters effectively preserved the fiction of their capture. They were 'clapped up . . . upon suspitions' and as the Committee of Estates reported to the Scots commissioners in London, in the nearest approach to an official account available, Leslie garrisoned Home Castle 'and finding grett slowness and disobedience to all publick orders in the Mers and Teviottdale it has beine thought fitt for a tyme to secure the persones of the Earls of Home and Roxburgh.'[4] For the first time since leaving Bothwell Montrose must have realized the full enormity of the odds against him. 'All these were great disheartenings to any other but to him, whom nothing of this kind can amaze. With the small forces he has presently with him, he is resolved to pursue David Leslie, and not suffer him to grow stronger,' wrote Spottiswood to Digby whom he proceeded to scold for failing either to prevent Leslie's advance into Scotland or to send troops to Montrose's assistance. The letter adequately captures the air of unreality which pervaded the Montrose camp in those days before Philiphaugh. The idea that he should 'pursue' David Leslie was ludicrous and he made no attempt to do so. He spent two indecisive days at Stichill before advancing from Kelso up Teviotdale to Jedburgh. Leslie withdrew to Haddington fearing that Montrose might strike out for the north. Jedburgh is no great distance from the English border; as close as Montrose would ever come to the southern kingdom again. Uncertain about the situation in England, and with Leslie to his rear, he could not risk an advance to the south. He decided to attempt to supplement his forces, which numbered about six hundred, in Dumfriesshire. His route lay up Yarrow through the passes of the Moffat hills.

On Friday 12 September the small army arrived at Selkirk, a sleepy little burgh perched on a hill above the Ettrick. A mile south-west of the town, across the water, there is a 'haugh', a low and level piece of ground, at the point where the Yarrow descending from its braes spills its waters into the Ettrick. Philiphaugh is best known now for the frequent battles in which Selkirk Rugby Football Club participates. There beside the river Montrose pitched camp. He ordered his foot to throw up a ditch beside the wood which skirted Harehead Hill and he retired to Selkirk. Border tradition, no less tenacious than that of the Highlands, relates that his hostess was boiling a sheep's head, cheerfully vowing that if it had been Montrose's head she would have taken care to hold down the lid. Apocryphal or not, the story accurately reflects the prevalent hostility of the soutars of Selkirk. There was no love for James Graham in this country.

Most of Montrose's apologists were dumbfounded by the disastrous failure of intelligence at Philiphaugh. There were persistent rumours that the enemy were in the vicinity but scouts sent out to investigate reported that there was nothing to be seen within a ten-mile radius. In fact Leslie was advancing with four thousand men down Gala Water. Montrose sat up late writing despatches to the king. Three miles north of Selkirk the tiny settlement of Sunderland guarded the confluence of Ettrick and Tweed. There during the night one of Leslie's advance parties surprised a dozen scouts led by Charteris of Amisfield who had arrived at Bothwell with Annandale and Hartfell. Eleven of his party were killed and Charteris himself escaped to Selkirk with difficulty. If Patrick Gordon is to be believed the refugee was accused of having been involved in a drunken brawl. But Gordon's explanation for the defeat that followed was that Montrose had overreached himself 'throw ane unwonted confidence and assurance'. He may have been correct, for it is difficult to attribute Montrose's failure of intelligence solely to the faithlessness of the Border barons; the blame must attach to the general himself. In the old days he would have camped with his men at Harehead, ready for action at a moment's notice; his scouts should have been on every hill watching for enemy fires and listening for the clink of metal on the still night air. His instincts should have told him to be wary of the locals in terrain with which he was unfamiliar. The most he did was to order a rendezvous at first light. He was too late.

His morning sleep was shattered by the news that Leslie was only a mile away. The latter had divided his forces: one party crossed the river and advanced along the right bank while Leslie led his division past Ovenscloss and Langlie under cover of darkness and an autumn mist to the camp at Philiphaugh. Montrose grabbed the first horse he could find and hurled himself down the hill and across the river to find a situation of near chaos. Groups of men stood all over the field in clutches of fifty and sixty. Some were vainly trying to catch their horses. Douglas's Borderers were already in flight. Some of the officers were still abed in Selkirk. One was Sir Robert Spottiswood who staggered out to find battle joined. In spite of the mist which Wishart and others have used to cloak Montrose's failure he obtained a clear view of the field from the town before he was captured. Only the Irish calmly awaited Montrose's command, 'readie to die and live with him as they had beene from the beginneing'. There was no time to do more than to place the foot on his left, their flank protected by Harehead Hill with the ditch to the fore. On the right he managed to muster some two hundred horse and the musketeers took cover behind hedges and hastily improvised trenches, all resolved 'to maintain the place till a noble death in the field of Mars sould give testimonie of ther courage and valour'.

Leslie launched two attacks on Montrose's right. During the first the horse defended themselves 'very gallantly about a quarter of an hour'. Montrose then called up his musketeers but the odds were overwhelming. Leslie led his horse against the Irish foot. The veterans of six victories calmly stood their ground absorbing the shock of heavy cavalry, and even the covenanting propaganda says 'the battle was very hotly disputed'. Two hundred Irishmen died behind the ditch at Philiphaugh. Montrose's horse were in tatters and Leslie's other division was by now advancing across the Ettrick, catching the royalists in a deadly cross-fire. 'It was a sight as melancholy as new to Montrose to see his troops fly before their enemies and indeed, this misfortune occasioned sundry impulses in his mind, which had like to have undone him.' But Montrose's resolve to sell his life dear was short-lived owing to the entreaties of his associates. Gathering a few horsemen around him, he cut his way out and fled past the 'dowie dens of Yarrow' to Minchmoor. Those on foot who tried to follow were caught and cut down near Newark Castle at a spot still known as Slain Man's Lea. Soon after leaving the field his party split up, Montrose going one way, Douglas and Airlie another, Crawford a third, to reassemble later.[5]

Covenanting propaganda gave ludicrously inflated estimates of Montrose's losses. Some claimed that three thousand had been killed while Robert Baillie reported that a thousand graves had been dug. Montrose later told Charles that he lost about two hundred men, a figure which possibly excludes those who were executed subsequent to surrender. The Irish bore the brunt of the casualties and those who surrendered on promise of quarter can have had few illusions about the fate which awaited them. One of the victors' newsletters states that one hundred of them were 'shot at post'. Fifty is probably nearer the mark. Even Gordon, who much admired their bravery, says that the Irish were too cruel, 'for they killed men ordinarily with no more feeling of compassion and with the same careless neglect that they kill a hen or a capon for supper'. They were also much given to 'filthie lust' and 'excessive drinking'. The truth from either side was almost irrelevant. As Leslie marched to Selkirk his army was told that 'divers young virgins were carryed away captives in the [royalist] army, with whom the soldiers committed filthiness in open places, the officers first taking and then the soldiers enjoying what they left'. Such stories are common to warfare the world over, but the devout exacted a terrible revenge. The camp followers had, of necessity, been abandoned – the 'boyes, cookes, and a rabble of rascals and women with their children in their arms'. Three hundred of them 'were cutte in pieces with such savage and inhumane crueltie as nether Turke nor Scithean was ever herd to have done the lyke'.[6] But in the eyes of the covenanters the spawn of Anti-Christ deserved no better fate. The Lord had delivered them into the hands of the godly who considered that they had a positive obligation to purge Israel of the plague. It was their belief; in their eyes no other explanation need be offered and for none other would their victims have asked. 'Behold when the enemie was thus ripe in sinne, the Lord cuts him off in an instant.' The Borderers were no less exultant.

> Now let us a' for Lesly pray,
> And his brave company!
> For they hae vanquish'd great Montrose
> Our cruel enemy.

Or so at least the ballad had it some years later. They could rejoice with Argyll that 'the Lord hath this day here at Philiphaugh appeared gloriously for his people'.[7] Among the captives were Ogilvie, Nat Gordon, and Sir William Rollo; so were Harry Graham and two of the Irish commanders Magnus O' Cahan and Major Thomas O' Lachan.

Nothing depresses like defeat. Montrose had lost several of his closest friends, his crack troops, and all of his baggage which contained letters to and from the king as well as a complete list of all who had entered his peace at Bothwell. In England Charles's advisers, drugged on a series of success stories, rejected the bitter truth. Yet things were not as hopeless as they at first sight appeared. Alasdair and Aboyne were still at large and many of the loyal clans would still, it was thought, be prepared to give their support. Montrose found the door of Traquair House locked against him. Lord Linton had been recalled by his father four days before the battle and Montrose doubtless sought some explanation. None was forthcoming. According to Wishart the two Stewarts, father and son, sat tight and silent within the house while Montrose went on to Peebles. From there, gathering stragglers *en route*, he took the ancient route through the Clyde gap and after crossing the river he joined up with Airlie, Crawford, and a party of horsemen. There was only one option open to them. The source of his success had always been the Highlands. Four days after the defeat at Philiphaugh he was at Buchanty in Glenalmond where exactly twelve months before Lord Kilpont had joined him on the eve of Tibbermore. It says much for Montrose's tenacity and strength of will that he was already attempting to reassemble an army. He ordered that 'straggling Irishes' be rounded up and sent to him. Douglas and Airlie were sent into Angus. It remained to coax Alasdair and Aboyne into rejoining him.

There is an element of tragi-comedy in the feud between Graham and Gordon which now apparently prevented a royalist resurgence. Perhaps, as Gilbert Gordon noted, 'great men's reasons are best known to themselves', but ever since his experiences in 1639 Huntly had borne a grudge against Montrose. Both men were jealous of their own commissions and each refused to yield to the other in the north. Burnet believed that Huntly's obsession with astrology led him to a passive fatalism. A more pressing concern may have been his star-inflicted bankruptcy. At Drumminor, close to the field of Alford, Montrose was joined by Aboyne and Drummond of Balloch with fifteen hundred foot and three hundred horse. From there he congratulated Huntly on his recent safe return from the north. Aboyne had conveyed his father's 'nobell and affectionat expressions concerning his Majesties service'. Montrose wrote, 'for tymes to come I am absolutly resolved to observe the way you propose, and in evry thing, upon my honour, to witness myself as your sone and faithful servant',[8] courtesies which Huntly interpreted too literally, in a sense never intended.

After Philiphaugh David Leslie marched to St Andrews. John Middleton, veteran of Brig o' Dee, who was at the time a general in the army of the covenant and would two years later engage for the king, was sent north to check the royalists. Huntly argued that it was essential to protect the district against Middleton's depredations. Lord Lewis Gordon arrived at Drumminor shortly after his brother but Huntly recalled both sons just as Montrose was about to commence what he hoped would be a triumphant march south. Valuable days were wasted in fruitless negotiations. By 23 October he was still at Braemar but he despatched envoys to treat with Huntly. Montrose ordered Robertson of Inver to convene an army at Dunkeld – 'And let me be advertised what you can hear of Sir Alexander MacDonald, or where he is.' Powrie Ogilvie and Captain Nisbet arrived in Atholl with messages from the king, ordering a rendezvous with Digby.

Charles was actually on his way to Scotland when he received news of Philiphaugh. The triumphant reunion of the royalists was then entrusted to Digby who arrived at Dumfries with fifteen hundred horse on 22 October. Even as Montrose prepared to join him he had retreated to the Isle of Man. Some weeks later Montrose received the apologies of his king. 'Though the successe hath not beene according to my wishes, yet that, nor nothing else, shall discourage me from seeking, and laying hold upon all occasions to assist you, it being the least part of that kyndness I owe you for the eminent fidelity, and generosity you have showed in my service.'

Montrose was, in any case, distracted from Digby by news of the fate of the Philiphaugh prisoners. Magnus O' Cahan and Major O' Lachan had been hanged on the Castlehill of Edinburgh. On 20 October, the day for which Montrose had summoned parliament, the Committee began to hear the case against the others at Glasgow. The first to suffer was Sir William Rollo, brother of Rollo of Duncrub. He had once escaped the covenanters before; he was captured after the battle of Aberdeen but was released in return for a promise to assassinate Montrose. Rollo had as little intention of keeping his promise as had the covenanters of allowing him to keep his head. Two others met a similar fate. Robert Baillie uneasily recalled that 'to this day no man in England has been executed for bearing arms against the parliament'. If the Committee suffered such qualms they were dispersed by the godly who demanded zealous execution of justice, 'that hereby God's wrath, which is greatly increased against the land may be turned away, the land purged of blood, the mourners in part comforted'. The Kirk urged the Estates in the name of 'Him who must judge the quick and the dead, to hear the voice of your Brethern's blood'.[9]

Toleration was not a word to be found in the Scottish vocabulary. The same sense of righteousness lay behind these petitions and the atrocities after Philiphaugh. The society which condoned both confidently anticipated a sympathetic hearing from its God, the same God who had destroyed the enemies of the Israelites in their thousands. He was a God who had selected Scotland for the task of preserving Reformation and leading the world to salvation. God had sent their foes to test his people; their reward was retribution. The frustrations of the kingless kingdom and of religious alienation coalesced in the covenant but the profound psychosis experienced by covenanting Scotland was largely created by Montrose's successes. In the minds of many his brilliant campaign delayed, if it did not completely destroy the possibility of, an accommodation with the king, and the rivers of blood which flowed from his six victories had to be avenged.

Montrose could do little to ease the plight of his comrades but he marched into Lennox with twelve hundred foot and three hundred horse to occupy the estate of Buchanan. Daily he led his troops out in full view of Glasgow and fired the surrounding countryside. He was temporarily successful and the trials were suspended but Leslie with a force of three thousand was not a man to be bluffed in this fashion. Montrose withdrew and the trials were switched to St Andrews.

James, Lord Ogilvie, feigning sickness, was permitted to receive a visit from his family. He exchanged clothes with his sister and, as a tearful girl, walked out of the castle to waiting horses and freedom; next day he joined Black Pate and Drummond of Balloch. Lord James and the others questioned the authority of the tribunal at St Andrews, demanding trial before parliament rather than a sectional committee. Ogilvie reminded the Committee that 'it is one of the fundamental laws and liberties of this kingdom, that peers of the kingdom and others cannot be judged upon the hazard of their life and state but by their peers', or by an ordinary judge. He also objected to the presence of Warriston whose bias was well known. The main defence of all the prisoners was that they had surrendered on promise of quarter. Some members of the tribunal were wavering in favour of relinquishing the business to a full parliament when Warriston intervened to remind them of their duty. 'He showed that the massacre of Kilsyth was never to be forgotten and that God, who was the just judge of the world, would not but judge righteously and keep in remembrance that sea of innocent blood which lay before his throne crying for vengeance on those bloodthirsty rebels, the butchers of so many innocent souls.'[10]

On Tuesday 20 January 1646 the defendants were executed. The decapitating device known as the 'Maiden' was taken to St Andrews specially for the purpose. Colonel Nat Gordon, who had been in constant attendance on Montrose since before Aberdeen, signed a paper confessing his sins but on the scaffold he disowned anything in it which was derogatory to the king. Sir Robert Spottiswood was an old man, secretary of state for Scotland (his seal of office was on his person when he was captured), who had joined Montrose very recently. He was a catholic who once advised Ewen Cameron to 'judge always of mankind by their actions – there is no knowing the heart. Religion and virtue are inseparable and are the only sure and infallible guides to pleasure and happiness.'[11] On the day before his death Spottiswood wrote to Montrose: 'This people having condemned me to die for my loyalty to his majesty and the respect I am known to carry towards your Excellence, which I believe, hath been the greater cause of the two of my undoing. Always I hope, by the assistance of God's grace, to do more good to the king's cause, and to the advancement of the service your Excellence hath in hand, by my death than perhaps otherwise I could have done, been living.' He perceived all 'the rubs and discouragements' which Montrose had suffered of late but believed that he would still succeed in restoring the Lord's anointed. 'One thing I must humbly recommend your Excellence, that as you have done always hithertill, so you will continue by fair and gentle carriage to gain the people's affection to their Prince, rather than imitate the barbarous inhumanity of your adversaries.' He was not permitted a speech on the scaffold. Invoking 'merciful Jesu', the saints, and the martyrs, he was struck off. Others were also executed but some were more fortunate; they were exchanged for royalist captives. It was through such an arrangement that Harry Graham was finally reunited with Montrose.

Montrose suffered yet another great loss when, retreating from Lennox in November 1645, he learned that Lord Archibald Napier had died at Fincastle north-west of Dunkeld at the age of seventy-three. They had not always agreed and their attitudes towards the covenant differed, but Napier's political philosophy had a great influence upon James Graham. Napier had long been disillusioned and disenchanted. If his hopes revived briefly after Kilsyth he must have once more been disgusted by the self-interest and fickleness of Montrose's 'seeming friends'. It is not known whether he took part in Philiphaugh and it seems likely that, worn out by the rigours and discomforts of prison, he remained behind while Montrose marched south. His heart was buried at Fincastle, his body in the churchyard at Blair Atholl. Montrose mourned him as a father. His grief over the loss of Napier and at the reports from Glasgow was channelled into a furious letter which he fired off to the ever-inactive Huntly. 'I hope I need not inculcate to your remembrance the danger the king and kingdom at present is in, and the misery that hangs over his and all faithful subjects' heads. Blame me not my Lord, if I can lay the fault on none but yourself and your son; first for hindering the supplies which the king sent; and next for the loss of those gallant and faithfull men, lately with so much cruelty butchered.'

November had brought one of the severest winters in living memory; the snow was deep but the ice on the frozen rivers and lochs was not quite thick enough to bear the weight of a man or a horse. Huntly was still dragging his feet and Montrose decided upon a weary march with the loyal men of Atholl through the passes to Angus and north to Strathbogie. He sought a conference with Huntly who, learning of his approach, removed himself to his customary winter residence at Bog of Gicht. Both Montrose and Huntly aimed to bring in the clans of the north, especially the MacKenzies. The weather and Huntly's disinclination alike conspired against any worthwhile activity; it was more important to try to secure a meeting at which plans for future efforts might be laid. Montrose followed Huntly to Kinnermony on the Spey and marched rapidly down river to meet him at the Bog. He eventually persuaded Huntly to agree to advance on Inverness, the Gordons taking castles as they moved along the coast, while Montrose marched inland, hugging the mountains. Judging from his correspondence, Montrose was fully aware that Huntly would have a greater chance of attracting the support of the northern clans than he would himself. His own personal disagreements with many of these clans as well as his recent record were against him, whereas Huntly's inactivity which Montrose deplored could be seen as a positive advantage. As his majesty's Lieutenant-General in the north George Gordon could now emerge to summon the northern clans and do his bit for the king. Throughout January Montrose badgered Huntly with questions. Glengarry had assured him that Seaforth would come in; why had Huntly not approached Seaforth? Had he contacted the Grants? Montrose also appealed to MacLean of Coll on which island James Boswell consulted the letters during his tour of the Hebrides in 1773.[12] Huntly has been accused of frittering his time away by besieging insignificant castles in settlement of private scores but he could reply that it was necessary to secure his route as he advanced, and that January and February were not, in any case, the best months for campaigning. Seaforth was active. He arranged a rendezvous with Glengarry, Lord Reay, Sir James MacDonald of Sleat, and the captain of Clan Ranald, at the end of January. Again the season was not propitious and although the 'meeting did not hold', Seaforth was reportedly still busy about the king's business in the north.

Montrose continued to seek news of Alasdair. Since August he had employed himself in terrorizing the west. The tenants of Arran and Bute were fleeing to Ayrshire in December in anticipation of his imminent arrival in these islands and the Countess of Eglinton feared that he would cross from there to the mainland.[13] From Bothwell Alasdair went to Kintyre 'and cleared it for himself, and he drove out of it the Clan Campbell and he erected Dunaverty as a place of strength'. Iain and Donald Muideartach went to Moidart from where they plundered the 'Rough Bounds'. MacLean of Duart returned to Mull while Alasdair himself 'spoiled Argyll and Cowal and the territories'.[14] Towards the end of the year Antrim crossed to Kintyre with a small force in fulfilment of his commission from the king who had been anticipating the arrival of an army from Ireland for some months. Ranald based himself at Dunaverty. The bards were overjoyed that he had returned to his ancestral territories.

> Welcome to the Earl with a fanfare, to himself and
> his army, as he comes to Scotland, to the land of
> his ancestors, a masterful, kingly folk: Clan Donald
> from Isla, rulers of the Islands of the warriors; they
> held sway over land and sea, a splendid company with banners.[15]

There was much activity throughout the hard winter of 1646. So hard pressed were the Campbells, 'driven by absolute want and in terror of MacDonald's power and threats of annihilation', that twelve hundred of them under Campbell of Ardkinglas raided Menteith and proceeded to besiege Strathample Castle.

They were joined by the Stewarts of Balquhidder, members of Clan Menzies and by other stray and starving Highlanders. Black Pate and Balloch, fearing an attack on Atholl, led seven hundred Athollmen against them. In a skirmish near Callendar the predators were routed and eighty of them were killed. The remainder fled to Stirling where Argyll found them, frozen and famished. He sent them into Renfrewshire to look for sustenance but the covenanters' hatred of the Gael extended to their own allies and they were sent back to Lennox to live off the land. The refugees remained a problem. The church of Kilmaronock in Strathendrick was forced to grant relief to 'the poor ones of Argyll . . . among us in great plenty'. Many were wandering through the parish 'in famine and nakedness'.[16]

In March Drummond of Balloch, the Laird of MacNab, and the young Lord Napier, all of whose estates had been threatened by the recent incursion, occupied the old Graham stronghold of Kincardine. Their purpose is obscure and they succeeded in bringing Middleton, armed with cannon from Stirling Castle, down upon them. They held out for a fortnight but when water and supplies were exhausted the three ringleaders escaped to join Montrose. The garrison, some fifty strong, surrendered; twelve of them were summarily executed while the castle was fired.

Middleton then returned to Aberdeen to rejoin the remainder of his forces; he was now in full command since Leslie had again been summoned to England. Montrose was delighted by the success of his colleagues but he resisted entreaties that revenge should be taken on those prisoners captured at Callendar. Huntly and Lord Lewis Gordon continued to rampage in the north, the latter based at Rothes. One who lived through these troubles was James Fraser of Phopachy near Inverness. He remembered Lord Lewis as 'a merciless cruell man', who fired dozens of cornstacks and barnyards throughout Moray. Lewis was supposed to guard against an advance by Middleton while Montrose, assisted by a number of MacKenzies and MacDonalds, besieged Inverness. If the northern capital fell Seaforth and the others would have no choice but to give their wholehearted support to the king. According to Fraser, Montrose had Inverness surrounded but, allegedly through the indolence or treachery of Lewis Gordon, he had no warning of Middleton's rapid approach from Aberdeen. So hastily did he abandon the siege that he was forced to leave behind precious cannon set up on Castle Hill. He fled across the Ness and marched through the Caiplich to Farley Forest on the border of Ross and Cromarty. Middleton followed through Inverness and along the main road to pitch camp in sight of the enemy. For two days messages passed between the two, neither feeling inclined to risk pitched battle. 'Montrose, after refreshing his forces, timous in a morning firing of his camp, escaped to the mountains.' The black smoke gave Middleton the first indication of his departure. There was no pursuit. Montrose took the long route via the wilds of Strathglass, crossing the Great Glen south of Loch Ness and marching up the south side of the loch through Stratherrick to arrive back on Speyside early in May. Somewhere in the hills he met Seaforth and the two men renewed the Kilcumin band. Copies were sent for subscription to MacDonalds, MacLeods, MacKays, Frasers, Camerons, and some of the covenanting clans besides. When news of it reached the general assembly Seaforth was excommunicated but the band itself meant no more than it had done before. As Montrose marched from Farley to Speyside the MacKenzies melted into the hills. During those weary months since Philiphaugh Montrose had achieved nothing. He had failed to establish contact with Alasdair; communications with potential supporters were miserable; his activities appeared as aimless as those of Huntly. Montrose was still understandably bitter about the Gordons. Huntly had sensibly taken Aberdeen after Middleton moved out but he swiftly abandoned the city once more. On 27 May Montrose made one last effort to interview George Gordon. He rode twenty miles at speed to Bog of Gicht but once again Huntly, hearing of his approach, fled. Montrose had had enough; he decided to leave the Gordons to their own devices. He had faced a great test as leader of the royalists in Scotland during the past months and without doubt he failed. As he would rediscover to his cost in 1650 his charm and appeal held few attractions for the men of the north.

The accommodation with Seaforth, for what it was worth, was in any case too late. After the failure of his projected march into Scotland Charles had withdrawn to Oxford where throughout the winter he watched the cause collapse around him. At the prompting of the French ambassador Montereul, he considered the possibility of an agreement with the Scots, hoping thereby to put pressure on parliament. Negotiations proceeded far enough for Charles to write a letter (though it is doubtful that he ever sent it) to Montrose urging that if he was satisfied that the covenanters really had declared for the king and that the Scottish royalists were protected by an amnesty, he should 'take them by the hand and use all possible diligence to unite your forces with theirs for the advancement of my service'. Like Montereul he failed to realize that there could be no accommodation with the Scots which granted such favourable terms to Montrose. On 26 April Charles left Oxford in disguise, making for he knew not where. His vague hopes of recruiting support came to nothing. When he heard from Montereul that the Scots might be prepared to modify their demands he rode into their camp at Newark in desperation, to be received by the Earl of Lothian who immediately demanded that Charles order the surrender of Newark, that he sign the covenant, and that he command Montrose to lay down his arms. The king refused on all, counts telling Lothian that 'he who had made him earl, had made James Graham a marquis'.[17] The Scots could now look forward to the king's eventual subscription of the covenant and his approval of the

presbyterian establishment in both countries and they withdrew with
their valuable, and unexpected, acquisition to Newcastle. To his credit
Charles still refused to repudiate Montrose. The covenanters were
equally insistent. It was claimed that his campaigns had caused £36,000
worth of damage, almost half a million pounds Scots, perhaps a modest
estimate. Montereul's suggestion, which had been floated before, that
Montrose and Alasdair should be allowed to pass to France was initially
rejected outright.[18] Montrose, however, was still Charles's trump – and
perhaps only – card. The covenanters were genuinely afraid of a
summer campaign with the joint forces of Montrose, Seaforth,
Alasdair, Huntly, and the clans. The Earl of Lanark, who had captured
Spottiswood at Philiphaugh, eventually persuaded his colleagues to
permit Montrose to go into exile if the king would command him to
disband. No provision was made for the others but on 2 June Montrose
received the letter he must have dreaded. 'You must disband your forces
and goe into France, where you shall receive my further directions. This
at first may justly startle you, but I do assure you that if, for the present,
I should offer to doe more for you, I could not doe so much . . .'

Montrose replied from Strathspey, promising humble obedience,

Only I must humbly beg your Majestie to be pleased to consider, that ther are
nothing remembred concerning the immunity off those who heave beane upon
your service; that all deeds, in ther prejudice, be reduced; and those of them
who stay att home, enjoy ther lyves and propertyes without being questioned;
for such as goe abroad, that they heave all freidome off transport; as also that
all prissoners be released, so that no characters of what hes happened remaine.
For when all is done that we can, I am much afraid, that it shall trouble both
those ther with your Majestie, and all your servands heir, to quit thir parts.
And as for my aune leaveing this kingdome, I shall, in all humility and obedience
endevoure to performe your Majesties command wishing never to see it
againe with myne eyes; willing, alsweale by passion, as action, to witness myself your Majesties most humble, and most faithful, subject and servand.

Such at least was the public declaration. There must have been much
reading between the lines going on and the important details were
confided to the bearer, whom Montrose instructed to assure the
king, that if he did not really wish the army to disband, he would hold
himself in readiness. It was with some such idea in mind that he
ordered Donald Robertson, Tutor of Strowan, to 'repair to us with all
possible diligence'. Two days after replying to the king he wrote to

Lord Reay from Corgarff telling him of the order to disband 'and this without any immunity for what is past or assurance for time to come'. He related how Huntly refused to act for the king but he assured Reay, 'I cannot be so base nor dishonourable to leave all who have engaged in the king's service in the mire . . . I resolve not to abandon you and Seaforth and all other friends. . . .'[19] Charles reassured Montrose that he was greatly concerned about the interests of his Scottish supporters and particularly about Montrose himself whom he was sending out of the country in order that he might 'returne home with greater glory, and in the meantime to have as honourable an imployment as I can put upon you'. He asked Montrose to instruct Huntly, Crawford, Airlie, Seaforth, and Ogilvie to lay down their arms.

At Newcastle Alexander Henderson tried to win the king over to the covenant. The need for some accommodation became, for the covenanters, increasingly pressing. They had frequently rancorous exchanges with the parliamentarians, many of whom were veering towards Independency. English and Scots alike were alarmed by the news from Ireland that Owen Roe O'Neill had defeated Monro at the battle of Benburb on 5 June. Three weeks later Argyll made a statesmanlike speech to the House of Lords in an attempt to pull the Scottish and English allies together. He thought that they had a unique opportunity to settle the religion, peace, and union of Scotland and England, but he urged the *via media*. 'Upon the one part we would take heed not to settle lawless liberty in religion, whereby instead of uniformity, we should set up a thousand heresies and schisms which is directly contrary and destructive to our covenant. Upon the other part we are to look that we persecute not piety, and peaceable men who cannot, through scruple of conscience come up in all things to the common rule; but that they may have such forbearance as may be according to the word of God, may consist with the covenant, and not be destructive to the rule itself, nor to the peace of church and kingdom.' Argyll, like a number of the covenanters, had come round to a point of view adopted by Montrose as early as 1639. Acceptance of the spirit of the covenant did not necessarily imply total acceptance of the ideas which it embodied. He said that Scotland and England had given reciprocal aid in the past.

Therefore let us hold fast that union which is so happily established betwixt us; and let nothing make us again two, who are so many ways one – all of one language, in one island, all under one king, one in religion, yea one in covenant; so that in effect we differ in nothing but in the name (as brethern do) which I wish were also removed, that we might be one if the two kingdoms think fit; for I dare say, not the greatest kingdom in the Earth can prejudice both so much as one of them may do the other.

He forbore to speak of the many jealousies between the two countries but he could not resist commenting upon the charge that Scotland was 'too much affected with the king's interest'. His attitude admirably sums up the Scottish sentiment with regard to the captive king. 'I will not deny, but the kingdom of Scotland, by reason of the reign of many kings hath a natural affection to his Majesty, whereby they wish he may be rather reformed than ruined; yet experience may tell their personal regard to him has never made them forget that common rule, "the safety of the people is the supreme law"; so likewise their love to monarchy makes them very desirous that it may be rather regulated than destroyed.'[20] With much of this Montrose would have agreed. He might also have approved some of the conditions for a treaty with the king which Argyll presented to the house. Episcopacy was to be abolished and the church reformed in line with the covenant and the Westminster confession. Montrose would have liked Charles to accept the covenant but he would have rejected the proposal that parliament should exercise control of the militia and the navy for twenty years and that parliament's resolutions should have the effect of law.

Charles undoubtedly feared that Graham would have none of the treaty. The king wrote to him on 16 July assuring him that 'according to that real freedom and friendship which is between us, as I cannot absolutely command you to accept of unhandsome conditions, so I must tell you I must believe your refusal will put you in a far worse estate than your compliance will'. He strongly urged him to accept 'for if this opportunity be let slip, you must not expect any more treaties; in which case you must either conquer all Scotland, or be inevitably ruined.' If he found the proffered conditions reasonable he could say that he accepted them by royal command; if he did not he could expect the king's (public) displeasure which would bring an army down upon him. Montrose must not be allowed to jeopardize the chance of peace. On 22 July he duly met John Middleton at a point on the Water of Isla to discuss a cessation. For two hours they stood together accompanied only by an attendant each to hold their horses.

There on the frontier of Highlands and Lowlands Montrose learned of the fate of himself and his fellows. He, Crawford, and Sir John Hurry were to be excluded from all pardon except safe conduct overseas in a vessel provided by the Estates, on condition they embarked before the beginning of September. All the rest of Montrose's supporters were to retain their lives and their estates, a significant concession considering that Argyll's list of persons to be excluded from pardon named MacLeod of Harris, the chief of MacKay, Huntly, Nithsdale, Carnwath, Aboyne, Ogilvie, and Alasdair. It is difficult to believe that Alasdair was pardoned and, indeed, Gilbert Gordon says that he was not. Others in time made their own peace with the covenant but they paid dearly for the privilege.

On 30 July at Rattray near Blairgowrie, Montrose said farewell to his small army. Wishart describes the episode in a rather affecting little tableau.

It was obvious to all that the king's authority ended that day. Everyone felt convinced that the order to disband had been extorted from the king under fear of some evil more imminent. As for themselves, whatever terms might be made for their safety, they would rather have borne the worst, than stand by, idle, dishonoured, spectators of the calamity which had befallen their sovereign ... Their grief was greatly enhanced by apprehensions of the fate that awaited their brave, successful and beloved general, torn from his king and country, from themselves and all true men. His soldiers fell at his knees, and besought him with tears, if the king's safety required him to quit the kingdom altogether to take them with him where he would. They were ready to live, to fight, and if it pleased God, to die under his command.

While individuals like Lord Napier wrote to the king offering faithful service, it may be suspected that most of Montrose's supporters would be relieved to see him go. Few had the will or the inclination to renew the exhausting campaigns. With Graham out of the way there might be peace in the land.

Montrose received one last letter from his king, lamenting that Charles could offer only verbal repayment for all his service. 'But I assure you that the world shall see that the real expressions of my friendship to you shall be an infallible sign of my change of fortune. As for your desires, they are all so just, that I shall endeavour what I can to have them all satisfied. . . . Defer your going beyond seas as long as you may, without breaking your word.' This last plea stemmed from the hope that some saviour might yet descend from the Highlands or from Ireland. Antrim and Alasdair might still advance from Kintyre; Huntly could organize in the north; Seaforth was rumoured to control eight thousand men. The royalist appetite for rumour, hope, and fantasy was insatiable. As it was, Montrose almost missed the boat. The promised vessel did not arrive in Montrose harbour until 31 August. The shipmaster, 'a boorish, stiff-necked champion of the covenant', refused demands that he sail at once, on the grounds that the ship required to be caulked and rigged. English men o' war were spotted off the Esk. Montrose suspected treachery and it was imperative that he escape as soon as possible. His agents found a small Norwegian bark in Stonehaven harbour. For a substantial payment her master agreed to transport Hurry, Balloch, Harry Graham, and several others. On the evening of 3 September the Norwegian captain Jens Gunnersen sailed his sloop into Montrose roads. A small cock boat rowed out to meet him and Jens took aboard the reverend James Wood and his poorly clad servant. The latter, James Graham, Marquis of Montrose, left Scotland as he had entered it in 1644 – in disguise.

13
PASSIONATE
EXILE

Good wishes to the illustrious Graham who though in exile is on the march; although some distance away, his tryst is to meet with us; wherever he be in camp in Spain or in Holland, who so wills let him drink a toast to Montrose.

Were Montrose to come to Ireland to join forces with us, with three score rigged ships and hempen ropes as reins upon them, with banners of satin and with King Charles' command, the fulfilment of that prophecy would bring us to life, as Thomas the Rhymer foretold.[1]

Iain Lom

Although hopes of a royalist resurgence appeared to have evaporated with the departure of Montrose, Alasdair mac Cholla pursued his own private war in the west. In future years needy petitioners and popular tradition alike combined to merge Alasdair's two invasions of Argyll. Following the first rampage Archibald Campbell, captain of Dun-staffnage, made a careful note of the losses suffered by his tenants. The sizes of all houses, barns, byres, and mills were measured according to the number of 'couples' – rafters or roof-beams – used in their construction. Thus, Ardchonnell, 'ane principall hous conteining fyve couples consisting of ane hall, ane chalmer (chamber), with three standing beddis, ane chymnie and ane cellar', was destroyed. Tenants' houses and byres totalling thirty-four couples, a kiln of three, and five barns of twenty-four couples also suffered. Fifty-seven bolls of meal, eighty-four of oats and horse-corn, and thirty-one of bear were looted from the same estate as were thirty-two cows, two stirks, fifty-three sheep and goats, and three plough horses. Similar quantities of victual and livestock were pillaged from nearby Achavaich while Barcaldine on the north side of Loch Etive was fired and plundered. The apprehensions of the inhabitants on Alasdair's second visit were fully realized when, according to local tradition, he left only one cow in the whole of Glassary. Yet George Campbell of Airds, sheriff-depute at Inveraray, opined, 'it is not the enemies that entered the country that is destroying the same – every neighbour is destroying another, partly through not drawing to a head and partly through joining with the enemy, so it is likely when forces comes that this country must be anew conquered.' He added that no provisions were to be found in the vicinity of Inveraray; Patrick Campbell, keeper of Barcaldine, had also exhausted his food supplies. In January 1645 parliament sent one thousand five hundred bolls of meal and three hundred bolls of malt 'to the garrisons and country people in Argyll'. The Marquis of Argyll later claimed that he collected no rents between 1644 and 1647.[2] Alasdair and Antrim virtually annexed Kintyre.

In February 1646 they were negotiating with the men of Bute and were rumoured to be contemplating a march to the Lennox by way of Loch Fyne and Loch Long. George Campbell urged Dunstaffnage to sound out the MacLeans, 'but do it so as that they may know there is nothing intendit for thame but destruction unless they submit in time'; he was also to investigate the situation in Appin and Glencoe. Even more alarming from the point of view of the faithful was that Anti-Christ once again reared his ugly head. Priests were once again active throughout Kintyre and the inner Hebrides. The synod of Argyll stated: 'The sword of the rebells quhilk hes bereft us of our freends, spoiled us of our goods, and burnt our dwellings, [and] the apprehension of a following famine . . . cannot parallell the bitterness that the feare of the sorest of all plagues, the removall of the light of the gospell, hes possessed our soules with.'[3] One, Murdoch MacKenzie, was negotiating with Alasdair and Antrim on behalf of Seaforth. MacLean, Clan Ranald and Sir James MacDonald of Sleat had also been approached, while Alasdair was planning military expeditions to Islay and Ardnamurchan. Because of the Troubles many ministers were unable to attend the synod and several of them with members of their flocks were solemnly excommunicated for compliance with the rebels. Among those who rallied to Alasdair's banner were the MacDougals of Dunnollie, the MacDonalds of Largie, Angus MacEachern of Kilellan, the MacKays of Ugadale, the MacNeills of Carskey, and some of the MacAllasters of Loup. Archibald Mór MacDonald of Sanda died in Alasdair's service while his son Archibald Òg followed him to Ireland.[4]

Antrim returned to Ireland in obedience to the king's commands but from his base at Dunaverty Alasdair ruled Kintyre for over eighteen months, the high point of his career. He not only held sway over his ancestral territories but he enjoyed the company of his brothers and his incorrigible old father Coll, now seventy-six years old. His presence greatly hindered Argyll's efforts to send relief to his beleaguered clansmen. When Archibald Campbell of Penmore was delivering meal to Castle Sween for distribution to Duntroon, Craignish, and Dunstaffnage the news that Alasdair's boats were in the mouth of Loch Tarbert forced him to beat a hasty retreat.[5] Although Mac Cholla suffered a minor setback when he failed to take Skipness Castle in Kintyre after a lengthy siege his secure hold on the area bred a careless over-confidence. When the Scots surrendered their king to the English parliament, David Leslie was free to eradicate the pocket of resistance in the west. With Argyll he advanced from Dunblane in the spring of 1647. On 5 May Alasdair issued a commission appointing his 'weelbeloved father' commander-in-chief over 'the lands of Yla and all other lands unto me belonging within the kingdom of Scotland, he my said father charging and commanding all the inhabitants of the said lands to all such employments as shall concern the advancement of his Majesty's service where occasion shall require. As also to man, victual, defend and keep the fort and garrison of Dunyveg against all manner of invasion of the enemy.'[6] Old Coll must have returned to Dunyveg with great pride and satisfaction after such a long absence but apart from this splendid gesture to his kindred Alasdair took few steps to defend himself against the invading army. On the evening of 24 May Leslie and Argyll, after a forced march of twenty miles down the west coast of Kintyre from Loch Tarbert, surprised him at Rhunahaorine Point not far from Largie Castle which he was presumably using as a temporary base. He lost eighty men including the last of his three Irish commanders Ranald Òg MacDonald, who was captured and subsequently executed at Inveraray. Mac Cholla, however, was well placed to escape across the narrow sound to Gigha and from there to Islay. Sir James Turner who served with Leslie because, according to his own account, 'I thought it duetie to fight against these men who first had deserted Montrose when he stood most in need of them', condemned Alasdair for placing three hundred of his best men in Dunaverty far to the south – 'if he had beene a soldier and not excessivelie besotted with brandie and aquavitae he sould have possessed the passes on this side of Kintyre.'[7] Perhaps he was right; it would be surprising if the heady achievements of the past three years had not taken their toll.

Leslie marched on Dunaverty where, warned by his chaplain of the curses which befell Saul for sparing the Amalekites, he butchered the three hundred despite a promise of quarter. He then crossed to Islay to find Dunyveg defended by its recently appointed captain though Alasdair had moved on to Ireland. Like Dunaverty, that crumbling fortress on a tooth of rock lacked an adequate water supply. Alasdair's detractors have condemned his apparently heartless abandonment of Coll Ciotach but that old man had survived much and he very nearly survived again. He talked with his old acquaintance, and gaoler, Campbell of Dunstaffnage, about the possibility of surrender on terms. On 29 June he sent out for 'four dollars worth of acquavitae', offering Dunstaffnage a dram or two in exchange for further parley. When he was asked if he intended Campbell to go into the castle or if he would come out, Coll fearlessly emerged to immediate arrest. He had served his purpose which was probably to give Alasdair time to win clear. In due course he was tried by Campbell of Airds, condemned, and hanged, according to tradition, from the mast of his own galley.

Alasdair survived his father by only a few months, As Lieutenant-General of Munster in the confederate army, he was part of the force which faced General Murrough O'Brian, Baron Inchequin at the battle of Knocknanuss in County Cork on 13 November. It has been said that he 'fell obscurely in some unrecorded provincial quarrel',[8] but the army in which he fought consisted of seven thousand foot and one thousand horse. Some said that he was cut off by fourteen troopers on a small hill; others – and these the Gaels will always believe – that he was shot through the head having been promised quarter.

> Stout Machabee from whom the double ty
> Of zeale and of unbounded loyalty,
> Too early for us on too blacke a day,
> Inforced the tribut which we all must pay.
> Whyle thy sterne countenance and stronge arme press'd
> The fates, but for a single interest.

Like lightning captiv'd fortune shot her smyles,
To wayte on thee in Scotland and her Iles.[9]

The clans of Kintyre attempted to make their peace with Leslie who, after sparing the garrison of Dunyveg for service in France, went to Mull. Lachlan MacLean had little alternative but to surrender the Irish who assisted him in the defence of Duart Castle. The Irish were executed and the chief was imprisoned. MacDonald of Glengarry had accompanied Antrim to Ireland from where he eventually made his way to the continent. At Dunaverty, Dunyveg, and Duart Leslie broke the power of the western clans, of those who, as MacMhuirich had it, 'did all the service'. At Knocknanuss there perished one of the greatest of Gaelic Scotland's warriors. Iain Lom was heartbroken;

I got news from Dungannon that has dimmed my sight, my utter woe that
Alasdair was dead:
And the truth from the harper when he landed at Port Patrick;
my mind made no glad response to his music.
Sad to me is the dispersing of the men of Islay and the
noblemen of Kintyre. . . .[10]

Time would prove that, with the execution of old Colkitto and the death of Alasdair mac Cholla, the men of Islay and the noblemen of Kintyre had indeed been dispersed for ever.

In the Lowlands the royalist situation was equally bleak. Legislation of January 1646 provided for the punishment of royalists whose 'prime supporters' were to be fined a minimum of two, and a maximum of six, years' rent. For those who assisted in any other way the fines ranged between six months and four years. A subsequent act allowed for imprisonment until such fines were paid. Rents and estates could be sequestrated or lands sold to pay fines, in which cases buyers' rights were secured.[11] Creditors of royalists were encouraged to advance their claims, a practice which bore heavily on those who had guaranteed the bonds of individuals who were now more often than not bankrupt. The Committee allegedly considered exhuming Napier's remains at Fincastle in order to pass sentence of forfeiture upon them. Lord Erskine, who had stood surety for him, was pursued for 'but a little summe of 40,000 merks, whereof £20,000 is assigned to the Advocates for their service donne the State'![12] Ecclesiastical sanctions aggravated the situation. Both Ogilvie and Seaforth were ultimately successful in having their sentences of excommunication relaxed, but the Grahams of Gorthie and Cairney took much longer to convince the assembly commissioners of their reformed ways. From Orleans in October 1647 Montrose wrote to his kinsmen of Fintry, Morphie, Inchbrakie, Gorthie, Balgowan, and Craigo,

I must take hold of this opportunity to show you the astonishment I have that people's malice should be so unjust and endless, that after I have suffered them (by my obedience to his Majesty's commands) to ruin and sack my own fortunes, that yet they would cast also against all those of my friends to smart me more than my own wounds, as particularly appears by this procedure against my nephew, Lord Napier, whose father, being bound with others for some of my debts, they yet (and though absent from the country) pursues for the whole, not out of any favour they intend to others, but making this once a preparative, they will use it as a leading case to fall on every one of you in the same kind and study your ruins to satisfy their malice against me, and meantime, reserve my estate to be disposed of at their own pleasure, which according to all laws both divine and human it should at the worst be employed for satisfaction of creditors and liberty of all parties burdened, what is all I desire, for if none suffer unjustly for me what they can do against myself cannot move me much. . . . Let me again entreat you to save yourselves and let no man be sufferer for me, so far as my own can go and trust me to God, and my own fortunes which cannot disappoint; wishing you people there may calm their malice, and let their experience make them more wise, for if innocency and patience cannot prevail, it may be I light upon a virtue that will be found fitter for their temper.

The letter was signed 'your most loving chief'.[13]

Montrose arrived at Bergen on 10 September 1646, making his way from there to Christiana 'by a wild and difficult route across the high rugged mountain ranges buried in perpetual ice and snow'. Despite their respective difficulties Charles had always maintained a regular correspondence with his uncle Christian IV of Denmark from whom he sought assistance in 1642. As part of Montrose's overall strategy, the following year Christian sent two shiploads of weapons and ammunition which were captured by the parliamentarians. Montrose still had high hopes of Christian who also ruled Norway and who was no longer preoccupied with a war with Sweden. Charles informed his uncle in February 1646 that he was reduced to the last extremity – 'the rebels are now endeavouring the total overthrow of monarchy and to substitute an oligarchy or rather a democracy.' He reminded Christian that his plight was of concern to all neighbouring kings and he begged him to send three or four thousand well-equipped infantry to England.[14] When Montrose learned that Christian was in Germany he proceeded through Holstein to Hamburg where he remained until the end of March. Charles had expected the marquis to make a landfall in the Low Countries; he urged him to go to Paris to consult with his queen. The latter's court in exile was plagued with bickering, jealous courtiers who were increasingly bewildered and hesitant following the Scots' surrender of Charles in January 1646. According to Wishart Montrose had predicted the Scottish 'betrayal', hoping that the news might travel ahead of him to facilitate recruitment for the cause.

The marquis's own inclinations were signified by his gift of a sword to Charles. 'The more the saints sought to crush the good king and with him all royal authority, the more erect and firm he stood to restore the liberty and avenge the majesty of his sovereign.'[15] On learning for certain of Charles's confinement he hastened to Paris, where he ex-pected to receive instructions from the queen and a commission as the king's ambassador extraordinary to France. On both counts he was disappointed while the ill-considered suggestions of courtiers such as John Ashburnham increased his frustration. Montrose was adamant that any renewed assault must be properly organized, co-ordinated, and supplied. When Ashburnham suggested that Montrose should try to make his peace with the covenanters he replied 'that no man was readier to obey the king's instructions in all that was just and honourable, but not even the king should command his obedience in what was dis-honourable, unjust and destructive to his Majesty himself.' During a year spent in France the queen's fickleness and the intrigues of her court depressed him further; he thought that no person of honour and virtue would suffer themselves to 'live in so lewd and worthless a place'. During that time he struck up a friendship with Cardinal de Retz to whom he confided his distaste for court life and his financial inability to maintain the following of noblemen and officers who had accompanied him from Scotland. De Retz considered him 'the solitary being who ever realized to my mind the image of those heroes whom the world only sees in the biographies of Plutarch', a man possessed 'with a grandeur of soul that finds no parallel in the present age'.[16] Mazarin evidently concurred in part for although he was in corres-pondence with certain English royalists about the possibility of

supporting Montrose in an Irish campaign,[17] he offered the marquis
command of the Scots Guard in France and the post of Lieutenant-
General of the French army with the promise of promotion to Marshal
of France and the captaincy of the king's own guard. Although urged
by Napier to accept, Montrose considered any appointment below the
rank of Marshal a slight to his honour. He believed the offer was a ruse
to prevent his offering his services to Spain which was more sympathetic to Charles I than was France. Montrose's fame was spreading,
particularly after the publication of Wishart's *De Rebus* in Holland in
September 1647, although word-of-mouth reports of his deeds had
already aroused the admiration of Europe. The future Charles II was
less than enthusiastic. He required Montrose to suppress the book
because it accused several persons of quality of crimes of a high nature
and he could not afford 'patronage to accusations which render persons
of honour infamous before they be heard'.[18] Lord Napier proudly told
his wife that Montrose was held in 'huge esteem', sought out by many
distinguished visitors to France. He modestly added that 'it was ever
said that Montrose and his nephew was like the Pope and the Church
who would be inseparable.' Nor had Montrose lost any of his old
conceit. He was in an identical situation to that of 1643, advocating
action to a basically sympathetic but powerless queen. Intransigent as
ever he was convinced that his own destiny was inextricably bound up
with that of the king but those who came to worship at his shrine could
offer only praise; they had neither men nor money nor weapons to
give. When Henrietta Maria supported the Hamilton-led 'Engagement'
on behalf of the king, the parallel with 1643 was complete. He would
not associate with such suspect persons and he departed from France for
the court of her enemy, the Emperor, who satisfied honour by offering
him the baton of a field-marshal.

It soon transpired that the Scots had miscalculated in exchanging the
person of Charles for the guarantee of a presbyterian establishment in
England, for the army, which predominantly favoured Independency,
was increasingly gaining the upper hand. When in June 1647 the army
seized Charles the worst fears of some Scots were realized. Fearing for
his life Charles escaped to the Isle of Wight where, during the autumn
of 1647, he worked out a compromise with the very men of whom
Montrose was most suspicious, including Traquair, Lanark, Loudoun,
and Lauderdale. These men represented an uneasy coalition of moderate

opinion in opposition to the ambitious and exorbitant demands of the Scottish clergy. The negotiations concluded in a Scottish undertaking to intervene on the king's behalf to allow him to return to London in safety, honour, and freedom, in exchange for a three-year trial period of presbyterianism in England and a share in English trade. Burnet had a story that Charles secretly agreed to the Scottish annexation of Northumberland, Cumberland, and Westmorland which, if true, testifies to a basic unreality underlying the entire negotiations for even if the Scots won a decisive military victory it was extremely improbable that the English would prove receptive either to the presbyterian establishment or to the surrender of territory. However, by entrusting the military command to Hamilton, freed from imprisonment in 1646 to make his peace with the kirk by subscribing the solemn league, the Engagers ensured defeat, and their army was cut to pieces at Preston on 17 August 1648.

Argyll was implacably opposed to the Engagement because he did not believe Charles was to be trusted. Some royalists took comfort from the fact that Argyll depended upon 'the airie opinion of the clergie which once being excluded from the consultation of publict affaires will soone decay', though Traquair realistically advised that the ministers were the people to watch.[19] Although Argyll's party was in a minority it exerted an influence out of all proportion to numbers. Within a week of Preston he was in touch with Cromwell; he was also on hand to welcome the several thousand covenanters who marched upon Edinburgh from the west in the episode known as the 'Whigga-more Raid'. He was the obvious leader of the coalition of ministers and Whigs, 'the well affected party', as Cromwell called it. When the latter arrived in Edinburgh he was greatly impressed by, and as sub-sequent developments would show also learned from, Argyll's success in driving those in sympathy with the Engagement out of the Com-mittee of Estates – 'a lesser party of a parliament hath made it lawful to declare the greater part a faction.'[20] But Argyll was far from being an Independent and his alliance with Cromwell was short-lived. Despite his apparent success he had miscalculated in relying so exclusively on the support of the ministers; he was to regret that he neglected his earlier suspicions of their ambitions. It was about the time of the Engagement that according to his own testimony things started to go wrong. 'I did not look upon our intended reformation as any way taxable since it had the whole stream of universal consent of the whole nation; I never thought of those dire consequences which presently followed, till by that confusion my thoughts became distracted and myself encountered so many difficulties in the way that all remedies that were applied had the quite contrary operation.'[21] Such awareness, however, was retrospective. For the moment Argyll and the ministers set about the creation of the New Zion in Scotland's sole, and mercifully brief, experiment in theocracy.

When Montrose departed from Paris he left his nephew to cover his tracks by 'letting the word go that my uncle was gone to the country for his health', a ruse which apparently fooled even Wishart. Napier continued to visit the court, the playhouse, and the Academy, where he pursued his scholarly 'exercises'. When he learned that Montrose had reached Geneva he decided, in view of the high cost of living in Paris, to quit France for Brussels in the company of some fifteen of Montrose's associates, to await further orders, and to pine for his wife whose portrait 'in the breadth of a sixpence' he requested in order to place it in a small gold pendant alongside that of Montrose. From Geneva Montrose proceeded through the Tyrol and Bavaria to Vienna from where he wrote to Graham of Craigo on 29 June. Magdalen Carnegie had died earlier in the year, doubtless a sadly troubled woman. Montrose's reaction to her death is not recorded but he was concerned about the welfare of his children.

Though I have judged it against the times to hazard any correspondence of this kind, yet being informed of your pains and endeavours in all my affairs there, I cannot but adventure to give my thanks and withall desire (that since it has pleased God my children do come in your disposing that are my friends) you may be pleased to take such present course as they may be in the power of none but yourselves (as I make no doubt but you have already done) until I be able to acquaint you with my further resolutions ... your most loving chief.

Six months later Lord James petitioned the commissioners of assembly that since through the care of his late mother and his relations he had attended the schools, he might now be permitted to attend a university. Permission was granted though care was to be taken to 'try the qualification, affection and conversation' of his regents.[22]

Emperor Ferdinand III was not in Vienna. Montrose caught up with him at Prague which was soon to be besieged in the last major conflict of the bitter war which had begun there exactly thirty years before. Most of Europe was exhausted as negotiations which commenced at Münster and Osnabrück in 1644 ground towards a conclusion in the Treaty of Westphalia, but the Swedish general Königsmarck found sufficient energy for a descent on Bohemia. The imperialists were defeated at Zusmarshausen in May and their fortunes continued to ebb throughout the summer of 1648. Ferdinand was happy to recruit a man of Montrose's 'famous repute and experience in war' as the commission dated at Linz on the Danube described him.[23] He was given authority to raise levies for the service of the Emperor who also provided letters of introduction to his brother Archduke Leopold, Governor of the Spanish Netherlands, an area which was expected to prove a fertile recruiting ground. Montrose's intentions are none too clear. According to Wishart his sole object was to serve Charles – 'it was his wish to be near at hand in order to take advantage of any opportunity that might occur' – but just what he had in mind is not divulged. The marquis seems to have been intent upon sounding for himself the depth of potential support for Charles, which probably accounts for the lengthy route he followed from Vienna, moving eastwards along the Danube to the Hungarian capital of Pressburg, to Cracow, and so to Danzig. The international network of Scots which covered Europe included several substantial Polish communities. Wealthy expatriate merchants, or soldiers of fortune, might be just the men to finance, or fight for, Charles Stewart. From Danzig Montrose sailed to Copenhagen and a favourable reception from Frederik III who had succeeded Christian the previous February. He then crossed to Jutland and took ship for Groningen in the Netherlands, travelling overland to Brussels in time to learn of Archduke Leopold's defeat at the battle of Lens by Louis de Bourbon, duc d'Enghien, Prince of Condé.

Earlier in the year William, Prince of Orange, had been among those who advised Montrose that since the affairs of Charles were in 'so bad posture', he should serve France until the situation improved. John, Lord Belasyse, fled to Brussels after the battle of Preston where he met 'his old friend' Montrose, and they 'swore not to part'. Since Condé had 'a great esteem for them both, they applied themselves to him to serve the King of France; but before conditions could be agreed upon the marquis attempted in Scotland some designs which did not take effect.'[24] It is not improbable that Condé and Montrose did seek one another out. Disappointed in his expectations of Leopold, the marquis perhaps decided that the future lay after all with France; he was certainly prepared to recruit allies from all quarters. He must have been cheered by the realization that his fame and reputation were his greatest assets but he was to be disappointed once again for the court in exile was still torn by internal strife and from the one worthwhile and potentially successful royalist offensive Montrose was pointedly excluded.

The Marquis of Ormonde arrived in Paris from Ireland in March 1648. When Inchequin declared for the king within six months of his victory at Knocknanuss, the moment seemed propitious for a royalist coalition which would include some of the catholic confederates. The Prince of Wales commissioned Ormonde to lead the renewed assault. He was empowered to grant any concessions necessary to recruit the adherence of the confederates including initially the abolition of all anti-catholic legislation, though that sweeping offer was later withdrawn in favour of granting concessions made in any former treaty.[25] Throughout the following year royalist hopes continued to be pinned on Ireland to which Ormonde duly returned. Prince Rupert was to provide him with naval backing and it was obviously in hopes of being granted a piece of the action that Montrose decided to contact '*Robert le Diable*'. 'When your Highness shall be pleased to know that I was ever a silent admirer of you and a passionate affecter of your person and all your ways, you will be pleased to allow me recourse to your goodness and generosity, and the rather that your Highness sees I am for the present at such distance with all interests, as no end but naked respect can now prompt me to it!' Rupert replied in the fashionable, similarly effusive cavalier style and so a correspondence of some months commenced. Montrose must have been uncomfortably aware that he belied the optimistic designation which he had reserved for himself in the cipher he was then using; so far '*Venture Faire*' expressed only his hopes. He also approached James, Duke of York, the future James II and VII who, like the Prince of Orange, assured him of his friendship and esteem which, however flattering, did not ease his predicament. Nor could Rupert, who had his hands full with a mutinous fleet, spare time for a private meeting. Montrose's language became more heightened the more convinced he became of his own rejection as letters were conveyed in the greatest secrecy between Rupert and himself by Sir John Hurry who bore the scars of Preston. He announced his intention of returning to the Imperial court 'in regard there is nothing of honour amongst the stuff here, and that I am not found useful for his Majesty's service in the way of home'. Rupert should not conceive his 'passionate servant' 'slackened of the invincible desire I have vowed ever to retain to serve you'. He had no interest in compromise of any kind. They must strive 'to gain or lose the whole'. Montrose was indeed 'an enthusiast in whom political allegiance had become a religion'.[26]

By mid-January Montrose's enthusiasm had infected the Prince of Wales who instructed the chancellor Edward Hyde, future Earl of Clarendon, the magnificent chronicler of the Great Rebellion, to have discussions with the marquis. Clarendon basically admired Montrose though he believed that he was unduly elated by his own great deeds: 'he was then a man of *éclat*, had many servants, and more officers, who had served under him'. The chancellor may have been over-severe when he asserted that Montrose expected the queen to maintain his company 'with some lustre by a liberal assignation of moneys' but the maintenance of his retinue was a pressing problem. Montrose was delighted that at last his voice had been heard. 'There can be nothing said but I am most ready to own it, wherein the least point of your Highness's service can be concerned. . . . I shall only beg your highness to believe that, as I never had passion upon earth so strong as that to do the King your father service, so shall it be my study, if your Highness command me, to show it redoubled for the recovery of you; and that I shall never have friend, nor enemy, but as your pleasure and the advancement of your service shall require.'[27] He informed Rupert of his apprehensions about certain Scottish envoys. Although the marquis favoured a descent upon Scotland he would have no truck with the Engagers believing them capable of betraying both Charles and his son, but he advised Rupert to discover their intentions – 'it were better to find out their mine that you might the better know how to labour your's.' The queen, who still retained a considerable affection for the Hamiltons, tended to favour a royalist campaign in Scotland and it was suggested that Rupert's fleet might be used for that purpose, but while her son was inclined to agree with her, he fully realized that Montrose would not be party to any accommodation with the Engagers. Clarendon prepared a declinature, formally declining Montrose's offer of service; it was never used but it may have been intended for the eyes of Lanark and Lauderdale. The Prince of Wales was in no position to reject any possible alliance or offers of assistance; he therefore kept all options open. Montrose was about to set out for Sevenburg near The Hague to meet Clarendon when he was stopped in his tracks by a message from the chancellor himself. Charles I had been executed on 30 January 1649.

'When news of this monstrous parricide was confirmed, and there remained no more room for hope, his grief became passion, his anger was heightened to fury, and his noble spirit was so overwhelmed that his limbs stiffened and he fainted in the midst of his attendants, falling down like one dead.' When he had recovered a little he groaned, 'We must die, die with our gracious king. May the God of life and death be my witness, that henceforth life on earth will be bitterness and mourning.' He locked himself in his chamber for two days after which Wishart discovered on a scrap of paper a poem which adequately indicates the unbalanced state of his mind. There is a terrible splendour about its savage primitivism reminiscent of that to which the clans gave vent on the fields of Inverlochy and Auldearn.

> Great, Good and Just, could I but rate
> My Grief to Thy too Rigid Fate!
> I'd weep the World in such a Strain,
> As it would once deluge again:
> But since Thy loud-tongu'd Blood demands Supplies,
> More from Briareus Hands, than Argus Eyes,
> I'll tune Thy Elegies to Trumpet sounds,
> And write Thy Epitaph in Blood and Wounds!

The heinousness of the crime demanded not the tears of Argus's hundred eyes, but the swords wielded by the hundred-handed Briareus. Montrose mourned the sad little man who put on two shirts in case the mob should think he shivered from fear on that cold January day, a king who was neither great, good, nor just, but he also lamented the death of an ideal of society, the demise of a civilization personified by that king, whose passing released in him the very feelings of bloody barbarism that he condemned in Charles's executioners. Montrose undoubtedly believed with Gordon of Ruthven that 'the kinge of Scots is kinge of men both because he is not intituled efter the countrie as other kinges, but efter the natione, as lykwayes it is not his wealth or

great revenues that mantains his royall dignitie and so long continew-
ance of his throne, but the resolutione, the curradge, and the valour
of his subjects.' Even the most anti-monarchical ministers in covenanting Edinburgh, where the Prince of Wales was immediately proclaimed Charles's successor, recognized that the killing of the king
represented an attack on the Scottish people. Very few Scots, however,
adopted such a simplistic approach to the problem of the king's death
as did Montrose. In his exquisite grief he usurped the task of God –
'Vengence is mine, I will repay'. It could be argued that the seeds of
Montrose's destruction had been present from the beginning for such
usurpation was tyranny, a sin which also beset his boyhood hero
Alexander the Great towards the end of his life. In Montrose's favourite book, Ralegh quoted Seneca's assessment of Alexander with
approval. 'Nothing simply considered by it selfe beseemes a man. We
must regard what, to whom, when, why, where, and the like; without
which considerations no act can be approved. Let honours bee proportioned unto the persons: for whereas vertue is ever limited by
measure, the excesse is as faultie as the defect.' All factors considered,
Montrose emerged from the experience of the king's death with 'too
much excesse'. Always a violent man he believed in violent retribution.
His uncomplicated approach to politics combined with his self-conceit
and his single-mindedness cast him in the role of Avenger. As he told
Clarendon,

The griefs that astonish speak more, with their silence, than those that can
complain. And although we could never justly look for other but such tragic
effect, yet the horridness of the thing doth bring along too much wonder not
to be admired – never enough complained of . . . It will be no more time to
dally. For if affection and love to the justice and virtue of that cause be not
incitements great enough, anger and so just revenge, methinks, should wing us
on.

He would write Charles's epitaph 'in blood and wounds' or perish in
the attempt.[28]

Montrose believed that the appearance of Lanark, Lauderdale, and
others at The Hague so soon after the king's execution was not only
intolerable but also signified Charles II's ruin. In due course he met the
chancellor secretly. Clarendon had been impressed by Montrose's
'modesty and deference to the opinion and judgement of other men',
when he encountered him at Oxford in 1643, 'but he had since that

time done so many signal actions, won so many battles, and in truth made so great a noise in the world, that there appeared no less alteration to be in his humour and discourse than there had been in his fortune.' The marquis did not doubt for a moment that the king would find his service acceptable and in spite of Clarendon's pleas he insisted on appearing at The Hague where several Scots such as Lauderdale, who considered that Scotland would never forgive James Graham for the savagery of his campaigns, refused to stand in the same room with him. Several commentators testified to the factions which split The Hague during the spring of 1649. In addition to Lauderdale and Lanark (who succeeded to the dukedom after Hamilton's execution on 9 March), Seaforth, Callendar, Lord Sinclair, and Lord Napier were present. Some tried to persuade Charles to subscribe the covenants, a course strongly opposed by Montrose who favoured 'the way of force as agreeing better with both conscience and honour'. He believed that 'if once we engage the business is half done', but he confided his misgivings to Rupert whom he hoped the king would join in Ireland. It was reported that Montrose abhorred even the most moderate of his countrymen but Charles was urged to adopt his suggestions 'as the man of the clearest honour, courage, and affection to his service'. The queen begged Montrose to unite with all of his countrymen who entertained iust indignation at the late king's fate, but he would not be moved.[29]

The Scottish parliament met at Edinburgh on 5 January. It prescribed a solemn fast and humiliation and the resubscription of the covenants. The Act of Classes prohibited all who had supported the Engagers from holding office for a period commensurate with their degree of commitment. Argyll predicted that the act would represent 'the breaking of the malignants' teeth'. Early in the month parliament instructed the Scots commissioners in London that if sentence was pronounced on the king they were to register their dissent and protest. When news of the execution reached Edinburgh on 5 February Chancellor Loudoun, dressed in a black velvet gown, immediately proclaimed Charles king of Great Britain, France, and Ireland on condition that he gave satisfaction concerning religion, the union, and the peace of the kingdom in terms of the covenants. It was agreed to send representatives to The Hague while parliament pushed ahead with the creation of the new Scotland. Death was decreed for witchcraft, blasphemy, worshippers of false gods, beaters and cursers of parents, and for those guilty of incest according to the Book of Deuteronomy. Lay patronage was abolished, a significant triumph for the ministers who also obtained legislation augmenting their stipends. There was an act concerning the poor and an act forbidding the export of victual due to 'the sad conditioun of the meane and poor people . . . throw great scairstie and darth'. Three hundred merks were set aside to pay 'some able and sufficient man for drawing up, compiling, and writing the history, records and chronicles of the time'. Argyll and Warriston among others were commissioned to 'revise and considder all the lawis statutes and actis of parliament of this kingdom'. Codification of Scots law was to be the corner-stone of the new society.[30]

In February Thomas MacKenzie of Pluscardine, brother of Seaforth, joined with some of his clan, some MacKays, and Sir Thomas Urquhart of Cromarty to drive a covenanting garrison from Inverness. Two months later they were joined by Donald MacKay, second Lord Reay, and General Middleton, as well as a number of Gordons intent on avenging their chief, who had been beheaded on 22 March having appropriately admitted, 'I am broght hither to undergoe the execution of ane decrie given against my lyfe, for having spent some litle, and indeede too litle tyme therofe, in demonstrating my obedience, and in endevouring to have done some service to our sacred soveraigne.'[31] The royalists were cut off and defeated at Balvenie; there were no reprisals; the vanquished survived to receive the thanks of their king and an invitation to join Montrose when he arrived in Scotland.

Meanwhile the 'brethern' had arrived at The Hague to invite Charles's subscription to the solemn league. They demanded that the covenant be subscribed in the three kingdoms, that presbyterianism be well and truly established, and that he should assent to the settlement of civil matters by parliament and of ecclesiastical matters by general assemblies. It was with some truth that a commentator observed that Charles had been proclaimed king in Scotland 'with such limitations and restrictions against his exercise of royal power that they have only given him the name and denied him the authority'. There was a further condition which he found totally unacceptable; they demanded the removal of 'the most bloody murderer of our nation . . . this cursed man whose scandalous carriage, pernicious counsels and contagious company, cannot fail to dishonour and pollute all places of his familiar access and to provoke the anger of the most high God against the same'.[32] The object of all this vituperation had recently been commissioned as Lieutenant-Governor and Captain-General of all the royal forces in Scotland. Lieutenant-Governor Montrose was asked by his king for his views on the commissioners' proposals. He saw no harm in Charles accepting the National Covenant but subscription of the solemn league would constitute the king's 'shame and ruin . . . being nothing but a condemning of your royal father's memory'. He considered that since Charles succeeded by hereditary right they had no business to proclaim him king as if he succeeded by conditional election, just as they had no right to insist that parliament and assembly should hold sway to the point where the king 'should signify nothing'. In his view they had connived at the king's murder and were now intent upon killing all friends to monarchy. Montrose's hardened attitudes blinded him to reason; the commissioners wished as fervently and sincerely for the covenanted king as did Montrose to avenge his father.

Elizabeth of Bohemia, 'Queen of Hearts', wrote from her palace at Rhenen to warn Montrose that she had learned by chance of the Prince of Orange's intention to influence the king in the commissioners' favour. According to her youngest daughter Sophia, future consort of the Elector of Hanover, Montrose was one of the many royalist exiles who thronged the court at Rhenen. She recalled him as 'a man of great ability who believed everything to be attainable by courage and honour', including it would appear the hand of her elder sister Princess Louise. The story may represent no more than gossip. The vivacious nineteen-year-old Sophia was currently preoccupied in fighting off the lecherous overtures of Charles Stewart and her assertion that Montrose was one who 'sought their fortune in my service' seems a little far-fetched since she was in no position to advance her own fortune let alone that of others. Louise was twenty-seven, an amiable girl so devoted to painting that while working on her canvases 'she neglected herself sadly – one would have said her clothes had been thrown on her'. She is said to have attended the painting school at Utrecht of Gerard van Honthorst, the highly acclaimed portrait painter who followed the style of Caravaggio. It was possibly through Louise's agency that Honthorst painted the well-known portrait of Montrose in black armour, surely conceived as the depiction of 'a candidate for immortality'. *Gerardo dallo Notti*, so named for his painting mainly night pieces, was an appropriate artist to convey the deep sense of mourning in the life-size portrait. It has been plausibly suggested that it was this portrait for which Elizabeth of Bohemia thanked Montrose in a letter of June 1649. 'I have hung it in my cabinet to fright away the brethern', a reference to approaches made by the Scots commissioners to the 'First Dochtour of Scotland', beseeching her intervention with Charles. In ten letters, generously spiced with warmth and wit, written between June and January, she kept 'Jamie Graeme' as she called him informed of the fortunes of her son Rupert, of diplomatic activity, and of contemporary gossip. She did not mention Louise, who never married. She became Abbess of Maubuisson and lived until 1709. According to Sophia Montrose was to have her hand if his expedition to Scotland was successful.[33]

On 23 April Montrose received another royal commission; he was invested with full power and authority to negotiate in Charles's name with the Emperor and all other kings, princes, generals, free states, and army commanders. It was an appropriate honour for Montrose's projected campaign now became the subject of diplomatic activity throughout the whole of Europe. The time should have been propitious for recruitment, for central and northern Europe teemed with mercenaries starved of food and pay. All soldiers sought arrears of pay. German towns and principalities, extremely short of cash, attempted to raise loans wherever possible, notably from Frankfurt whose wealth was in danger of being gobbled up by the disbanded mercenaries of the Duke of Bavaria. The local populations found the burden of quartering unbearable. 'These peoples hardly see yet any difference between a suspension of arms and open war; to some the latter would be more tolerable.'[34]

In January 1649 Charles sent Patrick Ruthven, Earl of Brentford, who had travelled far since his defence of Edinburgh Castle in 1640, to negotiate supplies of men, money, and munitions, as well as a shipload of corn for Ireland, from Queen Christina of Sweden; by March he reported 'a promise of arms and ammunition, which must not appear to be sent immediately from the Queen'. Sir John Cochrane, on a similar mission to the Duke of Courland, intimated Frederik of Denmark's sympathies. The latter's Lord Chamberlain Corfitz Ulfeld was then at The Hague to negotiate a treaty regulating trade through the Sound. He gave Montrose a loan of five thousand rix dollars paid in diamond rings. In a letter to Ulfeld concerning this transaction,

Montrose gave the first positive indication of his intentions. He had recommended four possible places for a Scottish landing to Hurry – Strathnaver, Cromarty, the Spey estuary, and Aberdeen. He mentioned the need for cannon, gun-carriages, and a frigate, though he was somewhat embarrassed to ask for more in view of Ulfeld's generosity. 'I am afraid we may appear too keen though too unprepared. We are in such straits that it seems very little will go right for us.' Every little helped but Montrose admitted he was a poor suppliant. It can be no coincidence that Charles wrote next day (12 April) thanking MacKenzie of Pluscardine for his good service and urging him to continue 'until we shall have meanes and opportunity to give you and your friends such further encouragement as shall be necessary, which we expect and intend to do with all convenient speed'.[35] There was one further connection. Donald, first Lord Reay, chief of MacKay, was in Copenhagen in January and February 1649 where he probably died.[36] He must have been involved in some way in the negotiations, so explaining Montrose's unfortunate choice of Strathnaver, Mackay country, as a point from which to launch his campaign. The other sites were chosen because of their proximity to MacKenzie's centre of activity.

But agents were active further afield in the Stewart cause. The queen signed a pass for Patrick Guthrie, a veteran of 1644–5, to go to Italy to sound opinion. Ludovic, Earl of Crawford, reported from Madrid that Charles could expect a substantial loan from the king of Spain who was outraged by the execution. Crawford protested that though he might gain all the wealth of the East and West Indies, he would 'rather choose with bread and water' to serve Charles than any king alive. The Portuguese ambassador at The Hague advised Charles to grant liberty of conscience to his subjects and to approach Rome for aid.[37] Secrecy, however, was a scarce commodity, difficult to preserve. In April one of Montrose's bearers Mr William Orde was arrested in Angus by Leslie. By the beginning of May it was rumoured that the marquis was bound for Scotland with Seaforth 'whose brother is now the chief opposer of Argyll and his faction'. Seaforth was another of Elizabeth of Bohemia's darlings – 'my Highlander', as she called him.

Montrose received another commission from Robert Long, the king's secretary, in May, 'to treat for foreign levies and supplies of all natures, and to transport and conduct them accordingly' as well as a special commission to negotiate with specific German towns and principalities.

Long was also requested to make out ambassadorial papers for Harry Graham and Johan Adam von Karphen, a Hessian with long experience of the wars. Montrose sent personally accredited representatives to Sweden, Saxony, and Denmark. The whole of northern Europe was to be scoured for men and money and, as if to emphasize the fact, the marquis was commissioned as Charles's ambassador extraordinary to foreign powers.[38] In June Cochrane claimed that support had been promised by Brandenburg, Mainz, Cologne, Hesse, Neuburg, Mecklenburg, Luneburg, France, Spain, Denmark, Portugal, and Sweden. Little wonder that he wrote, '*nous sommes ici dans un nouveau monde*'.[39]

That the 'new world' did not endure was due to total confusion in royalist planning and to the embarrassment, financial and political, of a number of well-wishers who lacked the ability or intention or both to honour their promises. On 15 June Charles was forced to leave The Hague since his presence threatened Dutch relations with England. Montrose accompanied him to Brussels where the two men parted; Charles went on to Paris, St Germain's, and eventually Jersey while Montrose returned to The Hague. In future months Charles continued to assure the marquis of his good intentions as he actively negotiated with the Scots commissioners. 'I entreat you to go on vigorously, and with your wonted courage and care, in the prosecution of those trusts I have committed to you, and not to be startled with any reports you may hear, as if I were otherwise inclined to the presbyterians than when I left you. I assure you I am still upon the same principles I was, and depend as much as ever upon your undertaking and endeavours for my service, being fully resolved to assist and support you therein to the uttermost of my power.' The extent of Charles Stewart's commitment to principle is one of the conundrums of British history, though he undoubtedly believed, as did Montrose, that the cause was greater than any one man. During their last weeks together the two men worked out a strategy of sorts, so causing Lord Jermyn, who favoured a compromise with the Scots, considerable anxiety.

The ground upon which a nearer agreement with Scotland was despaired of was the giving Montrose a commission of Lieutenant-General with instructions to solicit several princes for means for it, and being furnished therewith to constrain Scotland to those things in our behalf, that we could not obtain by treaty. Montrose is gone about this undertaking with great assumptions of being in estate to make an attempt suddenly upon Scotland; but I am fully persuaded that he will not be able to put himself into a condition for it so soon, if ever, as he is willing to say he shall. There was much division amongst those that served the king at the Hague about these things.[40]

Montrose had often expressed his willingness to serve his king in any way possible. He was aware from the outset that the purpose of his campaign was to put pressure on the Scots commissioners, to prolong the treaty negotiations until he could secure his position in Scotland, and if possible to avert the need for a treaty altogether. In a declaration published towards the end of the year he called upon all who loved their God and their king to resolve, like Joab, 'to play the men for their people, and the cities of their God, and let the Lord do whatever seemeth him good, wherein, whatsomever shall behappen, they may at least be assured that dead or alive, the world will give them thanks.'[41]

At The Hague Brentford reported that the promised Swedish arms were not yet available. Much of Montrose's difficulty stemmed from a general confusion about precisely for whom weapons and money obtained throughout Europe were intended. The Swedish consignment for example, was meant for Ormonde's sole use, but through Long Montrose made arrangements to have it divided equally between Ormonde and himself. He borrowed a further seven thousand five hundred rix dollars from Ulfeld and on 11 July he gave him a receipt for delivery of a quantity of weapons and ammunitions which included fifteen hundred each of muskets, swords, pikes, and cutlasses, as well as fuses, powder, lead, twenty-six cannon, and sixteen hundred cannon balls. When Ulfeld later fell foul of the Danish authorities he claimed that had Montrose not 'expressed some words' tending to a 'misprision [contempt] of him', he had intended to lend a further thirty thousand rix dollars of his own money 'and had prepared the way for it'.[42] Although he was reasonably well supplied with weapons Montrose's difficulty was that he lacked hard cash to pay his soldiers. On 22 July he urged the Elector of Brandenburg to pay a loan promised to Harry Graham and Von Karphen. For unknown reasons – though Frederick William probably just did not have the money – the loan was not forthcoming. Montrose had decided to send an advance party of some two hundred men under the Earl of Kinnoul to establish a base at Orkney just across the Pentland Firth from Strathnaver, but Ulfeld's money had already been spent and even with a supplementary loan advanced by Captain John Griffith and Baron von Heenvliet, there was barely enough money to send them on their way. Kinnoul spent his time practising archery with Queen Elizabeth at Rhenen. A letter from Henrietta Maria protesting her esteem and admiration – 'and I must exact the same sentiments from yourself' – may imply that he had asked her, rather shortly, to assist with the fund-raising. James, Duke of York, expressed his pleasure that Charles had 'found an occasion of employing you, being confident you have a heart full of zeal and affection to his service', but good wishes were no substitute for concrete assistance. Montrose's separation from Charles undoubtedly damaged his efforts, making it harder to solicit aid when the king's intentions were widely suspected.

Nonetheless, with or without adequate funds, it was essential that the campaign be launched as soon as possible if it was to have any hope of attaining its objective for the Scots had renewed active negotiations. To this end a declaration was published at Copenhagen on 9 July, possibly the source of Montrose's disagreement with Ulfeld since it was potentially of considerable embarrassment to the Danish king. It was a call to action, warning all to enter the king's peace by 5 November and signifying Montrose's intention to march through Scotland to England. It exhorted all good subjects 'by all ties sacred and civil, by the duty they owe to God, by their loyalty to their sovereign, by their love to their native country, and by their tender affection to their dear wives, children and posterity, that they make their speedy repair to Enderness [Inverness] in Scotland, or to any other place upon my march, and to join with me in this pious and honourable engagement.' He still intended to capitalize on Pluscardine's initiative and mid-August found him urging Seaforth's personal participation: 'I am just now setting out and intends to recover thir delays by the best dispatch I can.'[43]

Since June Cochrane had been assuring Courland of Montrose's imminent arrival in Hamburg. The marquis left the Low Countries for that city at the end of August. Before doing so he decided that further delay was intolerable. Ill-prepared as he was the advance party must be sent to Orkney before the season became too late. So far all the ambitious negotiations for an impressive expedition to Scotland had yielded only promises and one old ship 'new vamp't without a gun'. In that ship Kinnoul with one hundred and eighty men set sail from Amsterdam for Kirkwall while Montrose went north to raise more money and men. Kinnoul reached Orkney at the end of September after a hazardous and tempestuous voyage of three weeks, buffeted by storms and pursued part of the way by a parliamentary frigate. So began the last campaign.

14
THE LAST
CAMPAIGN

*There have been few men that have put an end to great undertakings:
God did not even suffer that great prophet, who spoke to him face to
face, to introduce his people into the land which he had promised;
he reserv'd the honour thereof to Joshua, his successor. In a word;
whatever has had a beginning, still contains a sort of corruption in the
principles of its generation; and the most perfect creatures in the world,
are still sensible of the nothing from whence they had their rise.*

Menteith of Salmonet

The islands of Orkney were conveniently situated for an attack on
the north of Scotland yet remote enough to be outside the orbit of
covenanting influence. 'Your lordship is gaped after with that expectation that the Jews look after their Messiah,' Kinnoul informed
Montrose, 'and certainly your presence will restore your groaning
country to its liberties and the king to his rights.' At Kirkwall Kinnoul
was joined by Captain John Hall of Leith, who defected from the
covenant with two ships. All, however, was not well. Kinnoul's uncle
Robert Douglas, seventh Earl of Morton, followed a hospitable reception at Birsay with a demand that his nephew resign his commission
to himself. Morton's father, Argyll's father-in-law, who was noted for
his royalist sympathies, had received a royal charter of the earldom of
Orkney and the lordship of Shetland in 1643, redeemable by the crown
on payment of £30,000. He died at Kirkwall in 1648. His successor
was loyal, but sensitive. He was rather jealous of Kinnoul, while both
men were suspicious of Lieutenant-Colonel George Drummond, whose
father was described as 'Morton's enemie, and is gone to the south to
shunne ingaging in this bussines'. Drummond, for his part, told

Charles II that 'those who are your Majesty's loyall subjects here, feare an absolute commission to the earle of Morton may wrong your service'. He confided his fears to another correspondent: 'The way of our stating the country [Orkney] was by a well affected party in this place, with the assistance of a few, which we brought allong with us, so that my Lord Morton, was forced either to join with us, for the king, or els to quit the illands.' Since arriving in Orkney Drummond had visited the mainland, where 'some of them are in armes already and the rest only atends Montrose's comming, which I wish may bee suddenly'. He was probably the son of George Drummond of Balloch who married Agnes, sister of Archibald, first Lord Napier, and who had performed stalwart service in 1644–5. George senior survived until the 1650s but his son, according to a Drummond history written in 1681, was 'cruelly shot to death by order of the Committee of Estates in time of the civil wars'.[1]

Two declarations issued by Montrose in the second half of 1649 contain little that is new but they do represent the articulation of his philosophy on the eve of the last campaign. Because of the aspersions and calumnies heaped upon his head he determined to 'open the book of my soul and clearly deliver the very sense of my heart'. He regretted the censure of the Church – 'Such is the unhappy fate of some men that even their best actions are clothed with scandal, and their most faithful services rewarded with disgrace', a point he would reiterate on the scaffold. He protested no intention of harm to kirk or kingdom, swearing that he would confine himself to 'the affairs of the sword', avoiding interference in matters of policy and state. A long and familiar list recited the crimes of the rebels. 'And as if they had made a covenant with Hell to banish modesty . . . they overthrew the foundation of government, even in that instant that they declared to maintain it, and are entered into a solemn agreement to abolish monarchy, and in the room thereof to establish an eternal anarchy.' After 5 November none who failed to enter the king's peace would be pardoned. 'I will with all violence and fury, pursue them and kill them as vagabonds, rogues and regicides . . . not leaving one of their cursed race, if possible, to breathe upon the face of the earth.'[2]

From Hamburg Montrose went to Denmark. His communications were hopelessly overstretched, for Charles was in Jersey while his supporters were scattered in England, France, and the Netherlands.

Contacts with Orkney and Scotland, where Colonel Sibbald was arrested on a mission in November, were difficult. Sir James Turner, who arrived in Hamburg to offer more positive royal service than he had in Kintyre and the Hebrides, sent a letter to his wife with Sibbald telling her to give him some money, 'and he had his head chopped off not long after at the Cross of Edinburgh and so I lost both my friend and my money'.[3] Ormonde received a wildly optimistic report concerning the success of Montrose's diplomatic activity. It claimed that the Emperor, Denmark, Sweden, Courland, Brunswick, and Hanover had all promised assistance and that twenty thousand loyalists, including Leslie's own troops, were preparing to join Montrose in Scotland. Reality as usual was less rosy. Hopes of co-operating with Rupert were shattered when he was driven out of Kinsale following Cromwell's bloody campaigns in Ireland. Montrose did meet Frederik of Denmark at Flensburg but, having been referred to the Danish Council at Copenhagen and frustrated by further non-committal statements, he sent a testy letter to the Danish king. 'Delays are the worst of all evils. What your Majesty shall please to do will be doubled by being done soon. In such affairs a refusal that sets us free to act is better than a promise that ruins us.'[4]

Neither promise nor refusal was forthcoming; by November he was in Gothenburg, where he resided with one man who was conspicuously active in the Stewart cause, Johan or Hans Maclier, the wealthiest merchant in Sweden. The latter had his own reasons for supporting the royalists. He was a Scot whose real name was John MacLean, and he was the younger brother of Sir Lachlan MacLean of Duart; he thus 'chose an indirect way of fighting for his family against Argyll'.[5] The MacLeans, as ever, were more resolute than the Mac-Kenzies, though Montrose continued to believe in *MacCoinnich* himself – 'For what friendship you heave beene pleased to doe me the honor to witnes I will make you the faithfullest returne my lyfe can doe, and if it please God I los it not very suddenly, I shall be sure not to dye in your debt.' The relentless cycle of disappointment and delay was perhaps beginning to condition him to defeat in the *'Venture'* on which he was about to embark.

Early in December Captain John Hall arrived from Orkney to deliver another blow. Kinnoul and Morton had both died of an illness within a few days of each other. Hall had picked up two hundred mercenaries in Copenhagen. Montrose decided that irrespective of inadequate preparation the time had come for action. On 15 December he informed Seaforth that he was about to sail for Scotland. Maclier had hired a Swedish merchantman. Three ships from Stralsund had either arrived at, or were on their way to Gothenburg, carrying an estimated six hundred mercenaries. But again he was forced to delay to allow Maclier time both to acquire two other ships and to persuade Peder Ribbing, provincial governor of Gothenburg, that he had authorization to take possession of a consignment of arms purchased from the Swedish crown. During his residence in Sweden Montrose took care to avoid causing Queen Christina any political embarrassment. He made no attempt to see her and for similar reasons he transferred his mercenaries to Marstrand in Norway. Maclier, whose diplomatic activities proved much more successful than those of the professionals, secured food supplies for them. By mid-January a number of Montrose's officers, including Harry Graham, the new Earl of Kinnoul, and Lord Eythin, a veteran of the Swedish wars who was given command of a supporting expedition, had arrived in Gothenburg. Hall and Kinnoul sailed for Orkney with the Marstrand ships on 14 January. Montrose would have followed but he had been warned to expect an express from the king and the waters of the Gota froze, trapping his ship. A royalist English envoy who visited him in early February reported that he awaited only a fair wind to sail to Scotland. 'I meet everywhere many good men for the king, but all very poor, and the truth is Montrose is not able to entertain soldiers on this side of the sea.'[6]

In mid-February the faithful Maclier addressed a letter to Montrose aboard the frigate *Herderinnan*. Three ships from Courland would arrive by the end of the month to be crewed by some of Captain Hall's men left behind for the purpose. Detailed lists show the use Montrose made of the weapons supplied by Maclier. Thus 1536 muskets, 20 barrels of bullets, and 400 stones of mutch accompanied Kinnoul to Orkney, as well as 2720 swords, 100 sets of cavalry armour, and 1500 pikes, but a proportion of the weapons was left behind to supply Eythin's force. It is clear therefore that in spite of all the effort and activity on the part of Montrose and the others his expedition was not over-equipped.[7] He eventually sailed himself in late February. His standard was typical of the man: 'of white damaske, on it a lyon on a steep rock going to leap from one steep rock to another, and betwixt the two rocks a great river; the motto: *"Nil Medium"* '.[8]

By the end of October 1649 the covenanters had reopened negotiations with Charles, so panicking the English into recalling Cromwell from Ireland. Wishart told Napier that they offered Charles 'present possession' of the whole kingdom of Scotland 'at so easie a rate as the forsaking of one man'. When Count Henry of Nassau arrived at The Hague to belittle Montrose's progress in Denmark, Holstein, and Hamburg, Elizabeth of Bohemia, 'passionately affected to Montrose his ends', sincerely hoped that he was deliberately indulging in fabrication in order to mislead the Scots commissioners. It was rumoured that Charles intended to go to either Ireland or Scotland. By the second week of February it was common knowledge in Paris that the king had conferred the Order of the Garter upon Montrose along with reassurances about his negotiations with the Scots. Charles also sent a 'public letter' to Montrose which was published in France during the second half of February though the marquis did not receive either letters or Garter until he reached Orkney. The public letter told Montrose of the overtures from Scotland and indicated that Charles had agreed to meet the Scots at Breda on 15 March.

And to the end you may not apprehend that we intend, either by anything contained in those letters, or by the Treaty we expect, to give the least impediment to your proceedings, we think fit to let you know, that as we conceive that your preparations have been one effectual motive that hath induced them to make the said address to us, so your vigorous proceeding will be a good means to bring them to such moderation in the said Treaty as probably may produce an agreement, and a present union of that whole nation in our service. We assure you therefore, that we will not before or during the Treaty, do anything contrary to that power and authority which we have given you by our commission, or consent to anything that may bring the least degree of diminution to it. And if the Treaty should produce an agreement, we will, with our uttermost care, so provide for the honour and interest of yourself, and of all that shall engage with you, as shall let the whole world see the high esteem we have of you ... We require and authorise you therefore to proceed vigorously and effectually in your undertaking; and to act in all things in order to it, as you shall judge most necessary for the support thereof and for our service in that way; wherein we doubt not, but our loyal and well affected subjects of Scotland will effectually join with you, and by that addition of strength either dispose those that are otherwise minded to make reasonable demands, to us in the Treaty, or be able to force them to end it by arms, in case of their obstinate refusal. To which end we authorise you to communicate and publish this our letter to all such persons as you shall think fit.[9]

Montrose's agent in Paris took it upon himself to publish the letter, in order, some thought, to hinder the treaty. Others believed that Charles should have sent it 'from his owne mouth to Montrose his ear . . . with all imaginable secrecy', since the publication was bound to antagonize the covenanters. The contingent at The Hague thought that Charles intended the suppression of Argyll's government in any case, and that he was simply playing for time, keeping the commissioners 'drousy, till Montrose can get into some considerable posture', choosing rather to 'lose the Argyllians in Scotland by the discovery, than the Montrosians by the concealment of his intentions'.[10] Since Charles arrived in France in February to consult his mother at Beauvais he presumably approved the letter's publication, but whatever the truth of the matter, the letter's existence betrays a cynical manipulation of men and lives. Private correspondence from the king urged Montrose to disregard adverse reports of his activities – 'Depend upon my kindness and proceed in your business with your usual courage and alacrity, which I am sure will bring great advantage to my affairs, and much honour to yourself.'

In spite of Charles's assurances many of Montrose's supporters, such as Callendar, Sinclair, and Napier, were very uneasy. They urged a military solution to the problem, insisting that recruits would be found in Leslie's army, among ex-Engagers and in the ranks of those weary of the 'kirk-yoke'. Montrose could depend upon those who had participated in Pluscardine's rising. Middleton had promised support as had Lord Lewis Gordon, now Marquis of Huntly since Aboyne had predeceased his father at Paris. Urquhart of Cromarty, Monro of Lemlair, Earl Marischal, Lord Ogilvie, and the loyal clans of Badenoch and Atholl would rally to the royal standard. Greater numbers would appear if the king himself was present. 'And these arguments they urge with the more vehemencie because they know that if the Prince agree with the Argyllians, some or other of them will be sacrificed for the peace offering.'[11] Montrose's well wishers would have preferred that if a sacrifice was required, the marquis should oblige rather than themselves. They were prepared to use him as, even at the peak of his success, they had never allowed him to use themselves. With the notable exception of Napier, who was anxious to join his uncle, the exiled noble courtiers were prepared for the moment to regard Montrose as an expendable Messiah. As a newsletter put it, 'The truth is, there was never poor Prince so fitted with counsellors and company; he hath such with him, as, if he will be ruled by them, are able sooner to lose him ten kingdoms (if he had them) than to recover one.'[12]

Montrose received Charles's letters on 23 March. Before he replied he took three days to reflect on his predicament. At least two supply ships had been wrecked losing valuable weapons and ammunition. Although there were further hopes of support from Middleton the leadership in Orkney was racked by disputes. Powrie Ogilvie told him that too much authority had been placed in young hands, 'quho treulie hes not witt to governe themselffis, lett alone to advance the weill of his Majestie's service'. The arrival of Kinnoul (himself no greyhead) had partly salvaged a potentially dangerous situation, but the problems persisted. Harry May, a servant of James, Duke of York, brought his master's good wishes to Orkney along with the king's letters. When James Graham picked up the pen to write what would be his last letter to his sovereign, the tone was subdued and his thoughts were of death. He thanked the king for the honour conferred upon him (he did not know that it had also been given to Hamilton), 'for which I can make your Majesty no other humble acknowledgement, but with the more alacrity and bensell [vigour] abandon still my life to search my death for the interests of your Majesty's honour and service, with that integrity and clearness as your Majesty and all the world shall see that it is not your fortunes in you, but your Majesty in whatsomever fortune, that I make sacred to serve'. He advised the king to beware of the craft used against him, 'chiefly in this conjuncture'. He counselled him to 'hear the zealous opinions of your faithful servants who have nothing in their hearts, nor before their eyes, but the joy of your Majesty's prosperity and greatness, which shall ever be the only passion and study of your most sacred Majesty's most humble, faithful and most passionate subject and servant'. On the same day he wrote to Seaforth thanking him for his 'noble and friendly carriages, for which believe I will serve you with my life, all the days it shall please God to lend me it'. He told him he was about to go to the Scottish mainland. 'I shall tender your friends and interests, as my own life, and still live, or die, my Lord, your cousin and faithful friend and servant.'[13] Both of these letters were written by a man aware that his days might be numbered, by one who manifestly did not 'fear his fate too much', who did not lament his own destiny, but who mourned the king's wrong-headedness in betraying all for which he had fought. Charles was guilty of a sell-out. Tom Sydserff stated that Montrose's greatest fault was his insatiable desire for honour, 'which he did pursue with as handsome and heroic action as ever any did'. The king's intentions were not honourable. The survivors of Carbisdale later declared 'how much the heart of Montrose was broken before the fight in the very thoughts that the king and the Scots would agree'.[14] In a world where King Stewart and King Covenant were at one, there was no place for James Graham; in that world he had no desire to live.

During two weeks in Orkney Montrose based himself at Kirkwall. Harry May put his force at about two thousand when he told Secretary Nicholas that 'all things proceed with much expectation . . . the importunity of the country has been very extraordinary for our entering'. Huntly and Middleton were consulting with Marischal; it was thought that even if Huntly proved a 'superficial friend', the Gordons would turn out in strength. On 26 March Montrose commissioned James Maitland as captain of a troop of horse in the regiment of Colonel Thomas Gray, a veteran mercenary now returning to his native country after an absence of thirty-four years. David Guthrie who had accompanied Montrose into exile was commissioned major of foot.[15] Montrose's officers also included Harry Graham, Colonel William Johnston, recently employed on continental embassies and soon to be appointed governor of Orkney, John Spottiswood younger, of Dairsie, and John Lisle, another fellow exile who was shortly to command the meagre royalist cavalry. Menzies of Pitfoddels, a catholic, was the standard bearer. Others included Crichton of Frendraught, a very recent convert to royalism, and Captain Mortimer, who fought on opposite sides at Aberdeen, and Powrie Ogilvie, John Douglas, son of the Earl of Morton, Drummond of Balloch younger, the Hays of Naughton and Dalgetty (both fighting for their chief Kinnoul), Sir John Hurry, and a number of Dutch and German mercenaries. Some English merchant seamen were forced to sign an oath of allegiance to Charles II at Kirkwall; a few accompanied the expedition. According to Kirkwall's protestation of loyalty at the

Restoration, the town supplied sixty fully armed men for the campaign as well as a garrison of one hundred under Johnston's command. Eight hundred from the rest of Orkney also accompanied the army south.[16] May's estimate notwithstanding, Montrose's total force could barely have exceeded sixteen hundred men.

Aboard the *Herderinnan* in Scapa Flow Montrose issued Hurry with his orders on 9 April. He was to sail with the evening tide to Caithness, 'choosing the most convenient place for landing as occasion shall serve'. If unopposed his force of five hundred (he succeeded in gathering only three hundred together) was to march directly to the Ord of Caithness, north of Kildonan, where the coastal plain ends as the hills drop sharply into the North Sea. His alternative, should he meet with resistance, was to proceed to Strathnaver on the north coast, which failing, 'you are to apply a little higher betwixt that and Kintail which places are all for the king', an instruction which has been interpreted to mean Assynt but which more probably refers to Kintail MacKay, the Kyle of Tongue.[17] A few days later when Hurry had secured the Ord, the remainder of the force crossed the Pentland Firth, utilizing 'all the ships, barks and boats' of Kirkwall, traditionally landing at John o' Groats and marching along the coast to Thurso where Montrose issued a declaration to the gentlemen and heritors of Caithness on 14 April.

He also issued three warrants to Captain Hall who was granted the first vessel he could capture as compensation for his losses; he was promised the command of a squadron of ships at the earliest opportunity; and he was ordered to seize ships belonging to Hamburg which had presumably been seen in the vicinity: if they offered any resistance Hall was to 'pursue, take, kill, sink and destroy all those men, loading goods and commodities belonging to the said vessels'.[18] Harry Graham was left to coax the men of Caithness into submission while Montrose marched south to Dunbeath Castle close to the Ord. Alexander Sinclair of Brims, Hugh MacKay of Dirled, and Hucheon MacKay of Scourie rallied to the standard to be sent to recruit further local support at Tongue, promptly abandoned by Captain William Gordon who fell back to Dunrobin. Sir John Sinclair abandoned Dunbeath to the care of his wife and hastened south to alert the Earl of Sutherland to the invasion. Lady Catherine, a daughter of Fraser of Lovat, put up a spirited but brief defence before being permitted to withdraw with her baggage. Sutherland organized a half-hearted resistance to Hurry at the Ord but he was unwilling to challenge the royalists without assistance and he retreated to Ross leaving strong garrisons in his castles at Dunrobin, Skelbo, Skibo, and Dornoch. He also sent some of his men 'to the hills and heights of the country with their cattle and goods to preserve them from the enemy'.

From Dunbeath Montrose advanced cautiously down the coast to Garty, only some four miles south of the Ord where he camped, covering eight miles next day to spend the night at Kintradwell. A further nine miles took him to Dunrobin which defied surrender. The slowness of his march was dictated by the transportation of cannon, but he was also handicapped by uncertainty about Sutherland's precise movements and he did not wish to push too far ahead of expected reinforcements. His difficulties were aggravated when a party of invaders straying between the castle and the sea was captured by the garrison. Having camped at Rhives at the foot of Beinn a' Bhragie, he cut up Strathfleet to Rhaoine and from there to Gruids, south of Lairg, where he awaited the levies from Tongue; only Sinclair of Brims came in.

On receiving news of the invasion David Leslie ordered a muster at Brechin for 25 April, pressing northwards from Angus by forced marches. In the meantime he charged his northern commanders to hinder the royalist advance. The main command lay with Archibald Strachan, an interesting individual ('heretofore but a driver of ale from Musselburgh into Edinburgh')[19] with a reputation for sectarianism. He had been employed by Argyll as a go-between with Cromwell and had distinguished himself by defeating MacKenzie of Pluscardine at Balvenie. He was a ruthless soldier, unafraid of Montrose's reputation. From his winter base at Inverness he wrote to James Guthrie, one of the leading ministers, to complain of the severe financial burdens imposed on the commonalty, of malignancy in the army, of unsatisfactory pay, and of 'unreconcilable differences amongst the forces who cannot join together against another common enemy'. He was unhappy about arrangements for the levy and, satisfied that the Lord had shown what could be done by the few at Balvenie – 'the Lord is strong and mighty and as he hath done will do valiantly by weak means and in small appearances' – he had no doubt that God would grant the destruction of James Graham, 'if he land near this quarter'.[20]

In April his troop, together with that of Colonel Gilbert Ker, was stationed at Brahan and Chanonry, in Ross, a presence which, with the covenanting garrison in Eilan Donan, accounts for the inaction of the MacKenzies during the last campaign. He was joined in Ross by Lieutenant-Colonel Hackett and Captain Cullace with thirty-six musketeers from Lawers' regiment. He also secured the services of two local lairds who had been on the losing side at Balvenie: Colonel John Monro of Lemlair, with his son Andrew, and David Ross, laird of Balnagowan, supplied between them four hundred of their kindreds.

Montrose completely failed to understand that the balance of power had shifted in the north. The covenant had been kind to John Gordon, seventh Earl of Sutherland, whose long feud with the MacKays ground to a relentless conclusion when he obtained a sequestration of Strathnaver in August 1649. He also had designs on estates which MacKay had sold to Robert Monro of Achness. In 1647 parliament withheld assurances from Monro of Achness and his son Hugh and from Lord Reay, Hugh MacKay of Dilred, and MacKay of Scourie until 'they restore the Earl of Sutherland to the peacable possession of his lands and goods taken from him'. Their title was perfectly legal, but like Argyll Sutherland could command the resources of the covenant to further his own interest. It was no coincidence therefore that, with the exception of Lord Reay himself, all those mentioned were among the few who actually turned out for Montrose in 1650. Monro of Achness and his three sons joined him before Carbisdale to be appointed as scouts, while the others were supposedly recruiting in the north. Other families such as Monro of Lemlair and the Rosses decided that the future lay with Sutherland, although their recent association with Pluscardine led Montrose to anticipate their support. Local clan politics was one of the main reasons for the disaster at Carbisdale. Montrose 'sent Hurry to Balnagowan who espoused the cause', while Major Lisle was ordered to 'find the gentry of the shire'. Gordon of Sallagh says that Montrose was 'espyed and found out by the travel [travail] and diligence of Colonel John Monro of Lemlair and his son Captain Andrew Monro who incoraged the troops to goe on'. Some treachery is implied by the local tradition that the Lemlair Monros took no part in the battle until the outcome was known. According to Menteith, Montrose awaited 'the raising of a regiment of four hundred men which he ordered', a figure which tallies exactly with Gordon's estimate of the numbers mustered by Monro and Ross. He makes Montrose stay for some days at Carbisdale 'expecting to hear from Pluscardine and the Earl of Seaforth's friends, who promised him their assistance'. When Monro of Achness assured Montrose that there was only one troop of horse in the whole of Ross, that information, coupled with the immediate expectation of being joined by the four hundred, encouraged him to warn Sutherland that 'although he spared to burne and spoyl his countrie at this time, yet before it were long, he should make his own neighbours undoe him'.[21] At a hastily convened council of war at Tain it was decided that Sutherland should return north to defend his own country against Harry Graham while Strachan and the others advanced against the royalists.

Two otherwise compatible accounts of the battle are in flat contradiction over Montrose's position. Gordon of Sallagh states that he camped at Carbisdale for some days; a newsletter, 'The True Relation', probably based upon Strachan's own report, says that the royalists had marched from Strathoykel to Carbisdale. If Montrose had been well entrenched Strachan would not have found his task so easy. All the descriptions suggest that the marquis was taken unawares, on the move, possibly expecting to link up with the local levies. Montrose forded the Oykel just west of the point where it is joined by the Cassley, to march along the south bank of the river. The railway village of Culrain sits in the middle of the battlefield of Carbisdale, a name now preserved only by Carbisdale Castle, a splendid Gothic edifice looming on the shoulder of Creag a' Choineachan, but which once designated the shallow valley formed by the Culrain Burn in its short course from Loch a' Choire to the sea. For several miles above Invershin the Oykel seems unable to decide whether it is a river or a loch, flowing slow and deep between its marshy banks. At Invercharron two and a half miles south of Culrain the River Carron joins the Kyle of Sutherland. The village is situated in the middle of level ground roughly triangular in shape, bounded on the north and west by the densely wooded slopes of Creag a' Choineachan and the low wooded slopes of the 'Scroggie Wood', on the east by the Kyle and on the south by the Culrain Burn. Montrose marched through the narrow pass between the Creag and the Kyle into the centre of the triangle, facing south-east towards Bonar Bridge and the Dornoch Firth. His force numbered about twelve hundred men of whom only about forty were cavalry, commanded by Major Lisle.

The engagement at Carbisdale was less a battle than a rout. On Saturday 27 April Strachan arrived at Kincardine, about five miles from Culrain and south across the Kyle from Bonar Bridge. He was uncertain whether to push on that day or delay until the Monday since he refused to infringe the Sabbath, but he also feared that if he awaited reinforcements from Leslie, the enemy would take to the hills. Once informed of Montrose's exact position 'they concludit to feight that wicked crew with the force they had', suitably refreshed with prayer and a blessing at three in the afternoon. Both Sallagh and Menteith state that Montrose was ambushed but as S.R. Gardiner long since pointed out, Sallagh must have mistaken Strachan's position for he placed him at Wester Fearn, south of Kincardine and a good six miles from the battle site, 'concealed by the broom'. Andrew Monro reported that Montrose's cavalry were out looking for the single troop of horse to which Achness had alerted him. Local tradition relates that the Monros and the Rosses advanced up Strathcarron to shelter behind the ridge of Feith Tharsuinn where they awaited the outcome of the battle. The story may imply that Andrew actually conversed with Montrose, deliberately misleading him as to Strachan's numbers. Andrew certainly advised Strachan that only one troop of horse should show itself while the others remained in concealment. It is otherwise difficult to understand how Montrose's twelve hundred were so completely demolished by fewer than three hundred men, even allowing that most of them were mounted. Strachan simply advanced along the shore of the Kyle, hidden by the broom and scrub. Montrose was roughly in the position of the modern village when he saw Strachan at the head of a hundred horse crossing the Culrain Burn. He ordered his men to take up positions on the wooded hillside skirting the level ground while he sent Lisle forward to investigate. Before the royalist foot could reach the shelter of the woods Strachan charged. A hundred cavalry were more than a match for forty. Lisle's horse broke, driving back against their own infantry in confusion. Hackett and Ker charged from their cover to support Strachan. Hurry commanding the centre could do little to make a stand although the battle-hardened mercenaries attempted a volley. In a matter of minutes the royalists were demolished. Menzies of Pitfoddels, Guthrie, Ogilvie, and Lisle were all killed in the first charge. Two hundred Orcadians drowned while trying to swim the spring-swollen waters of the Kyle. A bullet hit Strachan's belt buckle; apart from a few wounded he lost one over-enthusiastic trooper who perished in the Oykel. 'The Monros and the Rosses entering the wood did kill many.' On the lower slopes of Creag a' Choineachan the defeated were hunted down. In two hours over four hundred royalists were killed; over four hundred and fifty prisoners were taken. In the commotion Montrose was wounded in several places, his horse shot from under him. The proud insignia of the Garter was abandoned on the field to be picked up by the victors. Crichton of Frendraught, himself bleeding in two places, pressed his own horse on the marquis, reminding the unwilling recipient that 'the preservation of his person was keeping life in the cause'. With Kinnoul, Sinclair of Brims, and Sir Edward Sinclair, an Orcadian, the Lieuten-ant-Governor of Scotland swam the Kyle. In this disastrous, humiliat-ing, undignified rout the military career of James Graham ended; not even the pen of Wishart could have discovered any glory in it.[22]

For three days and two nights Montrose, disguised as a shepherd, wandered in the wilds of Strathoykel without food or shelter. Sallagh asserts that Kinnoul died of his wounds or exposure or both; his where-abouts after Carbisdale are a complete mystery for it is attested that he lived until 1677. Sinclair of Brims apparently went back to his own country alone, though Menteith believed that he was the means of Montrose's betrayal. The marquis and Edward Sinclair struggled blindly up the strath to a reception as inhospitable as the stark Suther-land mountains themselves. All Christ-like figures require their Judas. According to royalist martyrology Montrose found his in Neil MacLeod of Assynt. He received milk and bread at a shieling in the vicinity of Cnoc na Glas Choille, south-east of Loch Urigill. A guide offered to take him to Reay country and instead led him to Ardvreck Castle on the shores of Loch Assynt. Iain Lom was in no doubt of the guilt of 'Neil from dreary Assynt'.

> You and your father-in-law, that Goodman of Lemlair, although you should both be hanged it would not be sufficient blood-price for my loss.
>   You are a stripped branch of the perjured apple-tree without fruit or honour or comeliness, ever engaged in murdering one another, you are the leavings of [sword] thrusts and dirks.

The death should be about you, despicable one, for you have sinfully sold the truth for Leith meal, most of which had gone sour.[23]

Royalist literature persisted in the fiction that Montrose expected to receive shelter from his 'friend' Neil, and was therefore betrayed by him. Neil succeeded his grandfather Donald in 1646. Since he did not come of age until 1649 it is unlikely that he ever met Montrose. The MacLeods of Assynt were one of those clans which decided to throw in their lot with the Earl of Sutherland who had recently appointed Neil sheriff-depute of Assynt. In 1646 Ardvreck was besieged by the MacKenzies. The evidence therefore suggests that Neil would favour Sutherland in opposition to Seaforth or Montrose. When the marquis arrived at Ardvreck Neil was besieging Dunbeath with Sutherland and he had been warned by his brother-in-law Andrew Monro of Lemlair to keep a look-out for stray royalists in general, and James Graham in particular. The reward of £20,000 first offered for Montrose in 1644 was presumably still available – the sum was subsequently mentioned in parliament as appropriate remuneration for MacLeod's services – and in addition Neil was voted approximately five thousand pounds worth of meal, a particularly acceptable commodity because, at that time, there was near famine in the north. Neil subsequently received the captaincy of Tongue, the old MacKay stronghold. These supplementary awards were fitting since Montrose was, if anything, more of a wanted man in 1650 than he had been in 1644–5. 'Betrayal' is a loaded word and despite the fact that 'Ardvreck's Shame' is still apparently an emotive topic after three centuries, it is irrelevant. Montrose had anticipated the much more valuable support of the MacKays, the Monros, the Rosses, and the MacKenzies, whose chief he called 'friend' in the last recorded letter of his life. Wounded, famished, defeated, and alone he perhaps had reason, but no right, to delude himself with expectations of assistance from Assynt. Christian Monro placed her captive in the dungeon at Ardvreck, summoned her husband from Dunbeath and sent runners to Leslie at Tain. On 4 May Major-General Holburn arrived to take custody of the prisoners. Neil was understandably deaf to Montrose's bribes and cajolings; the MacKenzies already had designs on his estates; if he alienated Sutherland, the MacLeods of Assynt faced total destruction. Neil carried the stigma of treachery to the grave. He was tried twice on the charge of betraying Montrose but was never found guilty. Two years after his death his estates passed to Seaforth.[24]

As Montrose set out on his last long march he was embarking upon a kind of eerie pilgrimage through his own career. From now until he stepped off to eternity his actions and bearing were consciously theatrical, inescapably recalling Burnet's assessment that he was 'stately to affectation, took upon him the port of a hero too much, and lived as in a romance'. He was concerned that in the last act of the great drama of his life, he should not fail the groundlings. On 5 May Holburn led his prisoners out of Ardvreck down the long strath to Glen Cassley, where Montrose had awaited the northern levies, along the north bank of the river to Invershin, and then through Balblair to Skibo Castle three miles from Dornoch. There, tradition says, he was treated to high comedy, for the irate lady of the castle beat Holburn over the head with a leg of mutton to teach him better manners when he neglected to give the marquis precedence at table. After two days he was ferried to Tain, where he was transferred to the custody of David Leslie to be conveyed to Beauly. Leslie's outstanding military abilities perhaps highlight the deficiencies of Montrose's very different brand of general-ship. Of all Cromwell's opponents he was to come closest to defeating him in 'the brunt or essential agony of the battle of Dunbar'. He had recently refused the offer of the carldom of Orkney but he became a king's man in 1650 and Lord Newark ten years later.

At Beauly Montrose met some of the other casualties of Carbisdale. Sir John Hurry, 'a robust, tall, stately fellow, with a long cut in his cheek', had fought his last battle, as had John Spottiswood, but Gray and Mortimer were to be spared. Many foreign mercenaries, some Englishmen, and one or two Orkney ministers were also among the captives. Leslie pushed north to mop up the last pockets of resistance. A number of Montrose's papers were seized when he retook Dunbeath. Harry Graham fled through Caithness to Orkney whence he and Johnston took ship for the continent. Captain Cullace crossed the firth to demolish the last royalist stronghold of Noltland Castle on the extreme north-west point of Westray. There George Drummond, among others, was captured; he was shipped back to Caithness 'to be shot at a post'.[25] By 21 May 281 royalist prisoners were confined in Edinburgh.

On 8 May Montrose was at Brahan where the previous century the famous seer Coinneach Odhar had allegedly prophesied doom for the

MacKenzies. James Fraser of Phopachy was one of those who saw the marquis as he was taken south. 'He set uponn a little shelty horse without a sude [saddle], but a quilt of raggs and straw, and pieces of roaps for stirrops, his feet fastened under the horse belly, with a teather and a bit halter for a bridle, a ragged old dark reedish plaid, a muskatire on each side, and his fellow prisoners on foot after him.'26 At Inverness he began to show a fever. The townsfolk, some curious, some contemptuous, gathered to witness the living legend. An old woman shrieked at him to look at the houses he had burned during the siege in 1646, 'yet he never altered countenance'. At the mercat cross when offered wine he chose water. As he left the northern capital which had always defied him the provost Duncan Forbes of Culloden expressed sorrow for his circumstances. 'I am sorry for being the object of your pitty,' was the reply. As he passed through Moray, close to the site where Alasdair had held off the Campbells in the enclosures at Auldearn, many came to greet him, though Fraser possibly exaggerates in saying he 'was overjoyed to see those about him' for they included many gentlemen who were loyalists come lately, including Thomas Mac-Kenzie of Pluscardine who had ignored any instructions he may have received from his brother. At Keith where he had faced Baillie before Alford a tent was set up in the fields so that Mr William Kinanmond could preach from the covenanters' favourite and bloodiest biblical book. 'And Samuel said, as thy sword hath made women childless, so shall thy mother be childless among women. And Samuel hewed Agag in pieces before the Lord in Gilgal.' Montrose might have said with Agag, 'Surely the bitterness of death is past', but he listened awhile before turning his back. 'Rail on!' said he. That night 'Agag' requested, and was given, permission to sleep in the fields as in his campaigning days.

From Keith the party advanced through Garioch and Strathdon, the district of so many marches and counter-marches since 1639. Tradition says he spent a night at Pitcaple, where he refused an offer of escape, but there is no certainty about the route, though he seems to have avoided Aberdeen, the city he saved to sack. When he reached Southesk's castle at Kinnaird he was permitted to see his two younger children for the last time. They had seen little of him in their short lives. James was in exile in Flanders. Robert was to end his days fighting on the continent, while Jean never married. An age had passed since the carefree days of early marriage at Kinnaird. The irascible old Southesk was now seventy-five; he had eight years to live. Fraser, who knew little of Dundee, says that the townsfolk 'were so farr from insulting him that the whole town expressed a great deal of sorrow for his condition' but it is doubtful if they had forgotten the hectic visit of Alasdair and his 'Irishes' in 1645.

At Dundee Montrose exchanged his sheltie for a ship which conveyed him to Scotland's Jerusalem. On Saturday 18 May he landed at Leith to be mounted on a cart horse and led up the Water Gate to Holyrood, forty persons 'of quality' marching behind him on foot. He was met by the city magistrates, the town guard, and the hangman, who informed him of the decision of a hastily convened parliamentary committee. He was to be 'tied with cords upon a cart, bare-headed' and led up the Royal Mile, the hangman riding upon the cart horse. The prisoner replied quietly that he would 'go to it', his only regret being that through him the king should be dishonoured. As the procession passed 'there appeared in him such majesty, courage, modesty and even somewhat more than natural, that those common women who had lost their husbands and children in his wars, and who were hired to stone him, were upon the sight of him so astonished and moved, that their intended curses turned into tears and prayers.' At Moray House, however, Lady Jean Gordon, Countess of Haddington, 'did publicly insult and laugh at him', eliciting a remark from the crowd that she should be in the cart for her adulteries. The same balcony held Lord Lorne and his new-wed wife Mary Stewart, daughter of the Earl of Moray whose hospitality they all enjoyed. As the cart passed by, the eyes of Montrose and *MacCailein* himself met briefly through a partly drawn blind.

He was lodged in the Tolbooth. Parliament sent representatives to question the prisoner who refused to answer till he knew how things stood with the king. They returned to consult their colleagues about an appropriate reply; it was decided both to tell him the truth and to defer sentence until Monday. On their second visit Montrose begged rest: 'The compliment they had put upon him that day was something tedious.'

There was no comfort in the news from Breda, where negotiations had dragged on since 15 March. It was clear initially that 'some good news from Montrose, that he were in any hopeful posture, would soon spoil the treaty with these commissioners', but in the absence of such news Charles would have no alternative but to 'close with them, as well as he can, and expect what time may bring forth to deliver him of his bonds'. Some thought that Montrose might usefully be employed in Ireland but his own supporters dismissed the suggestion, asserting that Montrose would retire to the Highlands before he would lay down arms. On 12 April it was reported that terms had all but been agreed. Charles's ignorance of Montrose's progress had 'brought him to obedience to supposed necessity', though it was thought that 'he and Montrose are too well assured of each other to mistake one another's actions'. On 26 April Charles was still demanding a pardon for 'that anathematized arch rebel' James Graham, while trying to prolong negotiations to allow James time to increase his following. Agreement was finally reached on 1 May when Charles accepted the terms offered the previous year. A perceptive reporter distinguished the essential hollowness of the agreement on the day it was concluded.

[The Scots] say they find nothing but vanity and lightness in him [the king] and that he will never prove a strenuous defender of their faith. And 'tis evident still that he perfectly hates them, and neither of them can so dissemble it, but each other knows it, and 'tis a matter of pleasant observation, to see how they endeavour to cheat and cozen the other. .... They hate the thing Monarchy, but they must have the name of it ... they must make a property of him, no other will serve them for a shadow to stalk their ends by.[27]

Two days later Charles sent letters to Montrose commanding him to lay down arms. 'You cannot reasonably doubt of my real intention to provide for your interests and restitution with my utmost care; and though I may not be able to affect it for the present, yet I do not despair of doing it in a little time, nor of having an occasion to employ you more honourably, and more advantageously than in your present design.' So his 'private' letter; the public one ordered him to cease all acts of hostility and immediately lay down arms, disband, and withdraw himself and his forces from Scotland.

It has been argued that Charles had received assurances about Montrose's safety from Argyll[28] but the flaw in the theory is that, if it is correct, Argyll jeopardized the agreement with the king by letting Montrose die. Although Charles did not sign the solemn league until 23 June his subscription of the document was, as Montrose had predicted, the king's 'shame and ruin ... nothing but a condemning of your royal father's memory, joining all your dominions in rebellion, by your consent against you, and in effect a very formal putting hand on yourself'. Charles believed that it was 'sometimes needful to hold a candle to the devil', and that Scotland and his throne were worth a covenant. His protestations to the contrary notwithstanding, there is every indication that he abandoned Montrose with the same cynicism which allowed him to accept the solemn league. If Montrose was one of the noblest servants of monarchy, Charles Stewart was one of the worst representatives of kingship. His order to disband was tantamount to a death warrant; he had no way of knowing of Montrose's progress. The bearer of the letters Sir William Fleming might have reached the marquis in the aftermath of another Kilsyth or bottled up in Inverness or Perth with people like Strachan and Guthrie screaming for the blood of the Amalekites. Fleming's instructions defied imagination. If he found that the prevailing party in Scotland was not satisfied with the concessions he had granted, Montrose was not to demit arms; if on the other hand they had accepted the conditions only to force Montrose to capitulate then he was to do as he pleased. If Scottish royalists did not agree with the terms they were to join Montrose. If Montrose was strong he was not to disband, if weak he was, and if disbanded his soldiers were somehow to be 'entertained in other troops'. Montrose would have required Napier's logarithms to work out the possible permutations. The fact that he was willing to be sacrificed does not exonerate the king. On hearing vague reports of Carbisdale Charles wrote to the Scottish parliament 'showing that he was heartily sorry that James Graham had invaded this kingdom, and how he had discharged him from doing the same; and earnestly desires the Estates of Parliament to do himself that justice as not to believe that he was accessory to the said invasion in the least degree.'[29] Fortunately Montrose was spared both receipt of the instructions and knowledge of the depths of Charles's faithlessness; he was spared the final tragic realization that so far as he was concerned the cause was not worthy of the man. It was left to a foreign king, Louis XIV, to attempt intervention for his life at the request of De Retz, pleading that 'he has done no more than devote himself, in a most generous spirit, to his paramount duty in fulfilling the commands of the king, his sovereign lord'. The day after the letter was written, news reached Paris that Montrose was dead.

Throughout the Sabbath the prisoner was pestered by ministers and 'parliament men'. He told them that his journey from Leith was 'the most honourable and joyful that ever he made'. The following morning the ministers again descended upon him. Patrick Simson later related his memories of the occasion to Robert Wodrow. They accused him of pride, of raising war, ravaging his country, and causing bloodshed. He refuted the charges 'handsomely as he could well do, intermixing many Latin apothegms'. As David took strange company to defend himself in difficult times, said Montrose, so had he employed Irish papists. Unpaid soldiers could not be restrained from spoil. If possible he would have avoided the bloodshed for 'he would rather it had all come out of his own veins'. To the charge of having breached the covenant he replied, 'the covenant which I took I own it and adhere to it. Bishops I care not for them. I never intended to advance their interest.' The solemn league was another matter which had led to the king's murder and the overturning of government. When the ministers explained that such developments were due to sectarians he told them that error was infinite. He expressed his regret that his actions had proved offensive to the church with which he would dearly have liked to be reconciled. 'But since I cannot obtain it on any other terms – unless I call that my sin which I account to have been my duty – I cannot, for all the reason and conscience in the world.'[30]

The spiritual repast was followed by a breakfast of bread dipped in ale after which he dressed carefully to hear doom pronounced in Parliament House. When the charges against him were read out he made an eloquent reply. 'My care has always been to walk as became a good Christian, and a loyal subject. I did engage in the first covenant and was faithful to it.' His Cumbernauld Band had attempted to foil those who cloaked their aims to wrest authority from the king under religion. When a faction of Scots decided to assist the English rebels the king had commissioned him to create a diversion. He said that no blood had been spilled save in battle, that he had personally saved many thousand lives, and that 'never a hair of a Scotsman's head that I could save, fell to the ground', three claims he would have found difficult to prove and against which there is considerable evidence. The 1650 expedition was intended to 'accelerate the treaty' between the king and the Scots, 'by his Majesty's just commands'. 'I may say that never subject acted upon more honourable grounds, nor by so lawful a power, as I did in these services. Let me be judged by the laws of God, the laws of nature and nations, and the laws of the land. If otherwise I do here appeal from you, to the righteous Judge of the World, who one day must be your judge and mine, and who always gives out righteous judgements.'

Warriston then read the sentence. He was to be hanged at the Cross of Edinburgh with the *De Rebus* and his declarations round his neck. After three hours he was to be cut down, 'headed and quartered', the head being displayed on the Tolbooth and the legs and arms at the gates of Stirling, Glasgow, Perth, and Aberdeen. If he repented his body would be buried in Greyfriars, if not in a common grave on the Burgh Muir. When he made to speak he was silenced by Loudoun. Throughout he behaved 'with a great deal of courage and modesty, unmoved and undaunted as appeared, only he sighed several times and rolled his eyes alongst all the corners of the House'. He may have flinched on realizing he was to be hanged; a man of his rank would have expected decapitation.

Argyll once observed that 'whatever honour we have at the crime, we immediately forget and pity the criminal when he comes to suffer' and Montrose was determined not to disappoint his audience as he prepared with the greatest care for the final curtain. As he was brushing his hair on the morning of Tuesday 21 May he was asked why he was so careful of his locks. 'My head is yet my own. I will arrange it to my taste; tonight, when it will be yours, treat it as you please.' The thirty-foot gallows predicted by Rothes had been erected; the minutely detailed accounts for its construction survive. As the moment approached drums and trumpets alerted the town guard and a detachment of soldiers. There were fears of a rescue bid as the victim learned to his amusement. 'What, am I still a terror to them? Let them look to themselves, my ghost will haunt them.' He devoted the greatest attention to his dress, wearing 'fine scarlet, laid over with much silver lace, his hat in his hand, his hands and cuffs exceeding rich, his delicate white gloves on his hands, his stockings of incarnate silk, his shoes with ribbons on his feet. To be short, nothing was here deficient to honour his poor carcass, more beseeming a bridegroom than a criminal going to the gallows.'[31]

It was a short walk down the High Street to the scaffold. He made no farewell speech but the son of Sir Robert Gordon of Gordonstoun noted his last remarks and sentiments in shorthand. He said little that he had not said before. He submitted himself to God and forgave his tormentors. In his view Charles I had lived a saint and died a martyr. 'I pray God I may end as he did. If ever I would wish my soul in another man's stead it should be his.'

I doe bot follow the light of my owne conscience, which is kendled to the working of the good spirit of God that is within me. I thank him, I goe to heavinis throne with joy, and he sufferis me not to feir the terrouris of death, and furnishes me with confidence and courage to embrace it, even in [its] ugliest shape. I desyre your charitie and prayeris: I sall pray for you all. I leive my soull till God, my service to my Prince, my good will to my freindis, and my name and charitie to you all.[32]

There was little to add to the poem which he wrote during his imprisonment.

> Let them bestow on ev'ry airt a limb;
> Open all my veins, that I may swim
> To Thee my Saviour, in that crimson lake;
> Then place my pur-boil'd head upon a stake;
> Scatter my ashes, throw them in the air;
> Lord (since Thou know'st where all these atoms are)
> I'm hopeful, once Thou'lt recollect my dust,
> And confident Thou'lt raise me with the just.

Since the ministers refused to pray for him as an excommunicate, he prayed for himself. Observing custom he gave the hangman four pieces of gold. Wishart's *History* and the declarations were tied round his neck. 'I love this more than my badge of being knight of the garter,' said he. 'Nay more my honour than a chain of gold.' His arms were pinioned, leaving his hands free. He ascended the ladder 'in a very stately manner'. As the executioner adjusted the noose round his neck he asked, 'how long shall I hang here?' On a prearranged hand signal he was pushed off.

An English commentator expressed astonishment that Montrose's countenance did not alter even as he was turned off the ladder. 'It is absolutely believed that he hath overcome more men by his death in Scotland, than he would have done if he had lived,' he wrote. 'For I never saw a more sweeter carriage in a man in all my life.' Argyll was less impressed. He spent a sleepless night before the execution while his wife gave birth to a daughter, 'whose birthday is remarkable', he told Lothian, 'in the tragic end of James Graham at this Cross. He was warned to be sparing in speaking to the king's disadvantage, or else he had done it. He got some resolution after he came here, how to go out of this world, but nothing at all how to enter into another.'[33] The presbyterian brand of Christianity knew little charity, though if monarchy claimed a martyr in Montrose, the covenant took Campbell eleven years later.

In fulfilment of the sentence the body was quartered and its parts duly distributed. The trunk was placed in a short box and buried on the Burgh Muir. Two days later Lady Napier arranged to have the grave reopened and his heart removed to be embalmed in a gold casket. Montrose had admitted that he would prefer his head 'standing on the ports of this town, for this quarrel, than to have my portrait in the king's bed-chamber'. He had his wish, for his head was well and truly fixed to the spike on the Tolbooth, a cross spike being inserted to ensure it was not stolen. At least one Cromwellian soldier used it for target practice, the shot dislodging not the head but a chunk of masonry which killed a drummer shopping in the luckenbooths below. It was a fatal object for David Graham of Gorthie died a few hours after removing it from the spike in 1661. It was shortly replaced by the head of *MacCailein Mór*.

Argyll crowned Charles in 1651 but the king did not forget the indignities to which he was subjected in Scotland and when Campbell hastened south to greet the 'merry monarch' at the Restoration, he was clapped in the Tower and shipped to Leith. As he lay in Edinburgh Castle awaiting trial Charles decreed that Montrose's remains be reassembled for honourable burial. Argyll, in no doubt of the verdict which awaited him, was a thoroughly disillusioned man. 'They are very miserable who have nothing but a heap of years to prove they have lived long, but infinitely unhappy are they who survive their credit and reputation,' he told his son. 'There is no better defence against the injuries of fortune and vexation of life than death.'[34]

Charles II attempted to purge his own guilt by ordering for Montrose the most splendid funeral that Scotland had ever seen. A largely new generation of the Scots nobility gathered to pay their last respects to the man who in life had embodied the noble virtues and qualities of their rank and station which so few could bring themselves to imitate. In brilliant sunshine the procession moved up the Royal Mile from Holyrood to St Giles, led by two conductors in mourning and twenty-four of the city's poor holding the arms of Graham. Sir Harry Graham rode in full armour carrying the colours of his house on the point of his lance. Behind him walked the servants of friends and relations and behind them representatives of all the branches of the Grahams with their colours and mourning banners. A great black horse of war and a horse of state were led unmounted. Individual Grahams bore Montrose's spurs, gauntlets, helmet, corselet, and banner. Next came the arms of the 'eight branches', four from his mother's side and four from his father's – Dirleton, Angus, Methven, Gowrie, Marischal, Wigtown, Perth, and Montrose. Then came the Lord Provost of Edinburgh with the baillies and burgesses, the members of parliament, and the nobles. Montrose's own arms were paraded, followed by a riderless horse of mourning, trumpeters, pursuivants and heralds, his secretaries, his physician, and his chaplain. Graham of Killearn carried his parliament robes, Graham of Cairney his baton, Inchbrakie the insignia of the Garter, Morphie the marquis's crown, and Fintry the purse. Lord Lyon preceded the coffin, which was carried by fourteen earls, while a further twelve bore the pall. James, second Marquis of Montrose and his brother Robert marched beside the coffin 'as chief mourners in hoods and long robes carried by two pages, with gentlemen bareheaded on every side'. They were followed by 'nine of the nearest in blood, three and three' – Douglas, Marischal, Wigtown, Southesk, Drummond, Madderty, Napier, Rollo, and Luss. John Middleton, parliamentary commissioner 'in an open coach' brought up the rear. As Montrose's remains were laid to rest in St Giles, in the grave of his grandfather the viceroy, volleys were fired in salute. Honour had finally been satisfied.

Huntly, Seaforth, Campbell of Glenorchy, Wigtown, Traquair, Southesk, Crawford, Atholl, Balcarres, Balmerino, Hamilton, and Napier had not survived to witness the spectacle. Sutherland lived on for one year, Loudoun for two, Airlie for three, Frendraught for four, Marischal for ten, Lauderdale for eleven, and Callendar for thirteen. The second marquis was thirty-five when he died. In 1665 he was forced to sell Auld Montrose to pay off his father's debts and so the estate and the title parted for ever. After Charles II left Scotland in 1651 no other reigning monarch visited the country until 1822. The legacies of the covenanting revolution included the continued deterioration of relations between Highlands and Lowlands, religious schism, and the survival of the demand for constitutional reform. The debate about the nature of kingship went on until, in 1689, Charles's brother James was deemed by the Convention of Estates to have forfeited the crown. He had invaded 'the fundamental constitution of this kingdom, and altered it from a legal limited monarchy, to an arbitrary despotic power'. The wheel had turned full circle in the ultimate triumph of the ancient ideal of the Scottish constitution for which Montrose had fought and died. To posterity he bequeathed his name and his charity. No man can do more.

NOTES AND REFERENCES

I THE MAKING OF AN EARL

1 G.W.S.Barrow, *Robert Bruce and the Community of the Realm of Scotland* (London 1965), p. 439.
2 Historical Manuscripts Commission (H.M.C.), *Graham of Fintry*, p. 188.
3 Scottish Record Office (S.R.O.), GD 220 A.7.4.6.
4 H.M.C., I–II, App., *Montrose*, p. 168; S.R.O., GD 220 B.2.3.5.
5 Mark Napier (ed.), *Memorials of Montrose and His Times*, 2 vols (Edinburgh 1850), I, 26.
6 S.R.O. GD 220 B.2.3.3.
7 *Register of the Privy Council of Scotland* (R.P.C.), 14 vols (Edinburgh 1877–98), V, p. 387; H.M.C., *Graham of Fintry*, p. 113; H.M.C., X, App. IV, *Muncaster*, pp. 234, 262.
8 S.R.O. GD 220 B.2.2.2/3.
9 David Calderwood, *The History of the Kirk of Scotland* (ed.) T.Thomson, 7 vols (Edinburgh 1842–9), VII, p. 38.
10 R.Cant, *The College of St Salvator* (Edinburgh 1950), pp. 174–5.
11 On Lindsay see Lord Lindsay, *Lives of the Lindsays or a Memoir of the House of Crawford and Balcarres*, 2 vols (London 1849), II, pp. 3–4. On the Rosicrucians, Francis A.Yates, *The Rosicrucian Enlightenment* (London 1972) passim.
12 W.Wilson, *The House of Airlie*, 2 vols (London 1924), II, p. 10.
13 Quoted W.A.Gatherer (ed.), *The Tyrannous Reign of Mary Stewart* (Edinburgh 1958), p. 5.
14 Napier, *Memorials*, I, p. 124.
15 Henry Guthry, *Memoirs* (2nd edn, Glasgow 1747), p. 112.
16 Wilson, *Airlie*, II, p. 14.
17 D.Thomson, *The Life and Art of George Jamesone* (Oxford 1974), p. 90.

2 TOWARDS A REVOLUTION

1 S.R.O., GD 112 39.4.475.
2 Mark Napier, *Memoirs of the Marquis of Montrose* (Edinburgh 1856), p. 89. For Indictment see *Selected Justiciary Cases 1624–1650* (ed.) S. Gillon (Edinburgh 1953), pp. 213–18.

3 W.Fraser, *The Chiefs of Colquhoun and their Country*, 2 vols (Edinburgh 1869), I, p. 241.

4 Napier, *Memoirs*, p. 87.

5 George Wishart, *Memoirs of the Most Renowned James Graham, Marquis of Montrose Translated from the Latin of the Rev Doctor George Wishart* (Edinburgh 1819), pp. 517–18.

6 Edmund Goldsmid (ed.), *The History of the Devils of Loudoun*, 3 vols, *Collectanea Adamantaea*, XXI (Edinburgh 1888), III, pp. 29–38.

7 John Major, *A History of Greater Britain* (ed. and transl.) A.Constable (Edinburgh 1892), p. 215.

8 D.Laing (ed.), *The Works of John Knox*, 6 vols (Edinburgh 1895), IV, pp. 528–9.

9 A.Hamilton, *De Confusione Calvinianae sectae apud Scotos* . . . (Paris 1577), p. 60. I am grateful to Dr Arthur Williamson for drawing my attention to this reference.

10 George Buchanan, *De Jure Regni Apud Scotos* (1843 edn), cap. XVIII in (transl.) D.Mcneill, *Art and Science of Government among the Scots* (Glasgow 1954), p. 29.

11 H.R.Trevor-Roper, 'George Buchanan and the Ancient Scottish Constitution', *English Historical Review Supplement*, 3 (1966), p. 42.

12 Archibald Campbell, Marquis of Argyll, *Instructions to a Son* (Glasgow 1743), p. 6; Napier, *Memorials*, II, p. 52.

13 Quoted T.D.Robb, 'Sixteenth Century Humanism as Illustrated in the Works of George Buchanan', in *George Buchanan: Glasgow Quatercentenary Studies* (Glasgow 1907), p. 178.

14 James I, *The Political Works* (ed.) C.H.McIlwain (Cambridge 1918), pp. 53–70.

15 Carmichael's letters are conveniently gathered in D.Laing (ed.), *The Miscellany of the Wodrow Society*, I (Edinburgh 1844), pp. 409–48.

16 David Stevenson, *The Scottish Revolution 1637–1644* (Newton Abbot 1973), p. 48.

17 Sir Thomas Craig, *De Unione Regnorum Britanniae Tractatus* (ed. and transl.) C.S.Terry (Edinburgh 1909), pp. 440–68.

18 James I, *Works*, p. 329.

19 R.P.C., VIII, p. 745.

20 *A Copie of a Letter from the nobility of Scotland* . . . (London 1607); R.P.C., VII, p. 536.

21 Calderwood, *History of the Kirk*, VI, p. 36.

22 R.P.C., VII, p. 164n.

23 R.P.C., VII, p. 485.

24 Calderwood, *History of the Kirk*, VI, pp. 581–2.

25 *Correspondence of Sir Robert Ker, Earl of Ancram and William, third Earl of Lothian* (ed.) Earl of Lothian (Edinburgh 1875), I, p. 37.

26 R.P.C., *New Series*, 8 vols (Edinburgh 1899–1908), I, p. 193.

27 *Correspondence of Ancram and Lothian*, I, p. 42.

28 Napier, *Memorials*, I, pp. 10–13.

29 *Acts of the Parliaments of Scotland* (A.P.S.) (eds) T.Thomson and C.Innes, 12 vols (London 1814–75), V, pp. 232–3.

30 James Maidment (ed.), *The Poetical Remains of William Lithgow* (Edinburgh 1863) (facsimile reprint).

31 W.Cobbett (ed.), *State Trials*, 10 vols (London 1809), III, pp. 603–4.

32 R.Baillie, *The Letters and Journals* (ed.) D.Laing, 3 vols (Edinburgh 1841–2), I, pp. 2, 4.

33 George Wishart, *The Memoirs of James Marquis of Montrose 1639–1650* (transl. with introduction, notes etc.) Alexander D.Murdoch and H.F. Morland Simpson (London 1893), p. 518.

34 P.Heylyn, *Cyprianus Anglicus or the history of the life and death of William, Archbishop of Canterbury* (London 1671), p. 373.

35 S.R.O., GD 220 B.4.2.7; B.4.2.14; Napier, *Memoirs*, p. 136.

36 Gordon Donaldson, *Scotland, James V to James VII* (Edinburgh 1965), p. 300.

37 H.M.C., *Laing*, I, p. 172; *Correspondence of Ancram and Lothian*, p. 42.

38 Napier, *Memorials*, I, pp. 216–17.

39 Napier, *Memorials*, II, pp. 43–9.

40 J.Gordon of Rothiemay, *History of Scots Affairs from MDCXXXVII to MDCXLI* (eds) J.Robertson and G.Grub, 3 vols (Aberdeen 1841), I, p. 33.

3 CAVALIER FOR THE COVENANT

1 W.Balcanquhal, *A Large Declaration Concerning the Late Tumults in Scotland* (London 1639), pp. 50–2.

2 Gordon of Rothiemay, *Scots Affairs*, I, p. 46.

3 *Calendar of State Papers, Domestic, Charles I* (C.S.P.D.), 25 vols (London 1858–76), (1638–9), p. 454.

4 John, Earl of Rothes, *A Relation of Proceedings Concerning the Affairs of the Kirk of Scotland* (Edinburgh 1835), p. 119. See also D.Stevenson, 'The Financing of the Cause of the Covenants 1638–51', *Scottish Historical Review*, LI (1972), p. 89.

5 Stevenson, *Revolution*, p. 89; *The Black Book of Taymouth with other papers from the Breadalbane Charter Room* (ed.) C.Innes (Edinburgh 1855), p. xxi; Guthry, *Memoirs*, p. 41.

6 H.M.C., XI, App. VI, *Hamilton*, p. 95.

7 H.M.C., XXI, *Hamilton Supplement*, p. 50; David Dalrymple, Lord Hailes, *Memorials and Letters Relating to the Reign of Charles I* (Glasgow 1766), p. 40; Ian Grimble, *Chief of Mackay* (London 1965), pp. 3–4.

8 R.P.C., X, pp. 113–18.

9 J.L.Campbell, 'The Letter Sent by Iain Muideartach, Twelfth Chief of

Clan Ranald to Pope Urban VIII in 1626', *Innes Review*, IV (1953), pp. 110–16.

10 George Hill, *An Historical Account of the MacDonnells of Antrim* (Belfast 1873), pp. 254, 444.

11 H.M.C., IX, Pt II, *Traquair*, p. 255.

12 H.M.C., *Hamilton Supp.*, p. 47.

13 W.Knowler (ed.), *The Earl of Strafford's Letters and Despatches*, 2 vols (Dublin 1740), II, pp. 290–1; H.M.C., XII, App. Pt II, *Cowper*, II, pp. 213–14; H.M.C., App., Pt VIII, *Atholl*, p. 24.

14 *Large Declaration*, pp. 157–72.

15 *Large Declaration*, pp. 173–81.

16 *Large Declaration*, p. 167; Knowler, *Letters and Despatches*, II, p. 291.

17 Gordon of Rothiemay, *Scots Affairs*, I, p. 151.

18 Gordon of Rothiemay, *Scots Affairs*, I, pp. 151–2; *Large Declaration*, pp. 240–2. Baillie, *Letters and Journals*, I, p. 133.

4 THE CURSE OF MEROZ

1 C.S.P.D. (1638–9), pp. 406–10.

2 Printed in Andrew Stevenson, *The History of the Church and State in Scotland from the Accession of King Charles I to the Restoration of King Charles II*, 2 vols (Edinburgh 1754), II, pp. 686–95.

3 Sir R.Gordon of Gordonstoun and G.Gordon of Sallach, *A Genealogical History of the Earldom of Sutherland* (Edinburgh 1813), p. 489.

4 Gordon of Rothiemay, *Scots Affairs*, II, p. 193.

5 John Spalding, *Memorialls of the Trubles in Scotland and in England 1624–1645*, 2 vols (Aberdeen 1850), I, p. 135; H.M.C., *Laing*, I, pp. 202–3.

6 Gordon, *Sutherland*, p. 489; Gilbert Burnet, *Memoirs of the Lives and Actions of James and William, Dukes of Hamilton and Castle-herald* (Oxford 1852), p. 113.

7 *Johnston of Warriston's Diary 1639* (ed.) G.M.Paul (Edinburgh 1896), p. 411.

8 Baillie, *Letters and Journals*, I, p. 409; H.M.C., XII, App. Pt VIII, *Atholl*, pp. 24–5.

9 Gordon of Rothiemay, *Scots Affairs*, II, p. 222.

10 Gordon of Rothiemay, *Scots Affairs*, II, p. 232.

11 Gordon, *Sutherland*, p. 489.

12 M.Wood (ed.), *Extracts from the Records of Edinburgh 1626–1655*, 2 vols (Edinburgh 1936), I, p. 214.

13 Baillie, *Letters and Journals*, I, p. 83.

14 Spalding, *Trubles*, I, p. 197; Gordon, *Sutherland*, pp. 491–2.

15 C.S.P.D. (1638–9), p. 58. On Huntly's alleged faithlessness see pp. 15, 39, 50–1, 59, 66, 72, 97, 99.

16 C.S.P.D. (1638–9), pp. 124, 146, 282.

17 Baillie, *Letters and Journals*, II, pp. 441–2.

18 H.M.C., VI, App., *Cumming*, p. 698.
19 Spalding, *Trubles*, II, App., pp. 486–9.
20 C.S.P.D. (1639), p. 386.

5 THE TEARS OF XERXES

1 Charles I, *His Majesties Declaration Concerning his Proceedings in Scotland* (London 1640), pp. 7–9.
2 C.S.P.D. (1639), pp. 395, 399, 407–8, 419; Robert Mentet (Menteith) of Salmonet, *The History of the Troubles of Great Britain* (transl.) James Ogilvie (London 1735), p. 49; Guthry, *Memoirs*, pp. 1–2.
3 Gilbert Burnet, *Bishop Burnet's History of His Own Time*, 3 vols (Edinburgh 1753), I, p. 39; Burnet, *Hamiltons*, p. 188.
4 S.R.Gardiner (ed.), *Hamilton Papers* (London 1880), pp. 94–8; *Argyll Transcripts*, Inveraray Castle 19.7.1639. (For convenience items of Argyll correspondence cited from Inveraray Castle are referenced as *Argyll Transcripts*, which are housed in the Cherry Park at the castle. The Argyll Muniments are currently being reclassified.)
5 H.M.C., IX, App., *Traquair*, p. 250.
6 C.S.P.D. (1639), p. 453; Gordon of Rothiemay, *Scots Affairs*, III, pp. 36–61.
7 C.S.P.D. (1639), p. 453; H.M.C., *Traquair*, p. 250.
8 Napier, *Memorials*, I, pp. 217–18.
9 H.M.C., *Traquair*, p. 249.
10 Guthry, *Memoirs*, p. 65.
11 Napier, *Memorials*, I, p. 253.
12 A.P.S., V, pp. 263, 266–7, 286.
13 Sir J.Balfour, *Historical Works*, 4 vols (Edinburgh 1824–5), II, p. 363.
14 H.M.C., *Montrose*, p. 169; Warriston's letter is wrongly dated to 1639 in Hailes, *Memorials*, p. 52. See also Napier, *Memoirs*, p. 228.
15 S.R.O., GD 220 B.8.4.10; B.7.5.2; B.8.6.1; B.8.5.1; B.8.5.9.
16 Gordon of Rothiemay, *Scots Affairs*, III, pp. 100–5; Charles I, *Declaration* (1640), pp. 37–9, 54.
17 Burnet, *History*, I, p. 39; the letter is printed in Charles I, *Declaration* (1640), pp. 57–9; in H.M.C., *Traquair*, pp. 253, 255; in C.S.P.D. (1639–40), p. 610; and Spalding, *Trubles*, I, p. 266.
18 H.M.C., *Erskine*, p. 638.
19 C.S.P.D. (1639–40), p. 555; *Argyll Transcripts*, 15.2.1640.
20 *Argyll Transcripts*, 13.2.1640, 4.3.1640; bond of friendship in H.M.C., *Argyll*, pp. 482–3.
21 H.M.C., *Traquair*, pp. 253, 255.
22 C.S.P.D. (1640–1), p. 375.
23 *Argyll Transcripts*, 26.12.1639.
24 A.P.S., V, pp. 288–326; Balfour, *Historical Works*, II, pp. 373–9.
25 Argyll, *Instructions to a Son*, p. 126.

26 Napier, *Memoirs*, p. 236.
27 C.S.P.D. (1640–1), pp. 10, 53.
28 Napier, *Memorials*, II, p. 477.
29 H.M.C., *Argyll*, pp. 491–2.
30 *Argyll Transcripts*, July 1640; Wilson, *Airlie*, I, pp. 220–1.
31 Annie M.Mackenzie (ed.), *Orain Iain Luim. Songs of John MacDonald, Bard of Keppoch* (Edinburgh 1964), pp. xxiii, 10 11.
32 Napier, *Memorials*, I, pp. 254–5. Also printed in Baillie, *Letters and Journals*, II, pp. 467–8. Laing noted a copy in the Balcarres MSS. and he possessed another in a contemporary hand. See also H.M.C., *Traquair*, p. 257. There are slight, but insignificant, differences in each of the copies.
35 Lithgow, *Poetical Remains*, p. xxviii.

6 THE TRIALS OF JOB

1 Napier, *Memorials*, I, p. 359.
2 C.S.P.D. (1640), p. 612.
3 C.S.P.D. (1640), pp. 616, 617, 621, 622.
4 Spalding, *Trubles*, I, pp. 321–31.
5 C.S.Terry, *The Life and Campaigns of Alexander Leslie* (London 1899), pp. 110–38; Hailes, *Memorials*, pp. 81–106; H.M.C., X, App. Pt IV, *Powis*, p. 393; H.M.C., XII, App. Pt II, *Cowper*, p. 260; H.M.C., *Various Collections*, II, pp. 256–7.
6 C.S.P.D. (1640–1), pp. 15, 29, 35, 85.
7 Burnet, *Hamiltons*, pp. 228–9.
8 C.S.P.D. (1640–1), pp. 206–7; Balfour, *Historical Works*, II, pp. 403–4.
9 Napier, *Memorials*, I, pp. 303–4.
10 Napier, *Memorials*, I, pp. 268–71; II, pp. 54–5.
11 Napier, *Memorials*, II, pp. 43–53.
12 Napier, *Memorials*, I, pp. 296–301, II, pp. 475–7.
13 Napier, *Memorials*, I, pp. 272–3.
14 *Correspondence of Ancram and Lothian*, pp. 126–7.
15 Balfour, *Historical Works*, III, pp. 27–30.
16 H.M.C., *Traquair*, p. 255; Napier, *Memorials*, I, p. 360.
17 Napier, *Memoirs*, p. 267. See also Mark Napier, *Montrose and the Covenanters*, 2 vols (London 1838).
18 H.M.C., XIII, App. Pt I and II, *Portland*, I, p. 24.
19 Napier, *Memorials*, I, p. 292.
20 Wigton Papers in *Miscellany of the Maitland Club*, II, Pt I (Edinburgh 1840), pp. 428–9.
21 Balfour, *Historical Works*, III, pp. 40–1.
22 Thomas Carte (ed.), *Collection of Original Letters and Papers . . . found among the Duke of Ormonde's Papers*, 2 vols (London 1739), II, p. 5; H.M.C., *Salisbury–Cecil*, XXII, p. 364.

23 Baillie, *Letters and Journals*, I, p. 391.
24 H.M.C., *House of Lords*, IV, p. 164.
25 J.B.Paul, *The Scots Peerage*, 9 vols (Edinburgh 1904–14), VI, pp. 517–18; Spalding, *Trubles*, II, p. 76.
26 R.P.C., VII, p. 154.
27 C.S.P.D. (1641–3), p. 139.
28 H.M.C., *House of Lords*, p. 168; Baillie, *Letters and Journals*, I, p. 392.
29 A.P.S., V, p. 448.
30 H.M.C., *Traquair*, p. 243; Napier, *Memorials*, I, pp. 317–18.

7 THE ADVENTURE BEGINS

1 S.R.O., GD 220 C.1.2.2, B.7.5.4, B.7.8.11, B.8.2.11.
2 Spalding, *Trubles*, II, p. 99.
3 Napier, *Memorials*, I, pp. 352–62.
4 Napier, Memorials, I, pp. 475–8; H.M.C., *Montrose*, pp. 168–9.
5 H.M.C., *Cowper*, p. 308; cf. H.M.C., *Ormonde*, II, p. 5.
6 Napier, *Memorials*, II, p. 56.
7 *Letters to the Argyll Family* (ed.) A.Macdonald (Edinburgh 1839), p. 37.
8 Napier, *Memorials*, II, pp. 60–1.
9 Napier, *Memorials*, II, pp. 58–9.
10 E.F.Hart, 'The Answer Poem of the Early Seventeenth Century', *Review of English Studies*, VII (1956).
11 J.L.Weir (ed.), *Poems of James Graham, Marquis of Montrose* (London 1938), no. V. The poem is discussed in Napier, *Memorials*, II, pp. 463–9, and Napier, *Memoirs*, App. II. See also W.Chappell, *Popular Music of the Olden Time*, 2 vols (London 1859), I, pp. 378–81, and note by Edward Rimbault, 'The Great Marquis of Montrose's Song', *Notes and Queries*, 4th Series, XII (1873), p. 522. On the genre, H.M.Richmond, 'The Intangible Mistress', *Modern Philology*, LVI (1959).
12 Napier, *Memorials*, II, pp. 71–2.
13 Burnet, *Hamiltons*, pp. 263–7.
14 Spalding, *Trubles*, II, p. 224.
15 E.Hyde, Earl of Clarendon, *The History of the Rebellion and Civil Wars in England begun in the year 1641* (ed.) W.D.Macray, 6 vols (Oxford 1888), II, p. 519.
16 H.M.C., VI, *Cumming*, p. 681; Gordon, *Sutherland*, p. 590; *Spalding Club Miscellany*, I (Aberdeen 1841), p. 52.
17 Burnet, *Hamiltons*, pp. 271–2.
18 Carte, *Ormonde*, I, pp. 19–20.
19 Spalding, *Trubles*, II, pp. 243–50; H.M.C., *House of Lords*, pp. 93–4; H.M.C., *Portland*, I, pp. 121–3; H.M.C., *Hamilton Supp.*, pp. 68–9; Baillie, *Letters and Journals*, II, pp. 74–5.
20 Napier, *Memorials*, II, pp. 77–8. cf. Carte, *Ormonde*, I, p. 19.

21 H.M.C., III, *Rollo*, p. 407.

22 A.P.S., VI, p. 41.

23 Menteith of Salmonet, *History of the Troubles*, pp. 148–9.

24 Napier, *Memorials*, I, pp. 220–1, II, pp. 119–21.

25 H.M.C., *Montrose*, p. 172; Hill, *MacDonnells*, pp. 266–7.

26 W.J.Watson, 'Unpublished Gaelic Poetry', *Scottish Gaelic Studies*, III (1931), pp. 143–59.

27 *Argyll Transcripts*, 22.5.1643.

28 James, eleventh Lord Somerville, *Memorie of the Somervilles*, 2 vols (Edinburgh 1815), II, pp. 288–331; Napier, *Memorials*, II, pp. 135–7.

29 Napier, *Memorials*, II, pp. 141–5.

30 H.M.C., *Cumming*, p. 686.

8 THE FIRST STRANGE COURSING

1 Quoted Aidan Clarke, 'The Earl of Antrim and the First Bishops' War', *The Irish Sword*, IV (1963–4), p. 112.

2 *Calendar of Clarendon State Papers*, 4 vols (Oxford 1872–1932), I, pp. 165ff.

3 *An Teachdaire Gaelach*, 2 vols (Glasgow 1830–1), II, pp. 61–2; for a variant see Angus Matheson, 'Traditions of Alasdair Mac Colla', *Transactions of the Gaelic Society of Glasgow*, V (1958), pp. 21–3.

4 Spalding, *Trubles*, II, p. 385; Caoimhin O'Danachair, 'Montrose's Irish Regiments', *The Irish Sword*, IV (1963–4).

5 B.O'Ferrall and O.O'Connell (eds), *Commentarius Rinuccinianus. De Sedis Apostolicae Legatione ad Foederatos Hiberniae Catholicos per annos 1645–1649*, 5 vols (Dublin 1932), I, pp. 458, 463; William Forbes-Leith, *Memoirs of Scottish Catholics during the xviith and xviiith centuries*, 2 vols (London 1909), I, pp. 266–7, 281–2.

6 Forbes-Leith, *Scottish Catholics*, I, pp. 287–8; Patrick Gordon of Ruthven, *A Short Abridgement of Britane's Distemper MDCXXXIX to MDCXLIX* (Aberdeen 1844), p. 63.

7 C.S.P.D. (1625–49), p. 629.

8 Gordon of Ruthven, *Britane's Distemper*, p. 70.

9 Mackenzie, *Orain Iain Luim*, p. 29.

10 Gordon of Ruthven, *Britane's Distemper*, pp. 76–8.

11 Napier, *Memorials*, II, pp. 146–7.

12 Hugh MacDiarmid, *Scottish Eccentrics* (London 1936), p. 284.

13 C.S.P.D. (1641–3), p. 305.

14 C.A.Patrides (ed.), *Sir Walter Ralegh, The History of the World* (London 1971), p. 46.

15 Napier, *Memorials*, II, pp. 147–8.

16 Napier, *Memorials*, II, pp. 312–17. Accounts of the battle: *A True Relation of the Happy Successes of His Majesty's Forces in Scotland* . . . (London 1644); Wishart, *Memoirs of Montrose*, pp. 58–62; Menteith of Salmonet, *History*

of the Troubles, pp. 171–3; Spalding, *Trubles*, II, p. 403; Gordon of Ruthven, *Britane's Distemper*, pp. 73–5; Carte, *Ormonde*, I, pp. 73–4.

17 *Argyll Transcripts*, 4.9.1644.

18 G.M.Fraser, *The Old Deeside Road*, Publications of the Aberdeen Natural History and Antiquarian Society, 3 (1921), pp. 24–5.

19 L.B.Taylor (ed.), *Aberdeen Council Letters*, 3 vols (Oxford 1952), II, pp. xxv, 380. See also Spalding, *Trubles*, II, p. 406.

20 Spalding, *Trubles*, II, p. 410.

21 Accounts of the battle: Spalding, *Trubles*, II, pp. 406–13; Wishart, *Memoirs of Montrose*, pp. 66–9; Gordon of Ruthven, *Britane's Distemper*, pp. 80–4; Carte, *Ormonde*, I, p. 173; *True Relation*.

22 Gordon of Ruthven, *Britane's Distemper*, pp. 86–7.

23 T.M., *Blood for Blood or Murders Revenged* (Oxford 1661); Napier, *Memorials*, II, p. 240.

24 C.S.P.D. (1649–50), pp. 265–6.

25 *Correspondence of Ancram and Lothian*, I, p. 178.

26 Wishart, *Memoirs of Montrose*, p. 77.

27 H.M.C., *Cumming*, p. 682.

9 THE SHAKING OF MacCAILEIN MÓR

1 James Fraser, *Chronicles of the Frasers; being the Wardlaw Manuscript* (ed.) William Mackay (Edinburgh 1905), p. 289.

2 Gordon of Ruthven, *Britane's Distemper*, pp. 94–6; Forbes-Leith, *Scottish Catholics*, I, p. 306.

3 'Book of Clanranald' (*Clanranald*) in Alexander Cameron, *Reliquiae Celticae* (ed.) A.MacBain and J.Kennedy, 2 vols (Inverness 1892–4), II, p. 181.

4 Forbes-Leith, *Scottish Catholics*, I, p. 306.

5 E.G.Cody (ed.), *The Historie of Scotland, wrytten first in Latin by John Leslie, Bishop of Ross and translated in Scottish by Father James Dalrymple*, 2 vols (Edinburgh 1884), I, p. 95.

6 Wishart, *Memoirs of Montrose*, p. 81; Spalding, *Trubles*, II, p. 443; Baillie, *Letters and Journals*, II, p. 263.

7 Napier, *Memorials*, II, pp. 175–6.

8 Forbes-Leith, *Scottish Catholics*, I, p. 312.

9 Forbes-Leith, *Scottish Catholics*, I, p. 317.

10 *An Historical and Genealogical Account of the Clan MacLean, by a Senachie* (London 1838), p. 124.

11 D.Thomson, *Introduction to Gaelic Poetry* (London 1974) p. 131.

12 Gordon of Ruthven, *Britane's Distemper*, pp. 57, 100; Forbes-Leith, *Scottish Catholics*, I, pp. 320–1. Argyll's heir, the ninth earl, referred to this prophecy in a letter of 17 October 1663 to Campbell of Glenorchy. 'One prophecie may now be looked on, as I ever did, to be false – that there

should be no more Earle of Argyll. But I thank God and his Majestie that have made more than one false prophet in this matter.' (S.R.O., Breadalbane Letters, 965.)

13 Napier, *Memorials*, II, pp. 172–3.
14 H.M.C., X, Pt VI, *Braye*, p. 160.
15 *Argyll Transcripts*, 3.9.1644; *Wardlaw Manuscript*, pp. 289–90.
16 *Argyll Transcripts*, 31.1.1645.
17 John Buchan, *Montrose* (London 2nd edn 1938), p. 190.
18 *The New Statistical Account of Scotland* (N.S.A.), 15 vols (Edinburgh 1845), XV, 'Kilmonivaig', p. 509.
19 Gordon of Ruthven, *Britane's Distemper*, p. 100.
20 A.Cameron Miller, 'Montrose in Lochaber', *The Celtic Monthly*, XVIII (1911), p. 204.
21 *Account of Clan MacLean*, p. 126.
22 Mackenzie, *Orain Iain Luim*, pp. 21–5.
23 A.MacLean Sinclair, *Mactalla nan Tur* (Sydney 1901), p. 2. Translation by Dr John MacInnes.
24 Forbes-Leith, *Scottish Catholics*, I, p. 322.
25 Napier, *Memorials*, II, pp. 175–9.
26 Napier, *Memoirs*, p. 491.
27 Clanranald, p. 185.
28 Forbes-Leith, *Scottish Catholics*, I, pp. 323–4.
29 Baillie, *Letters and Journals*, II, p. 418.
30 Sir James Turner, *Memoirs of his own life and times MDCXXXII–MDCLXX* (ed.) T.Thomson (Edinburgh 1829), p. 14.

IO THE FREEDOM OF A KINGDOM AND A CROWN

1 Napier, *Memorials*, II, pp. 183–92.
2 Spalding, *Trubles*, II, p. 456.
3 S.R.Gardiner, *History of the Great Civil War 1642–49*, 3 vols (London 1888–91), II, p. 160; Sir Thomas Hope, *Diary of Public Correspondence 1633–45* (Edinburgh 1843), p. 218.
4 Menteith of Salmonet, *History of the Troubles*, p. 199.
5 *An Extract of Several Letters from Scotland concerning the defeat given to the Rebel Forces under the command of James Graham at Dundee* (London April 1645), p. 4.
6 Wishart, *Memoirs of Montrose*, p. 93.
7 *Extract of Several Letters*, p. 6.
8 Baillie, *Letters and Journals*, II, p. 418.
9 Napier, *Memorials*, II, pp. 184–5.
10 Napier, *Memorials*, II, p. 181.
11 Gardiner, *Civil War*, II, p. 160.
12 Spalding, *Trubles*, II, p. 473.

13 H.M.C., *Laing*, I, p. 248.
14 Gordon, *Sutherland*, p. 525.
15 Mackenzie, *Orain Iain Luim*, p. 27.
16 Accounts of the battle: Wishart, *Memoirs of Montrose*, pp. 98–103; Gordon of Ruthven, *Britane's Distemper*, pp. 121–7; Spalding, *Trubles*, II, pp. 473–4; Gordon, *Sutherland*, p. 525; *Clanranald*, pp. 188–93; *Wardlaw Manuscript*, pp. 296–7.
17 Buchan, *Montrose*, p. 215.
18 *Wardlaw Manuscript*, p. 297.
19 N.S.A. XIII, 'Auldearn', p. 11.
20 Mackenzie, *Orain Iain Luim*, p. 27.
21 Baillie, *Letters and Journals*, II, p. 417.
22 Napier, *Memorials*, II, p. 204.
23 Accounts of the battle: Wishart, *Memoirs of Montrose*, pp. 108–11; Gordon of Ruthven, *Britane's Distemper*, pp. 128–31; *Clanranald*, p. 195; Baillie, *Letters and Journals*, II, pp. 417–18; W.Douglas Simpson, 'The Topographical Problem of the Battle of Alford', *Aberdeen University Review*, VI (1919).

II ASCENT TO THE MERIDIAN: KILSYTH

1 Baillie, *Letters and Journals*, II, p. 304; A.P.S., VI, pp. 429–37.
2 *The Statistical Account of Scotland*, 21 vols (Edinburgh 1791–9) (O.S.A.), XVIII, 'Kilsyth', p. 215.
3 H.C.B.Rogers, *Battles and Generals of the Civil Wars 1642–51* (London 1968), p. 253.
4 *Account of Clan MacLean*, p. 134.
5 Baillie, *Letters and Journals*, II, pp. 422–3; cf. Gardiner, *Civil War*, II, p. 267, and Buchan, *Montrose*, p. 234.
6 Thomson, *Gaelic Poetry*, p. 51; Baillie, *Letters and Journals*, II, p. 422; *Clanranald*, p. 201.
7 W.J.Watson, 'Unpublished Gaelic Poetry', *Scottish Gaelic Studies*, II (1927–8), pp. 89–91.
8 N.S.A., VIII, p. 148; O.S.A., XVIII, p. 298.
9 W.Fraser, *The Red Book of Grandtully*, 2 vols (Edinburgh 1868), I, p. 142.
10 Napier, *Memorials*, II, p. 222.
11 S.R.O., Records of Parliament, PA, 36.
12 Cobbett, *State Trials*, V, p. 1427.
13 Napier, *Memorials*, II, pp. 325–32.
14 Mackenzie, *Orain Iain Luim*, pp. xxvii, 59.
15 Terry, *Life of Leslie*, p. 367.
16 H.M.C., *Portland*, pp. 259–60, 272.
17 Napier, *Memorials*, I, p. 224, II, p. 233.
18 John Knox, *Works* (ed.) D.Laing, 6 vols (Edinburgh 1846), V, p. 32;

John Calvin, *Institutes of the Christian Religion* (transl.) Henry Beveridge, 2 vols (London 1962), I, p. 179.

19 H.M.C., IV, *Denbigh*, p. 272.
20 Napier, *Memorials*, I, pp. 215–29.
21 H.M.C., *Braye*, p. 160.

12 DESCENT TO DECADENCY: PHILIPHAUGH

1 Wishart, *Memoirs of Montrose*, p. 138; H.M.C., *House of Lords*, p. 101; A.P.S., vi, Pt II, p. 580.
2 S.R.O., PA 38, 39.
3 *A More Perfect and Particular Relation of the Late Great Victorie in Scotland* . . . (London September 1645), p. 1.
4 H.M.C., *Denbigh*, pp. 272–3; H.M.C., *Portland*, I, p. 268.
5 The fullest accounts of the battle are *A More Perfect Relation*; Wishart, *Memoirs of Montrose*, pp. 142–5; Gordon of Ruthven, *Britane's Distemper*, pp. 158–62.
6 Gordon of Ruthven, *Britane's Distemper*, p. 160.
7 John Willcock, *The Great Marquess. Life and Times of Archibald* . . . *Marquess of Argyll* (Edinburgh 1903), p. 387.
8 Napier, *Memorials*, II, pp. 237–8.
9 Napier, *Memorials*, II, pp. 245–51.
10 Wilson, *Airlie*, II, pp. 56–7.
11 James MacKnight (ed.), *Memoirs of Sir Ewen Cameron of Locheill, Chief of Clan Cameron* (Edinburgh 1842), pp. 78–81.
12 Buchan, *Montrose*, p. 264n.
13 H.M.C., X, App. Pt I, *Eglinton*, p. 55.
14 *Clanranald*, p. 203; Gordon of Ruthven, *Britane's Distemper*, p. 199.
15 A. and A.MacDonald, *The MacDonald Collection of Gaelic Poetry* (Inverness 1911), pp. 46–7. Translation by Dr John MacInnes.
16 J.Guthrie Smith, *Strathendrick and Its Inhabitants from Early Times* (Glasgow 1876), p. 131.
17 Turner, *Memoirs*, p. 41.
18 J.G.Fotheringham (ed.), *The Correspondence of De Montereul and the Brothers De Bellièvre, French Ambassadors in England and Scotland 1645–8*, 2 vols (Edinburgh 1898–9), I, p. 199; *Calendar of Clarendon State Papers*, I, p. 312.
19 George Mackay, 'Two Unpublished Letters from James Graham . . . to Sir Donald Mackay . . . ', *Juridical Review*, LIII (1941), p. 310.
20 *House of Lords Journal*, VIII, pp. 392–6.

13 PASSIONATE EXILE

1 Mackenzie, *Orain Iain Luim*, p. 29.
2 *Joint Print of Documents in Causa His Grace the Duke of Argyll against Angus*

John Campbell of Dunstaffnage and Another, Court of Session First Division (Edinburgh 1911), pp. 165–7, 171–3; A.P.S., VI, Pt I, pp. 498, 643.

3 C.Duncan MacTavish (ed.), *Minutes of the Synod of Argyll 1639–51*, 2 vols (Edinburgh 1943), I, pp. 62, 100, 148. See also A.Mitchell and J.Christie (eds), *The Records of the Commissions of the General Assemblies, 1646–9*, 2 vols (Edinburgh 1892–6), I, pp. 66–8, 71–2.

4 S.R.O., GD 92.83, petition of Archibald MacDonald of Sanda. I am grateful to Dr Francis Burton for this reference. Cf. A.McKerral, *Kintyre in the Seventeenth Century* (Edinburgh 1948), pp. 46–7.

5 *Joint Print*, pp. 176–7.

6 S.R.O., PA 7.23.2.49.

7 Turner, *Memoirs*, pp. 45, 238.

8 Napier, *Memoirs*, p. 603.

9 *Commentarius Rinuccinianus*, II, p. 786.

10 Mackenzie, *Orain Iain Luim*, p. 37.

11 A.P.S., VI, Pt I, pp. 203, 209–10, 220.

12 Napier, *Memorials*, II, p. 305; H.M.C., X, App., *Stirling–Maxwell*, p. 79.

13 H.M.C., *Graham of Fintry*, pp. 248–9.

14 'Forty Seventh Annual Report of the Deputy Keeper of the Public Records', *Parliamentary Papers* 37 (London 1886), App. II, pp. 55, 73, 74.

15 Napier, *Memorials*, II, p. 303; Wishart, *Memoirs of Montrose*, p. 191.

16 Menteith of Salmonet, *History of the Troubles*, p. 509; Napier, *Memoirs*, p. 61.

17 H.M.C., VIII, *Marlborough*, p. 27.

18 H.M.C., *Pepys*, p. 207.

19 Gardiner, *Hamilton Papers*, p. 164; *Montereul Correspondence*, II, p. 377.

20 Quoted H.N.Brailsford, *The Levellers and the Puritan Revolution* (London 1961), p. 362.

21 Argyll, *Instructions to a Son*, p. 5.

22 H.M.C., *Graham of Fintry*, pp. 249–50; *Records of Commissioners*, II, p. 123. On Magdalen's death see Buchan, *Montrose*, p. 263n.

23 Napier, *Memoirs*, p. 670n.

24 H.M.C., *Montrose*, p. 173; H.M.C., *Ormonde*, II, p. 396.

25 H.M.C., *Pepys*, p. 212.

26 S.R.Gardiner, 'The Last Campaign of Montrose', *The Edinburgh Review*, CLXXIX (1894), p. 124; Rupert's correspondence in Napier, *Memorials*, II, pp. 355–73.

27 Clarendon, *History*, V, pp. 14–15; Napier, *Memorials*, II, p. 365.

28 Wishart, *Memoirs of Montrose*, p. 228; Weir, *Poems of Montrose*, no. XI; Gordon of Ruthven, *Britane's Distemper*, p. 220; *Ralegh's History of the World*, p. 319; Napier, *Memorials*, II, pp. 368–9.

29 H.M.C., *Leyburn-Popham*, p. 10; H.M.C., *Ormonde*, I, pp. 232, 238–40; Napier, *Memorials*, II, pp. 310–11.

30 A.P.S., VI, Pt II, pp. 296, 299, 363, 409.

31 *Maitland Club Miscellany*, II, Pt II, pp. 442–3.

32 Carte, *Ormonde*, I, p. 261; Napier, *Memorials*, II, p. 375.

33 *Memoirs of Sophia, Electress of Hanover 1630–80* (transl.) H.Forester (London 1888), pp. 14–15, 22–3; L.M.Baker, *The Letters of Elizabeth of Bohemia* (London 1953), pp. 167–74; Carola Oman, *Elizabeth of Bohemia* (London 2nd edn 1964), pp. 375–6.

34 H.M.C., *Pepys*, pp. 234–6, 240–1.

35 Bodleian Library, Oxford, Clarendon MSS. fol. 37, no. 169; Wishart, *Memoirs of the most renowned Montrose* (1819), p. 440.

36 Grimble, *Chief of Mackay*, pp. 156–7.

37 H.M.C., *Montrose*, p. 176; H.M.C., *Pepys*, pp. 251, 256.

38 H.M.C., *Pepys*, pp. 253–4, 257–8; Wishart, *Memoirs of Montrose*, p. 251; James N.M.MacLean, 'Montrose's Preparations for the Invasion of Scotland and Royalist Missions to Sweden 1649–51', in *Studies in Diplomatic History. Essays in memory of David Bayne Horn* (eds) R.Hatton and M.S.Anderson (London 1970), pp. 9–10.

39 *Miscellany of the Scottish History Society*, I (Edinburgh 1893), p. 173.

40 Carte, *Ormonde*, I, p. 300.

41 *Records of Commissioners*, II, p. 447.

42 Clarendon MSS. fol. 48, no. 1878; see also fol. 48, 1889.

43 *Records of Commissioners*, II, p. 444; Napier, *Memorials*, II, p. 390.

14 THE LAST CAMPAIGN

1 Wishart, *Memoirs of Montrose*, pp. 256–7; S.R.O., GD 220.6, letter of George Drummond. He is identified in William Drummond, *The Genealogy of the Most Noble and Ancient House of Drummond 1681* (Glasgow 1889), p. 61. George Drummond of Blair who married the daughter of George Graham, Bishop of Orkney was also in Orkney in 1650, but he was a covenanter (Drummond, *Genealogy*, pp. 282–3). The provost of Kirkwall at this time was also named George Drummond (John Mooney, *Charters and Other Records of the City and Royal Burgh of Kirkwall* [Kirkwall 1948], p. 124).

2 *Records of Commissioners*, II, pp. 441–4.

3 Turner, *Memoirs*, p. 92.

4 Wishart, *Memoirs of Montrose*, p. 264.

5 MacLean, 'Montrose's Preparations', p. 17, n5.

6 C.S.P.D. (1649–50), p. 505.

7 MacLean, 'Montrose's Preparations', p. 25 n85.

8 S.R.Gardiner (ed.), *Letters and Papers Illustrating the Relations between Charles II and Scotland in 1650* (Edinburgh 1894), p. 6.

9 Napier, *Memorials*, II, pp. 411–12.

10 Gardiner, *Charles II and Scotland*, pp. 11–14.

11 Gardiner, *Charles II and Scotland*, pp. 26–7; Wishart, *Memoirs of Montrose*, p. 290.

12 Gardiner, *Charles II and Scotland*, p. 33.

13 Gardiner, *Charles II and Scotland*, pp. 42–3; Napier, *Memorials*, II, p. 415

14 H.M.C., *Leyburn-Popham*, p. 73.

15 S.R.O., GD 220.3.196, GD 220.6.1.

16 Mooney, *Charters of Kirkwall*, pp. 87–9.

17 Gardiner, 'Last Campaign', p. 284; Grimble, *Chief of Mackay*, p. 161.

18 S.R.O., GD 220.3.200, 3.202, 3.203.

19 M.V.Hay (ed.), *The Blairs Papers 1603–1660* (London 1929), p. 29.

20 Wishart, *Memoirs of Montrose*, pp. 302–3.

21 Menteith of Salmonet, *History of the Troubles*, p. 511; Gordon, *Sutherland*, p. 553.

22 Accounts of the battle: Gordon, *Sutherland*, pp. 552–5; Menteith of Salmonet, *History of the Troubles*, p. 511; Balfour, *Historical Works*, IV, pp. 8–12; Wishart, *Memoirs of Montrose*, pp. 306–9; Gardiner, 'Last Campaign', pp. 140–8.

23 Mackenzie, *Orain Iain Luim*, p. 59.

24 The fullest investigation of 'the betrayal' is Wishart, *Memoirs of Montrose*, App. XIII. See also 'Trial of Neil MacLeod' in Gardiner, *Charles II and Scotland*, App; Gordon, *Sutherland*, p. 534; *Wardlaw Manuscript*, pp. 344–5. The most recent and highly tendentious account is Bee Jay (S.Barker Johnson), *3 Centuries of Falsehood Exposed* (Golspie 1970) expanded in *Scotland's Shangri-la* (Gairloch 1972), pp. 238–73.

25 Wishart, *Memoirs of Montrose*, p. 500. On the aftermath of Carbisdale see Wishart, App. I.

26 *Wardlaw Manuscript*, pp. 353–4.

27 Gardiner, *Charles II and Scotland*, pp. 53–4, 64, 74, 78–9.

28 Gardiner, 'Last Campaign', pp. 154–6.

29 Napier, *Memoirs*, pp. 761–2; Balfour, *Historical Works*, IV, p. 23.

30 Napier, *Memoirs*, pp. 787–8.

31 John Nicholl, *A Diary of Public Transactions and Other Occurrences, chiefly in Scotland from January 1650 to June 1667* (ed.) D.Laing (Edinburgh 1836), p. 13.

32 *Maitland Club Miscellany*, II, Pt II, 487–9.

33 Napier, *Memoirs*, p. 763.

34 Argyll, *Instructions to a Son*, p. 89.

INDEX

Abercorn, James 2nd Earl of 158, 224
Aberdeen 4, 18, 21, 33, 47, 54, 55, 56, 63,
65, 66, 68, 69, 71, 72, 73, 74, 75, 76, 78,
79, 82, 140, 147, 163, 181, 189, 190, 192,
193, 200, 212, 230, 240, 245, 246, 271,
283, 292, 297; battle of 164–8, 170, 172
Aberuthven 7, 8, 112, 130
Aboyne, James Gordon, Viscount 65, 66,
72, 73, 74, 76, 77, 78, 79, 138, 139, 140,
141, 145, 146, 163, 169, 199, 200, 202,
204, 207, 209, 210, 211, 213, 214, 215,
218, 220, 223, 233, 238, 239, 250, 281
Act of Revocation 23, 35–6, 40
Airlie, James Ogilvie, 1st Earl of 90, 91,
96, 147, 162, 163, 165, 166, 180, 181,
183, 194, 214, 215, 216, 218, 220, 237,
238, 248
Airlie Castle 95–6, 119, 131, 195
Airth, William Graham, Earl of 85, 124,
128, 159, 222, 224, 300
Alasdair mac Cholla, see MacDonald
Alexander the Great 1, 8, 71, 135, 266
Alford, battle of 208, 209–11, 213, 219,
239, 292
Almond, James Livingstone, 1st Lord, see
Callendar
Angus 12, 67, 77, 90, 91, 94, 95, 131, 147,
159, 163, 169, 170, 200, 207, 213, 238,
243, 271, 285
Angus, James Douglas, Earl of 22, 300
Angus mac Ailin Duibh 215
Annandale, James Murray, 2nd Earl of
141, 222, 232, 235
Anne, Queen 15
Antrim, Ranald MacDonald (or Mac-
Donnell), Earl of 50, 53, 139, 140, 141,
144, 145, 146, 150, 152, 153, 232, 244,
251, 253, 254, 256
Appin 173, 178, 181, 182, 253
Arbroath Declaration (1320) 23, 31
Ardnamurchan 51, 53, 193, 253
Ardvreck Castle 289, 290, 291
Argyll 90, 152, 153, 174, 175, 176, 177, 178,
179, 181, 186, 230, 244, 253

Argyll, Archibald Campbell, 8th Earl and
1st Marquis of (formerly Lord Lorne) 11,
22, 27, 47, 49, 53, 54, 55, 57, 58, 59, 63,
66, 70, 71, 74, 84, 85, 87, 89, 90, 91, 92,
93, 94, 95, 96, 98, 101, 105, 108, 110,
113, 114, 115, 117, 120, 121, 122, 123,
124, 125, 126, 127, 128, 129, 132, 133,
136, 138, 141, 147–9, 150, 153, 154, 158,
162, 163, 168, 169, 170, 171, 172, 174,
175, 176, 178, 179, 181, 182, 184, 185,
186, 188, 189, 194, 207, 216, 217, 220,
221, 223, 229, 232, 234, 238, 244, 248–9,
250, 252, 253, 254, 260, 261, 267, 268,
271, 278, 281, 285, 286, 293, 294, 297,
298, 299
Articles, Lords of 84–5, 86, 88, 90, 92
Assynt 181, 284, 289
Atholl 75, 95, 156, 159, 160, 169, 170, 172,
173, 183, 184, 200, 208, 209, 213, 231,
239, 243, 244, 281
Atholl, John Murray, 28th Earl of 75, 77,
94, 98, 113, 120, 147, 300
Auld Montrose 2, 4, 12, 15, 16, 66, 79, 80,
118, 129, 132, 136, 163, 189, 300
Auldearn, battle of 11, 190, 201–6, 211,
213, 265, 292
Ayrshire 97, 215, 224, 243

Bacon, Sir Francis 27, 31, 227
Badenoch 94, 169, 170, 172, 175, 207, 209,
210, 281
Baillie, Robert (author of Letters and
Journals) 39, 43, 55, 59, 66, 73, 82, 106,
114, 115, 133, 138, 140, 141, 150, 162,
177, 190, 191, 196, 205, 237, 240
Baillie, General William of Letham 178,
179, 190, 195, 196, 197, 199, 200, 201,
205, 206, 208, 209, 210, 211, 213, 214,
215, 216, 217, 218, 219, 292
Balcarres, Alexander, 2nd Lord Lindsay
of 21, 210, 218, 219, 300
Balcarres, David 'the Rosicrucian', 1st
Lord Lindsay of 13–14
Balcarres' Horse 190, 193, 210, 218, 220

Balfour, Sir James of Denmylne 92, 93
Balgowan 9, 12, 17, 18, 160
Balmerino, James Elphinstone, 2nd Lord 39, 43, 93, 136, 170, 190, 195, 300
Balvenie Castle 69, 172, 207, 268, 285, 286
Berwick 35, 38, 49, 79, 80, 81, 82, 83, 89, 91, 234; pacification of 79, 80
Blackness 33, 34, 57, 125
Blair Atholl 156, 175, 193, 200, 242
Bog of Gicht 69, 74, 169, 189, 243, 246
Borders 1, 95, 104, 145, 151, 205, 231, 235, 236, 238
Bothwell 222, 223, 224, 227, 231, 232, 234, 235, 238, 244
Boyd, Robert, 8th Lord 97, 108
Braco 9, 12, 13, 14, 17, 40
Braemar 75, 155, 207, 239
Brechin 58, 66, 82, 168, 195, 196, 198, 285
Breda 280, 293
Brentford, Patrick Ruthven, Earl of, *see* Ettrick
Brig o'Dee, battle of 77–8, 149, 239
Bruce, King Robert 2, 23, 94
Brussels 261, 262, 272
Buchan, John 4, 134, 165, 197
Buchanan, George 14, 25–8, 29, 35, 42, 62, 110–11, 116
Buchanan's Regiment 200, 203
Burleigh, Robert Arnot, 2nd Lord Balfour of 92, 163, 164, 165, 166, 167, 217
Burnet, Gilbert (historian) 8, 22, 23, 45, 49, 81, 82, 239, 260, 291
Burnet, Sir Thomas of Leys 163, 170

Callendar 244, 245
Callendar, James Livingstone, Earl of (formerly Lord Almond) 97–8, 102, 107, 124, 125, 126, 128, 147, 150, 179, 224, 267, 281, 300
Calvin, John 14, 24, 53, 62, 155, 227
Cameron, Ailean mac Dhomnaill Dhuibh, chief of Locheil 179, 181, 187; Ewen of Locheil 179, 216, 241
Camerons 155, 179, 245; of Glen Nevis 173, 178; of Locheil 179, 182;
Campbell, Archibald, Marquis of Argyll, *see* Argyll; Archibald of Dunstaffnage 182, 252, 253, 255; Archibald of Penmore 254; Duncan of Auchinbreck 176, 182, 184, 185; George of Airds 253, 255; Lady Mary 141; Sir Mungo of Lawers 141, 203, 205; Neil 193; Patrick of Barcaldine 253; Sir Robert of Glenorchy 19, 54, 82, 96, 148, 175, 300; Captain 205; Colonel 205
Campbells 5, 47, 50, 52, 53, 71, 94, 95, 118, 147, 148, 153, 155, 168, 169, 172, 174, 175, 176, 177, 179, 180, 184, 185, 187, 203, 216, 244, 292; of Ardkinglas 244; of Glen Faochain 186; of Inverawe 96, 177; of Skipness 185, 186

Campbell of Lawers' Regiment 147, 181, 200, 203, 204
Carbisdale, battle of 283, 286, 287–9, 291, 295
Cardross 2, 199, 200
Carlipis, Thomas 19–21
Carlisle 49, 89, 139, 146, 147, 156, 163, 169, 199, 225, 232
Carmichael, James 29–30
Carnegie, Agnes 16; Alexander 16; David, *see* Southesk, Earl of; David 16; Elizabeth, Lady Balvaird, 16; Lord James, later 2nd Earl of Southesk 16, 222; John 16; Katherine 16; Magdalen, *see* Montrose, Countess of; Lady Margaret, Countess of Southesk 16; Margaret 16; Marjorie, Viscountess Arbuthnott, 16
Carnwath, Robert Dalziel, 1st Earl of 141, 145, 146, 250
Cassilis, John Kennedy, 6th Earl of 105, 125, 195, 215, 224, 232
catholics 154, 158, 174, 175, 180, 229, 263
Charles I 6, 15, 19, 20, 21, 30, 34, 35–6, 37–8, 39, 40, 41, 42, 43, 45, 48, 49, 50, 51, 52, 53, 61, 62, 63, 66, 72, 74, 77, 79, 80, 81–2, 83, 84–5, 86–7, 88–9, 90, 92–4, 99, 100, 104, 106–7, 107, 108–9, 115, 117, 119, 120, 121, 122, 125, 126, 127, 128, 129, 132, 133, 135, 136, 137, 140, 144, 151, 154, 158, 159, 168, 178, 187, 195, 199, 208, 225, 226, 228, 231, 237, 238, 239, 240, 246, 247, 248, 249, 250, 257, 259, 260, 262, 265–6, 298
Charles II 106, 229, 259, 263, 264, 265, 266, 267, 268, 269, 270, 271, 272, 273, 274, 277, 280, 281, 282, 283, 294, 295, 296, 299, 300
Charles Louis, Elector Palatine, 107, 115, 116, 121
Charteris of Amisfield 147, 235
Christian IV of Denmark 257, 258, 262
Clan Ranald 50, 51, 52, 53, 148, 173, 177, 182, 183, 184, 202, 204, 209, 213, 214, 218, 219, 220, 225, 243, 253
Clarendon, Edward Hyde, 1st Earl of 48, 264, 265, 266, 267
Claverhouse 9, 12, 17
Clydesdale 199, 215, 222
Cochrane, Colonel Sir John 107, 108, 115, 118, 121, 123, 124, 125, 126, 128, 146, 270, 272, 274
Colla Ciotach, *see* MacDonald
Colonsay 51, 53, 152
Colquhoun, Sir John of Luss, 5, 7, 9, 13, 18, 19–21, 300
Committee of Estates (formerly Tables q.v.) 91, 92, 93, 94, 107, 113, 114, 117, 118, 119, 120, 132, 133, 141, 150, 163, 165, 172, 178, 184, 189, 190, 200, 208, 215, 216, 234, 240, 241, 256, 260, 277
Condé, Louis de Bourbon, duc d'Enghien, Prince of 262, 263

Convention of Estates 36, 140, 141, 142, 301
Conway, Edward, Viscount, 91, 104, 105
Copenhagen 262, 271, 274, 278, 279
Courland, Duke of 270, 274, 278, 279
Court of Session 32, 36, 231
Covenanters 99, 103, 107, 114, 115, 117, 121, 122, 123, 127, 132, 136, 138, 139, 140, 141, 149, 155, 158, 160, 167, 189, 190, 196, 204, 207, 209, 217, 228, 230, 231, 234, 240, 244, 246, 247, 248, 258, 280
Crabstone 164, 165
Craig, Sir Thomas 30–1, 35, 37
Crawford, Ludovic Lindsay, 16th Earl of 123, 124, 125, 126, 127, 128, 145, 146, 195, 224, 233, 237, 238, 248, 250, 271, 300
Crawford's Regiment 218, 220
Crawford-Lindsay, *see* Lindsay, Earl of
Crichton of Frendraught, James, Lord 166, 168, 283, 289, 300
Crichtons of Frendraught 72, 165, 166, 170
Cromwell, Oliver 22, 148, 225, 229, 260, 278, 280, 285, 291
Culrain 287, 288
Cumbernauld 13, 18, 97
Cumbernauld Band 97–9, 108, 112, 118, 120, 121, 128, 131, 222, 296

Dalziel, Captain Francis 146
De Retz, Cardinal 258, 295
Dee, River 43, 77, 167, 170, 207, 212
Deeside 71, 75, 147, 163, 164, 169, 206, 209
Denmark 144, 150, 257, 272, 277, 278, 280
Deveron, River 66, 172, 190, 207
Digby, George, Lord 234, 239, 240
Don, River 167, 209
Donaldson, Margaret 112, 161
Douglas, John (harpist) 193; John (son of Morton) 283; William, 1st Marquis of 22, 158, 222, 231, 232, 234, 236, 237, 238, 300; Sir William of Cavers 205
Drum 71, 163, 169, 170
Drummond, George of Balloch 147, 209, 224, 232, 239, 241, 244, 251, 277; Lieutenant-Colonel George (son of Balloch) 276, 277, 283, 291; James 88; James, Lord 98, 159, 160, 222; Sir John 159, 162, 166, 172; William of Hawthornden 109, 224; Sir William of Riccarton 116; Captain 203, 204, 205
Drummonds 181, 300
Dumbarton 13, 73, 105, 224
Dumfries 146, 147, 239
Dunaverty 244, 254, 255, 256
Dunbar, battle of 291
Dunbeath 284, 285, 290, 291
Dunblane 40, 141, 254
Dundaff 2, 10, 216
Dundee 9, 12, 17, 64, 68, 77, 88, 162, 163, 195–7, 198, 293

Dunfermline, Charles Seton, 2nd Earl of 32, 81, 170
Dunkeld 49, 113, 115, 161, 172, 195, 196, 198, 214, 215, 239, 242
Dunnottar 66, 77, 147, 194
Dunstaffnage 177, 182, 254
Dunyveg 254, 255, 256
Dupplin, Lord, *see* 3rd Earl of Kinnoul

Edgehill, battle of 136
Edinburgh 3, 4, 12, 30, 38, 39, 43, 45, 47, 48, 49, 52, 55, 58, 62, 72, 73, 75, 80, 81, 83, 88, 89, 90, 91, 96, 103, 105, 107, 108, 116, 118, 119, 123, 125, 132, 133, 172, 176, 179, 190, 207, 214, 223, 224, 234, 240, 266, 267, 278, 285, 291, 297
Edinburgh Castle 74, 86, 89, 91, 105, 114, 118, 189, 223, 270, 299
Eglinton, Alexander Montgomery, 6th Earl of 215, 224, 232
Elcho, David Wemyss, Lord 11, 159, 160, 161, 162, 218
Elgin 43, 188, 189, 200, 206
Elizabeth of Bohemia 5, 15, 93, 269, 270, 271, 274, 280
Engagers or Engagement 259, 260, 264, 267, 281
England 15, 27, 30, 32, 33, 37, 62, 74, 83, 88, 92, 95, 99, 102, 103, 104, 110, 112, 127, 132, 133, 134, 136, 137, 140, 143, 151, 152, 165, 168, 178, 187, 195, 225, 226, 229, 230, 231, 233, 235, 238, 240, 245, 248, 258, 259, 260, 272
Erskine, Lord 98, 133, 147, 222, 256; of Dun 58–9, 170; of Pittodrie 79
Ettrick, Patrick Ruthven, Lord (later Earl of Brentford) 86, 89, 91, 105, 270, 273

Farquharson, Donald of Monaltrie 75, 155, 171, 181, 193, 194, 204, 210, 211; James of Inverey 209
Farquharsons 75, 77, 94, 184, 189, 213
Ferdinand III, Emperor 259, 261, 262, 270, 278
Fettercairn 66, 194, 195
Fife 13, 62, 67, 133, 136, 147, 159, 161, 165, 215, 216
Fife levies 215, 216, 218, 221
Fintry 9, 12, 17
Five Articles of Perth 34, 35, 55, 56, 59, 83
Fleming, John, Lord 222; Sir William 295
Flodden 2, 78, 103
Forbes, Alexander, 2nd Lord of Pitsligo 168, 209; Major Arthur 163; Duncan of Culloden 292; of Craigievar 165, 166, 172; of Tolquhon
Forbeses 63, 71, 75, 147, 148, 165, 170
Forfar 15, 63, 64, 95, 103
Forres 169, 188, 200, 201
Forth, Firth of 74, 76, 96, 113, 215, 216, 217

France 22, 23, 32, 89, 124, 247, 256, 258, 259, 261, 262, 263, 267, 272, 277, 280, 281
Fraser, Andrew, 2nd Lord, 166, 168; James of Phopachy 245, 292, 293
Frasers 63, 64, 71, 75, 147, 165, 166, 181, 201, 206, 245
Frederick the Elector Palatine 5
Frederick William, Elector of Brandenburg 273
Frederick III of Denmark 262, 270, 278
Fyvie, skirmish at, 170, 171, 184, 198

Galloway, Alexander Stewart, 1st Earl of 98
Gardiner, S. R. 165, 288
Geddes, William 13
General Assembly 3, 16, 33, 43, 46, 55, 80, 83, 88, 92, 113, 121, 133, 134, 268
Geneva 29, 261
Germany 36, 77, 258
Glamis 17, 98
Glasgow 7, 13, 47, 58, 217, 221, 222, 232, 240, 241, 242, 297
Glasgow Assembly 58–60, 64, 66, 80, 82, 83
Glencoe 173, 174, 176, 178, 253
Glen Dochart 175, 183
Gordon, George, 2nd Marquis of Huntly, see Huntly; George, Lord 65, 72, 163, 165, 168, 169, 180, 188, 189, 190, 194, 196, 198, 199, 200, 204, 205, 207, 209, 210 211, 212; Gilbert of Sallagh (historian) 73, 203, 205, 239, 250, 286, 287, 288, 289; of Haddo 148; Lord James, Viscount Aboyne, see Aboyne; James of Rhynie 200, 204, 205, 211; James of Rothiemay (historian) 65, 66, 70, 73, 82, 93, 99; John 196; Lord Lewis (later 3rd Marquis of Huntly) 75, 77, 163, 165, 166, 168, 189, 198, 239, 245, 281, 283, 300; Major Nathaniel 147, 163, 165, 166, 167, 172, 188, 192, 193, 202, 207, 209, 210 218, 220, 223, 238, 241; Patrick of Ruthven (historian) 155, 156, 165, 166, 171, 184, 188, 193, 196, 205, 208, 209, 211, 214, 217, 220, 222, 226, 229, 230, 234, 235, 237, 265; Sir Robert of Gordonstoun 137, 297; Robert of Straloch 69, 71, 74, 75; Captain William 284
Gordons 52, 53, 63, 71, 72, 75, 139, 163, 168, 169, 170, 178, 181, 185, 188, 189, 192, 195, 202, 203, 204, 207, 208, 210, 211, 217, 220, 233, 243, 246, 268, 283; of Glenlivet 75
Gowrie Conspiracy 3–4
Gowrie, William Ruthven, 1st Earl of 3; John Ruthven, 3rd Earl of 3, 300
Graham, Beatrix (sister) 5, 159; of Cairney 161, 257, 300; of Craigo 136, 257,

261; David (son) 130; David of Fintry (d. 1593) 3; David of Fintry 9, 88, 120, 130, 136, 257, 300; Sir David de 1; David of Gorthie 130, 131, 161, 257, 299; Dorothea (sister) 6, 13, 141; Elizabeth (sister) 6; of Hallyards 3; Sir Harry (half-brother) 7, 151, 207, 224, 238, 242, 251, 272, 273, 279, 283, 284, 286, 291, 300; James, 5th Earl and 1st Marquis of Montrose, see Montrose; Lord James (son), 2nd Marquis of Montrose, see Montrose; James (secretary) 118; Jean (daughter) 130, 292; Sir John de 2; John (brother) 4; Lord John (son) 130, 166, 167, 181, 189; John (son of Graham of Morphie) 22; John of Balgowan 9, 88, 130, 161, 257; John of Orchil, 9, 18, 88, 130, 161; John (minister) 112–13, 130; Katherine (sister) 6, 19–21; of Killearn 300; Lilias (sister) 5, 21, 86, 224; Murdo (page) 7; Patrick of Inchbrakie (Black Pate) 9, 12, 130, 151, 156, 159, 161, 213, 241, 244, 257, 300; Sir Richard of Netherby 116; Robert (son) 130, 189, 292, 300; Sir Robert of Morphie 9, 17, 18, 22, 47, 130, 131, 257, 300; Walter of Duntroyne 18; William de 1; William (page) 7; William of Braco 9, 10, 88, 130, 161; Sir William of Claverhouse 9, 14, 18, 23, 88, 130
Grahams 2, 8, 10, 16, 17, 99, 100, 152, 160, 181, 216, 244, 300; of the Borders 9
Grants 63, 155, 181, 188, 189, 243
Gray, Lord 124, 128; Colonel Thomas 283, 291
Great Glen 173, 178, 180, 181, 187, 245
Gunn, Colonel William 77, 78, 79
Gustav Adolph, King of Sweden 22, 160, 165
Guthrie, Major David 283, 288; James 285, 295; Patrick 271
Guthry, Henry 49, 57, 80, 97, 114

Hackett, Lieutenant-Colonel 286, 288
Haddington 29, 115, 235
Haddington, Thomas Hamilton, 1st Earl of 16; Lady Jean Gordon, Countess of 293
Hague, The 265, 266, 267, 268, 270, 271, 272, 273, 280, 281
Hall, Captain John 276, 278, 279, 284
Hamburg 258, 274, 277, 278, 280, 284
Hamilton, James, 3rd Marquis and 1st Duke of 22, 37, 40, 47, 48, 49, 50, 51, 54, 58, 59, 74, 75, 76, 77, 80, 87, 90, 93, 96, 97, 114, 117, 122, 123, 124, 125, 126, 127, 128, 133, 136, 138, 140, 141, 144, 146, 150, 259, 260, 264, 267; John 88; William, 1st Earl of Lanark and 2nd Duke of, see Lanark

Harris 51, 52, 173
Hartfell, Lord Johnstone of Lochwood, 1st Earl of 98, 146, 222, 232, 235
Hebrides 50, 51, 52, 53, 91, 145, 243, 253, 278
Heidelberg 5, 21
Henderson, Alexander 43, 45, 46, 48, 58, 62–3, 76, 141, 142, 248
Henrietta Maria, Queen 132, 133, 137, 140, 141, 143, 258, 259, 264, 267, 271, 274
Henry, Prince 15, 33
Heritable jurisdictions 35, 52, 90
Highlanders 103, 138, 162, 174, 177, 181, 186, 195, 196, 289, 213, 215, 232, 244
Highlands 49, 72, 73, 139, 141, 145, 152, 174, 175, 177, 187, 189, 205, 213, 214, 221, 225, 232, 235, 238, 250, 251, 294, 301
Hill of Buchanty 159, 238
Holburn, Major-General 290, 291
Holyrood 31, 48, 125, 127, 129, 199, 293, 300
Home, James, 3rd Earl of 98, 125, 126, 128, 223, 231, 234; Lieutenant-Colonel Robert 124, 126, 127
Home's Regiment 218, 219, 220, 221
Hope, Sir Thomas of Kerse 115, 116, 117
Huntly 169, 170, 171, 206, 208
Huntly, George Gordon, 2nd Marquis of 47, 55, 63, 64, 65, 66, 67, 68, 69, 70, 72, 73, 74, 75, 79, 82, 83, 85, 90, 94, 138, 139, 140, 141, 145, 147, 148, 151, 152, 155, 158, 163, 168, 169, 171, 209, 210, 218, 233, 239, 242, 243, 245, 246, 247, 248, 250, 251, 268; Lewis Gordon, 3rd Marquis of, *see* Gordon
Hurry, Lieutenant-Colonel John 125, 126, 127, 128, 190, 193, 195, 197, 198, 199, 200, 201, 203, 204, 205, 206, 250, 251, 264, 271, 283, 284, 285, 286, 288, 291

Iain Lom, bard of Keppoch, *see* Mac-Donald, John
Inchbrakie 9, 17, 160
Inchequin, General Murrough O'Brian, Baron 255, 263
'Incident', the 123–7, 128, 146, 190
Innes, Laird of 90, 188
Inveraray 90, 96, 176, 177, 186, 253, 254
Inverlochy, battle of 179, 180, 181, 182, 183–7, 189, 190, 193, 195, 225, 265
Inverness 64, 169, 178, 181, 187, 189, 200, 203, 205, 206, 207, 243, 245, 268, 274, 285, 292, 295
Inverurie 67, 69, 70, 73, 74, 168, 170, 192
Ireland 28, 37, 53, 74, 86, 128, 138, 140, 143, 144, 145, 148, 152, 154, 174, 179, 182, 195, 202, 228, 229, 230, 244, 248, 251, 254, 255, 256, 263, 267, 278, 280, 294

Irish or 'Irishes' (followers of Alasdair mac Cholla) 154–5, 156, 160–1, 167, 171, 173–8, 183, 196–7, 202, 205, 208, 209, 210, 214, 216, 229, 233, 236, 237, 238, 256, 293
Irish Rebellion 128, 132, 153
Islay 50, 51, 52, 53, 253, 254, 255, 256
Italy 22, 23, 168, 271

James VI and I 2, 3, 4, 7, 10, 15–16, 27–8, 29, 30, 31, 32–5
James, Duke of York, later James VII and II 263, 274, 282, 301
Jamesone, George 4, 18
Jermyn, Lord 272
Johnston, Archibald of Warriston 45–6, 48, 55, 58, 66, 76, 81, 87, 93, 129, 229, 241, 268, 297; Colonel William 283, 284, 291; Lieutenant 75, 77, 78,

Keir 94, 141, 142, 143, 147
Keith 208, 209, 292
Keith, George 194; Robert 170; William, 6th Earl Marischal, *see* Marischal
Keppoch 9, 96, 173, 181, 182
Ker, Lord (son of Earl of Roxburgh) 122, 123, 125; Colonel Gilbert 286, 288; Lady Mary 16
Kilcumin Band 180–1, 189, 245
Kildrummy 70, 165, 208
Killiecrankie, battle of 51, 181, 216
Kilpont, John Graham, Lord 126, 159, 160, 162, 238
Kilsyth, battle of 151, 215, 216–21, 222, 224, 225, 226, 231, 241, 242, 295
Kincardine 2, 5, 7, 8, 12, 13, 18, 40, 118, 136, 160, 244
Kinghorn, John Lyon, 2nd Earl of 68, 69, 70, 88, 98, 121
Kinnaird 12, 15, 16, 17, 18, 19, 21, 64, 292, 293
Kinnoul, George Hay, 2nd Earl of 88, 141; George, 3rd Earl of (formerly Lord Dupplin) 161, 172, 273, 274, 275, 276, 278; George, 4th Earl of 279, 282, 283, 289
Kintyre 50, 53, 244, 251, 253, 254, 255, 256, 278
Kirkcudbright, Thomas, Earl of 98, 126, 128, 195
Kirkwall 274, 283, 284
Knocknanuss, battle of 255, 256, 263
Knox, John 23, 24–5, 28, 46, 227

Lambie, John 12, 13, 22, 118, 130
Lanark, William Hamilton, 1st Earl of (later 2nd Duke of Hamilton) 127, 128, 136, 141, 144, 215, 217, 247, 259, 264, 265, 266, 282, 300
Laud, William, Archbishop of Canterbury 55, 106, 117

Lauderdale, John Maitland, 1st Earl of 58, 89; John Maitland, 1st Duke of 22, 259, 265, 266, 267, 300
Lauderdale's Regiment 218, 220
Leith 10, 48, 81, 105, 126, 127, 224, 276, 290, 293, 296, 299
Lennox 25, 240, 242, 244, 253
Lennox, Esmé Stewart, Duke of 3, 29; James Stewart, 4th Duke of 47, 48, 82, 110, 116, 117, 121, 123, 126
Leslie, Alexander, later 1st Earl of Leven 64, 65, 67, 71, 72, 80, 81, 89, 95, 96, 97, 102, 103, 104, 105, 107, 108, 116, 126, 128, 141, 145, 146, 149, 225, 226; David, General (later Lord Newark) 11, 226, 234, 235, 236, 237, 239, 241, 245, 254, 255, 256, 271, 278, 281, 285, 288, 290, 291
Leven's Regiment 179, 184, 186
Lewis 148, 189
Linlithgow 127, 223, 228
Linton, John Stewart, Lord (later 2nd Earl of Traquair) 222, 238
Lisle, Major John 283, 286, 288
Lithgow, William 14–15, 20, 37–8, 39, 100–1, 135
Lochaber 94, 96, 155, 173, 174, 181, 182, 184, 231
Loch Awe 96, 175, 176
Loch Ness 180, 181, 182, 187, 245
Loch Tay 96, 175, 200
London 12, 15, 17, 21, 30, 33, 34, 37, 38, 40, 78, 88, 102, 106, 107, 116, 117, 132, 226, 230, 234, 260, 267
Long, Robert 271, 272, 273
Lorne, Lord, *see* Argyll; Archibald Campbell, Lord (later 9th Earl of Argyll) 293
Lothian, William Ker, 3rd Earl of 81, 106, 115, 168, 170, 171, 172, 179, 246, 299
Lothian's Regiment 168, 181, 195, 203, 204
Loudoun, John Campbell, 2nd Lord and 1st Earl of 43, 49, 81, 82, 89, 92, 97, 103, 122, 125, 126, 137, 226, 259, 267, 297, 300
Loudoun's Regiment 195, 200, 203, 218, 219, 221
Louise, Princess 269, 270
Lour, David, Master of 98; Sir John Carnegie, Lord 98, 121
Lovat, Hugh, 7th Lord Fraser of 169, 206, 284
Low Countries or Netherlands 36, 93, 132, 137, 258, 274, 277
Lowlanders 174, 175, 176, 181, 187, 227, 228, 229
Lowlands 51, 52, 151, 155, 174, 181, 187, 195, 205, 215, 221, 232, 233, 250, 256, 301

MacAllasters of Loup 253
MacBreck, Father James 154, 155, 171, 175, 180

MacCailein Mór, *see* Argyll
MacCulloch, Captain 149, 150
MacDonald, Alasdair mac Cholla Ciotaich 51, 53, 96, 152–3, 154, 155, 156, 160–1, 165–6, 169, 173, 174, 175, 176–7, 180, 183, 184–6, 193, 194, 196, 197, 198, 200, 202–6, 207, 209, 213, 216, 218, 222, 223, 224, 225, 230, 232–4, 238, 239, 243–4, 246, 247, 250, 251, 252–6, 292, 293; Alasdair mac Iain Chathanaich 50; Alexander (brother of Antrim) 139; Angus, son of Alan Dubh 174; Angus of Dunyveg 52; Angus, chief of Glengarry 183, 209, 243, 256; Angus of Knoydart 173; Archibald MacColl 90; Archibald Mór of Sanda 253–4; Archibald Og of Sanda 254; Colla Ciotach or Colkitto 51, 52, 90, 140, 152, 177, 185, 207, 254–5, 256; Donald Balloch 179; Donald Glas of Keppoch 96, 173, 181; Donald, Lord of the Isles 214; Domnhuill MacAonghais mhic Alasdair of Glengarry 50, 155, 183; Donald Muideartach of Clan Ranald 213, 214, 220, 243, 244; Sir Donald of Sleat (Donald Gorm) 50, 51, 90, 140, 152, 155; Dougal of Clan Ranald 148; Iain of Keppoch 148; Iain Muideartach, Captain of Clan Ranald 50, 52, 53, 173, 176, 183, 185, 213, 220, 244; Colonel James 154, 183, 211; Sir James of Dunyveg 52, 152; Sir James of Sleat 152, 155, 243, 253; John (Iain Lom), bard of Keppoch 9, 96, 156, 181, 183, 185, 225, 256, 289; quoted 156, 185, 204, 206, 225, 256, 289–90; John Lord of the Isles 148; Ranald, Earl of Antrim, *see* Antrim; Ranald (macDomnuill) 203–4; Ranald Og 154, 254; Sorley Boy 50, 184
MacDonalds 50, 53, 117, 154, 173, 183, 185, 186, 202, 204, 245; of Antrim 49, 154; of Coigach 181; of Glencoe 173, 183; of Glengarry 182, 183, 213; of Islay 51; of Keppoch 155; of Largie 253; of Sleat 155
MacGregor, Donald 197; Patrich Caoch 181, 220
MacGregors 5, 175, 181, 213, 225
MacIain of Ardnamurchan 51, 52
MacIntosh of that ilk, 136, 201
Mackay, Donald, 1st Lord Reay, chief of 50, 65, 90, 145, 243, 248, 250, 271, 286; Donald, 2nd Lord Reay 268; Hucheon of Scourie 284, 286; Hugh of Dirled 284, 286; of Ardnacross 203
Mackays 245, 268, 271, 286, 290; of Ugadale 253
MacKenzie, Captain 206; George, Earl of Seaforth, *see* Seaforth; Murdoch 253; Sir Thomas of Pluscardine 188, 268, 271, 274, 281, 285, 286, 290, 292

MacKenzies 64, 181, 189, 203, 205, 243, 245, 246, 278, 286, 290, 292
MacKinnon of Strathordale 51, 52
MacLean, Donald, son of Hector Og 219–20; Eachann Bacach 179; Ewen of Treshnish 179, 185, 202, 218, 219; Hector Og, chief of 51; John, *see* Maclier; Sir Lachlan of Duart 52, 53, 90, 117, 140, 179, 180, 183, 213, 244, 253, 256, 278; Murdo 222; of Ardgour 179; of Coll 52, 179, 243; of Kingairloch 179; of Kinlochaline 179; of Lochbuie 52, 181
MacLeans 53, 155, 179, 181, 183, 213, 216, 218, 219, 225, 253, 278
MacLeod, Donald of Assynt 290; John of Dunvegan and Harris 51, 52, 53, 173, 250; Neil of Assynt 289, 290; of Lewis 52
MacLeods 155, 245; of Assynt and Gairloch 181, 290
Maclier, Johan or Hans 278. 279
MacMhuirich, Cathal 220; Neil (historian) 161, 173, 183, 186, 196, 202, 203, 205, 210, 211, 217, 256
MacNabs 175, 181, 183, 213
MacNeill, of Barra 52
MacNeills, of Carskey 253; of Gigha 52
MacPhee of Colonsay 51
MacPhersons 155, 162
Madderty, Master of 147, 159, 160, 300
Maitland, Captain James 283
Major, John (historian) 23, 24, 25, 28, 188–9
Mar 136, 198, 200, 207
Mar, John Erskine, 19th Earl of 89, 98, 128, 216, 222, 224
Marischal, William Keith, 6th Earl 54, 66, 68, 74, 75, 76, 77, 79, 98, 140, 168, 170, 194, 281, 283, 300
Marston Moor, battle of 150, 151, 178, 184, 190, 199, 226
Mary, Queen of Scots 2, 20, 23, 25, 61
May, Harry 282, 283, 284
Mearns 17, 67, 68, 75, 147, 194, 213, 214
Melville, Andrew 14, 29, 34, 46; James 33, 34
Menteith, Robert of Salmonet (historian) 99, 161, 186, 196, 231, 234, 286, 288, 289
Menzies of Pitfoddels 283, 288
Menzieses 159, 244
Mercer, Sir James 105, 106
Merse, the 125, 232, 234
Methven 9, 40, 112, 123, 156, 214, 215, 300
Middleton, John (later 1st Earl of) 78, 239, 244, 245, 246, 249, 268, 281, 282, 283, 300
Mingarry Castle 155, 169, 173
Monro (or Munro), Andrew of Lemlair 286, 288, 290; Christian (wife of Neil MacLeod of Assynt) 290; Hugh of

Achness 286; Colonel John of Lemlair 281, 286, 287, 289; Robert of Achness 286, 287, 288; Major-General Robert 139, 153, 230, 248
Monros 63, 181, 201
Montereux, Jean de 246, 247
Montrose (town of) 4, 5, 9, 10, 12, 17, 68, 69, 130, 193, 195, 251
Montrose, 1st Earl of 2; 2nd Earl of 2; John Graham, 3rd Earl of 2, 10, 32, 40, 300; John, 4th Earl of 1, 3, 4, 7, 8, 9, 10, 16, 20, 32, 36, 41; James Graham, 5th Earl and 1st Marquis of, birth 1, 4–5, 10; ancestry 1–4; childhood and education 7–8; at university 8, 10–15; his kindred 9–13; gambling 11; generosity 11–12; marriage 4–5, 15–18; portraits 18, 269–70; served heir 10; relations with Colquhoun 5, 19–21; Grand Tour 21–3; appearance and character 21–2, 40, 157–8, 226–7; supports Covenant 23; political philosophy 27, 41–2, 109–12, 180–1, 228–30, 296–7; returns to Scotland 39–40; meets Charles 40; motives for supporting Covenant 40–1; elected to Tables 43; sent to Aberdeen 54–5; 'Montrose's Protestation' 55–7; at Glasgow Assembly 58–60; disagrees with Southesk 63–4; expedition to Aberdeen and Turriff 64–6; meets Huntly's representatives 66–7; devises 'blue band' 68; enters Aberdeen 68–9; his moderation 69; negotiations with and arrest of Huntly 69–74; excluded from amnesty 74; returns to Aberdeen 75–7; battle of Brig o' Dee 77–8; takes Aberdeen 78–9; with king at Berwick 81–2; suspected by Covenanters 81–2; at assembly and parliament 83–5; supports Traquair 84–5; corresponds with king 86–7; debts 88, 130; relations with and suspicions of Argyll 48, 93, 95; Cumbernauld Band 96–8; doubts 100–1; enters Newcastle 104; corresponds with Charles 106–7; suspected 108; relations with Napier 6, 109–10; accused by Committee 113–15; arrested and imprisoned 115–18; libel against 118–19; the 'Incident' 123–6; released 128–9; family 130, 257, 292; trial 131–2; overtures to king 132; poetry 134–5; meets Queen 137–8; quarrel with Hamilton 138–9; York plot 139–40; breaks with Covenanters 141–2; Solemn League and Covenant 142–3; at Oxford 143–4; commissioned 145; marches north 145–6; takes Dumfries 146–7; siege of Morpeth 149–50; disappointments 150; in Strathearn 156; joined by Alasdair 156; Tibbermore 159–62; murder of Kilpont 162–3; Aberdeen 163–8; Fyvie 170–1, truce 171;

INDEX

Montrose—*contd.*

descent on Argyll 174–7; in Lochaber 177–8; Kilcumin Band 180–1; flank march 182–3; Inverlochy 184–7; at Elgin 187–8; joined by Gordon 188–9; forfeited 190; marches south 194–5; attacks Dundee and retreats 196–8; rendezvous at Cardross 199; Auldearn 201–6; Alford 209–11; raids Fife 215–16; Kilsyth 216–21; camp at Bothwell 222; and Iain Lom 224–5; remonstrance 228–30; deserted by clans and Gordons 233–4; Philiphaugh 235–8; retreats 239; in Lennox 240–1; trial of associates 241–2; joins Huntly 243; siege of Inverness 245; communications from Charles 246–8; cessation 249–50; leaves Scotland 250–1; Norway and Germany 257–8; France 258–9; Vienna 261; Denmark and Netherlands 262; contacts Rupert 263–4 and Clarendon 264; reaction to king's execution 265–6; suspicious of covenanters 267 who demand his removal 268–9; Elizabeth of Bohemia and Princess Louise 269–70; letter to Ulfeld 270–1; embassies 272; campaign launched 274–5; declaration 277; diplomatic activity 278; in Orkney 279–83; in Scotland 284–5; Carbisdale 286–9; captured 289–90; taken south 291–3; imprisoned in Tolbooth 293–6; executed 297–8; funeral 299–300; quoted 27, 41, 83, 87, 119–20, 142, 157–8, 164, 177, 184–5, 199, 204–5, 247, 257, 261, 265, 266, 294; poetry quoted 8, 14, 17, 44, 87, 135, 139, 151, 226–7, 298; mentioned 39, 44, 45, 46, 80, 90, 91, 92, 127, 136, 179, 191, 192, 194, 231; James Graham, 6th Earl and 2nd Marquis of 163, 189, 224, 231, 261, 292, 300; Magdalen Carnegie, Countess of 15, 16, 17, 18, 19, 95, 130, 261

Moray 67, 155, 172, 181, 188, 203, 245, 292

Morpeth 103, 104, 149, 150

Morphie 9, 12, 17, 18

Mortimer, Captain 155, 166, 193, 283, 291

Morton, William Douglas, 6th Earl of 11, 47, 122, 126, 141; Robert Douglas, 7th Earl of 276, 278, 283

Mugdock 2, 5, 10, 19, 118

Mull 154, 179, 203, 213, 244, 256

Murray, Robert 40, 112, 113, 123; William 123, 124, 125, 126, 127

Nairn 201, 206

Napier, Archibald, 1st Lord 6, 7, 9, 13, 17, 22, 23, 37, 40, 44, 88, 94, 98, 108, 109, 110, 115, 116, 117, 118, 119, 121, 128, 133, 141, 147, 199, 223, 228, 242, 256, 277; Archibald, 2nd Lord (formerly

Master of) 147, 199, 210, 216, 223, 244, 250, 257, 259, 261, 267, 280, 281, 282, 300; John of Merchiston 6, 46, 295; Lady 299; Mark 6, 20, 109, 134, 228

Naseby, battle of 208, 225

National Covenant 23, 27, 29, 40, 42, 43, 44–7, 50, 54, 56–7, 74, 75, 76, 83, 84, 85, 92, 97, 99, 100, 107, 108, 118, 121, 126, 131, 132, 133, 140, 143, 147, 174, 180, 181, 188, 206, 228, 240, 242, 246, 248, 249, 268, 269, 296

Negative Confession 29, 46, 56, 57, 70

Newburn, battle of 104–5, 178

Newcastle 74, 91, 93, 99, 102, 104, 105, 106, 107, 108, 116, 120, 149, 178, 199, 207, 247, 248

Newcastle, William Cavendish, Earl and Marquis of 137, 139, 140, 145, 146, 149, 150

Nithsdale, Robert Maxwell, 1st Earl of 91, 105, 139, 140, 141, 145, 146, 158, 250

nobility of Scotland 23–7, 33, 34, 38, 40, 129, 145, 188

North Esk, River 66, 193, 195

O'Cahan, Major Christopher 171; Magnus 154, 171, 183, 184, 197, 211, 238, 240

Ogilvie, Lady Helen 95–6, 223; James, 1st Earl of Airlie, see Airlie; James, Lord 14, 17, 64, 91, 94, 95, 119, 124, 126, 137, 140, 141, 145, 146, 151, 223, 224, 231, 232, 238, 241, 248, 250, 256, 281; James 224; Powrie 239, 282, 283, 288; Sir Thomas 162, 166, 183, 184, 186; of Inverquharity 166, 172;

Ogilvies 94, 96, 165, 215, 218, 220

O'Lachan, Major Thomas 166, 210, 238, 240

O'Neill, General Owen Roe 154, 248

Orange, William, Prince of 262, 263, 269

Orchil 9, 12, 13, 17, 18

Orkney 273, 274, 275, 276, 277, 278, 279, 280, 282, 283, 284, 291

Ormonde, James Butler, Marquis of 138, 263, 273, 278

Oxford 143, 144, 145, 151, 152, 225, 231, 246, 266

Oykel, River 287, 288, 289

Paris 15, 23, 66, 168, 258, 261, 263, 272, 280, 281, 295

Parliament 81, 84–6, 88, 92–3, 106, 107, 108, 113, 119, 121, 122, 123, 127, 131, 171, 267

Perth 3, 12, 17, 34, 63, 66, 95, 112, 130, 159, 160, 161, 162, 163, 179, 190, 196, 214, 295, 296

Perth, John Drummond, 2nd Earl of 98, 159, 222, 300

Philiphaugh, battle of 11, 98, 170, 230, 231, 234, 235–8, 239, 240, 242, 246, 247

324

Poyntz, Major-General Sir Robert 138, 226
Preston, battle of 260, 262, 264
Privy Council 3, 4, 32, 33, 35, 36, 40, 79, 84, 132, 133, 134, 136, 137, 140

Ralegh, Sir Walter 8, 159, 266
Reay, Lord, *see* Mackay
Reformation 5, 23, 24, 28, 32, 35, 103, 143, 175, 240
Restoration 49, 158, 181, 229, 284, 299
Rhunahaorine Point, battle of 254
Rinuccini, John Baptist 154
Ripon 106, 107
Robertson, Alexander of Lude 161; Donald of Strowan 247; John 162; of Inver 207, 239
Robertsons 155, 181
Rollo, Sir James of Duncrub 6, 13, 18, 88, 141, 142, 151, 184, 300; Sir William 151, 156, 165, 166, 168, 238, 240
Rome 22, 38, 39, 112, 271
Rosicrucians 13–14, 21
Ross 90, 245, 285, 286, 287
Ross, David of Balnagowan 286, 287; Patrick 130
Rosses 63, 181, 201, 286, 288, 289, 290
Rothes, John Leslie, 6th Earl of 35, 37, 43, 45, 47, 49, 54, 74, 81, 85, 89, 92, 93, 100, 103, 105, 106, 110, 113, 114, 117, 297
Roxburgh, Robert Ker, 1st Earl of 16, 44, 58, 122, 125, 126, 128, 141, 223, 231, 234
Royalists 125, 127, 132, 133, 136, 141, 144, 146, 147, 162, 170, 196, 197, 206, 208, 216, 226, 246, 256, 268
Rupert, Prince 150, 190, 263, 264, 267, 270, 278
Rutherford, Samuel 21, 43, 46, 47
Ruthven (family) 3–4, 7

Scotland, 1, 2, 5, 6, 15, 16, 20, 21, 23, 24, 27, 28, 29, 30, 31, 32, 33, 37, 39, 40, 42, 45, 46, 47, 50, 62, 63, 73, 77, 81, 83, 86, 93, 97, 99, 103, 106, 107, 109, 111, 112, 115, 116, 122, 123, 125, 127, 129, 131, 132, 133, 134, 135, 137, 138, 139, 140, 141, 142, 143, 144, 145, 146, 149, 150, 152, 153, 155, 158, 159, 161, 163, 167, 174, 175, 178, 186, 187, 188, 190, 199, 205, 212, 217, 222, 223, 225, 226, 229, 230, 232, 234, 239, 240, 241, 246, 248, 249, 251, 254, 256, 258, 261, 262, 264, 267, 268, 269, 270, 271, 272, 273, 274, 276, 278, 279, 280, 281, 293, 294, 295, 298, 299, 300
Seaforth, George MacKenzie, 2nd Earl of 50, 53, 90, 98, 117, 118, 121, 139, 147, 152, 169, 180, 181, 188, 189, 200, 203, 206, 243, 245, 246, 247, 248, 251, 253, 256, 267, 268, 271, 279, 282, 290, 291, 300

Selkirk 235, 236, 237
Seneca 7, 159, 266
Sibbald, Lieutenant-Colonel William 95, 151, 156, 278
Sinclair, John, 6th Lord 118, 147, 267, 281; Alexander of Brims 284, 285, 289; Sir Edward 289; Sir John 284
Sinclair's Regiment 149
Solemn League and Covenant 142–3, 145, 147, 228, 266, 268, 269, 294, 295, 296
Somerville, Lieutenant-Colonel 149, 150
Sophia, Princess (later consort of the Elector of Hanover) 269, 270
Southesk, David Carnegie, 1st Earl of 4, 5, 12, 15–16, 19, 22, 44, 58–9, 64–5, 85, 91, 147, 189, 292, 293, 300
South Esk, River 4, 12, 198, 200, 251
South Shields 102, 150
Spalding, John (historian) 65, 69, 70, 73, 147, 148, 164, 167, 168, 171, 196, 198, 205
Spey, River 155, 169, 189, 200, 207, 243, 271
Speyside 168, 245, 246, 247
Spottiswood, John, Archbishop of St Andrews 36; John of Dairsie 283, 291; Sir Robert 146, 224, 231, 233, 234, 236, 241–2, 247
St Andrews 8, 10 11, 13, 14, 15, 17, 18, 86, 95, 98, 99, 118, 239, 241
Stewart, Alexander 125, 126, 128; Sir Andrew of Blackhall 108, 115, 116, 117, 128, 224; Prince Charles Edward 225; James 139; James of Ardvoirlich 162, 163; Jean 125; John of Appin 183; John of Ladywell, commissary of Dunkeld 113, 114, 115, 116, 117, 118, 120, 121, 131; Sir Lewis 59, 91, 121, 224; Mary 293; Thomas 161; Lieutenant-Colonel Walter 115, 116, 117, 118, 120, 121, 122, 128, 131; Captain William 125, 126, 127, 128; of Ballintoy 153; of Grantully 221
Stewarts 51, 99; of Appin 173, 178, 181, 183, 213; of Atholl 94, 155, 181; of Balquhidder 244
Stirling 10, 11, 18, 44, 147, 214, 216, 224, 244, 245, 297
Stirling, Sir George of Keir 94, 98, 108, 115, 116, 117, 121, 128, 133, 141, 147, 199, 223, 224; William Alexander, 1st Earl of 199
Stonehaven 65, 194, 251
Stormont, Sir Mungo Murray, 2nd Viscount 98, 113
Strachan, Archibald 285, 286, 287, 288, 289, 295
Strafford, Thomas Wentworth, Earl of 55, 57, 86, 104, 106, 116, 120, 122, 128
Strathbogie 55, 72, 73, 77, 155, 168, 170, 171, 172, 194, 198, 200, 207, 209, 210, 213, 243

Strathdearn 188, 193, 194
Strathearn 2, 5, 9, 11, 12, 13, 151, 159, 198
Strathnaver 148, 271, 273, 284, 286
Strauage, William 7
Struthers, William 14
Sutherland 77, 181, 289
Sutherland, John Gordon, 7th Earl of 118, 119, 138, 169, 201, 203, 284, 285, 286, 287, 290, 300
Sweden 257, 272, 278, 279
Sydserff, Archibald 88, 130, 224; Tom 21–2, 283

Tables 43, 44, 48, 54, 58, 59, 62, 63, 67, 68, 75, 81, 91, 95
Tain 287, 290, 291
Tay, River 67, 159, 195, 196, 214
Tibbermore, battle of 11, 159–61, 165, 184, 214, 222, 238
Tower of London 4, 89, 92, 97, 299
Traquair, John Stewart, 1st Earl of 16, 37, 44, 45, 58, 81, 82, 83, 84, 85, 86, 88, 106, 115, 116, 117, 119, 129, 132, 222, 223, 231, 234, 238, 259, 260, 300
Treaty of London 106, 122, 133, 143
Tullibardine, Patrick Murray, 3rd Earl of 76, 160, 218

Turner, Sir James 14, 155, 190, 254, 278
Turriff 55, 64, 65, 66, 77, 171, 190, 192
Tweed, River 35, 97, 99, 102, 145, 235

Ulfeld, Corfitz 270, 271, 273, 274
Union of the Crowns 2, 15, 30–8
Urquhart, Sir Thomas of Cormarty 268, 281

Wales 178, 225, 231
Wallace, William 2
Warriston, *see* Johnston
Wauchope, Sir John of Niddrie 184
Wigtown, John Fleming, 3rd Earl of 9, 13, 18, 22, 94, 97, 117, 222, 224, 300
Winton, George Seton, 3rd Earl of 158 222
Wishart, George (biographer) 4, 6, 18, 99, 106, 144, 161, 162, 165, 171, 172, 177, 196, 198, 200, 202, 205, 210, 214, 217, 223, 233, 234, 236, 238, 250, 258, 259, 261, 262, 265, 280, 289, 298
Wodrow, Robert 109, 296,

York 105, 107, 132, 137, 138, 139, 140, 146
Yorkshire 137, 226, 231